The Institutions of the European Union

The New European Union Series

Series Editors: John Peterson and Helen Wallace

The European Union is both the most successful modern experiment in international cooperation and a daunting analytical challenge to students of politics, economics, history, law, and the social sciences. The EU of the twenty-first century will be fundamentally different from its earlier permutations, as monetary union, eastern enlargement, a new defence role, and globalization all create pressures for a more complex, differentiated, and truly new European Union.

The New European Union series brings together the expertise of leading scholars writing on major aspects of EU politics for an international readership.

The series offers lively, accessible, reader-friendly, research-based textbooks on:

EU Policy-Making

The EU's Institutions

The History of European Integration

Theorizing Europe

The EU's Member States

The EU as a Global Actor

The European Union: How Does it Work?

The Institutions of
the European Union

Edited by

John Peterson

and

Michael Shackleton

OXFORD
UNIVERSITY PRESS

OXFORD
UNIVERSITY PRESS

Great Clarendon Street, Oxford OX2 6DP

Oxford University Press is a department of the University of Oxford.
It furthers the University's objective of excellence in research, scholarship,
and education by publishing worldwide in

Oxford New York

Auckland Bangkok Buenos Aires Cape Town Chennai
Dar es Salaam Delhi Hong Kong Istanbul Karachi Kolkata
Kuala Lumpur Madrid Melbourne Mexico City Mumbai Nairobi
São Paulo Shanghai Singapore Taipei Tokyo Toronto

and an associated company in Berlin

Oxford is a registered trade mark of Oxford University Press
in the UK and in certain other countries

Published in the United States
by Oxford University Press Inc., New York

British Library Cataloguing in Publication Data

Data available

Library of Congress Cataloging in Publication Data

Data available

ISBN 0–19–870052–0

1 3 5 7 9 10 8 6 4 2

Typeset in Swift and Argo
by RefineCatch Limited, Bungay, Suffolk
Printed in Great Britain by
T. J. International Ltd,
Padstow, Cornwall

Outline contents

Part III **Integrating Interests**

Detailed contents

Preface

This book is the second to appear in the Oxford University Press New European Union series, after Helen and William Wallace's milestone in the EU literature, *Policy-Making in the European Union* (4th edition). We can only hope that our book lives up to the high standard set for the series by the Wallace and Wallace collection. If it does, it is not least due to the ever-valued advice, support, and encouragement of Helen Wallace as series co-editor. She also cheered us up when all seemed to be going wrong.

We owe a huge debt to our colleagues at Oxford University Press for helping to keep the project on track. The professionalism of Miranda Vernon and Sophie Rogers in seeing the book through the production process was exemplary. Above all, we are grateful to Angela Griffin, whose commitment to this project has made a deep impression on us and inspired us to put the ball in the goal.

Our authors have invariably worked to a high standard. Almost all have patiently coped with our active editorship and constant urgings to respect the next deadline. We have learned much from them (especially Philippe de Schoutheete) and are enormously grateful to each for the part they played in making this project a success. We also are in debt to Caroline Wilding for preparing the index and Brenda James for assembling and editing the bibliography.

Our final expression of thanks is to our families—Elizabeth, Miles, and Calum in Scotland and Katie, Lucy, and (especially) Jan in Brussels—for putting up with our absences from home while working on the project and the late nights working on the book when we *were* at home. Our constant and sometimes long phone calls and e-mails to each other made each of us distracted strangers in our own homes on many occasions.

The sad death of Jan Shackleton's mother just before the book was finished reminded us of what really counts most in life, and it is *not* the EU's institutions. None the less, we hope this book is good enough both to stimulate our readers and to convince our loved ones that it was worth it.

Figures

Exhibits

Tables

Abbreviations

Here we list the abbreviations for EP party groups in the 1999–2004 Parliament only. See chapter 12 for details on groups that existed beforehand.

ACP	African, Caribbean, and Pacific countries
ADAR	Audit Developments and Reports
AFSJ	Area of Freedom, Security, and Justice
AG	advocate-general
APA	Administrative Procedure Act
BBC	British Broadcasting Corporation
BSE	bovine spongiform encephalitis (mad cow disease)
CAP	common agricultural policy
CCP	common commercial policy
CEECs	countries of central and eastern Europe
CFI	Court of First Instance
CFSP	common foreign and security policy
COA	Court of Auditors
COCOR	Commission de Coordination du Conseil des Ministres
CoR	Committee of the Regions and Local Authorities
Coreper	Committee of Permanent Representatives
Coreu	Correspondant Européen (EPC communications network)
COSAC	Conférence des Organes Spécialisés dans les Affaires Communautaires
CPMP	Committee for Proprietary Medicinal Products
CSCE	Conference for Security and Cooperation in Europe
CVMP	Committee for Veterinary Medicine
DECODE	Designing the Commission of Tomorrow
DG	Directorate-General (European Commission)
EBRD	European Bank for Reconstruction and Development
EC	European Community
ECA	European Court of Auditors
ECB	European Central Bank
ECHO	European Community Humanitarian Office

ECtHR	European Court of Human Rights
ECJ	European Court of Justice
Ecofin	(Council of) Economic and Finance Ministers
Ecosoc	Economic and Social Committee
ECSC	European Coal and Steel Community
EDD	Europe of Democracies and Diversities
EDF	European Development Fund
EDG	European Democratic Group
EEA	European Environmental Agency
EEC	European Economic Community
EFA	European Free Alliance
EFGP	European Federation of Green Parties
EFTA	European Free Trade Association
EIB	European Investment Bank
EIF	European Investment Fund
ELDR	European Liberal, Democratic, and Reform Party
EMEA	European Agency for the Evaluation of Medicinal Products
EMI	European Monetary Institute
EMS	European Monetary System
EMU	economic and monetary union
EP	European Parliament
EPC	European Political Cooperation
EPP	European People's Party
ERT	European Roundtable of Industrialists
ESC	Economic and Social Committee
ESCB	European System of Central Banks
ESDP	European Security and Defence Policy
EU	European Union
EUL–NGL	European United Left–Nordic Green left
Eurostat	EU statistical office
FPÖ	Austrian Freedom Party
GAC	General Affairs Council
G/EFA	Greens/European Free Alliance
GTP	General Tariff Preferences
ICJ	International Court of Justice

IGC	Intergovernmental Conference
IMF	International Monetary Fund
IO	international organization
JHA	justice and home affairs
LI	liberal intergovernmentalism
MEP	member of the European Parliament
Nato	North Atlantic Treaty Organization
NI	new institutionalism
NPM	new public management
NRA	national regulatory authority
OAU	Organization of African Unity
OJ	*Official Journal of the European Communities*
OJ L	*Official Journal of the European Communities*, Law Series
OLAF	Office de la Lutte Anti-Fraude (Fraud Prevention Office)
OMC	open method of coordination
ONP	open network provision
Perm reps	permanent representations
OSCE	Organization for Security and Cooperation in Europe (formerly CSCE)
Phare	Pologne-Hongrie: Assistance à la Restructuration des Économies (extended to other CEECs)
PES	Party of European Socialists
PoCo	Political Committee
PSC	Political and Security Committee
QMV	qualified majority voting
SCA	Special Committee on Agriculture
SEA	Single European Act
SEM	Sound and Efficient Management
SGCI	Secrétariat général du Comité interministériel pour les questions de coopération économique européenne
SIS	Schengen Information System
SNAs	sub-national authorities
SOA	Statement of Assurance
SPD	German Social Democratic party
SRO	self-regulatory organization
Tacis	Technical Assistance for the CIS Countries

TAO	Technical Assistance Office
TEC	Treaty of the European Community
TEI	Technical Group of Independent Members
TEU	Treaty on European Union
TGI	Technical Group of Independent Members
UCLAF	Unité de Co-ordination de la Lutte Anti-Fraude (anti-fraud unit)
UEN	Union for the Europe of the Nations
UK	United Kingdom
UN	United Nations
Unprofor	United Nations Protection Force in Bosnia
US	United States
WEU	Western European Union
WTO	World Trade Organization

List of Contributors

KIERAN ST CLAIR BRADLEY *Legal Service, European Parliament*

PHILIPPE DE SCHOUTHEETE *University of Louvain*

FIONA HAYES-RENSHAW *College of Europe (Bruges)*

CHARLIE JEFFERY *University of Birmingham*

KNUD ERIK JØRGENSEN *University of Aarhus*

BRIGID LAFFAN *University College Dublin*

JEFFREY LEWIS *Oklahoma State University*

KATHLEEN R. McNAMARA *Princeton University*

GIANDOMENICO MAJONE *University of Pittsburgh*

JÖRG MONAR *University of Sussex*

NEILL NUGENT *Manchester Metropolitan University*

JOHN PETERSON *University of Glasgow*

TAPIO RAUNIO *University of Helsinki*

MICHAEL SHACKLETON *Secretariat, European Parliament*

Editors' note

We have had to make decisions on a number of presentational issues and adopted the following conventions:

- the book follows the numbering of the treaty articles that emerged from the Treaty of Amsterdam and was maintained in the Treaty of Nice. When reference is made to an earlier period, the previous treaty article number may be used but always with the new treaty number (unless the article no longer exists).

- we use the initials TEU to refer to articles in the Treaty on European Union, or those which lie outside the scope of the European Community Treaty (notably the provisions on a Common Foreign and Security Policy—and more recently the European Security and Defence Policy—as well as police and judicial cooperation in criminal matters, the so-called second and third pillars). The initials TEC are used to refer to first pillar articles within the Treaty establishing the European Community.

- the book went to press shortly after the Irish referendum of June 2001, which saw Irish voters reject the Treaty of Nice. The changes referred to as arising out of that Treaty are therefore included on the assumption, rightly or wrongly, that it (or something like it) will eventually be ratified in a form similar to that agreed to in December 2000.

Chapter 1
The EU's Institutions: An Overview

John Peterson and Michael Shackleton

Contents

Summary

The European Union (EU) straddles accepted categories of political organization. It is less than a federation and more than a regime, a kind of confederation but not yet a *Gemeinschaft*, neither state nor 'ordinary' international organization. What sets the EU apart, above all, is its unique institutions. This chapter introduces contending definitions of 'institution' and shows how neoinstitutional approaches to the study of politics can help us make sense of the EU's institutions. Understanding the EU means understanding the inter-institutional cooperation *and* competition that occurs as the EU's institutions perform their three core functions: providing political direction, managing the Union, and integrating interests.

Introduction

The institutions of the European Union (EU) reflect directly the Union's most fundamental goals. Put simply, the EU exists to provide collective goods—such as an internal market, a single currency, and international power—which the Union's member states cannot deliver (or not as well) on their own. This enterprise has led to the creation of common EU institutions, including many that closely resemble no other bodies found at the national or international levels. This chapter is organized around the argument that the EU cannot be understood without intimate knowledge of its institutions: what they do, how they work, and how they cooperate and compete.

The EU remains one of the most elusive of all subjects of study in the social sciences. It straddles accepted categories of political organization: less than a federation and more than a 'regime' (Wallace 1983), something like a confederation but not yet a *Gemeinschaft* (Chryssochoou 2000), certainly not a state but not an 'ordinary' international organization either (Peterson 2001). The EU is a unique experiment embedding the national in the European, and the European in the national (Laffan *et al.* 2000).

Most work on European integration highlights the highly variable capacity of the EU to govern effectively in the different phases of its development. The standard version of that development suggests that Europe integrated surprisingly rapidly in the 1950s and early 1960s. Then, in the 1970s and early 1980s, the European Community (as it then was) became immobilized by economic crisis and a set of rules that made effective decision-making almost impossible. During this period of so-called Eurosclerosis, it seemed the Community could accomplish nothing very important. Then, dramatically, European integration was given fresh impetus by the 1992 Single Market project, which sought to transform (then) twelve national economies into a single, seamless European one. Before the project's target date for completion, even more dramatic changes were unleashed by the collapse of the Warsaw Pact and, subsequently, the Soviet Union in 1989–91. West European governments responded by agreeing the Maastricht Treaty, which contained bold commitments to economic and monetary union, a 'common' European foreign and security policy, and a political union. Suddenly, it seemed the EU could accomplish *anything* (Laffan *et al.* 2000: 4).

These twin perceptions of total breakdown and dramatic advance are both products of short-termism. They also reflect failed imagination: lack of it during the Eurosclerosis period, overactivity after that. In retrospect, the Community may have progressed further in the early 1980s and made far less progress in the years leading up to 1992 than was apparent at either time. The EU has always been somewhere between inert and ideal. In the 1990s, it was unable to avert or control the violent breakup of the Yugoslav federation and the subsequent conflict in Kosovo, it failed to solve Europe's chronic unemployment problem, and was scorned by many European citizens (and leaders) for failing to deal firmly with accusations of nepotism and fraud. But by 2000 it had made measurable strides towards consolidating democracy to its East and South, kick-starting an economic revival, and launching the single currency, the euro.

What spans the EU's successes and failures, its potential and shortcomings, its state-centrism and European-ness, is the EU's unique institutions. All have evolved and some have been transformed in the fifty years since the era of Schuman, Monnet, and the other post-war Founding Fathers, but the Founders' blueprint is still readily visible in the EU's institutions today. This hangover from the past raises thorny questions. Are the EU's institutions suited to modern tasks and innovative new policies? Or are they more likely to preserve policies long past their sell-by dates? Perhaps most importantly, can the EU's institutions—whose democratic legitimacy has always been weak—overcome the ingrained habits of fifty years and earn the respect and loyalty of European citizens?

Before we address these questions let us make clear what we mean by the term 'institution'. There is no one single, uncontroversial definition but rather a variety of contending definitions. Article 7 of the Treaties of the European Community (TEC) follows the European tradition of defining institutions as organizations which enjoy special legal status, and designates five: the European Parliament (EP), Council of Ministers, Commission, European Court of Justice (ECJ), and Court of Auditors. If we used this legal definition, this book would be much shorter and narrower in focus than it is. Alternatively, institutions might be defined as bodies that enjoy both legal status and a set of clearly defined powers. This definition would lead us, bizarrely, to cover the Court of Auditors but *not* the European Council, because the latter's powers are so vaguely defined.

Quite a lot of academic work defines institutions in a still broader sense, as 'extending beyond the formal organs of government to include standard operating procedures, so-called soft law, norms and conventions of behavior' (Bulmer 1994: 355). According to this perspective, 'institutions do not think, have preferences or act, but are sets of commonly accepted formal and informal norms that constrain political actors' (Marks 1996: 22). Thus, virtually anything that is accepted as 'normal' could be considered institutionalized. Coverage of all that fits under this definition in the EU would result in a book far longer than this one.

Our strategy for cutting through this thicket of competing definitions is to combine two approaches. First, we conceive of institutions as arenas where power and influence are exercised, regardless of the precise legal status of the organizations or bodies that preside over them. Second, we invite our readers to think of institutions not just in terms of specific people and premises but also as rules and practices that influence and constitute human behaviour.

This chapter begins by explaining why the study of institutions has been brought 'back in' to the study of politics (but also economics and law) in recent years. We then develop the argument that the EU's institutions provide an essential and revealing window into Europe's politics. Our next task is to consider how and why the Union's institutions, many of which were there at the creation of the European project, have changed yet endured over time. Finally, we set out some of the book's major themes, and conclude by offering advice on how this book might be read.

Why study institutions?

The social sciences came of age in the early twentieth century by focusing intensely, often exclusively, on institutions. Particularly in political science, the overwhelming emphasis was on formal structures of government and systems of law-making. Political analysis began—and often ended—by describing political institutions in great detail. Methodology was generally not a matter for debate nor was the behaviour of political leaders, officials, or citizens. As Rhodes (1995: 42) suggests, 'the focus on institutions was a matter of common sense, an obvious starting point . . . and therefore there was no need to justify it. The assumptions and practices in the study of political institutions were taken for granted.'[1]

Everything changed in the 1950s and early 1960s. First, the so-called behavioural revolution was unleashed (see Sanders 1995). Behaviouralists criticized the traditional emphasis on institutions as too narrow, unscientific, atheoretical, and even ethnocentric, tending to assume that Western institutions were innately superior. Traditional institutionalist analysis not only failed to explain policy or power, because it did not cover all of the relevant variables that determined politics. It also suffered from 'hyperfactualism': reverence for 'facts' meant that political science suffered from theoretical malnutrition (Easton 1971).

For behaviouralists, institutions were relatively uninteresting compared to the *behaviour* of political actors. Institutions had no political interests or personalities of their own. In a sense, behaviouralism assumed that institutions were just a car waiting for a driver. What was far more interesting than studying the car was studying the behaviour of the agents—political leaders, parties, voters— competing to seize power, control the institutions, and drive the car. Behaviouralists sought to make political science a true science, often through the use of statistics and quantitative analysis. Institutions—leaving aside some notable exceptions (such as Allison 1971)—more or less disappeared from the radar screens of most political scientists.

The second big change was a shift in the study of international relations.

Traditionally, scholarship had focused mostly on competition (especially military) between sovereign states in what was assumed to be a Hobbesian and anarchic international system (see Morgenthau 1948). However, the post-war creation of the United Nations (UN), the Bretton Woods institutions (the General Agreement on Tariffs and Trade, World Bank, and the International Monetary Fund, or IMF) led to a blossoming of scholarship on international cooperation. In time, Europe became the primary focus of this scholarship as the continent embarked on ambitious, even radical experiments in (especially economic) integration (see Haas 1968, Lindberg 1963, Deutsch *et al.* 1957). Multi-state institutions, or international organizations (IOs), became firmly established as areas of investigation in the study of international relations

Yet, with the dawning of the so-called 'Second Cold War' (Halliday 1983), it seemed clear that most IOs—including the then (supposedly) Eurosclerotic European Community—were relatively weak and unable to foster much meaningful cooperation. The empirical and theoretical focus shifted towards explaining renewed, Reagan-era competition between states, especially the United States and Soviet Union (see Waltz 1979). Europe was politically and—along with institutionalism—academically marginalized.

Then, beginning in the mid-1980s, institutions were rediscovered in the study of both comparative politics and international relations as well as, eventually, European integration. A groundswell of academic momentum stoked principally by Skocpol (1985) and March and Olsen (1989) led comparativists to bring the state, and its institutions, 'back in' to the study of politics. In some respects, the so-called 'new institutionalism' was a rebellion against behaviouralism. Neoinstitutionalists insisted that political behaviour was determined in fundamental ways by the nature of political institutions, how they are constructed, and how power is distributed between them.

The basic neoinstitutionalist argument is that institutions matter: they define group loyalties in any political system and thus help determine how political debates are structured. They are *not* just cars waiting for political interests to drive them. The form and shape of institutions have a powerful impact on how smoothly the car runs, which roads it can take, and how sure we can be that the car will not break down.

In particular, institutions, even ones that are formally apolitical, develop their own interests, agendas, and priorities in ways that often resist control by formally political actors, such as governments. Actual policy outcomes often bear the fingerprints of institutional *agency*—defined as the determined pursuit of defined choices—more than of the preferences of governments. One reason why is that the policy priorities of governments are often less than well defined, thus allowing ample scope for formally apolitical institutions to set the agenda and persuade governments that their institution's preferred policy solutions serve the overtly political agenda of political leaderships.

The new institutionalism is more a *perspective* on politics than a fully developed theory. It offers insights into politics, even if many of them are commonsensical, which other approaches miss. Perhaps most importantly, the new institutionalism offers concepts that travel: both between academic disciplines—economics (see North 1990) and law (Stone Sweet and Caporaso 1998) as well as politics—and between the national and international.

Neoinstitutionalism thus has emerged as a leading perspective on European integration and politics, and an alternative to state-centric or intergovernmental approaches derived from the study of international relations (see Grieco 1995; Moravcsik 1998a). The latter assume, reasonably, that the EU has a strong inter-governmental backbone and that policy debates are mostly debates between national actors pursuing national interests. Yet, arguments over EU policy are largely fought out far from national capitals and governments. Nearly all actors in EU politics have multiple identities and mixed loyalties, to their member state, political party, or the interests of the policy sector in which they work. Institutional affiliations thus give actors a sort of anchor or orientation that may override others and become a primary source of motivation and interest. In the EU, institutional orientations are a source of order because they serve to aggregate interests in a system that otherwise could descend into chaos. Neoinstitutionalist treatments argue that EU politics has to be understood in terms of inter-institutional competition between, above all, the Council of Ministers, the European Commission, and the European Parliament (EP), and not just in terms of intergovernmental competition.

Many variants of institutionalism exist (see Hall and Taylor 1996; Peters 1996) and most have been applied to the study of the EU. Bulmer's historical institutionalist approach (1994; Armstrong and Bulmer 1998) yields insightful treatments of EU governance, particularly concerning the single market. It highlights the importance of evolving institutional norms in EU policy-making, such as the norm that the Council usually aims to achieve unanimity on any measure regardless of whether qualified majority voting (QMV) is applied (see also Golub 1999). Such norms often constrain political decision-making and produce 'path dependence'— a concept central to all variants of institutionalism—in the sense that 'initial policy choices may restrict subsequent [policy] evolution' (Armstrong and Bulmer 1998: 55). Pierson's (1996) analysis of the EU's historical evolution argues that member states can become 'locked-in' and unable to alter or escape from decisions which set the EU on a given policy path. The EU's institutions become empowered as guardians of long-established EU policies, and thus 'are not simply passive tools of the Member States' (Pierson 1996: 132).

Historical institutionalism is probably the leading, but by no means the only, version of neoinstitutionalism used by scholars to make sense of the EU. Fligstein (1997; Fligstein and Brantley 1995; Fligstein and McNicol 1998) develops a sociological variant of institutionalism, which focuses on how the treaties and organizations of the EU shape and limit debate, specifying which issues are open for legislation and mobilization by organized interests (the internal market) and which generally are not (most issues related to social welfare). Garrett and Tsebelis (2000) present a sort of rational choice institutionalism that defies the messiness of EU governance by seeking to explain it with synthetic formal models. Pollack (1997) draws on principal-agent theories which examine how and why governments, or 'principals', solve collective action problems by delegating functions to international institutions, which then act as their 'agents', although usually with a variety of mechanisms put in place to control or monitor their behaviour (see also Majone 2000).[2]

The point is not that the only, or even best, way to study institutions in the EU or any other political system is to deploy some variant of neoinstitutionalism; indeed, the contributors to this volume deploy a range of different theoretical approaches to understanding and explaining 'their' institution. The point is rather that institutions are worth studying because, as is now widely acknowledged across all the social sciences, institutions matter: they determine political, economic, and legal outcomes in ways that are often crucial.

Why study the EU's institutions?

If institutions matter in determining politics in any political society, they may matter even more in the European Union than in other systems. Why? We can think of at least six reasons.

First, the EU's institutions remain young—fifty years at most and often far less—and are fundamentally experimental. They have been subject to an endless bout of tinkering since the late 1980s when European integration was relaunched, with many effects that are clear in EU policy outcomes (see Peterson and Bomberg 1999: 31–59). But in many respects it is surprising how little they have changed over time, and thus how deeply ingrained are their institutional cultures and established norms.

Second, the EU's institutions matter because they are the vehicles used by the Union's member governments to enforce the terms of the bargains they make with each other (see Moravcsik 1998a). Put simply, the EU's institutions exist to manage the enormous interdependence that binds together its member governments. Yet, while the Union's institutions may be viewed in theoretical terms as agents of their political masters, they are *not* just cars waiting for drivers. The powers they have accrued over time—arising from what is known as the *acquis communautaire*, or the full set of rights and obligations deriving from EU treaties, laws, and regulations—give the Union's institutions substantial autonomy. They are an important reason why European states continue to respond to their interdependence by cooperating (while competing, sometimes fiercely, over the details) and avoiding outright conflict.

Moreover, as a third observation, the EU's institutions do not simply manage. More than the international secretariats of any other IO, the EU's institutions possess rational-legal authority to make rules. They also create social knowledge in less formal ways, by defining shared European tasks, creating new categories of actors (such as refugees or 'EU citizens'), forming new interests for actors or reshaping old ones, and transferring new models of political and administrative organization across Europe (Barnett and Finnemore 1999). The EU's institutions thus have the capacity to provide political direction to the Union. Of course, most of this direction comes from the governments of the member governments themselves and is channelled via the European Council and Council of Ministers (for Agriculture, Industry, and so on). But there is scope here too for agency by the Commission and Parliament, each of which has its own political agenda and priorities which cannot be reduced to the sum total of those of the EU's member governments. Furthermore, the Commission, Parliament, and other EU institutions also act to integrate political and social interests, including those of actors who either oppose or act independently of their 'home' government. Certainly, it is easy to overestimate the extent to which the EU has given rise to a Brussels-based system of politics in which national interests or institutions are marginalized or blended together. As Helen Wallace (2000: 7) argues:

> much of EU policy is prepared and carried out by national policy-makers and agents who do not spend much, if any, time in Brussels. Rather what they do is consider how EU regimes might help or hinder their regular activities, and apply the results of EU agreements on the ground in their normal daily work. If we could calculate the proportions, we might well find that in practice something like 80 per cent of that normal daily life was framed by domestic preoccupations and constraints. Much the same is true of the social and economic groups, or political representatives, who seek to influence the development and content of EU policy.

At the same time, the EU has given rise to a multi-level polity in which the boundary between politics in national capitals and Brussels often is so blurred as to be insignificant. The Union's institutions have aided and abetted this blurring by providing opportunities for interests, including ones that have lost arguments or lack influence at the national level, to join their counterparts across Europe in pursuing common objectives. Many truly pan-European interests have been nurtured, sometimes manufactured, by the Union's institutions. The European Union gives political interests another crack at influence, not least because its institutions all encourage—actively or accidentally—pan-European mobilization.

Fourth, the EU's institutions fascinate because they are powerful yet mostly unloved by European citizens. During the difficult days of the early 1990s, the British Minister of State for European affairs, Tristan Garel-Jones, spoke of his ambition to make British citizens feel a sense of ownership of the EU.[3] Particularly given his own parliamentary constituency of Watford—not, he conceded, one of the most cosmopolitan parts of Britain—the challenge was to convince 'Watford man' (and woman) to think of the EU's institutions in the same way as they thought of the British Gas Board (at least before the 1990s when it became the subject of charges that it had become chaotic and indifferent to public needs). That is, to consider the EU's institutions as public-spirited, professional, and committed to improving the quality of life of average Brits, and other Europeans. Above all, the Union's institutions would be viewed as *belonging* to European citizens.

Yet, a low sense of ownership on the part of EU citizens clearly persists (see Chryssochoou 2000). Arguably, popular disillusion with the EU's institutions is no more severe—some evidence suggests less—than is disillusion with national political institutions and politics (see Hix 1999*b*: 138; Shackleton 1997). But it is hard to deny that progressively lower turn-outs in EP elections, declining trust in the European Commission, and rejection of the Maastricht and Nice Treaties by (respectively) Danish and Irish voters in referenda show that the EU's institutions have become dysfunctional, in much the same way as the institutions of less successful IOs (Barnett and Finnemore 1999). Like their counterparts in the IMF or UN, the EU's institutions often seem obsessed with their own internal rules and neglectful of their missions. An important reason to study the EU's institutions is that we are encouraged to think of how to improve them.

Fifth, the EU's institutions not only link Brussels to national EU capitals. They also link Europe to the wider world of international politics and, particularly, the extensive network of IOs that is now an essential feature of the international system. As the world's largest trading power, the EU is a crucial (if often berated) member of the World Trade Organization (WTO). Its recent steps towards equipping itself with a defence capability have required extensive interactions with the North Atlantic Treaty Organization (Nato). The EU itself—as opposed to its separate member governments—is increasingly the voice of Europe in IOs ranging from the UN to the Group of Eight (G8) to the Korean Economic Development Organization. The Union's institutions are increasingly more powerful actors in the so-called 'international community', a world once entirely and exclusively dominated by sovereign states.

Sixth and somewhat paradoxically, EU politics are largely a product of competition between its institutions—each of which has its own identity and interests—but the Union's institutions are profoundly and inescapably interdependent. The EU's decision rules are designed to foster collective responsibility for the Union's policies, and little of importance may be agreed without the joint consent of the Commission, EP, and Council—with appeal to the ECJ always likely when such consensus is *not* achieved. The Council remains the EU's main policy-maker, but Ludlow (1992) insists that a strong, active Council actually requires a strong, active Commission. Meanwhile the increasingly ubiquitous co-decision procedure makes the EP a politically and legal co-legislator with the Council in most areas of EU competence (see Shackleton 2000).

Thus, the EU's institutions cannot be studied as separate and autonomous entities. In practice, they form a network bound together by a set of formal and informal rules (see Keohane and Hoffmann 1991). In this network, the behaviour of each is heavily conditioned by the behaviour of others. Even an institution that is formally designated as independent, such as the European Central Bank (ECB), cannot be understood without reference to the decisions taken by the European Council and the Council of (Economic and Finance) Ministers at its inception. In line with new institutionalist assumptions, these decisions have heavily structured the kind of decisions the ECB can now take.

Institutional interdependence is clearly uneven across policy sectors. For example, the EP has little power to determine the common agricultural policy (CAP). The Commission, for its part, acts with considerable power and independence in competition policy. There exists no single mode of EU policy-making (see H. Wallace 2000), and the traditional Community method—which gives distinct and exclusive powers to the Commission, EP, and Council—increasingly seems under threat by new and distinct institutional arrangements for relatively new EU policies such as economic and monetary union (EMU), the Common Foreign and Security Policy (CFSP), or Justice and Home Affairs. In these and other areas, member governments have chosen *not* to 'Communitarize' cooperation using traditional institutional divisions of labour, but rather have chosen new and experimental types of institution, often ones that reserve for national decision-makers an upper hand. One upshot is that the EU is becoming more *polycentric*, with more, more diverse, and more independent centres of power and control (Peterson and Bomberg 2000). Increasingly, the EU's institutional diversity makes it look like a collection of different polities, as opposed to a single, unified one.

In short, if the EU has emerged as a polity in its own right, it is a highly differentiated one about which it is fiendishly difficult to generalize. None the less, two generalizations about the Union and its institutions *do* tend to hold. One is that the EU lacks hierarchy. For the most part, the EU lacks the authoritative control to impose policy solutions on its member states.

Second, as Nugent (1994: 298) argues, formal meetings of the Union's institutions, such as the Council, often fail to facilitate meaningful bargaining:

[they] tend to be formal and structured ... they are often, in themselves, not very well equipped to produce the training, the concessions, and the compromises that are so often necessary to build majorities, create agreements and further progress. As a result they have come to be supported by a vast network of informal and unstructured channels between EU actors.

As such, the EU is a hothouse for a dizzying variety of policy networks, or informally linked clusters of policy stakeholders, which facilitate bargaining between representatives of its institutions as well as other kinds of actor. EU policy networks vary enormously across its different policy sectors, ranging from loosely constituted issue networks (the membership of which varies between issues) to tightly integrated policy communities (whose memberships remain consistent regardless of the issue). But the overriding point is that we must be intellectually and analytically nimble in approaching EU politics, not least because we encounter such diversity in the way the Union's institutions interact and bargain in different policy sectors.

'Frustration without disintegration': the persistence of the EU system

We have argued that the EU's institutions are both important and essential to understanding the European Union, but also that the EU is marked by considerable institutional weakness and dysfunction. European citizens who express stronger support for a united Europe in the abstract than for the EU in practice[4] exhibit a sort of collective, common sense. It is perfectly plausible to be pro-European but to believe that the EU's institutions do not work very well.

Part of the problem is political. Without a government (or opposition), the Union often seems unable to steer the European project in a decisive, committed way. For one thing, the project has always depended for its sustenance on appearing, at least, to be apolitical, consensual, or uncontroversial. For another thing, and in contradiction to the chimera of 'apolitical-ness', the EU now features stiff competition between its institutions to steer the project, often in ways that vary and are incompatible with each other.

A second and related problem is managerial. The 1980s saw the Commission under the presidency of Jacques Delors show genuine political leadership. However, Delors and his college of Commissioners took little interest in the efficient management of the Commission. The administrative rot that had sprouted during the Delors years (see van Buitenan 2000) was worse than nearly any academic analysis acknowledged in the 1990s (see Peterson 1997). Amidst charges of mismanagement and nepotism, the collective resignation of the Commission under Delors's successor, Jacques Santer, in March 1999 was a low point in the institutional history of the EU. It illustrated clearly that the EU's lack of hierarchy and reliance on informal networks had serious costs. For students of public management, it has always been axiomatic that 'pluralistic policy networks are under-managed because the constituent organisations do not invest in the capacities needed to manage their mutual interdependence' (Metcalfe 2000: 13). For students of the EU specifically, it is hard to resist Metcalfe's (2000: 13) conclusion that 'the substandard performance of the system is everyone's problem and no-one's responsibility'.

Yet, the aftermath of the fall of the Santer Commission showed that the EU is sometimes capable of determined, collective political agency. Meeting only a week or so after Santer's resignation, European leaders chose unanimously to nominate Romano Prodi, the former Italian Prime Minister, as Santer's replacement (while also agreeing a seven-year budget for the EU and showing considerable solidarity on Kosovo). The EP confirmed both Prodi's nomination and the new Commission by overwhelming majorities

Hopes for a more politically potent Commission, raised by Prodi's appointment, vanished quickly. For instance, the report of three 'wise men' (Dehaene *et al.* 1999) commissioned by Prodi, which called for radical institutional reforms ahead of enlargement, was rebuffed by the European Council. Insiders at the November 1999 Tampere European Summit expressed shock at how the Spanish Prime Minister, Jose Maria Aznar, brusquely told Prodi: 'we don't need your wise men. *We* are your wise men!'[5] Prodi and the Commission seemed marginalized at the subsequent Lisbon and Nice Summits in 2000 as European leaders first embraced an ambitious economic reform plan to make the EU the 'world's most dynamic economy', and then agreed yet another institutional overhaul via the Treaty of Nice.

One view of these developments would hold that they reflect a time-honoured pattern of swings in the locus of political leadership in the EU. Another would contend that European governments have clawed back for themselves the power to be the true political masters of the EU. The Commission—in the absence of Delors's genius for channelling national preferences for the EU's own ends—and Parliament have both become emasculated. If this latter interpretation is accepted (it is *not* by all of this volume's contributors), this latest swing in the locus of political leadership has occurred for three reasons.

First, a primary function of the EU's institutions, integrating political interests, has often *not* been abetted and sometimes has been actively resisted by member governments. Naturally, perhaps, EU governments wish to retain their own, favoured, primary relationships with voters and interest groups. The result is that the EP and Commission lack their own, independent sources of authority and support. They also lack resources. The EP has nothing approaching the resources of say, the US Congress (with its large Congressional Research Service, General Accounting Office, etc.). The Commission remains shackled by close to zero-growth in its personnel and budget.

Second, the EU almost never makes a hard decision today that can be put off until tomorrow. The radical reforms favoured by Prodi and his 'wise men' were mostly eschewed by European leaders in agreeing the Treaty of Nice even though the EU's institutions, created for six member states, seemed to require a radical overhaul if the Union was to function with twenty-seven or more member states. Yet, European leaders—perhaps to mollify critics of the remarkably convoluted

Treaty of Nice—surprised few observers by agreeing that yet *another* Intergovernmental Conference (IGC) to negotiate Treaty reform be held in 2004.

Third and finally, the path dependency with which the EU's institutional system
is imbued seems to be accepted with a good measure of weary resignation by EU
governments. 'Frustration without disintegration' (see Scharpf 1999) is an apt
description for how the EU's institutional system remains sub-optimal but never
stops working. The desire amongst European governments to make the Union
work better, but to avoid a genuine process of state-building, reflects deep-rooted
hesitation to create an EU that challenges states as the primary loci of political
authority in Europe.

These institutions and this book

As we have shown, following the EU's Treaties to the letter would mean that this
book would only contain five chapters. It would thus provide a very incomplete
picture of the EU's institutional landscape, missing out the European Council, the
European Central Bank, the Committee of Permanent Representatives, the Committee of the Regions, and the new European agencies, along with institutions
which have grown up around the CFSP and justice and home affairs policy. Regardless of what the Treaties say, these bodies are all either powerful or remarkable or
both, and thus all are the subjects of chapters that follow. Our coverage is not
exhaustive and not every institution is covered in equal depth. Nevertheless, the
book brings under one roof comprehensive analysis of the increasingly complex
institutional structure responsible for decisions which have a growing influence
on the lives of European (and non-European) citizens.

One way to approach the EU's institutions would be to adopt a rather 'pure'
version of neoinstitutionalism, and thus look beyond formal organizations to
focus on the rules and norms that structure social interactions in EU decision- and
policy-making. In its organization, at least, this book takes a somewhat narrower,
more focused approach by organizing chapters around specific EU organizations
or policy-specific clusters of institutions. Nevertheless, none of our authors neg-
lects the rules and norms which govern the work of the institutions. In particular,
all of our contributors grapple with the interaction of 'their' institution with
others in the EU system, and the changing rules and norms that preside over these
interactions. Whatever the geographical distance between them (and such distance is a marked feature of Union institutions), the EU's institutions are highly
and intricately interconnected. One of the central tasks of this book is to explore
this interconnectedness.

Table 1.1 An institutional timeline[a]

Start of activities		Title of institution	Location
1950			
	1952	**Council of Ministers**	Brussels/Luxembourg
	1952	**ECSC High Authority**	Luxembourg
	1952	**European Court of Justice**	Luxembourg
	1952	**ECSC Parliamentary Assembly**	Strasbourg/Luxembourg
	1958	**European Commission**	Brussels/Luxembourg
	1958	**Economic and Social Committee**	Brussels
	1958	**European Investment Bank**	Luxembourg
	1958	**Committee of Permanent Representatives (Coreper)**	Brussels
1960			
	1962	European Parliamentary Assembly changes its name to **European Parliament**	Strasbourg/Luxembourg/ Brussels
	1965	Merger Treaties create a single **Commission**	Brussels/Luxembourg
1970			
	1974	**European Council** (formally established by Paris Summit)	
	1975	European Centre for the Development of Vocational Training	Berlin (since 1994 Thessaloniki)
	1975	European Foundation for the Improvement of Living and Working Conditions	Dublin
	1977	**European Court of Auditors**	Luxembourg
1980			
	1989	**Court of First Instance**	Luxembourg
1990			
	1990	European Environment Agency	Copenhagen
	1994	**Committee of Regions**	Brussels
	1994	Office for Harmonization in the Internal Market	Alicante
	1994	Translation Centre for Bodies in the European Union	Luxembourg
	1995	**European Ombudsman**	Strasbourg
	1995	European Training Foundation	Turin
	1995	Community Plant Variety Office	Angers
	1995	European Agency for Safety and Health at Work	Bilbao
	1995	European Agency for the Evaluation of Medicinal Products	London
	1995	European Monitoring Centre for Drugs and Drug Addiction	Lisbon
	1998	European Monitoring Centre on Racism and Xenophobia	Vienna
	1998	**European Central Bank**	Frankfurt
	1999	European Anti-Fraud Office (OLAF)	Brussels
2000			

[a] Institutions in bold are designated in the Treaties.

Each chapter is also sensitive to the importance of the historical development of each EU institution and how it has assumed its role in the Union's institutional network. As Table 1.1 shows, this network has developed over fifty years, with 'younger' EU institutions struggling to establish themselves *vis-à-vis* more established bodies and less powerful bodies constantly seeking to extend their influence. Thus, another central purpose of this book is to show how and why the positions of individual institutions have advanced and receded over time, within an overall pattern of considerable fluctuation. What emerges clearly is that today's debates about how the EU should work are often not new ones: they echo debates that date back as far as the 1950s.

The EU's institutions have always, from the EEC's earliest origins, operated in a highly contested environment. There is no universal agreement about what the European Union is or ought to be, and never has been. Is it a particularly elaborate IO that enables states to achieve certain goals more efficiently than they could otherwise do? Or does it now transcend the state, in some areas emerging as more than the sum of its parts? Since academics as well as practitioners (see Exhibit 1.1) give different answers to these questions, they inevitably disagree as to what the Union's institutions—individually and collectively—are there to do.

One thing should be clear from our analysis thus far: the EU's institutions cannot simply be seen as a purely functional set of bodies designed to achieve certain common purposes. If they were, they could be judged purely on the basis of efficiency. Yet, European integration has become a highly political exercise, and the EU's institutions have evolved into highly political animals. Arguments about how to make the EU more efficient often ignore widespread doubts about the legitimacy of the Union as a whole.

The question of legitimacy encourages us to consider the relationship of the institutions with the wider public beyond. As the range of action of the Union has developed and with it the range of institutions, so public acceptability of the EU institutional system has become a far more salient issue. Calls for the application of the criterion of consent, in the same way as it is applied within national democratic systems, have become more frequent. As a result, this book challenges its readers to look beyond debates about what each institution should do. Changing relations between, say, the European Council and Commission President (who is actually a full member of the European Council) are important. But they cannot be divorced from wider debates about the governance of the Union as a whole.

Exhibit 1.1 Perceptions of the EU's institutions[a]

'The fusion of interests in the European Community is being achieved through a new mechanism of institutions which it is only slight exaggeration to call a constitutional framework' (Walter Hallstein, 1962).

'Rien n'est possible sans les hommes, rien n'est durable sans les institutions' (Nothing is possible without men, nothing lasts without institutions) (Jean Monnet, 1976).

'What a model our institutions, which allow every country irrespective of its size to have its say and make a contribution, offer the nations of Eastern Europe' (Jacques Delors, 1989).

'1992 emerged because the institutions of the Communities, especially the Commission, were able to exercise policy leadership' (Wayne Sandholtz and John Zysman, 1989).

'Supranational institutions—above all, the European Commission, the European Court, and the European Parliament—have independent influence in policy-making that cannot be derived from their role as agents of state executives' (Gary Marks, Liesbet Hooghe, and Kermit Blank, 1992).

'As has always been true in domestic politics, new governments in member states now find that the dead weight of previous institutional and policy decisions at the European level seriously limits their room for maneuver' (Paul Pierson 1996).

'Supranational entrepreneurs have only a rare and secondary impact . . . the EC has not banished power politics from Western Europe' (Andrew Moravcsik, 1998).

'First the engine was key individuals with vision. Then the Commission became the motor for Europe, a common institution helped along by the Franco-German alliance, particularly in the 1980s, when Delors' special relation with European leaders brought in the Single Market and EMU. But since Maastricht the Community has run down hill. Nice was a caricature of what should have happened' (Alain Lamassoure 2000).

[a] Years indicated are those of delivery (of speeches) or publication. References to each quote (several taken from excerpts reproduced in 'readers') in the order they appear in the exhibit are as follows: Weigall and Stirk 1992: 125; Monnet 1976: 441; Nelson and Stubb 1998: 60–1, 197, 277–8, 318; Moravcsik 1998a: 485; *The Parliament Magazine*, 22 Jan. 2001.

Conclusion

Students of the EU will find a curious scarcity of works that cover the full range of the EU's institutions. Most leading EU texts offer a straight review of what the Treaty designates as institutions, with one chapter each on the Council, Commission, EP, and so on. Less weighty institutions, such as the Court of Auditors and Committee of the Regions, tend to be covered in a composite, 'lest we forget' chapter.

This book abstains from a standard, one-institution-per-chapter dash across the EU's institutional landscape. Instead, we offer three grouped sections of chapters that examine how different institutions provide political direction, manage the Union, and integrate interests. Each chapter begins with an analysis of the origins and development of the institution specified, followed by an overview of its structure and functions. Each author then reflects on 'their' institution's powers, before considering the (crucial) question of how it fits into the EU's wider institutional network. Each explicitly confronts the question of which theories of European integration and EU governance help us best to understand the institution, how it works, and how it has developed over time. None ignores the crucial question of how their institution is likely to be changed by enlargement.

Some EU institutions—particularly the Commission, Council, and EP—perform more than one function, and thus analysis of them is spread across more than one chapter. The reader who wants to understand the institutions 'one by one' (or teacher who wants to teach them that way) should not hesitate from reading, say, Chapter 4 on the college of Commissioners together with Chapter 7 on the Commission's services. But we would encourage the reading of chapters together in the sections into which they are grouped. The effect, we hope, is to help the student of the EU's institutions to come to grips with the intensity of both inter-institutional cooperation *and* competition in the performance of the Union's three 'core' functions, and thus to come to grips with the politics of European integration.

Notes

1 The story of the social sciences that we present here is one that fits the English-speaking world better than the European continent, where intellectual trajectories have been rather different (see Jørgensen 2000).

2 Arguably (and certainly in strict legal terms), it is incorrect to describe the EU's institutions as 'agents' as they have been attributed wide discretion—not only executive power—and their powers cannot be clawed back by governments, short of closing down the EU altogether. We are grateful to Kieran Bradley for making this point to us.

3 Here we paraphrase from an address delivered by Garel-Jones to the 30th anniversary conference of the *Journal of* *Common Market Studies* held in Edinburgh on 20–2 November 1992 (see Garel-Jones 1993).

4 Consistent majorities of European citizens express precisely this view in biannual Eurobarometer surveys of public opinion (available from—**www.europa.eu.int**).

5 Interviews, Brussels, December 1999. Two caveats must be made. First, Aznar was apparently rebuked for this remark by the summit chair, the Finnish President Martti Ahtisaari. Second, in line with the Dehaene report's urgings, the negotiations on a new Treaty *were* widened to embrace issues beyond those 'left over' from the Amsterdam Treaty negotiations: that is, the size of the

Commission, national voting weights on the Council, and the extension of qualified majority voting. Interestingly, an analysis of the negotiations which ultimately produced the Treaty of Nice, written by an official in the Council's Secretariat-General, contains only one fleeting mention of the Dehaene report (Galloway 2001: 30), and appears to assign it little importance.

Further reading

For alternative perspectives on the EU's institutions, see Warleigh (forthcoming) and (in French) Doutriaux and Lequesne (2000, updated 4th ed. due in 2002). The best and most comprehensive coverage of the institutions given in any basic EU text is Nugent (1999). Good overviews of the neoinstitutionalist literature—in which March and Olsen (1989) remains seminal— are Hall and Taylor (1996) and Peters (1996). Essential applications of neoinstitutionalism to the EU are Pierson (1996), Pollack (1997), and Armstrong and Bulmer (1998).

Armstrong, K., and Bulmer, S. (1998), *The Governance of the Single European Market* (Manchester: Manchester University Press).

Doutriaux, Y., and Lequesne, C. (2000), *Les Institutions de l'Union Européenne*, 3rd edn. (Paris: La Documentation Française, collection Réflexe Europe).

Hall, P. A., and Taylor, R. C. R. (1996), 'Political Science and the Three New Institutionalisms', *Political Studies*, 44/5: 936–57.

March, J., and Olsen, J. (1989), *Rediscovering Institutions* (New York: The Free Press).

Nugent, N. (1999), *The Government and Politics of the European Union*, 4th edn. (Basingstoke and New York: Palgrave).

Peters, B. G. (1996), *Institutional Theory in Political Science* (London and New York: Continuum).

Pierson, P. (1996), 'The Path to European Integration: A Historical Institutionalist Analysis', *Comparative Political Studies* 29/2: 123–63.

Pollack, M. (1997), 'Delegation, Agency and Agenda-Setting in the European Union', *International Organization*, 51/1: 99–134.

Warleigh, A. (forthcoming), *Understanding European Union Institutions* (London and New York: Routledge).

Web links

The European Commission's web site— **www.europa.eu.int**—is the place to start any search for basic information on the EU's institutions, as it contains links to all of the web sites of the Union's other institutions. The European Research Papers Archive (ERPA) is a valuable research tool, offering access to papers posted on the web sites of several leading EU research institutes (including the European University Institute in Florence, Italy, and the Harvard Law School), and reliably containing work in the neoinstitutionalist vein: **www.eiop.or.at/ erpa**. Work by Bulmer, a leading neoinstitutionalist EU scholar, can be accessed at **www.les.man.ac.uk/ government/journals/epru/epru-wp.html**

Part I

Providing Direction

Chapter 2
The European Council

Philippe de Schoutheete

Contents

Summary

Since its creation in 1974, the European Council has played a fundamental role in the development of European integration. It gives political guidance and impetus to the Union, takes the most important decisions, gives high visibility to external policy positions and declarations, and puts the seal of approval to significant documents. Its composition gives it an intergovernmental character, yet successive decisions at that level have increased the supranational character of the Union. The European Council has been, over a quarter of a century, a formidable locus of power, but it seems to be reaching the limits of its capacity, particularly in treaty-making. It cannot, by itself, solve present and future problems of European governance.

Introduction

The composition of the European Council is specified in Article 4 TEU: it brings together heads of state or government (a formula designed to cover the situation of the French and Finnish presidents, who are both heads of state and chief executives) and the President of the Commission. They are assisted by the ministers for foreign affairs and a member of the Commission. When the European Council deals with questions linked to economic and monetary union, finance ministers are invited.[1] They either replace or sit alongside Foreign Ministers (both cases have been known to occur). Apart from a very small number of civil servants, nobody else participates in the meeting. This is the essence of the European Council: a limited number of political figures, headed by the chief executives of all member states, meeting in a closed room with no assistants.

A certain number of conclusions can be drawn from the definition in Article 4 TEU:

- The European Council is not simply a specific form of the Community institution known as the Council. The Rules of Procedure of the Council do not apply. The composition is different: the President of the Commission is *de jure* a member of the European Council, whereas the Council consists exclusively of representatives of the member states (Article 203 TEC), even if, *de facto*, a representative of the Commission is always present.

- It follows that, in formal terms, the European Council is not a *Community* institution (it is not specifically mentioned in Article 7 TEC which specifies five such institutions). The European Council is indeed mentioned in the European *Union* Treaty (Article 4 TEU) but separately from the other institutions (Article 5 TEU). Such ambiguity is not dispelled by Article 3 TEU which says that the Union 'shall be served by a single institutional framework'. Is the European Council part of that framework? Some participants might say yes, but others would say definitely not.

It can be argued that participants in a European Council fulfil the description of the Council as given by Article 203 TEC: 'a representative of each Member State at ministerial level'. It has, therefore, generally been acknowledged that it could, if it so wished, exercise the powers vested in the Council by the Treaties, and should then respect Council procedures. In fact it has refrained from doing so, to the point where the European Council could be viewed as operating in important respects 'outside the main institutional structure' (H. Wallace 2000: 20). None the less, it is abundantly clear that no book on the EU's institutions would be complete without a chapter dedicated to this peculiar body, which plays such a major role in European affairs.

From a legal point of view it is clear that when heads of government met in Brussels on 2 May 1998 to decide on the adoption of a single currency they met not as a European Council *stricto sensu*, but as a Council in the formation of heads of state and government (Article 121 TEC). It could also be argued that when meeting in Amsterdam in June 1997, or in Nice in December 2000, they did not constitute the European Council but a top-level meeting of two Intergovernmental Conferences (Article 48 TEU). These legal niceties, however, are not understood by public opinion, and are frequently ignored even by participants. For the purpose of analysis they are neglected in the rest of this chapter.

Origins

Heads of government have always played an important role in the development of European integration. Consider the observation of the legendary Belgian Foreign Minister, Paul-Henri Spaak (1969: 95), at a meeting in Paris in February 1957, on the eve of the signature of the Treaty of Rome, where heads of government had to settle the last politically sensitive issues: 'It went on day and night. I had to run from one to the other, pleading, looking for compromises. Finally at dawn on 20 February a solution was found.' This sounds no different from some present-day European Councils!

In 1969 a summit held at The Hague opened the way for British accession and initiated an effort at foreign policy coordination called 'European Political Cooperation' (see Chapter 10). Other summits were held in Paris in 1972 and Copenhagen in 1973. But it was at Paris in December 1974 that it was decided to have regular meetings of what was to become the 'European Council'. The first such meeting was held in Dublin in March 1975. Two to four meetings have been held every year since then and by the end of 2000 heads of government had met seventy-five times in this format.

Two basic objective reasons can be put forward as justifications for the Paris Summit decision:

- Community institutions were felt not to be working as well as they should, especially since the Luxembourg compromise of 1965 was in practice blocking majority voting. The first enlargement of the Community (Britain, Ireland, and Denmark) was likely to make decision-making more ponderous. The creation of a regular (as opposed to an occasional) source of strategic direction and political impulse made sense in this context.

- Foreign ministers were (already!) finding it difficult to coordinate the activities of a growing number of Council formations. Moreover European Political

> **Exhibit 2.1** The origins of the European Council, Paris, December 1974
>
> 'Recognizing the need for an overall approach to the internal problems involved in achieving European unity and the external problems facing Europe, the Heads of Government consider it essential to ensure progress and overall consistency in the activities of the Communities and in the work on political co-operation.
>
> The Heads of Government have therefore decided to meet, accompanied by the Ministers of Foreign Affairs, three times a year, whenever necessary, in the Council of the Communities and in the context of political co-operation. The administrative secretariat will be provided for in an appropriate manner with due regard for existing practices and procedures.
>
> In order to ensure consistency in Community activities and continuity of work, the Ministers of Foreign Affairs, meeting in the Council of the Community, will act as initiators and co-ordinators. They may hold political co-operation meetings at the same time.'
>
> Source: Bulletin of the European Communities, 2 (1974)

Cooperation posed a problem.[2] Some member governments, France in particular, were insisting that Community institutions should have no authority whatsoever in this new activity. Clearly some form of overall coordination would be needed if the 'European Union', as it was beginning to be called, was to develop in a coherent manner in various directions. Introducing the heads of government as the ultimate source of authority, with foreign ministers at their side, was felt to be the only way, or the least controversial way, to ensure coordination and consistency.

As is frequently the case for important decisions, personalities also played a role in the creation of the European Council:

■ Valéry Giscard d'Estaing had been elected President of the French Republic in May 1974. Committed to European integration, he had played, as Finance Minister, a significant role in the early years of the Community. He was determined to go on doing so and the creation of the European Council was a convenient way of achieving this objective (see Giscard d'Estaing 1988). He put his power and energy behind the project, and convinced the new West German Chancellor, Helmut Schmidt, who had also been Finance Minister and with whom he had a good relationship, to endorse it.

■ Something similar to the European Council had been proposed by de Gaulle in the Fouchet negotiations of the early 1960s.[3] It had been rejected, notably by the Benelux countries, as threatening Community institutions and introducing a *directoire* of bigger member states. Jean Monnet, whose influence in all Community countries was considerable, came to the conclusion that regular meetings of heads of government were needed. In 1973 he suggested that they should meet as a provisional government of Europe: 'The point is to place the responsibility for things with the heads of government, since it's they who have the last word . . . [we need] to return again to the springs of power' (Monnet 1978: 505, 509). Since the institutional system that the Benelux countries wanted to safeguard had in fact been conceived by Monnet, twenty-five years before, his credibility was high and his views were instrumental in securing the agreement of the smaller member states.

In any institutional framework the regularity of meetings makes a fundamental difference. Before 1974 summit meetings were important occasions where significant decisions were taken, but with little or no lasting impact on the working of Community institutions. Since then, and increasingly as time has gone by, European Council meetings have come to mark the rhythm of EU activities. Commission papers are put forward, Council reports approved, parliamentary resolutions voted in view of this or that European Council. Early on it was recognized as 'the most politically authoritative institution of the EC' (Bulmer and Wessels 1987: 2). The effect was not to give exclusive authority to the European Council but, even in the absence of legal texts, to give it a leading role in the European integration process: 'The biannual meetings of Heads of State and Government top the pyramid of power' (de Schoutheete 2000: 26). This fact is acknowledged also by those who wish the Union to develop in the direction of a federal state, as evidenced by the Spinelli[4] draft treaty approved by the European Parliament in February 1984. Article 32 of that draft proposed to give broad powers to the European Council and was more specific about these powers than the Single European Act or Article 4 of the Union Treaty as it stands today.

Composition and working methods

The restricted composition of the European Council is described in the Introduction to this chapter. There is, however, a small amount of flexibility: when a foreign minister is absent a junior minister (even, in rare cases, a permanent representative) may take his seat. The Prime Minister of France sometimes replaces, and sometimes assists, the President of the Republic. Over the years a limited number of officials from the presidency, the Council Secretariat, or the Commission have gained a seat in the room, or even, in the case of the Secretary-General of the Council, at the table. On these matters, as in others, the presidency has a certain margin of appreciation. Two delegates per delegation are issued with red badges, which allow them to enter the meeting, in order to submit a note or whisper a message, but they may not stay.

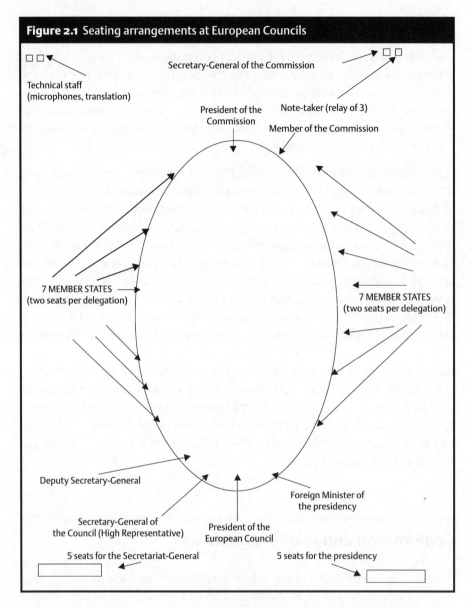

Figure 2.1 Seating arrangements at European Councils

Secretary-General of the Commission

Technical staff
(microphones, translation)

President of the
Commission

Note-taker (relay of 3)

Member of the Commission

7 MEMBER STATES
(two seats per delegation)

7 MEMBER STATES
(two seats per delegation)

Deputy Secretary-General

Foreign Minister of
the presidency

Secretary-General of
the Council (High Representative)

President of the
European Council

5 seats for the Secretariat-General

5 seats for the presidency

Proceedings are relayed to the outside world by a system of note-takers. An official from the Council Secretariat sits in the room and takes notes. Every quarter of an hour he is replaced, and goes out to brief orally the Antici group (personal assistants of the permanent representatives) who are sitting in an adjacent room, in the red zone where other members of national delegations do not have regular access. Each Antici[5] then transmits his notes to his own delegation, in another part of the building known as the blue zone. This indirect dissemination of information guarantees that national delegations know something of the proceedings inside, but with considerable delay and in a way which makes direct attribution of specific words to any participant nearly impossible. Such an extraordinary system would not have survived if heads of government were not happy with the result, namely that they operate at some distance, both in space and time, from the views and comments of their own civil servants.

Peter Ludlow has compared the physical arrangements at a European Council 'to a vast temple in some oriental rite' (Ludlow 2000: 15). Within the precincts are innumerable journalists and foreign diplomats, who have received special clearance, are professionally interested in the proceedings, but have no access to the temple itself. Inside the temple, and within the first veil (blue zone), are the national delegations who get indirect information on the ritual. A select few of these (junior ministers, permanent representatives) can penetrate a little further in the sanctuary (red zone) to get closer to the action. But even they have only occasional access to the inner sanctum where the high priests officiate in seclusion.

Although there are exceptions (the Nice European Council lasted four days) typical European Councils usually extend over a two-day period. On the first day, after a family photograph, the President of the European Parliament addresses the European Council. This custom, introduced in the late 1980s, has a highly symbolic value for the Parliament but rarely has, in practice, a significant impact on the proceedings. For the rest of the day, including lunch, the full European Council meets to debate the different points on the agenda. In the evening heads of government and foreign ministers usually separate for dinner. Foreign ministers will normally discuss a few specific points of international relations. Prime ministers will frequently have a freewheeling discussion on European affairs, recalling the fireside chats of the early European Councils.

The European Council is not bound by specific procedures. If the discussion gets bogged down the presidency may well interrupt the meeting and hold bilateral conversations (known as 'confessionals') with each delegation. The President can also encourage two or more delegations to get together to solve a specific problem. Any procedural suggestion which seems likely to get results is usually accepted, at least on an experimental basis.

In the course of the evening a small group of officials from the presidency, the Council Secretariat, and the Commission will be working on draft conclusions. An initial text, including points which need to be mentioned whatever the outcome of the discussions, is prepared by the Council Secretariat well before the European Council meets. It needs to be completed and amended in view of the first day's discussion. The final draft must be available in all official languages at dawn. In the 1970s, all member governments participated in this drafting exercise. After a number of mishaps it was thought more expedient to entrust it to the presidency and the Council Secretariat, much to the relief of national delegations.

At dawn on the second day draft conclusions are distributed to delegations, and each head of government will look at them over breakfast, discussing specific points with their assistants. Then the European Council convenes and spends most of the morning, and if necessary part of the afternoon, finalizing the conclusions. Traditionally these texts are known as 'presidency conclusions' but the time spent on them shows that everyone is aware of their importance for the daily working of the Union. In one exceptional case (Athens in 1983) disagreement was such that no conclusions could be drafted.[6]

In recent years it has become customary to invite heads of government from candidate countries for lunch and a brief session on the second day of most European Councils. This custom again has a highly symbolic value for the candidate countries but does not, in practice, usually lead to major decisions. A possible exception to the rule was the 2001 Gothenburg Summit, when the presence of candidate countries' heads of government may have encouraged the European Council to accelerate the timetable for eastern enlargement.

The last, but certainly not least important, act of a European Council is to give press conferences. Frequently, each national delegation gives its own press conference to a vast number of journalists who commute from one delegation to another. By comparing notes the press normally gets a clear picture of the actual debate. This led Roy Jenkins (1989: 75), President of the Commission from 1977 to 1981, to call European Councils 'a restricted meeting with full subsequent publicity'.

In the following days the President of the European Council, accompanied by the President of the Commission, reports to the European Parliament on the meeting. This exercise, prescribed by Article 4 TEU, tends to repeat information already available in the press. It therefore contributes to the general sense of frustration that the European Parliament entertains *vis-à-vis* the European Council, on whose activities it exerts no control and little influence. The European Parliament is listened to at the beginning of a European Council and informed of the conclusions after it has finished, but 'there is no evidence that either of these procedures produce much in the way of influence' (Nugent 1999: 203)

Although European Councils are brief moments of exceptional intensity—and the highlight of each successive presidency—they are, of course, prepared long in advance. This preparation is in the hands of the presidency, with the help of the Council Secretariat. Coreper (the Committee of Permanent Representatives) and the General Affairs Council try to coordinate issues and documents produced by various Council formations, and may have preliminary discussions on some points on the agenda. But political guidance is in the hands of the President of the European Council himself. Together with the Council Secretary-General, he normally makes a tour of capitals in the weeks preceding the meeting to clarify positions, test possible solutions, or suggest a form of words. On this basis he fixes the agenda and communicates it to his colleagues in a letter sent a few days before the meeting. This agenda is not absolutely binding, because there is no way of preventing a head of government from raising a subject he wants to raise. But in general terms the authority of the President is respected. It is in fact the presidency which 'drives' a European Council, in the knowledge that the best prepared meeting can be derailed by unforeseen events in the international sphere, such as a Balkan crisis.

In parallel, the Council Secretariat works confidentially, in close contact with the presidency and the Commission, on draft conclusions, incorporating both routine issues (greetings to the President of the European Parliament, reports to be approved, and so on) and potential solutions to the more controversial points which will be discussed by the European Council. It is this draft, completed and amended after the first day's discussions, that is the basis of presidency conclusions. Its quality is obviously important for the final result.

Three final points complete this brief sketch of the working methods of the European Council:

- *Informal meetings.* The first informal meeting was called by the Spanish presidency at Formentor (Mallorca) in September 1995 to discuss the issues of the ongoing IGC. Informal meetings are usually shorter than formal meetings, foreign ministers are not always present, there are no conclusions. The purpose is to allow for the sort of confidential exchange of views and brainstorming which a growing work load has gradually eliminated from regular meetings.

- *Thematic meetings.* In recent years there has been a tendency to call meetings on a specific subject such as justice and home affairs (Tampere, October 1999) or economic and social affairs (Lisbon, March 2000). This innovation reflects the growing involvement of the European Council in concrete policy issues. Thematic meetings of this sort are likely to increase in scope and frequency over time.

- *Primenet.* Heads of government themselves, and their immediate assistants (*sherpas*), obviously communicate directly by phone, fax, and e-mail, and this plays a certain role in the preparation of a European Council. At regular intervals suggestions have been put forward to formalize these links in some form of secretariat. One recent proposal called for a secure fax and videoconference system (codenamed 'Primenet') between offices of the heads of government. Such proposals face technical and linguistic difficulties, compounded by tacit yet resolute opposition from a variety of actors (foreign ministers, Commission, Coreper, and the Council Secretariat). Up to now nothing much has come of these proposals, but they seem likely to reappear in the future.

An example which gives food for thought is that of sanctions against Austria when the far right FPÖ party came into the government (in 2000). Because there was no basis in the Treaty for sanctions, and Community procedures were therefore unavailable, direct contact between heads of government was used to produce a decision of fourteen member governments in a matter of hours. A few weeks later, however, several heads of government were wondering whether their decision had not been too hasty. There can be disadvantages to direct and speedy decision making at the highest level.

Legal nature and characteristics

The legal nature of the European Council has been the object of much academic debate (see Taulègne 1993: 92–100). Part of the problem stems from the fact that for the first twelve years of its existence (1974–86), the European Council met, and exercised significant power, without any legal basis in the Treaties. In a highly structured legal system, such as the Community, this was indeed a strange phenomenon. The Single European Act specified the composition of the European Council but deliberately abstained from defining its role (De Ruyt 1987: 108–9). The Maastricht Treaty, slightly modified in Amsterdam, offers some description of its role, essentially in what are now Articles 4 and 13 TEU, but, as we shall see, this description is largely inadequate.

In a limited number of cases (for example, Articles 7 TEU and 121 and 122 TEC) the Treaty specifies that decisions must be taken by the Council meeting at the level of heads of state or government. In those cases the legal status of the meeting is clear. In all other cases the situation is ambiguous.

Perhaps the best way to visualize the European Council is to consider it not as an institution, in legal terms, but as a locus of power. This makes it easier to explain its main characteristics: its authority, its informality, the special relationship between participants including the impact of seniority, and finally its ambivalence.

- *Authority.* The European Council brings together political personalities who, in their national capacity, are ultimate decision-takers. Collectively they consider themselves, in the European context, as having a similar task. Essentially they come together to take decisions, and expect these decisions to be respected. Hence the specific nature of European Council conclusions. Strictly speaking they are not legally binding, but in fact they constitute a form of *soft law* which European institutions (Council and Commission) have to take into account and respect. Cases have been known where Councils (of Economic and Finance Ministers, Ecofin, in particular) circumvented European Council decisions, but these are the exception not the rule. In practice 'presidency conclusions' are highly respected documents with a real impact on the life of the Union.

- *Informality.* The European Council has always attached the highest importance to the informality of its meetings. It works on the basis of restricted sessions where heads of government and foreign ministers sit alone, face to face, frequently addressing each other by their first names. 'Keine Papiere, keine Beamte' (no papers, no civil servants) was one of the regular utterances of Helmut Schmidt when he was Chancellor of West Germany. His predecessor, Willy Brandt, wanted European Councils to be like a fireside chat (*Kamingespräch*).

Roy Jenkins considered the European Council as 'a surprisingly satisfactory body, mainly because it is intimate' (Jenkins 1989: 74). With time, meetings have tended to become more structured and specific papers are, in practice, actively debated. But the principle of privacy and direct contact, quite frequently confrontational, remains. Occurring at regular intervals this creates between participants a kind of mutual understanding that is unusual, at that level, in international affairs.

- *Unequal relationships.* In the abstract all heads of government are equal, just as their states have equal status in international law. But because the European Council is a locus of power, the fact that some participants have in fact more power (because they represent a bigger country) is immediately apparent and implicitly understood by all. Put simply, 'the intergovernmental nature of the European Council is more marked than that of the sectoral Councils' (Hayes-Renshaw 1999: 25). Thus, if smaller countries are sometimes diffident about the increasing power of the European Council, it is precisely because they know that they are less well protected at that level than in institutions governed by legal rules and strict procedures. The same is true for the Commission. When operating in the Council, the rights and prerogatives of the Commission are well defined and protected by the Treaty. At European Council level that is not the case. Some Commission Presidents (Jacques Delors in particular) have been able to exploit this lack of clarity to their advantage. Others have felt constrained by it.

- *Seniority.* Because participants are few in number and personal relations important, the balance of power in the European Council is influenced by seniority. Newcomers will not be able to pull their full weight at first meetings. Heads of government of smaller member states can expect to exert more influence after several years of being present, particularly after they led a successful presidency. The cases of Wim Kok, Prime Minister of the Netherlands since 1994, Jean Claude Juncker, Prime Minister of Luxembourg since 1995, Jean-Luc Dehaene, Prime Minister of Belgium from 1992 to 1999, are examples of representatives of smaller member states exercising considerable influence, certainly thanks to personal qualities but also because of their seniority.

- *Ambivalence.* Finally, viewing the European Council as a locus of power helps explain its ambivalence in institutional terms. Unlike other European institutions, its powers, procedures, decision-making process are not determined by the Treaty. It deals with whatever problem it wants to deal with, in the manner it judges most appropriate. Nowhere is its role clearly defined, yet that role is fundamental to the life of the Union. It can live with that ambivalence because it is bent on the exercise of power *de facto* and not on legally binding decision-making.

The European Council is generally considered as strictly intergovernmental, except when it acts formally as a Council. However it has been known to vote (in

Milan in 1985 to call the intergovernmental conference that was to lead to the Single European Act, with Britain, Denmark, and Greece opposing). Moreover the President of the Commission is *de jure* a member of the European Council (Article 4 TEU) and highly important decisions concerning the Community are taken at that level.

Perhaps because of this ambivalence, theories of European integration have some difficulty in accommodating the role of the European Council. Its composition and the power it wields would seem at first sight to confirm liberal intergovernmentalist (LI) theory, best developed by Andrew Moravcsik. LI explains European integration as a succession of bargains between the bigger member states, based on national interests, domestic politics, and the constraints of world environment. According to this view, 'the creation of the European Council was explicitly designed to narrow rather than to broaden the scope for autonomous action by supranational actors' (Moravcsik 1998a: 488). 'Its major consequence was to transfer policy initiative away from the more rule governed Commission and Parliament' (Moravcsik 1998a: 310). 'Bargaining outcomes reflect the relative power of states rather than supranational entrepreneurship' (Moravcsik 1998a: 485).

One may indeed consider, with Moravcsik, successive intergovernmental conferences as 'bargains' concluded by member governments at the highest level. But the net effect of these bargains, over two decades, has been a considerable increase in the powers of supranational institutions: more majority voting maximizing the power of initiative of the Commission, more legislative power for the Parliament through the cooperation and co-decision procedures, recognition of the primacy of European law thereby fortifying the position of the Court, creation of a European Central Bank with unparalleled independence. The Union has obviously more supranational elements today than it did in 1974. If supranational actors 'have only a rare and secondary impact' on negotiations (Moravcsik 1998a: 485), how is this transfer of power to be explained?

Historical institutionalism, on the other hand, considers that institutions, by themselves, 'structure political situations and leave their own imprint on political outcomes' (Thelen and Steinmo 1992: 9). According to this view, actors are assumed not to be entirely aware of, or concerned about, the long-term institutional consequences of the decisions they take. To explain in this way the integrative impact of the European Council over a quarter of a century presupposes, however, a lasting degree of political naïveté not normally associated with heads of government. We have seen that the European Council, unlike other institutions, is not bound by strict rules and procedures. It is master of its own agenda and can quite easily change one of its own decisions if unforeseen consequences become apparent. It does so quite frequently: for instance when in Edinburgh in December 1992 it decided to open new accession negotiations without respecting the conditions it had itself fixed six months earlier at Lisbon.

The fact is that theoretical models have difficulty reconciling the different and sometimes contradictory facets of European integration. That difficulty is perhaps most apparent when dealing with that all important yet ambivalent body: the European Council.

Functions

The role of the European Council is defined by the first indent of Article 4 TEU: 'it shall provide the Union with the necessary impetus for its development and shall define the general political guidelines thereof.' Article 13 TEU gives some further indication of the role of the European Council in foreign and security policy. Article 99 TEC gives it a role in the definition of broad economic guidelines and Articles 112, 121, and 122 TEC reserve to the heads of government certain specific decisions in the field of economic and monetary union. These articles were introduced by the Maastricht Treaty. They are partly based on a text adopted as a 'Solemn Declaration' (therefore not legally binding) at Stuttgart in 1983 (see Exhibit 2.2).

The extreme caution and diffidence with which the role of the European Council has been treated over the years is quite remarkable. What is particularly striking is that the 1983 Stuttgart declaration, which remains today the most elaborate text, even if not binding, on which member governments have ever agreed in this respect, is in fact totally inadequate. Functions of the European Council go well beyond the official texts.

Exhibit 2.2 Functions of the European Council, Stuttgart, June 1983

2.1.2 In the perspective of European Union, the European Council

- provides a general political impetus to the construction of Europe;

- defines approaches to further the construction of Europe and issues general political guidelines for the European Communities and European Political Co-operation;

- deliberates upon matters concerning European Union in its different aspects with due regard to consistency among them;

- initiates co-operation in new areas of activity;

- solemnly expresses the common position in questions of external relations.

2.1.3 When the European Council acts in matters within the scope of the European Communities, it does so in its capacity as the Council within the meaning of the treaties.

Source: Bulletin of the European Communities, 6 (1983).

Having no adequate textual references, we have no alternative but to concentrate on practice, and describe the role of the European Council as it is effectively exercised; that is, in terms of five main functions:[7]

- General political guidance and impetus
- Decision-making of last resort
- Visibility in external affairs
- Solemn ratification of significant documents
- Negotiation of treaty changes

Political guidance and impetus

The most traditional function of the European Council is to provide political guidance and impetus across the whole spectrum of Union activities. This was indeed the main reason given for its creation. It is mentioned both by the Tindemans report[8] (1976) and by the Stuttgart Declaration (1983) and is the sole function clearly described in the Treaty (Article 4 TEU). In the early texts the accent was put on ensuring consistency between Community affairs and other forms of European activity. At a time (before the Maastricht Treaty) when these branches were completely separated, the European Council was indeed the only place where some form of consistency could be ensured.

This task implies the right to launch new fields of activities. In Rome in December 1975 the European Council decided to initiate cooperation in the fight against terrorism and organized crime. In Hanover in June 1988 it appointed a group to look into economic and monetary union. At Lisbon in March 2000 it opened up a new field of action in social affairs and economic policy. Gradually it has acquired a sort of monopoly in this respect: 'Nothing decisive can be proposed or undertaken without its authority' (Taulègne 1993: 481).

Basically the European Council fixes the agenda of the European Union and is the place where strategic orientations are given. This is true for all fields of activity. Article 13(2) TEU specifies that it is the European Council which approves common strategies in the framework of CFSP, as it has done *vis-à-vis* Russia and Ukraine. As far as the Community is concerned, orientations leading to the completion of the internal market and to monetary union were defined at that level. Since the Maastricht Treaty, the European Council has devoted considerable time and effort to economic policy issues formerly dealt with by the Ecofin Council.

One example, among many, of political guidance is the momentous decision at Copenhagen in December 1993 on enlargement. At no other level would it have been possible to decide, with little or no public debate, to offer accession to central and eastern European countries (see Exhibit 2.3).

Exhibit 2.3 Political guidance on enlargement, Copenhagen, December 1993

'The European Council today agreed that the associated countries in Central and Eastern Europe that so desire shall become members of the European Union. Accession will take place as soon as an associated country is able to assume the obligations of membership by satisfying the economic and political conditions required.

Membership requires that the candidate country has achieved stability of institutions guaranteeing democracy, the rule of law, human rights and respect for and protection of minorities, the existence of a functioning market economy as well as the capacity to cope with competitive pressure and market forces within the Union. Membership presupposes the candidate's ability to take on the obligations of membership including adherence to the aims of political, economic and monetary union.'

Source: Copenhagen European Council. Presidency Conclusions. Point 7. A. (iii).

Decision-making

It was certainly not the initial intention of the member states that the European Council should serve as ultimate decision-taker, a court of appeal for settling problems too complex, or too politically sensitive to be resolved at the Council level. Quite the contrary: both the Tindemans report on European Union (1976) and the Dooge report[9] on institutional reform (1985) stated that this should *not* be the case. Official texts, like the Stuttgart Declaration (1993), steer clear of giving to the European Council a decision-making capacity. But in fact, over the years, that is exactly what it has acquired and exercised.

Examples abound. Successive European Councils wrestled in the early 1980s with the intractable British budgetary problem until a solution was finally found at Fontainebleau in June 1984. 'Virtually every decision that affected the development of the internal market since the early 1980s was taken by the European Council' (Sbragia 1991: 63). The 'packages' around the financial perspectives of the Union (Delors I, Delors II, Agenda 2000), which involve an element of distributive bargaining between member governments, have always been settled at the top level (see Exhibit 2.4). The same is true of decisions concerning the seat of European institutions, as taken at Edinburgh in December 1992 and in Brussels in October 1993. The same applies to the appointment of the President of the Commission or of the High Representative for CFSP.

The recent trend towards thematic European Councils (Luxembourg on employment, Tampere on justice and home affairs, Lisbon and Stockholm on economic and social policy) is an obvious confirmation of a tendency to debate specific concrete problems at the highest level.

The reason generally given for this evolution is the growing incapacity of the

Exhibit 2.4 Decision-making in the European Council, Berlin, March 1999

The Berlin European Council settled the financial perspectives (Agenda 2000) for the period 2000–2006. The following table (one of several) is indicative of the detailed decisions such an exercise implies.

. . .

11. An indicative financial framework for EU-21 as set out in Table B attached should accompany the financial perspective. It should include additional own resources resulting from the accession of 6 new member States, and set out in an additional heading 8 (enlargement) the total cost of enlargement for each of the years 2002–2006, expressed as maximum amounts in appropriations for commitments for agriculture, structural operations, internal policies and administration, as follows:

Heading 8 (Enlargement) (appropriations for commitments) (Mio. Euros 1999 prices)					
	2002	2003	2004	2005	2006
Heading 8 (Enlargement)	6.450	9.030	11.610	14.200	16.780
Agriculture	1.600	2.030	2.450	2.390	3.400
Structural operations	3.750	5.830	7.920	10.000	12.080
Internal policies	730	760	790	820	850
Administration	370	410	450	450	450

Source: Berlin European Council. Presidency conclusions. Part I.

General Affairs Council to coordinate the activities of other Councils. This failure compels the European Council to step in as arbiter. However, it is also the case that heads of government, though accepting in principle that their role should be one of mere guidance, have not in practice refused to deal in substance with the growing number of problems coming on their agenda. After all decision-making is a sign of power, and power is not something successful politicians tend to eschew.

External visibility

A century ago political messages to foreign authorities were almost exclusively sent through diplomatic channels. Today they are frequently addressed through the media and directed simultaneously at public opinion, at home and abroad, and to foreign governments. In this game the level at which the statement is delivered is highly significant: a point made by the President of the United States on the lawn of the White House may be identical in form and substance to one made by a State Department spokesman in his daily briefing, but the political impact and significance are completely different.

It is therefore natural that member governments should try to make use of high-level meetings to deliver political messages to the outside world. The very first

European Council, at Dublin in March 1975, approved a declaration on Cyprus and one on the Conference for Security and Cooperation in Europe (CSCE). In the words of the Stuttgart Declaration, the European Council 'solemnly expresses the [EU's] common position in external relations'. This has remained one of its primary tasks.

Over the years European Councils have approved a great number of such statements, covering events in all parts of the world and developments in all fields of diplomacy. Some have had a lasting effect, such as the launching of the Euro-Arab dialogue (Copenhagen, December 1973) or the establishment of a structured dialogue with countries of central and eastern Europe (Essen, December 1994). The European Council declaration at Venice in December 1980 marked a turning-point in the collective position of the member governments on the Middle East by recognizing the right of the Palestinians to self-determination and to a homeland. It was the European Council that decided the principle of sanctions against South Africa (The Hague, June 1986). Some of these statements are made at a time of existing or impending crisis, such as the one made in Berlin in March 1999 on the eve of Nato air strikes in Yugoslavia. Similarly the invitation addressed to President Trajkovski of Macedonia to attend the Stockholm European Council (March 2001), and the declaration approved on that occasion, was an attempt to avoid a potential crisis.

There is no doubt that member states have used the European Council effectively as a means of expressing forcefully common positions on international affairs. It is clear, for example, that the message demanding that the siege of Sarajevo be lifted, sent by the Cannes European Council in June 1995 (see Exhibit 2.5), would be taken seriously precisely because it was sent, in no uncertain terms, at the level of authority which might, if necessary, decide the use of force.

When acting in this external capacity the European Council operates in fact like a 'collective head of state' and this has been used as an argument in favour of a semi-permanent presidency of that body, to avoid the disadvantages of a six-month rotation (Quermonne 1999: 56–62). Whatever the merits of the argument, already formulated by President Giscard d'Estaing in 1978 (Jenkins 1989: 279), present trends do not seem to go in this direction. Most member states, especially the newer and smaller ones, are keen to keep the prospect of exercising their six-month presidency, and to exercise it precisely at that most prestigious level: the European Council. The decision to hold, after the next enlargement, all European Councils in Brussels[10] does not change the presidency system.

Solemn ratification

It is strange, in a way, that meetings initially conceived as a locus of power for taking strategic decisions, in a close circle characterized by informality, have gradually also become the place where formal ratification of important

Exhibit 2.5 Diplomatic statement agreed at Cannes EU Summit, June 1995

'Meeting in Cannes on 26 and 27 June 1995, the European Council sends the following message to the leaders and peoples of former Yugoslavia:

1. The European Union solemnly reaffirms its opposition to the settlement of the conflict in former Yugoslavia by force. It calls for a moratorium on military operations and for the conclusion of an agreement to cease hostilities.
2. Since the beginning, the European Union has lent its support to the efforts of the United Nations to contain the war, to come to the aid of the civilian population and to promote the peace process. It now wishes to emphasize its support for resolute action by UNPROFOR.

The European Union strongly advises all the parties in the conflict to refrain from placing obstacles in the way of the freedom of movement and action of UNPROFOR and of the humanitarian organizations bringing aid to the civilian population. It warns them that the peace forces are determined to overcome such obstacles. The siege of Sarajevo must be lifted. The European Union demands freedom of access to Sarajevo, its enclaves and the safe areas.'

Source: Cannes European Council. Presidency Conclusions.

documents is enacted. Each European Council regularly endorses a series of documents, reports, action plans, or contributions. They are submitted to the heads of government because they have been requested by a previous European Council, or because they apply a previous European Council decision, or simply because the authors (Council or Commission or Presidency) consider that the text needs to be approved at that level.

Exhibit 2.6 reproduces a lengthy list of documents submitted to the European Council at Santa Maria da Feira in June 2000. These are not all short briefs for ministers, and several run to more than a hundred pages. It can safely be assumed that many of them were not read by *any* member of the European Council. One or more will certainly have been discussed, but several will not have been mentioned at any time in the discussions. Their inclusion in the presidency conclusions has become a ritual, and ritualism is not a healthy sign for any institution. On several occasions individual heads of government have insisted that conclusions should only mention points effectively debated and documents strictly in relation with these. But bad habits creep back, political and bureaucratic pressure is strong, and rare are the presidency conclusions that can be said to apply those strict criteria.

Ultimate Negotiator

As we have seen, heads of government have always played some role in treaty negotiations, including in the negotiation of the Treaty of Rome. But over time

Exhibit 2.6 Documents submitted to the Feira European Council, June 2000

- Presidency report on the Intergovernmental Conference
  (CONFER 4750/00)
- Presidency report on strengthening the common European Policy on Security and Defence
  (9149/00)
- Council report on the Broad Guidelines of the economic policies of the member states and the Community
  (9164/00)
- Commission Report: Progress on financial services
  (8924/00)
- Council (Ecofin) conclusions on the Commission report on the implementation of the Action Plan for financial services
  (9280/00)
- EIB Innovation 2000 Initiative
  (9180/00)
- Commission Action plan: 'e-Europe 2002—An information society for all'
  (9097/00)
- Progress report by the High Level Working Party on strengthening cooperation for modernising and improving social protection
  (8634/00 COR 1 (en) COR 2 (gr))
- Contribution of the Council (Employment and Social Policy) on the follow up of the Lisbon European Council
  (9353/00)
- Presidency report on the White Paper on Food Safety
  (8899/00)
- Council (Fisheries) report on integrating environmental issues and sustainable development into fisheries policy
  (9386/00)
- EU-Action Plan on Drugs 2000–2004
  (9283/00)
- Priorities and objectives of the European Union for external relations in the field of Justice and Home Affairs
  (7653/00)
- Council Report on the Common Strategy on Russia
  (9405/00)
- Common Strategy on the Mediterranean
  (9404/1/00 REV 1)
- Report on the Western Balkans presented to the European Council by the Secretary-General/High Representative together with the Commission
  (3166/3/00 REV 3)
- Action plan for the Northern Dimension with external and cross-border policies of the European Union 2000–2003
  (9401/00)

Source: Feira European Council. Presidency Conclusions: annex VII.

that role has become predominant: the European Council has become 'the key forum for determining treaty reforms' (H. Wallace 2000: 20).

In the negotiation of the Single European Act (1985–6) the input of heads of government was limited. The main top-level decision was that the Act would indeed be 'single', that it would incorporate in one document articles relating to political cooperation *and* Community activities, which had been negotiated separately. This was an important decision in terms of political symbolism, and it was appropriate that it should be taken by heads of government. But the texts themselves had been negotiated and largely finalized at the level of officials or foreign ministers.

In the Maastricht negotiations (1990–1) several important points of substance were decided only at the highest level and at the last minute. The contribution of heads of government was therefore more significant than had previously been the case. Nevertheless a large amount of work had been done both by finance ministers, on the articles on monetary union, and by foreign ministers, notably on the second pillar relating to CFSP.

In the Amsterdam negotiations (1996–7), and again in the negotiations leading to the Treaty of Nice, foreign ministers had little impact. Practically all the problems not resolved at the level of personal representatives went to the European Council. Its direct contribution can be documented. By the time negotiations began on what was to become the Treaty of Amsterdam, the European Union had adopted rules on transparency and access to documents. This enables us to allocate responsibility for various parts of the text. As Exhibit 2.7 shows, the contribution of the European Council is very substantial, and not limited to basic issues.

Strengths and weaknesses

There is no doubt that the European Council has worked effectively over the years. For over a quarter of a century it has been the guiding force of the European integration process: 'the primary source of history making decision' (Peterson and Bomberg 1999: 33). Its existence has compelled top leaders 'to invest personal and political capital in the Union's development' (Bainbridge 1998: 192). Time and time again the most difficult problems have been debated, and solutions have been found, at that level. 'The headline making nature of the summits is sufficient to concentrate the minds of the participants and encourage them to reach agreement' (McCormick 1991: 116). It remains 'a mechanism indispensable to the working of the Communities' (Constantinesco 1992: 36). The European Union would not be what it is if heads of government had not been systematically involved in major decisions.

But top-level decision-making has of course its limits and its dangers. In the

Exhibit 2.7 The European Council as treaty negotiator, Amsterdam, June 1997

A comparison between document CONF 4000/97 of 12 June and document CONF 4001/97 of 19 June 1997 allows us to establish exactly what was the direct input of the Amsterdam European Council in what was to become the Treaty of Amsterdam. This comparison shows that the European Council itself brought significant changes in important aspects of the treaty such as:

- **Institutions**: introduction of a possible veto on closer cooperation (Article 11 TEC), elimination of proposed qualified majority voting on several articles (culture, environment, industry, free circulation, social security), a paragraph on transparency (Article 207 TEC), protocol 12 on seats of the institutions.

- **Visa, asylum, immigration**: introduction of QMV after five years for rules concerning the crossing of external borders (Article 67 TEC), specific rules for the United Kingdom, Ireland, and Denmark (Article 69 TEC and protocols 3, 4, and 5).

- **Foreign and security policy**: several points related to relations with WEU (Article 17 TEU and also protocol 1 and declaration 3 both on WEU), elimination of the possibility of closer cooperation in this pillar, elimination of an article on legal personality of the Union.

- **Justice and home affairs**: introduction of a possible veto on closer cooperation (Article 40 TEU), a system of opting in for the jurisdiction of the Court of Justice (Article 35 TEU).

On the other hand it may come as a surprise to find heads of government introducing, at their level, points which seem either trivial or self-evident, specially in the long list of declarations annexed to the Final Act:

- Declaration 4 indicating that two articles do not imply a transfer of competences,

- Declaration 5 indicating that the Political Committee should be able to meet at any time in the event of international crisis,

- The second indent of declaration 11 about philosophical and non-confessional organizations,

- Declarations 24 and 25 specifying that specific expenditures should fall within heading 3 of the financial perspectives,

- Declaration 37 on public credit institutions in Germany,

- Declaration 50 on the duration of the Ioannina compromise.

All these were introduced in the Final Act by the European Council itself.

words of Lord Carrington, 'to introduce into negotiations the top people of all is a hazardous and not always successful move' (Carrington 1988: 317). Dangers relate to the irretrievable character of mistakes. Limits relate both to the nature and the quantity of decisions to be taken.

Negotiation at the highest level is risky: miscalculations or tactical errors occur and cannot, in most cases, be corrected. In the absence of any written record, examples of such mistakes are not easily established. However, the case of the single currency (Exhibit 2.8) is relatively well documented.[11]

The limits of the European Council are particularly apparent when it modifies the Treaties. The important point, not always well understood even by partici-

---

Exhibit 2.8 A tactical error, Rome, October 1990

The main point on the agenda was the state of preparation of the IGC and in particular monetary union. A major point in the debate was whether the future currency (then called the ECU) should be:

- **A common currency**, or a currency circulating in parallel with, but not supplanting, national currencies (pounds, francs, marks, and so on).

- **A single currency**, or a currency taking the place of national currencies.

On this fundamental point no agreement was reached on the first day of the European Council. The draft presidency conclusions, circulated early on the second day, were based on the principle of a *common* currency. When questioned before the meeting started, the presidency answered that it had reluctantly come to the conclusion that the British Prime Minister would in no circumstance accept conclusions based on a *single* currency. Given the previous day's discussions it was difficult to question that judgement.

At the beginning of the meeting Mrs Thatcher declared that the presidency draft conclusions on monetary union were unacceptable, the United Kingdom would not be party to conclusions based on that draft and would need a separate paragraph in which the British point of view would be described.

This changed the deal completely. Frantic activity was noted in the corridors, with several delegations putting pressure on the presidency. The Italian Prime Minister, Giulio Andreotti, who was in the chair, stated in the course of discussion that the presidency had changed its mind and would propose conclusions based on the principle of a *single* currency. When Mrs. Thatcher protested, he answered (with a Sicilian smile) that since the UK would not be party to that part of the conclusions, and would have a paragraph of its own, it could hardly expect to influence the formulation preferred by other member states.

The European Council conclusions are as follows: 'The Community will have a single currency which will be an expression of its identity and unity.' A separate paragraph notes British dissent. If, as seems to be the case, the strategic objective of the British government at the time was to prevent the birth of a single currency, Mrs Thatcher made a serious tactical error. At this level tactical errors are irretrievable. Today the euro is a single currency.

pants, is that the work of the European Council as treaty negotiator is different in nature from its other functions. When it gives political guidance or impetus, when it makes foreign policy statements or takes note of documents, decisions are polit-ical, not legal. Even when it acts as decision-maker of last resort, the results are political. They receive legal form *ex post*, by a Council directive or regulation (such as for the structural funds) or by an inter-institutional agreement (for financial perspectives). 'The input of the European Council, which takes the form of a polit-ical decision, only has legal force once it has been adopted by the Council accord-ing to the relevant legislative procedures' (Hayes-Renshaw and Wallace 1997: 164). But when it acts as negotiator, the European Council is directly modifying the Treaty, the basic law of the Community. It is in fact legislating. That is a com-pletely different task.

The structure and the *modus operandi* of the European Council is well adapted to collective bargaining, to the definition of general guidelines, even to the drafting of political statements. It is not well adapted to a legislative function. Hectic night sessions with no assistants in the room, multilingual debate on texts which appear and disappear from the negotiating table without having been studied in depth, across-the-board compromises on unrelated issues at the break of dawn, cannot lead to clear legal texts. The complexity and confusion of the Treaties (thirteen protocols and fifty-nine declarations were annexed to the Amsterdam Final Act) must be partly attributed to the way in which they are negotiated. It took legal and linguistic experts, under the guidance of Coreper, two months to establish in legal terms what had been decided at Amsterdam. Several weeks of a similar exercise were undertaken after the European Council at Nice. The fact is that no civilized nation legislates in such an uncoordinated and risky way. The direct implication of the European Council in treaty negotiation is clearly essential, but sooner or later some discipline will need to be introduced in the procedure.[12]

Another obvious limit relates to the number of meetings: three times a year initially, later generally two, and, more recently, four. It is reasonable to assume that, in view of their other obligations, it would be impossible for heads of gov-ernment to meet more frequently, on a regular basis. But on the other hand it is far from clear that three or four meetings a year, however intense, are sufficient to deal effectively with a growing workload. Governing an increasingly complex multinational entity needs more regular and more frequent efforts. European Councils are frequently short of time. The fact that numerous documents are put on the agenda (and in presidency conclusions) without being discussed at all, seems to indicate that the system has reached the limits of its capacity. It also implies that the European Council is often unable to control the execution of its own decisions.

Finally the European Council works on the basis of consensus. It has 'placed political consensus at the centre of the integration process as a complement to the working of collective legal organs based on unanimity or majority voting' (Perez Bustamante and Palacio 1998: 11). But consensus, as a decision-making procedure, is relatively inefficient. European Councils frequently fail to reach decisions, creating 'left overs' (as after Amsterdam) or postponing decisions to a future date.

Conclusion

In many ways 'the whole European Union system revolves round the European Council' (Ludlow 2000: 15). The dates of its meetings, announced well in advance, mark the rhythm of the Union's various activities in the way religious feast days marked the rhythm of daily life in medieval Christendom. Foreign governments, the press, business organizations study Presidency conclusions to gauge the health, the dynamics, future orientations and potential actions of the Union.

In successive meetings over the years, it has largely fashioned the Union as we know it today. And the fact is that, even if the European Council is basically intergovernmental in nature, the system it has so largely contributed to establishing is not mainly intergovernmental. At the end of the century the Union is both much larger, much more integrated, and more supranational than it was in 1974. With hindsight it is clear, therefore, that Monnet was justified in advocating its creation. Those who feared, at the time, that it would lead to an intergovernmental system dominated by a *directoire* of major partners were proven wrong. 'The European Council worked its way into the Community decision making process without deeply undermining the institutional balance' (Werts 1992: 295).

What are the underlying reasons for this result? For most of the time since 1974, France and Germany have been governed by leaders strongly committed to their mutual cooperation and to furthering European integration. They found enough support for this ambition in the Benelux, in Italy, sometimes in Spain and Portugal, more recently in Finland, to push the Union forward, even in the face of winds of scepticism blowing from Britain or Scandinavia. Monetary union is a typical example. Moreover, for a long time, the Commission was chaired by Jacques Delors, who had developed a real talent for harnessing the power of the European Council to further the dynamics of integration (see Chapter 4). In the absence of any of these conditions the results would have been very different.

Because the European Council appears to be working effectively, alongside an institutional system that shows signs of stress, the temptation to increase its role is strong. Those tempted to follow this course include some, such as Joschka Fischer, the German Foreign Minister, who are ardent federalists. Equally tempted are those, such as Tony Blair, the British Prime Minister, who have a more intergovernmental approach. But the fact is that the European Council, however important its past, present, and future role, has come close to the limit of its potential. Its authority will no doubt be consolidated, but it is not a panacea for the ills of the Union. It will certainly play a significant role in resolving the problems of European governance. But it will only be a part of the solution to that most difficult problem.

Notes

1 This results from Declaration no. 4 annexed to the Final Act of the Maastricht IGC.

2 The early developments of political cooperation are described in de Schoutheete (1986: 21–36) and Nuttall (1992: 51–148).

3 This negotiation takes its name from French Ambassador Christian Fouchet, and has been studied by Bloes (1970) and, more recently by G. H. Soutou (1992: 126–43, see also the debate, pp. 185–91). For briefer accounts see de Schoutheete (1986: 14–20), Nuttall (1992: 37–46), or Bainbridge (1998: 264–6).

4 Altiero Spinelli, an Italian politician and member of the European Parliament, chaired a group of MEPs who submitted, and got approved by the Parliament in February 1984, a draft treaty on European Union. This first 'constitutional' treaty was never adopted by member states but it did have some influence on later developments, including the Single European Act.

5 This group, which plays an important role in the coordination of Coreper II activities, is named after Massimo Antici, an Italian diplomat who was, in 1975, its first chairman.

6 It is worth noting that European Council deliberations are in fact tape-recorded, but only the Secretary-General of the Council has access to the recording. In exceptional cases he will verify a specific point at the request of one or more delegations. This is particularly important when there is wide disagreement as to what was agreed at a European Council, as was the case after the meeting in Nice in December 2000.

7 These distinctions are somewhat arbitrary and they frequently tend to overlap. Some authors identify no less than nine different functions (Bulmer and Wessels 1987: 76–80). Elsewhere they are counted as three (Dinan 2000: 190), six (Nugent 1999: 201) or even twelve (Werts 1992: 120–22). This variety is, of course, a consequence of the absence of clear legal texts but basically the ground covered is the same.

8 Leo Tindemans was Prime Minister of Belgium in December 1974 when he was asked by the Paris Summit to draft a report on European Union, which he presented in early 1976.

9 James Dooge, a former Irish Foreign Minister, was asked by the Fontainebleau European Council in June 1984 to chair a group to draft a report on institutional reform. The report, presented in 1985, prepared the negotiation of the Single European Act.

10 Declaration 22 adopted by the conference and annexed to the Treaty of Nice reads as follows: 'As from 2002, one European Council meeting per Presidency will be held in Brussels. When the Union comprises 18 members, all European Council meetings will be held in Brussels.'

11 Information is provided mainly by a series of interviews conducted in 1997 by the British Broadcasting Corporation

(BBC) for the preparation of a documentary on monetary union called *The Money Makers.*

12 My personal views on this matter are explained in de Schoutheete (1993 and 1997).

Further reading

Bulmer and Wessels (1987) is now slightly dated but a new edition is announced in The European Union series published by Palgrave (formerly St Martin's Press, New York, and Macmillan, London). Taulègne (1993) has an in-depth legal analysis. Useful summaries can be found in Nugent (1999: 177-204), Bainbridge (1998: 191-7), Hayes-Renshaw and Wallace (1997: 158-72), and Dinan (2000: 188-91). In French, Constantinesco (1992) is interesting and has a good bibliography.

Bainbridge, T. (1998), *The Penguin Companion to European Union*, 2nd edn. (Harmondsworth: Penguin).

Bulmer, S., and Wessels, W. (1987), *The European Council* (London: Macmillan).

Constantinesco, V. (1992), *Conseil Européen*, in Répertoire de Droit Communautaire (Paris: Dalloz).

Dinan, D. (2000) (ed.), *Encyclopedia of the European Union* (London: Macmillan).

Hayes-Renshaw, F., and Wallace, H. (1997), *The Council of Ministers* (London and New York: Macmillan and St Martin's Press).

Nugent, N. (1999), *The Government and Politics of the European Union*, 4th edn. (Basingstoke and New York: Palgrave).

Taulègne, B. (1993), *Le Conseil Européen* (Paris: P.U.F.).

Web links

The Commission web site 'Europa' has a nine page description of the European Council: **http://ue.eu.int/en/info/eurocouncil**. It also gives, in all Community languages, the full text of presidency conclusions since the Corfu meeting in June 1994. Perez Bustamante and Palacio (1998) publish the full text, in Spanish, of all European Council conclusions since 1974.

Chapter 3
The Council of Ministers

Fiona Hayes-Renshaw

Contents

Summary

The Council is the EU's chief decision-making body, the place where national inter-ests are articulated, defended, and aggregated by ministerial representatives of all the member governments. It is presided over by each member state in turn, and is supported by a small secretariat in Brussels. Changes to qualified majority voting agreed at Nice will make decision-making in the Council more difficult, and will shift the balance in favour of larger member states for the first time in the history of the EU. Enlargement will require intensive socialization of the new members if the Council's work is not to be paralysed.

Introduction

Students of symbolism, were they to visit the sites of the various European institutions in Brussels today, would find plenty of material to fire their imaginations. The Commission's former home, the architecturally avant-garde Berlaymont building, has been stripped of its tons of extraneous asbestos, and is being rebuilt from the inside out, with the work due to be completed in 2003 at the earliest. In the mean time, the Commission and its services have been re-housed in over sixty different (mostly unprepossessing) buildings scattered around streets radiating out from the Rond Point Schuman, the former heart of the European Community's institutional district.

Directly opposite the Berlaymont building stands the rather severe but none the less imposing façade of the Justus Lipsius[1] building, the custom-built headquarters of the Council of Ministers. Its opaque windows and several entrances lend it an air of mystery and impenetrability, while a bizarre numbering system of the building's various levels could almost be construed as having been designed to confuse the non-initiated. Every working day, hundreds of national delegates file past the rather fragile-looking sculpture of Europa guarding the front gateway, and penetrate the building's curiously silent front courtyard, around which are ranged the meeting rooms of the Council, its committees, and working groups.

The back of the Justus Lipsius building, which contains the Council Secretariat's offices and work rooms, faces the custom-built buildings which are home to the European Parliament (EP) in Brussels. These imposing, inter-linked buildings span several blocks of a part of the city now targeted for redevelopment, and are a very physical symbol of the increased stature of the Parliament. Inside the building which houses the hemicycle, the venue for the EP's Brussels plenary sessions, stands a fantastic sculpture spanning several levels, seemingly unsupported, yet marvellous in its complexity—a rather ironic symbol at the heart of the EU's most democratic institution.

This chapter, which is divided into four main sections, examines in some detail the inhabitants of, and some of the visitors to, the Justus Lipsius building. First, the present-day Council is traced back to its origins in the 1951 Treaty of Paris. Second, the structure of the Council is explored, with a view to identifying those individuals who together constitute the various layers of the Council hierarchy. As this volume contains separate chapters on the European Council (Chapter 2) and on the Committee of Permanent Representatives (Coreper—Chapter 13), this chapter will concentrate on the remaining layers of the Council hierarchy—the ministerial Council, the working groups, the presidency, and the Council Secretariat. The third section describes the formal and informal powers of the Council, examines its relationships with the Commission and the EP, as well as its influence in the

EU, and confronts the frequently vexed question of the Council's accountability. Finally, the role played by the Council in the context of the EU as a whole is analysed, as are the challenges posed to the Council by enlargement, followed by a short concluding section.

The origins of the Council

The Council of the European Union can trace its origins back directly to the (Special) Council of Ministers provided for in the Treaty of Paris of 1951, which established the European Coal and Steel Community (ECSC). The creation of a body representing the governments of the member states was a direct and rather obvious attempt to temper the powers of the ECSC's innovative supranational High Authority, which later became the European Commission. When the founding treaties of the European Communities were negotiated and adopted some six years later, the blueprint of the ECSC was applied *mutatis mutandis*, and the Council of the European Communities was born.

Despite the shared name, the powers of the Council in the two bodies could not have been more different. The ECSC's Special Council was required merely to exchange information with and consult the High Authority (Article 26 of the original ECSC Treaty), while the 1957 Treaties of Rome establishing the European Economic Community (EEC) and the European Atomic Energy Community (Euratom) provided that the Council should 'ensure coordination of the general economic policies of the Member States and have power to take decisions' (Article 145 of the original EEC Treaty).

This altered role underlined an increased assertiveness on the part of the member governments *vis-à-vis* the more supranational elements of the European Communities, a confidence that has become still more marked in recent years. It is reflected not only in the additional powers that the Council has acquired, whether formally or informally, but also in the changes which have been made to the structure of the Council.

The Council hierarchy

The Council may be envisaged as a layered triangle, with the European Council at the top, followed by the Council of Ministers, Coreper and other senior preparatory groups, and, at the base, a large number of working groups. Heading each of these levels is the presidency, and the entire hierarchy is underpinned by a Secretariat-General.

The ministers

Although for legal purposes there is only one Council of Ministers, in practice it meets in sixteen different formations (see Table 3.1), depending on the items on the agenda. Each Council is composed of the relevant minister from each member state, as well as a representative of the Commission and a chairman.

The fact of there being a single Council for legal purposes means that any grouping of ministers may take a decision on any issue coming within the scope of the Council as a whole. So, for example, the Fisheries Council, which traditionally meets towards the end of December, frequently finds itself adopting pieces of legislation unrelated to fisheries, which are placed on its agenda by out-going presidencies anxious to maximize the number of decisions agreed during their term of office. Generally speaking, though, each Council discusses issues within its own field of competence.

A certain hierarchy is discernible among the various formations. Three Councils have traditionally met on a monthly basis, and have therefore been viewed as the most 'senior' formations — the General Affairs Council, made up of the foreign ministers of the member governments; the Economic and Financial Affairs (Ecofin) Council, composed of the ministers of finance or economic affairs (depending on how such issues are dealt with in each member state); and the Agriculture Council. The other main Councils meet from two to four times a year,

---

Table 3.1 Council formations

The Council meets in the following formations:
General Affairs
Agriculture
Economic and Financial Affairs
Environment
Transport and Telecommunications
Employment and Social Policy
Fisheries
Industry and Energy
Justice, Home Affairs, and Civil Protection
Internal Market, Consumer Affairs, and Tourism
Research
Budget
Culture
Development
Education and Youth Affairs
Health

Source: Council Decision to be found in *OJ* C 174/1–3 of 23 June 2000.

depending on the topics being discussed, and yet others are convened only once every six months or so. About 100 formal Council meetings take place every year, normally in the Council's headquarters in Brussels. However, as the result of an agreement with the Luxembourg government, ministerial meetings convened in April, June, and October are held in the European Centre in Luxembourg. The presidency may also schedule some ministerial meetings in its own country, especially informal ones.

The ministers are present in the Council in their capacity as the representatives of their respective governments for the issues being discussed. They are also authorized to commit their governments. In other words, if ministers agree to something in Council, it is understood that they have the support of their governments in so doing, and that the legislative act thus adopted will be implemented in their member state.

The presidency

The presidency of the Council rotates among the member states according to an established order (see Table 3.2). Each member state holds the post for a period of six months, beginning on 1 January or 1 July. The order of rotation is changed in the event of enlargement, when the new member states must be incorporated into the list.

Taking on the responsibility for the presidency of the Council directly affects large numbers of civil servants from the member state in question. A coordinating unit is normally created in the capital, which is responsible for ensuring coherence and consistency across the entire range of issues being discussed over the six-month period. The national permanent representation in Brussels comes into its

Table 3.2 Order of presidency rotation 2001–2008 (as envisaged before enlargement)

Year	January–June	July–December
2001	Sweden	Belgium
2002	Spain	Denmark
2003	Greece	Italy
2004	Ireland	Netherlands
2005	Luxembourg	United Kingdom
2006	Austria	Germany
2007	Finland	Portugal
2008	France	Sweden

own both before and during the half year in which that state takes on the presidency, becoming the operations centre for all Brussels-based activity. Its numbers are normally increased, sometimes significantly, in order to deal with the extra demands placed on it. For example, numbers in the French permanent representation were higher than usual in 2000, when France held the presidency from July to December (see Table 13.1).

There is some evidence to suggest that the most successful presidencies tend to be those where national officials forge close contacts with officials in the Commission and European Parliament (EP), and particularly with experienced officials in the Council Secretariat. The larger member states, who have considerable resources of their own, have frequently tried to run their presidencies from their respective capitals, with varying degrees of success. With far fewer resources at their disposal, the smaller member states have never had this option, and have therefore tended to rely to a much greater extent on officials from the EU institutions, particularly the Council Secretariat. There is little empirical evidence to support the suggestion that smaller member states tend to run more effective presidencies (although anecdotes abound), but it is true to say that the smaller member states are generally perceived (rightly or wrongly) as having fewer interests to pursue than their larger partners, and stronger incentives to seek consensus—a good trait in a presidency!

The Council Secretariat

The Secretariat-General of the Council is a relatively small and ostensibly politically neutral body, which underpins the entire Council hierarchy, providing it with vital logistical, technical, and administrative support. It is headed by a Secretary-General, who is appointed by the Council (in effect, the heads of state or government in the European Council) acting unanimously. The choice of an experienced politician, Javier Solana, in 1999 marked a departure from the tradition of appointing a diplomat to head the administrative arm of the Council, and bore witness to the changed role of the Secretary-General. Mr Solana is only the fifth person to hold this post since its establishment in 1952.

The structure of the Secretariat was changed towards the end of the 1990s in order to implement some of the provisions of the Treaty of Amsterdam, which added the role of High Representative for the Common Foreign and Security Policy (CFSP) to that of the Secretary-General, and created the additional senior post of Deputy Secretary-General, who is responsible for the day-to-day running of the Secretariat. The Council, acting unanimously, also appoints the latter. In 2000–1, a number of political and military units were created within the Secretariat under the direct responsibility of the Secretary-General, and a secure building close to the Justus Lipsius building was prepared to house officials responsible for CFSP, the Policy Unit, and the military and politico-military staff. The main body of the

Secretariat is divided into nine Directorates-General (DGs), the largest of which is responsible for administration. The other eight are organized on a functional basis, according to the Councils they serve, and the whole structure is served by a horizontal Legal Service.

The Secretariat is staffed by independent, international civil servants, recruited by open competition (the so-called *concours*) from among the nationals of the member states. The notable exceptions to this rule are part of DG E dealing with CFSP, the Policy Unit (both of which are staffed by a mixture of Secretariat and seconded national officials, reflecting the specifically intergovernmental nature of their work), and the most recent arrivals, the military staff, who are drawn from the ministries of defence of the member states. The number of officials in the Secretariat has changed over the years, in line with extensions in the scope of the Council's activities and successive enlargements (see Table 3.3).

What does the Council do?

The Council's main power is that of decision-making, which it fulfils in large part by reference to its internal rules of procedure.[2] These formal rules have been supplemented over the years by informal conventions and rules of the game, which govern the work of the Council, the presidency and the Council Secretariat.

The Council of Ministers

The Council of Ministers is the EU's principal legislative institution, being formally charged with decision-making across the three pillars that constitute the

Table 3.3 Council Secretariat staffing numbers		
Year	Total	of which A-grade officials[a]
1970	603	94
1975	1,475	161
1980	1,593	183
1985	1,790	188
1990	2,183	217
1995	2,446	273
2000	2,465	316

[a] A-grade officials are university graduates, who fulfil administrative and advisory duties in the Council hierarchy. By way of comparison, it is interesting to note that the EP Secretariat contained some 420 A-grade officials in 2000, significantly more than the Council Secretariat.

Source: Westlake 1999: 320 and 321 and Secretariat documentation.

Union. Specific decision-making procedures and voting rules apply to the different areas of Council activity (see below). In fulfilling its decision-making functions, the Council as a body represents and attempts to aggregate the interests of the member governments. Reconciling conflicting interests within the Council is achieved through a continuous process of negotiation, in the course of which the Commission proposal on the table is discussed in detail, national positions are articulated and defended, coalitions are formed, and compromises put forward. In addition to these internal negotiations, the Council must also engage in negotiations with the other institutions involved in the legislative process.

The Council's work is prepared by Coreper and one or more working groups of national officials (see Chapter 13 for a detailed discussion of the former, and Exhibit 3.1 for more information on the latter). At their meetings, the ministers adopt without discussion those items on the agenda that have been the object of agreement at Coreper or working-group level, and concentrate on those agenda items on which agreement has not been possible at lower levels of the Council hierarchy. At the end of the discussion in the Council, an item on the agenda may be adopted, referred back down to Coreper or one of its working groups for further discussion, or sent up to the European Council for a political input. Most of the detailed negotiation, therefore, and much of the actual agreement tends to occur at various levels below that of the Council itself. Some Secretariat officials have estimated that the ministers both discuss and decide on only about 10–15 per cent of all issues on the Council agenda. However, it is the ministers themselves who take (and the ministers alone who can take) the final decision in the name of the Council.

As the scope of the EU (and therefore the Council's work) has expanded, so the need to coordinate the work of the various Council formations has become more obvious and pressing. From the outset, the General Affairs Council, composed of the ministers for foreign affairs of each of the member governments, was given overall responsibility for coordinating the work of the Council as a whole, but it has not proved equal to the task, for a number of reasons.

The first has to do with the sheer volume of issues that end up on the GAC's agenda, which covers not only coordination but also foreign affairs. The formalization of CFSP and the greater representational role *vis-à-vis* third countries attributed to the GAC by the Maastricht Treaty in the early 1990s resulted in a steadily increasing number of external policy items on the GAC's agenda, a trend which continued throughout the decade. At the same time, the GAC was expected to coordinate the work of an increasing number of technical Councils, dealing with the rapidly expanding competencies of the EU, and entered as internal policy items on its agendas (see Table 3.4). Foreign ministers are interested, not surprisingly, in foreign affairs; they are already busy people, who have neither the time nor the expertise (and sometimes not even the inclination) to get involved in other issues. It is hardly surprising, therefore, that they have tended to focus

Exhibit 3.1 Council working groups

The working groups of the Council form the backbone of the system of European integration, for it is here that the substance of all Council decisions is first discussed, and the vital technical groundwork on draft legislation is carried out in the EU. Every working day, hundreds of national officials attend specialized working-group meetings in Brussels as representatives of their respective governments, operating on the basis of instructions received from their respective capitals and discussing Commission proposals article by article. About 70 per cent of the total number of issues in these proposals are the subject of agreement at working-group level, and are not discussed by either Coreper or the ministers again.

Each Council has at least one working group, and some of the busier or more broad ranging have several. The vast majority of the working groups are created by and answerable to Coreper. The results of their deliberations are sent to Coreper in the form of a report, detailing where agreement has been reached among the national delegates. No voting takes place in the working groups; instead, discussion continues until such time as it is clear to the President that a consensus in favour of a particular outcome has been achieved, or alternatively, that nothing further can be achieved at this lowest level of the Council decision-making hierarchy.

The main task of every working group is to reduce as much as possible the number of issues to be discussed at Coreper and ministerial level. Some of these groups are permanent and meet on a regular (weekly for the busiest) basis, while others may be set up on an *ad hoc* basis for a short period, or in order to deal with a particular issue. Keeping track of the exact number of groups in existence at any one time can be problematic, but according to the Secretariat-General there were some 180 in operation at the beginning of 2001.

A certain *esprit de corps*, similar to that perceptible in Coreper (see Chapter 13), is noticeable among the members of working groups that meet on a regular basis. The personal relations forged through continuous interaction between individuals in the group (many of whom may be long-serving members) eventually fosters an appreciation of differing points of view and a desire to reach agreement by consensus, in an attempt to keep everyone on board. Even in those groups which meet more infrequently, the knowledge of being the lowest and least political level in an ongoing process of negotiation removes the obligation to achieve agreement at any price and fosters an attitude of cooperation probably unmatched in other international organizations.

more on the agenda items relating to foreign affairs than those relating to coordination.

Second, the GAC has been assisted in this dereliction of duty by the European Council, to which issues which would otherwise have landed on the agenda of the GAC are now sent. Consequently, it is the European Council that increasingly sets the EU's agenda, with the GAC frequently being reduced to the position of senior organ of execution for the decisions of the heads of state or government.

Third, other specialist Councils have started to play a more central role, being better placed than the GAC to take high-level decisions on specialized dossiers.

Table 3.4 General Affairs Council agenda items

Year	Total number of items	External policy items as % of total	Internal policy items as % of total
1990	116	75	25
1991	69	82	18
1992	102	65	35
1993	141	71	29
1994	205	74	26
1995	291	86	14
1996	319	82	18
1997	279	77	23
1998	321	76	24
1999	403	72	28
2000[a]	217	78	22

[a] Figures apply to the period January–July only.

Source: Gomez and Peterson (2001: 60–1).

The most notable grouping in this area is Ecofin, which has come to play a central role in discussions (and rather meaty decisions) on such important issues as economic and monetary union and taxation.

Together, these developments have resulted in a diminution and contesting of the central role of the GAC. Arguably, it was unrealistic in the first place to expect the foreign ministers to be able to combine their specialist function with a coordinating one, but there is little consensus as yet as to who should assume responsibility for coordination in their stead. The creation of a Council of Ministers for Europe or a more senior, political level of Coreper has been mooted on various occasions, but with little hope of rapid implementation. In the mean time, a number of minor changes have been introduced in the working methods of the GAC in an attempt to make it more effective (see Gomez and Peterson 2001).

Voting in the Council

Ministers vote in the Council on the basis of simple majority, qualified majority, or unanimity, depending on the rules governing the issue in question laid down in the Treaties (see Corbett *et al.* 2000: 214–15). Under simple majority voting, which is normally used for procedural issues, each member state has a single vote, and eight votes are required to adopt a measure in the fifteen member EU. Decision-making in some policy areas (such as taxation) and for most questions concerned with the second and third pillars requires unanimity, under which any member state may veto the decision being taken.

Qualified majority voting (QMV) is fast becoming the most usual voting mechanism in the Council, and is credited with having speeded up EC decision-making in the 1980s (Teasdale 1996—but see Golub 1999 for an interesting, contradictory view). Under QMV, each member state is allocated a certain number of votes in approximate relation to its size, and thresholds for the attainment of a qualified majority and blocking minority are set (normally around 70 per cent and 30 per cent respectively—see Table 3.5).

The Treaty of Nice will in effect require a triple majority to be achieved for a decision to be adopted by QMV. This triple majority will be made up of (*a*) a

Table 3.5 QMV in the Council

Member state	Population	% of total population		EU-15 votes	% of total votes	EU-27 votes	% of total votes
		EU-15	EU-27				
Germany	82.038	22.86	17.05	10	11.5	29	8.4
United Kingdom	59.247	15.79	12.31	10	11.5	29	8.4
France	58.966	15.71	12.25	10	11.5	29	8.4
Italy	57.612	15.35	11.97	10	11.5	29	8.4
Spain	39.394	10.50	8.19	8	9.2	27	7.8
Poland	38.667	—	8.04	—	—	27	7.8
Romania	22.489	—	4.67	—	—	14	4.0
Netherlands	15.760	4.20	3.28	5	5.7	13	3.8
Greece	10.533	2.81	2.19	5	5.7	12	3.5
Czech Republic	10.290	—	2.14	—	—	12	3.5
Belgium	10.213	2.72	2.12	5	5.7	12	3.5
Hungary	10.092	—	2.10	—	—	12	3.5
Portugal	9.980	2.66	2.07	5	5.7	12	3.5
Sweden	8.854	2.36	1.84	4	4.6	10	2.9
Bulgaria	8.230	—	1.71	—	—	10	2.9
Austria	8.082	2.15	1.68	4	4.6	10	2.9
Slovakia	5.393	—	1.12	—	—	7	2.0
Denmark	5.313	1.42	1.10	3	3.5	7	2.0
Finland	5.160	1.37	1.07	3	3.5	7	2.0
Ireland	3.744	1.00	0.78	3	3.5	7	2.0
Lithuania	3.701	—	0.77	—	—	7	2.0
Latvia	2.439	—	0.51	—	—	4	1.2
Slovenia	1.978	—	0.41	—	—	4	1.2
Estonia	1.446	—	0.30	—	—	4	1.2
Cyprus	0.752	—	0.16	—	—	4	1.2
Luxembourg	0.429	0.11	0.09	2	2.3	4	1.2
Malta	0.379	—	0.08	—	—	3	0.8
Total EU-15	375.325	100.00	—	87	100.00	—	—
EU-27	481.181	—	100.00	—	—	345	100.00
QM				62	71.3	255	73.9
BM				26	29.9	91	26.4

Source: Adapted from tables in EP's initial analysis of the Draft Treaty of Nice (PE 294.737).

qualified majority of the weighted votes (255 votes out of a total of 345 in an EU of twenty-seven member states); (b) a majority of the member states (already implicit under the system of weighted votes); and (c) a demographic majority of at least 62 per cent of the total population of the EU. The effect of these provisions will be to make numbers (and percentages) increasingly important in determining whether or not a qualified majority or blocking minority can be achieved in the Council, and to increase the leverage of the larger member states in general, and Germany in particular.

But this obsession with numbers may be premature and rather academic. The mechanics of Council voting are interesting to outsiders, and talk of changing thresholds usually gives rise to a rash of articles containing complicated mathematical calculations about individual voting strength and possible winning coalitions. However, the reality is rather different. Voting in the Council can but does not always take the form of a show of hands. Instead, the President may allow all delegations to have their say on the point under discussion, then sum up and conclude the debate by asking whether any delegation is opposed to the decision reached. If no one objects, the measure is deemed to have been adopted in line with the President's conclusions. Even in those areas where qualified majority voting is required, consensus is the normal practice, and the acknowledged aim is to get as many member governments on board as possible; consequently, an actual vote is only taken in about one quarter of eligible cases (H. Wallace 2001).

The presidency

National officials readily admit that taking on the presidency of the Council is both a daunting and an exhilarating experience. Operating in the glare of a relentless spotlight, where even the slightest mistake can take on gigantic proportions, can be hugely stressful. When things are going smoothly, however, the effect can be intoxicating. This is particularly true for smaller states, who are not used to being listened to with such attention by their partners, or to playing such a central role in defining outcomes. One national official[3] spoke (only half-jokingly) of a malady which he termed 'post-presidency depression', the symptoms of which are brought on by the sudden silence of the telephone on 1 January or July, and the slowly dawning realization that you are no longer in the limelight, but merely one of the crowd again. The sudden fall in status can be dispiriting.

Exercising the presidency of the Council has always been an important task, but the demands placed on a presidency state today bear no comparison to those faced in the early years of the Community. Not only have the areas of internal and external activity in which the Council is involved increased, but with more member governments on board, negotiations are more time-consuming and can be very much more conflictual. Fulfilling all the duties required of a modern-day

---

Exhibit 3.2 Council presidency duties: a wide agenda

The main formal task of the presidency is the management of the Council's business over the period of six months during which it holds office. This involves a number of different duties:

■ Convening formal and informal meetings at ministerial and official level

■ Providing chairpersons for all meetings held at all levels of the Council hierarchy

■ Hosting one or more European Council meetings

■ Acting as spokesperson for the Council within and outside the Union

■ Acting as the main point of contact for the Commission, European Parliament, and other bodies involved in decision-making

■ Managing the CFSP in close association with the High Representative

■ Ensuring that all the Council's legislative and other obligations are met

■ Aiding the reaching of agreement in negotiations within the Council (with the help of Coreper, the Council Secretariat, and the Commission).

In fulfilling all these tasks, the presidency is assisted by the Council Secretariat, and works closely with the Commission services.

---

presidency (see Exhibit 3.2) for a period of six months can therefore present a rather frightening prospect, particularly for small or new member states.

Arguably, the main task of the presidency is to be (and, more importantly, to be seen to be) neutral. Specifically, this is achieved by the presidency member state fielding two delegations for each meeting: one to chair and manage the meeting, the other to articulate and defend the national position. This can place a heavy burden on national resources, particularly when a small member state is in the chair. The neutrality of the presidency is also displayed by its ability to put forward 'compromises from the chair' when negotiations get bogged down; in fact, it is often said that the 'real' negotiations only commence once the presidency compromise is on the table.

The impression that the presidency can impose its own interests on the rest of the EU, because of the scope for highlighting certain issues of particular interest to the incumbent presidency, is a false one. If a member state wishes a particular issue to come to fruition during its term in office, it must prepare the ground carefully in advance, bringing the other member governments and the Commission along with it. However, in attempting to highlight certain issues, the presidency member state needs to tread carefully, because its colleagues will not look kindly on a presidency which appears to use (or abuse) the office too flagrantly for its own ends. So, for example, the French presidency in the second half of 2000 opened itself up to criticism by manifestly pushing the interests of the larger member states in discussions on institutional reform.

With so much attention focused on the President-in-office, it has become a point of pride for the outgoing office-holders to be viewed by their colleagues as having conducted a 'good' presidency. Such judgements are obviously subjective, but a number of objective criteria can be employed as measuring devices. For example, it is possible to gauge whether Council business was dealt with efficiently and impartially, whether the main objectives outlined in the presidency programme (presented to the Parliament at the beginning of the six-month period) were achieved, whether European Council meetings (particularly the 'rounding-off' one at the end) were well managed and productive, and whether unpredictable events were dealt with calmly, efficiently, and effectively.

Depressingly for the practitioners, it has been suggested that assessing the success of a Council presidency is a bit like judging a rain-dancing contest: the presidential gallivanting may be spectacular, but the rain will come when it comes. In other words, the presidency may just happen to be in the right place at the right time. This judgement may be a bit harsh, ignoring as it does the amount of hard graft required to bring an issue to the point of decision, but it underlines the degree to which the agenda of any presidency is not by any means completely within its control.

The Council Secretariat

The Council Secretariat has two formal functions: conference organization and committee servicing. The vast majority of its staff (87 per cent) are engaged in conference organization, which involves convening meetings, preparing meeting rooms, and producing documents (which in turn requires the translation, photocopying, distribution, and archiving of tens of thousands of documents every year). The other 13 per cent of the Secretariat's staff are engaged in committee servicing, which involves drawing up agendas, preparing briefing notes for the presidency, advising the presidency on questions of procedure and legality, helping to draft amendments, note-taking, and producing minutes for all meetings held within the Council hierarchy. In fulfilling its functions, the Secretariat is at the service of the presidency, but is independent both of it and of the member governments.

So much for the formal role of the Secretariat; its informal role is much more nebulous (and more interesting). The Secretary-General, his Deputy, and Secretariat officials play an important, if intangible, role behind the scenes. They fulfil technical, advisory, and logistical duties and advise the presidency. They act as the memory of the Council, ensure consistency between successive presidencies, coordinate between the various Councils, and ensure that the work of the various preparatory bodies is coherent. They have even been known to perform important mediatory duties.[4] Their role is a vital one, which should not be underestimated.

Relationships with other institutions

The Council and the European Parliament

The introduction of the co-decision procedure in the 1990s transformed the Council–EP relationship from one of permanent confrontation to one of both formal and informal cooperation. Attitudes have clearly changed on both sides: the Council now manifestly takes the Parliament and its work more seriously, and the Parliament is less obsessive than in the past about obtaining more power—the link is obvious. The EP is now a real co-legislative authority with the Council, even if their cooperation is subject to complicated procedures, which can result in tensions between them. The fact that these tensions remain just that, and rarely flare up into full-scale inter-institutional battles, is a testament to the new spirit of interdependence which prevails between them, and is perceptible in the increased contact between the two institutions at all levels.

The co-decision procedure, if it is to operate smoothly and efficiently, requires constant contact between the main protagonists. Much informal negotiation goes on behind the scenes in advance of trialogue meetings (which bring together representatives of the Council, Commission, and Parliament at presidential and official level—see Chapter 5), and steps are taken to try to ensure that issues do not end up being discussed in the time- and resource-consuming process of full conciliation meetings.

Such active collaboration is a far cry from the seemingly endless disputes that appeared to typify the Council–EP relationship in the past, although glimpses were afforded now and again of what was possible when the Council and Parliament wanted the same thing. For example, the arrangements to integrate the five new German Länder into the Community were agreed in the space of just three months at the end of 1990 (Westlake 1991). But there is no question of the Council and Parliament being hand in glove on all issues. Rather, it is a case of the Parliament choosing its battles more judiciously than in the past.

The Council and the Commission

The improvement in relations between the Council and the Parliament in the co-decision procedure has had a knock-on effect on the Commission's dealings with both the Council and the Parliament. The EP is no longer the junior partner of the three institutions; it can now approach the Council directly, and is no longer dependent on the Commission as its interlocutor with the Council, as was the case before the introduction of the co-decision procedure. It is not as if the Parliament no longer needs the Commission; indeed, the support of the Commission can be helpful for both the Parliament and the Council in their dealings with each other, and the Commission is now well placed to play a brokerage role between them.

Relations between the Council and the Commission have always been typified by a complex mixture of cooperation and competition. EU observers who view the Union as a unique supranational experiment tend to talk up Council–Commission skirmishes, presenting them as battles for dominance. For example, much was made of the purported jockeying for position between Javier Solana (the Council's Mr. CFSP) and Chris Patten (Commissioner for External Relations) in the months after they took up their respective positions in 2000. Others point to the very reduced role played by the Commission in the second and third pillars (arguably the areas of greatest and most innovative activity in the Union today), while comitology[5] is frequently presented as an attempt by the member governments to keep an eye on what the Commission is doing, albeit to different extents, depending on the issue and type of committee in question.

The day-to-day reality of Council–Commission relations is much more mundane and reassuring, particularly as regards the first pillar. The two institutions are required to cooperate because they are so clearly interdependent. Thanks to its right of initiative, the Commission is responsible for producing the proposals on which most Council debates are based, but it is reliant on the Council (increasingly in tandem with the Parliament) to adopt the measures it has proposed. Accordingly, it attends meetings at all levels of the Council hierarchy in effect as the sixteenth delegation, acting both as protagonist and mediator in an attempt to have its proposals adopted. There is a direct correlation between the desire of the member governments to engage in greater integration and the degree of influence wielded by the Commission, in the sense that if one or more member governments are determined to block a legislative proposal the Commission's hands are tied. This is clearly the case where unanimity is required, but given the consensual instinct that informs decision-making in the Council, the Commission can be more influential in shaping the policy process when QMV applies. Like a pair of horses pulling a carriage, both institutions need each other in order to fulfil their functions properly.

Exerting influence in the Council

The Council is the Union's key decision-making institution. It is dependent on the Commission to provide it with legislative proposals and, in an increasing number of areas, on the EP as a co-decider on legislation, but no legislative decisions can be adopted without ministerial agreement. The Council's position in EU decision-making in particular and the Union in general is therefore central, endowing it with a large degree of influence over other institutions and authorities.

But the Council is not a monolithic body. It is composed of the representatives of fifteen very different governments, whose wide-ranging interests converge, conflict, overlap, and have to be reconciled on a daily basis across a broad spectrum of issues. The individuals who make up the Council represent member states that differ according to size, economic weight, length of EU membership, administrative culture, negotiating style, and attitude to European integration (*inter alia*). Yet somehow they manage to continue to reach agreement, more often than not by consensus.

Such agreement cannot be spontaneous, so who wields influence within the Council, and what form does this influence take? We have seen that the presidency is a neutral body, which risks the opprobrium of its collaborators if it tries to impose its narrow interests on them. The Franco-German axis is resurrected from time to time, and either hailed or deprecated for trying to lead the Council (and thereby the Union) in a particular direction. The European Council meets infrequently and discusses a limited number of issues, while the GAC has failed to fulfil its role as chief coordinator of the various Council formations. In order to determine who wields influence in the Council, therefore, we need to look at the formal voting mechanisms that govern its work, and the informal channels through which influence can also be exerted.

Where unanimity is the rule, influence is equally shared among the members of the Council: any can block agreement, so the interests of all have to be taken on board. Under QMV, numbers matter, and those member governments with the largest number of votes could be expected to wield the largest amount of influence. However, the EU's system of weighted majority voting is subtler than that. Safeguards have been built in to ensure that the smaller member states, working together, have as much chance as the larger ones to exert influence over the final outcome. Indeed, the big member states are frequently out-voted in the Council (see Table 3.6).

This illustrates a truism of EU negotiations. There is no enduring solidarity between the larger member states (or, for that matter, the smaller ones). Coalitions in the Council are constantly shifting, and tend to be issue-driven rather than power-driven, with consensus and compromise being, by and large, the name of the game. Certain member governments may have common or complementary goals or aspirations which may drive the Union for a period of time, but attempts to create and sustain a type of *directoire* at the heart of the Union fail to endure when they attempt to move from questions of overall direction of EU policy to the minutiae of the policies themselves (or vice versa).

Influence can be exerted by large and small member states alike in more informal ways, by putting forward compromise proposals acceptable to a majority of the member governments, by forming coalitions with like-minded states, and

Table 3.6 Losing the vote in the Council: number of votes where each EU country has been on the losing side (1996–2000)

Member State	Abstained	Voted against
Belgium	5	11
Denmark	2	20
Germany	14	37
Greece	2	9
Spain	10	8
France	6	12
Ireland	1	7
Italy	9	28
Luxembourg	5	3
Netherlands	4	22
Austria	2	8
Portugal	9	6
Finland	0	5
Sweden	0	14
United Kingdom	6	16
Total	75	206

Source: Council Secretariat.

by making their point of view known to the Commission, the presidency, and the Council Secretariat. Yet, the number of votes attributed to a member state continues to matter, as the rather unedifying scramble for votes at Nice in December 2000 amply demonstrated. The decisions on QMV which emerged from the Nice Summit did so only after some of the most heated and bitter exchanges ever witnessed in the EU. They were not helped by the existence of a decidedly non-neutral (large) member state in the chair.

This highly unusual taking off of the gloves was caused by real concerns on the part of the individual member governments about future influence in the Council. Not surprisingly, the final outcome did not please everyone, and it remains to be seen how the new system will operate in practice (assuming the Treaty of Nice is ratified). It is unlikely that decades of commitment to consensus will be ditched overnight, at least by the current member states, but enlargement may inject new dynamics into the process, affecting relative weight and influence in the Council.

The Council and accountability

The democratic accountability of the Council has always been an issue of concern to both proponents and detractors of the process of European integration. Whereas the members of the European Parliament are directly elected, the members of the Council take their seats ex officio in their capacity as national ministers, elected on issues that may be unrelated to those they are discussing and deciding upon in the Council. While the Commission can be voted out of office, the Council as a body has permanent tenure, although the individuals who make it up may (and frequently do) change in the wake of elections or cabinet reshuffles in their national capitals.

The presidency, on behalf of the Council, is accountable to the European Parliament. Presidency representatives attend the EP's plenary sessions during their term of office, where they answer questions put to them by members of the European Parliament (MEPs). The member state in question, represented by its prime minister or foreign minister, presents its presidency programme to the Parliament in advance of taking office, and sums up its achievements to the Parliament when it hands on the mantle to the next incumbent. Between plenaries, MEPs address written questions to the Council via the presidency, and ministers and officials from the presidency state attend EP committee meetings, where they inform the MEPs about ongoing negotiations in the Council.

Such appearances, however, have never succeeded in diminishing claims that the Council is an over-secretive body, operating far from the public gaze. Many have argued that this is a central reason for its success, but there is general agreement that more needs to be done to increase the institution's transparency, given the increasing importance of the decisions it is taking. Some measures were introduced in the early 1990s, but many were subsequently criticized for merely paying lip-service to the notion of transparency. These included:

- the televising of parts of some Council meetings—but the Council refused to allow the televising of votes, preferring to show (more boring) orientation debates on work programmes or major new legislative programmes;
- the publication of voting records—but, as mentioned above, more often than not a formal vote is not taken in the Council;
- the improvement of press briefings and information material—but they still do not include the political nuances which can only be gained from direct access to the negotiations themselves.

One area where a good deal of progress has been made, however, is on public access to documents (see Table 3.7), helped by the creation in 1999 of a register of

Table 3.7 Public access to Council documents			
	1997	**1998**	**1999**
Number of requests	282	338	889
Number of documents reviewed	2431	3984	6747
Percentage of documents supplied	78.3	82.4	85.6

Council documents, which is now posted on the Council's web site every day in the Union's eleven official languages. However, a central problem with this register is the scope of the documents it contains—or, to put it another way, what it does not contain. For example, the Council and the EP clashed in 2000–1 over the sensitive issue of disclosure of documents related to military and non-military crisis management. After intensive negotiations, a pragmatic solution was worked out in April 2001 as part of a larger agreement about access to documents in general. But this dispute may merely be an indication of things to come; the whole area of access to sensitive documents is bound to become more important as the emerging European Security and Defence Policy draws the member states and the Union's institutions into hitherto (for the EU) uncharted waters.

The Council in context

The Council and the larger 'EU system'

As the 2000 IGC drew to a close, and preparations for the 2004 IGC were put in train, national politicians queued up to voice their thoughts on the future of the EU's architecture, adding them to the melting-pot out of which will emerge the concrete ideas to be discussed at the next round of talks on treaty reform. The notions of subsidiarity, democratic accountability, transparency, proportionality, representativity, and flexibility will each be subjected to minute examination, as all interested parties have their say as the potential architects of the expanded Europe of the twenty-first century.

The Council, too, can expect to take its turn under the microscope, but suggested changes to its structure and working methods will owe much to the way in which the Council is perceived by the putative reformer. One long-term observer has described the Council as an 'institutional chameleon', attributing to it differentiated roles and properties, which give rise to different behaviours (H. Wallace 2001). As in the story of the blind men and the elephant (Puchala 1972), each of these roles is deemed to have relevance, but none on its own can explain the Council completely.

What are these differentiated roles, and what do they have to tell us about how the Council fits into the larger 'EU system' today? Wallace has suggested that the Council may be viewed in five distinct ways: as part of a tandem with the Commission, as a club of member governments, as the locus of persistent competition among the member governments for relative influence, as a non-monolithic arena through which networked governance operates, and as an institutional forum which delivers some EU policy regimes.

Our analysis of the Council in this chapter has highlighted two of these images—the Council as a club of member governments, and as the locus of persistent competition among the member governments for relative influence. As such, it has always been viewed as the central body for those who stress the importance of national interest as the factor explaining outcomes in the EU. Indeed, the Council as it exists and operates today may be viewed as the living symbol of the continuing power of the member states in the EU, and of the desire of the national governments to remain at the centre of the process of European integration. This is borne out by the fact that the areas of greatest innovation and movement in the EU today include those contained in the second and third pillars, where intergovernmentalism (and therefore the member governments) reign supreme. Since it is also representatives of the member governments who constitute the IGCs, which initiate constitutional reform in the EU, we can expect the Council to endure and to continue to play a central role in the larger EU.

Despite being the EU's intergovernmental institution *par excellence*, however, this chapter has also attempted to show that, in reality, the Council is a unique blend of the intergovernmental and the supranational. It represents member state interests that are aggregated under conditions frequently owing more to supra-nationality than to intergovernmentalism, and it is not necessarily the interests of the larger member states that determine the final outcome. The Council as an institution works closely with the Commission and the EP, both of whose views inform its work and impinge in important ways on the outcomes.

The Council and enlargement

Enlargement is no novelty for the EU, or indeed for the Council, which has had to adapt to new members on four separate occasions already. An increase in numbers has always necessitated adjustment in the Council and elsewhere, both in terms of socialization (of old and new members alike), and in terms of adaptation of working methods, systems, and structures. The forthcoming eastern enlargement will be no exception, although some disquiet has been expressed about the capacity of the EU to cope physically with such an unprecedented number of new arrivals, even if the enlargement is achieved in waves. Instructing such a large number of new recruits in the ways of the formal (and perhaps more importantly, the informal) procedures which govern the work of the Council hierarchy will be a time-consuming task, but the rapidity with which the new members become accustomed to the so-called Community method will have a direct effect on the work of the Council. The fact that all but two of the new recruits qualify as small member states for the purposes of weighted voting in the Council is also bound to focus attention on the question of the relative weight of large and small states in the Council.

Specific fears about the ability of the Council to cope with the effects of enlargement resulted in a far-reaching analysis of its structure and working methods towards the end of the 1990s. This gave rise to several critical reports and a large number of proposed reforms, but little concrete change. The number of Council formations was reduced, the working methods of the GAC were altered slightly to enhance its coordinating function, the Council's internal rules of procedure were redrafted to bring them up to date with current structures and practices, and agreement was reached on rules governing public access to documents. However, more fundamental problems and weaknesses facing the Council (such as the question of languages, how to deal with the mechanics of flexibility and how to increase transparency while preserving negotiating privacy) still remain to be addressed.

Conclusion

The abolition of the rotating presidency, a greater coordinating role for an enlarged Council Secretariat, a reduction in the number of Council formations to five with all others being sub-committees of a reformed GAC, the appointment of a Mr Euroland and a Ms JHA in addition to a Ms (sic) CFSP: these are some of the (more radical) changes envisaged for the Council by one EU observer (see Grant 2000). Other blueprints for an enlarged EU have been proposed by various prime ministers and foreign ministers, providing an interesting basis for a discussion on constitutional reform. This discussion can be expected to continue well beyond the 2004 IGC, and to be informed by the forthcoming enlargement of the EU.

It will also provide food for thought for theoretical analysts of European integration, who have traditionally had problems encompassing the Council in their accounts of the EU. Spanning as it does the intergovernmental and supranational camps, the Council embodies the enduring tension between the two approaches as explanatory tools for the construction of the EU: it brings together the representatives of the governments of the member states at ministerial and official level, who then frequently engage in behaviour which owes more to supranationality than to intergovernmentalism. The behaviour of these governmental representatives may owe more to sociology and anthropology than to regional integration theory (Rosamond 2000: 6), but the outcome of their conduct is a testimony to 'collective purpose, collective commitments and collective ideas' (Hayes-Renshaw and Wallace 1997: 2).

Yet realist observers of the Hoffmann (1966) and more recently the liberal intergovernmentalist (Moravcsik 1993) schools could neatly put paid to this cosy picture by pointing to the 2000 Nice Summit as an instance where national governments, when the chips are down, continue to rely on 'state interests' to inform their negotiating preferences. Indeed, it remains to be seen whether the Nice Summit will, in retrospect, be seen as merely the first, overt skirmish in a much larger battle for both intergovernmental and inter-institutional dominance in an enlarged EU, which will require the skills of sociologists and anthropologists rather than regional integration theorists to predict possible outcomes.

Eastern enlargement will not leave the Union or its institutions (in particular the Council) unchanged, both because of the numbers involved, and because of the differing cultural, political, and economic situations of the acceding and current member states. Pessimists predict that the retention of consensus as the preferred method of decision-making in the Council will result in paralysis, and that the changes to QMV agreed at Nice will make agreement more difficult to achieve, while granting greater influence to the larger member states. More optimistic observers foresee problems initially, but rely on the Council's informal conventions and processes to assist in the socialization of new members, as has occurred in the past.

In the first decade of the new millennium, the Justus Lipsius building in Brussels will accommodate officials and ministers from the acceding states. The Council will become a culturally and linguistically different—and far more diverse—institution, but with little or no visible external alteration. The imagery of this will not be lost on students of symbolism.

Notes

1 Justus Lipsius was an eminent sixteenth-century humanist, philosopher, and historian, who was born in Overijse, just outside Brussels. Although virtually unheard of today, he was just as famous in his day as Erasmus, his elder by several decades. A street named after him used to cross the site on which the Council's building now stands. The Justus Lipsius building was inaugurated in May 1995.

2 The Council's internal rules of procedure have been amended on a number of occasions. The most recent version was adopted by a Council Decision on 5 June 2000, and is to be

found in *OJ* L 149/21–35 of 23 June 2000.

3 Interview, Brussels, September 2000.

4 Sherrington (2000: 51) quotes one Council official who maintains that 90% of the time it is officials from the Council Secretariat rather than the presidency who find compromise solutions on specific proposals.

5 Comitology denotes the various types of committees (regulatory, consultative, and management) created to oversee the implementation of Community law, a power delegated to the Commission by the Council. These committees are composed of experts from the member states and chaired by a representative of the Commission. See Chapter 7 for an account of these committees, and Chapter 5 for an insight on Council–EP relations as regards comitology.

Further reading

The main works on the Council are Sherrington (2000), Hayes-Renshaw and Wallace (1997) (the main arguments of which are summarized in Hayes-Renshaw and Wallace 1995), and Westlake (1999). For an account of the Council in the 1990s, see Hayes-Renshaw (1999). See also Peterson and Bomberg (1999).

Hayes-Renshaw, F. (1999) 'The European Council and the Council of Ministers', in L. Cram, D. Dinan, and N. Nugent (eds.), *Developments in the European Union* (London: Macmillan).

—— and Wallace, H. (1995), 'Executive Power in the European Union: The functions and limits of the Council of Minsters', *Journal of European Public Policy*, 2/4: 559–82.

—— —— (1997), *The Council of Ministers* (London and New York: Macmillan and St Martin's Press).

Peterson, J., and Bomberg, E. (1999), *Decision-making in the European Union* (London and New York: Palgrave).

Sherrington, P. (2000), *The Council of Ministers: Political Authority in the European Union* (London: Pinter).

Westlake, M. (1999), *The Council of the European Union*, rev. edn. (London: Cartermill).

Web links

The Council's Secretariat-General Internet web site (which can be found at **www.ue.eu.int**) provides information on all its activities, and offers links to its 'Bookshop on line' where certain publications can be ordered, and to the Internet web site of each presidency (**www.ue.eu.int/presid**).

Chapter 4
The College of Commissioners

John Peterson

Contents

Summary

There is no institution, at any level of governance, which closely resembles the European Commission. It is distinctively hybrid in character: the EU's largest central administration and main policy manager, but also a source of political and policy direction. This chapter focuses on the college of Commissioners, appointed by EU member government to direct the work of the Commission as well as much of what the EU does more generally (Chapter 7 examines the Commission's permanent 'services' or Directorates-General). The college is the most political level of the Commission. Yet, Commissioners are unelected and the Commission is often portrayed as an unaccountable technocracy. If the Commission often seemed to be in a permanent state of decline after 1999, so did the notion of honest brokership and guardianship in EU policy-making more generally.

Introduction

The European Commission may be the strangest executive bureaucracy ever created. Despite claims that it can be understood using the accepted tools for analysing traditional bureaucracies (Page 1997), the Commission is in many respects a *sui generis* institution: there is nothing like it in any nation state or other international organization. Legally, the Commission is a single entity. In practice, however, it is a unique hybrid in two senses. First, it is given direction by a political arm, or college, of Commissioners, but the college is unelected. Second, the college exists alongside a permanent, formally apolitical administration, or what is known as the Commission's 'services' or Directorates-General (DGs), for whose work the college is held responsible. This book squarely confronts the Commission's duality by focusing here on the College and devoting a separate chapter (7) to the services.

Even if they are unelected, Commissioners 'are appointed via a highly politicised process . . . are almost invariably national politicians of senior status, and are expected to provide the Commission's political direction' (Nugent 2001: 3). At times, the college—the President, Commissioners, and their advisers—has provided political direction to European integration more generally, particularly during the earliest days of the EEC and again under the presidency of Jacques Delors in the 1980s, when the Commission pushed EU governments to embrace the vision of a 'Europe without frontiers'. At other times, the Commission has found itself marginalized in debates about Europe's future. Consistently, the Commission's role has been contested. It has always existed in a grey area between autonomy and dependence (Lequesne 1996; Edwards and Spence 1997*a*).

This chapter offers a broad overview of the changing role of the college of Commissioners. It is meant to be read alongside Chapter 7 on the Commission's services which, itself, echoes a central theme of this chapter: that the Commission is highly politicized, from top to bottom. As such, it faces enormous difficulties in performing its traditional roles as an independent, honest broker in EU policy-making and guardian of the EU's Treaties. Moreover, the very idea that the EU requires honest brokership and guardianship to work properly often seemed an anachronism by the early twenty-first century, thus raising the question of whether the Commission was in a permanent state of decline.

The origins and history of the college

The forerunner of today's European Commission was the High Authority of the European Coal and Steel Community (ECSC), whose first President was the legendary Jean Monnet (1978; see also Duchêne 1994). Monnet himself was one of the driving forces behind the bargain struck by the six founding member states of the ECSC in the 1951 Treaty of Paris to give the High Authority significant independent powers to regulate markets for coal and steel. The ECSC thus established that common European policies would be managed, and European integration given political impulse, by a non-partisan, central authority.

The High Authority was larger than Monnet wanted it to be: nine members— two from France and West Germany and one from all other member states (plus a co-opted ninth member)—instead of Monnet's preferred five. Thus, a precedent was created for national representation in what was meant to be a supranational administration. The High Authority was also much less nimble and more bureaucratic than Monnet desired (Nugent 2001: 21–2). Partly in protest, Monnet resigned before the end of his term.

The precise design of common institutions for the new European Economic Community (EEC) was one of the most difficult issues in negotiations on the 1957 Treaty of Rome. A Dutch proposal sought to give the EEC a supranational administration that would be more independent of control by member governments than the ECSC's High Authority. However, it ran into opposition, particularly from France, and ended up being 'almost the reverse of what was finally decided' (Milward 1992: 217–18). Compared to the High Authority, the new European Commission (the term 'High Authority' was discarded as too grandiose) was subjected to considerably stronger political control by a Council of (national) Ministers.

The Treaty assigned three basic functions to the Commission: overseeing the implementation of policies, representing the Community in external trade negotiations, and—most importantly—proposing new policies. The Commission's monopoly on the right to initiate policies, along with its prerogative (under what became Article 211 TEC) to 'formulate recommendations or deliver opinions on matters dealt with in this Treaty' effectively made it the 'conscience of the Community', or a source of ideas on new directions that the Community might take. Alongside the European Court of Justice (ECJ), the Commission was also designated as a guardian of the Treaty, and tasked with ensuring that its rules and injunctions were respected.

The early Commissions were small, consisting of just nine members, and united by a 'dominating sense of team spirit' (Narjes 1998: 114). Between 1958 and 1967, only fourteen different individuals served as Commissioners, with each initially supported by two *cabinet* advisers (and four advising the President). Walter

Hallstein became the Commission's first President after previously serving as the chief foreign policy adviser to the first Chancellor of the Federal Republic of Germany, Konrad Adenauer. Hallstein was both a political heavyweight and a forceful leader, repeatedly referring to himself as the equivalent of a 'European Prime Minister'. The Commission achieved considerable policy success during this period, laying the foundations for the common agricultural policy (mere agreement on the CAP was considered a 'success'), representing the Community in the successful Kennedy Round of world trade talks, and convincing member governments to accelerate the timetable for establishing the EEC's customs union.

A watershed in the history of the Commission was reached in 1965. A year away from a scheduled extension of qualified majority voting (QMV) in the Council, the Hallstein Commission proposed a new system of financing the CAP through 'own resources', or revenue directly channelled to the Community rather than cobbled together from national contributions. The plan proposed to give new powers both to the Commission, to redistribute funding between member states, and to the European Parliament (EP), to vet and approve the budget (see Chapter 5). It became a pretext for the French President, Charles de Gaulle, to register his opposition to what Hallstein called the very 'conception of the European Economic Community . . . a construct with federal tendencies' (quoted in Götz 1998: 158–9). Moreover, de Gaulle seized the opportunity to register his highly personal, almost obsessive hostility to Hallstein's federalist rhetoric and bold actions, which included receiving foreign ambassadors to the EEC with pomp, ceremony, and even a red carpet.[1] Above all, de Gaulle was adamant that 'the Commission must give up all idea of acting as a European government-in-waiting' (Tugendhat 1986: 77). Thus, France pulled out of virtually all Community negotiations for seven months, effectively precluding any important decisions from being taken.

The so-called 'empty chair' crisis ended with the Luxembourg compromise in 1966 (with Luxembourg holding the Council presidency). The agreement, released to the world only in the form of a press release, stated that 'where very important interests are at stake the discussion must be continued until unanimous agreement is reached'. Any member government could invoke the compromise in any negotiation if it felt its 'very important interests' risked being violated. The upshot was to give political blessing to unanimous decision-making in the Council, to instil a culture of disputes left unresolved, and generally to hobble the Commission.[2]

De Gaulle insisted that Hallstein be replaced as President of the Commission, which became a single, integrated administration for all three previously distinct 'Communities'—the EEC, ECSC, and the European Atomic Energy Community— in 1967. Headed by the low-key Belgian Jean Rey, the new model Commission initially contained fourteen members (reduced back to nine in 1970). The ensuing decade was a lean time for the Commission. Debates have persisted about, first, whether the Commission's most fundamental problem was weak presidential

Table 4.1 The Presidents of the Commission

Presidents (nationality[a])	Period of tenure
Walter Hallstein (D)	1958–67
Jean Rey (B)	1967–70
Franco Maria Malfatti (I)	1970–2
Sicco Mansholt (N)	1972–3
François Xavier-Ortoli (F)	1973–7
Roy Jenkins (UK)	1977–81
Gaston Thorn (L)	1981–5
Jacques Delors (F)	1985–95
Jacques Santer (L)	1995–9
Romano Prodi (I)	1999–present

[a] Note that the presidency has been held by a non-national of one of the original EEC-6 only once.

leadership (see Table 4.1) or the EEC's more general lack of dynamism, and, second, whether the Community actually achieved more than it is often given credit for in the 1970s (see Nugent 2001: 35–8). In any event, western Europe suffered through a series of economic crises, with the Community itself widely seen as beset by 'malaise'.

By the late 1970s, no European leader could plausibly argue that the Community was working well. A critical mass of member governments—numbering nine after the 1973 enlargement—was persuaded that the Commission should be led by a political figure, or one who was a potential prime minister in their own country. Thus, Roy Jenkins, a senior member of the United Kingdom's governing Labour Party, was appointed as President in 1977. Crucially, Jenkins was the first President to be nominated in advance of the college as a whole, thus giving him scope to influence the composition of his team.

The record of the Jenkins Commission was ambiguous. On one hand, Jenkins clearly 'did not have a high regard for some of his fellow Commissioners' (Nugent 2001: 39) and sought to elevate the position of the Commission presidency itself. Yet, member governments frequently disregarded Jenkins's own advice and preferences. There is little dispute that he 'was not a great success at running or reforming the Brussels machine' (Campbell 1983: 195), which Jenkins (1991: 449) himself described as 'dedicated but rigid'. On the other, Jenkins raised the external policy profile of the Commission by doggedly insisting (against French resistance) that the Commission President should attend Group of Seven economic summits. Above all, Jenkins could legitimately claim to be, along with the German Chancellor Helmut Schmidt and French President Valéry Giscard-d'Estaing, one of the founders of the European Monetary System (EMS), as his 'prompting role in public speeches and mediating role in behind-the-scenes meetings were vital' (Nugent 2001: 40). The EMS helped keep European currency values stable in the 1980s after enormous exchange-rate turbulence had contributed to the economic crises of the

1970s. The EMS was an important forerunner both to the 'freeing' of the Community's internal market and, later, monetary union.

Before the 1979 election of Margaret Thatcher as UK Prime Minister, Jenkins seemed likely to be the first Commission President since Hallstein to be reappointed to a second four-year term.[3] Afterwards, Jenkins's reappointment was made politically untenable by Thatcher's insistence on making the so-called 'British budgetary question' (arising from the size of its net EU budgetary contribution) a central preoccupation of the Community for no less than five years. The long-running row cast a cloud over the Commission presidency of the former Luxembourg Prime Minister, Gaston Thorn. The Thorn Commission made significant progress on accession negotiations with Spain and Portugal and stubbornly nagged member states about their collective declining, global competitiveness (see Thorn 1984; Tugendhat 1986). However, Thorn was a less than dynamic leader and his time as President marked a retreat in the direction of the lacklustre post-Hallstein Commissions.

Thorn was replaced in 1985 by the former French Finance Minister, Jacques Delors. Thatcher's own support for Delors would have been impossible if he had not played such a central role in France's economic policy U-turn of the early 1980s, when its Socialist government rejected traditional reflation, protectionism, and increased public expenditure in favour of market liberalism. Delors carefully reflected on how the Community could be relaunched via a dramatic, headline-grabbing, political project, eventually opting for a radical market liberalization programme. Working closely with the former British Trade Minister and new Commissioner for the 'internal market', Lord (Arthur) Cockfield (1994; see also De Clerq 1990), Delors urged that nearly all barriers to internal EU trade should be dismantled by the end of 1992. By seizing on converging preferences amongst Germany, France, and the UK for economic liberalization, privatization, and deregulation (Moravcsik 1991), as well as the strong support of the European business community, the 1992 project gave European integration renewed political momentum. The first substantive overhaul of the Community's founding Treaties was agreed in the Single European Act, which gave the Commission significant new powers—especially in its extension of QMV on the Council—after 1987.

Delors then convinced European leaders, despite the scepticism of many, at the 1988 Hanover European Council to give him a mandate to chair a high-level committee (of mostly central bankers) to relaunch long-dormant plans for economic and monetary union (EMU). Progress towards EMU was uninterrupted by the geopolitical earthquakes that subsequently shook the European continent in late 1989. On the contrary, Delors seized upon them to champion further advances for the Community. German unification was handled with great skill and speed by the Delors Commission (Spence 1991; Ross 1995), which also stepped forward to coordinate Western economic aid to the former Warsaw Pact states, ironically with more encouragement from the United States (US) than from EU governments.

By spring 1990, with another round of treaty revisions to create EMU on course, a joint letter by the French President, François Mitterrand, and German Chancellor, Helmut Kohl, threw their combined political weight behind the idea of separate, parallel set of negotiations to create a 'political union'. By this point Delors was accepted by Kohl, Mitterrand, and even Thatcher as a political equal in the European Council.

The second half of Delors's ten-year reign was a far less happy time for the Commission. Member governments agreed mostly intergovernmental mechanisms for making new internal security and foreign policies—the so-called second and third pillars—via the (Maastricht) Treaty on European Union, eschewing the idea of giving the Commission its traditional Community prerogatives in these areas. Delors also shouldered some of the blame for the 1992 Danish rejection of the new Treaty, after suggesting that the power of small states would inevitably be weaker in the EU of the future (Nugent 2001: 46–7). By the time Delors left Brussels in 1995, a critical mass of member governments wanted a less visionary and dynamic successor as Commission President.

A Franco-German proposal to replace Delors with Jean-Luc Dehaene, the Belgian Prime Minister and an avowed federalist, was vetoed by the UK. Instead, Jacques Santer, the Prime Minister of Luxembourg, was anointed with a clear understanding that his Commission (in his own words) would 'do less but do it better'. Yet, Santer inherited a full agenda, including the launch of the euro, eastern enlargement, another round of treaty reforms, and negotiations on the Union's multi-annual budget and structural funds for regional development. The Santer Commission handled most of these leftover issues well. Particularly its stewardship of the launch of EMU seemed 'enough to earn any Commission President a proud legacy' (Peterson 1999: 61).

In fact, Santer's legacy was hardly a proud one. For all of the dynamism of the Delors era, the Commission had placed much greater weight on policy initiation than on effective management. Presiding over an administration that had become inefficient and badly managed, Santer's tenure culminated in the dramatic mass resignation of the college in March 1999 after the publication of a report of a Committee of Independent Experts (1999), convened by the EP, on charges of fraud, mismanagement, and nepotism (see Exhibit 4.1). Many observers agreed, along with the German ambassador to the EU, that 'there's no more corruption here [in Brussels] than in any member state, including probably the UK'[4] (see also Peterson 1997). Still, Santer's fall from grace seemed to mark a defining moment in the Commission's evolution.

Santer's resignation in spring 1999 occurred at a particularly difficult moment. The Berlin summit, at which a series of major decisions on the EU's seven-year budget, structural funds, and agricultural reforms needed to be made, was just over a week away. The political crisis in the Balkans over Kosovo was deepening. The German Council presidency undertook a whirlwind tour of national EU

Exhibit 4.1 The fall of the Santer Commission

Jacques Santer's troubles began in earnest in late 1998[a] after the publication of a damning report of the Court of Auditors which suggested that large amounts of EU funds had gone missing in the previous budget year. At the same time, press reports began to circulate alleging that the Research Commissioner (and former French Prime Minister), Edith Cresson, had given plum advisers' jobs in the services to unqualified personal cronies.[b] Characteristically, Cresson dismissed them as part of an Anglo-German 'conspiracy'.[c] In the EP, a motion of censure was tabled— under its treaty powers to sack the entire Commission— which was defeated (by 293 votes to 232) after Santer accepted that a Committee of Independent Experts would investigate charges of fraud and mismanagement. At this point, according to Leon Brittan (2000: 10), a veteran of the Delors and Santer Commissions, the Commission began 'to sleepwalk towards its own destruction'. Santer told the EP that the college would implement the recommendations of the Experts' report, regardless of what they were, in an unusually clear sign of the Commission's political weakness.

The Experts had exactly five weeks to investigate the Commission, yet produced a report that was painstaking in detail. Its most serious charges—leaving aside those against Cresson—concerned improprieties that occurred during the Delors years. The bitter animosity between Delors and the Experts' chair, the former head of the Court of Auditors, André Middlehoek, was palpable in the report, which drew conclusions that seemed to go well beyond the evidence uncovered in its investigation. The report built to a crescendo with the devastating sound bite that it was 'becoming difficult to find anyone who has even the slightest sense of responsibility' for the work of the Commission (Committee of Independent Experts 1999a: 144). The EP's largest political group, the Socialists, announced that it would vote to sack all twenty Commissioners, thus making the outcome of the vote all but inevitable.

A series of efforts were mounted by individual Commissioners to isolate Cresson, including a bid by Santer to convince the French President and Prime Minister, Jacques Chirac and Lionel Jospin, respectively, to ask Cresson to resign. None succeeded. Thus, Santer urged that the entire Commission, as a collegial body, must resign. The President then was defiant in a press conference, claiming that the Experts' report was 'wholly unjustified in tone'.[d] Whether or not Santer's combativeness was politically ill-judged, his fate was sealed by a stroke of bad luck: an English interpreter mistakenly communicated Santer's claim (in French) that he was *blanchi*, or exonerated, from personal charges against him in the Experts' report, to the non-French press as a claim that he was 'whiter than white'.[e] It became widely seen as a political necessity that Santer had to go, and go quickly.

Ironically, the Commission had undertaken a series of internal reforms under Santer, and had become—on balance—better managed and more efficient than it had been under Delors (see Peterson 1999; Cram 1999a; Metcalfe 2000; Nugent 2000: 49–50). But the efforts were far from enough to cure the Commission of the administrative pathologies that had emerged and then festered under Delors. The Experts' report exposed the Commission as everyone's favourite scapegoat in Brussels. The Commission's lack of democratic legitimacy made it a weak sparring partner with the EP, with Santer (1999: 21) compelled to claim—incredibly—that he 'unreservedly' welcomed the Parliament's initial vote of censure 'as a sign that democracy is coming of age at the European level'. More generally, the fall of the Santer Commission showed that, in the words of one of Santer's disgraced Commissioners, 'in economic and monetary terms Europe is a giant in the world. But politically we are very young.'[f]

[a] In 1997, the EP passed a 'conditional' censure—mustering a two-thirds majority—of the Commission over its handling of the BSE ('mad cow disease') crisis and threatened an outright censure vote later in the year if the Commission did not meet its demands for a revamp of EU food and health policies (see Peterson and Bomberg 1999: 126–7).

[b] See *inter alia Libération* and *La Lanterne*, 28 Sept. 1998.

[c] Quoted in *Financial Times*, 16 Mar. 1999.

[d] Santer was not alone in making this claim. The respected Belgian Commissioner for Competition Policy, Karel van Miert, attacked the Experts' report as 'unjust and incorrect' (Santer and van Miert both quoted in *Financial Times*, 17 Mar. 1999). For his part, Brittan (2000: 11) insisted that the Experts had added 'unnecessary and crude journalistic icing . . . to what was a perfectly well-baked and freestanding cake'.

[e] Compare how Santer is quoted in *Le Monde* and *Financial Times*, 17 Mar. 1999.

[f] Unattributed quote in *Financial Times*, 17 Mar. 1999.

capitals to prepare the ground for a swift decision on replacing Santer. In Berlin, after ten minutes of discussion, the European Council agreed that the new Commission President should be the former Italian Prime Minister, Romano Prodi.

Prodi moved quickly to assemble a new college. He was by no means free to choose his own team, but nevertheless had more influence over the college's composition than most of his predecessors had enjoyed. Prodi also took advantage of new powers granted to the President in the Treaty of Amsterdam (see below), for which Santer had fought successfully, to demand that each nominee provide a written promise to resign at Prodi's request. He ended up with a less charismatic college than Santer's, but one in which expertise was matched to portfolio to an extent unseen in the Commission's history (see Table 4.2).

One EU ambassador spoke for many in Brussels in claiming that 'the economic team in this Commission—Solbes, Lamy, Liikanen, Bolkestein and Monti—is collectively the best the Commission has ever had'.[5] One of Prodi's two Vice-Presidents (see Table 4.2), Neil Kinnock, led the college's drive to implement an ambitious series of internal reforms of the Commission. Prodi himself helped shift the debate on eastern enlargement to the point where EU governments—at the 1999 Helsinki Summit—decided to open accession talks with no fewer than twelve applicant states on a more or less equal basis.

Yet, the Prodi Commission often seemed afraid to put a foot wrong, particularly after several early public relations gaffes—particularly Prodi's description of the Commission as a 'European government' and himself as a 'European Prime Minister'—caused political backlash. Kinnock's administrative reform programme encountered (predictably) bitter resistance in the services, where morale seemed to sink ever lower. The Commission was clearly marginalized in the negotiations that yielded the Treaty of Nice (see Exhibit 4.2). The most charitable comment that

Table 4.2 The Prodi Commission

Commissioner (nationality)	Portfolio(s)	Relevant previous post
Romano Prodi (I)	President (without portfolio)	Italian Prime Minister
Neil Kinnock (UK)	Administrative reform (Vice-President)	UK Labour Party leader
Loyola de Palacio (E)	Relations with EP; transport; energy (Vice-President)	Spanish Agriculture Minister
Franz Fischler (A)	Agriculture and fisheries	Austrian Minister of Agriculture
Erkki Liikanen (Fin)	Enterprise and information society	Finnish Finance Minister
Mario Monti (I)	Competition	Economics Professor
Michel Barnier (F)	Regional policy; institutional affairs	French Minister for Europe
Frits Bolkestein (N)	Internal market	Chair of Dutch Liberals
Philippe Busquin (B)	Research	Belgian Minister of Education
David Byrne (Ir)	Consumer protection	Irish Attorney-General
Anne Diamantopoulou (Gr)	Employment and social affairs	Greek Industry Ministry (chief official)
Pascal Lamy (F)	External trade	Head, private office of Jacques Delors
Poul Nielson (Dk)	Development and humanitarian aid	Danish Development Minister
Chris Patten (UK)	External relations	Governor of Hong Kong
Viviane Reding (L)	Education and culture	MEP
Michaele Schreyer (D)	Budget	Environment Minister, (Senate of) Berlin
Pedro Solbes (E)	Monetary affairs	Spanish Finance Minister
Günter Verheugen (D)	Enlargement	German Minister for Europe
Antonio Vitorino (P)	Justice and home affairs	Portuguese Deputy Prime Minister
Margot Wallström (S)	Environment	Swedish Social Affairs Minister

Exhibit 4.2 The Commission and the Treaty of Nice

After the December 2000 Nice summit, the Commission's Secretary-General, David O'Sullivan, issued a sombre assessment of the outcome in a memorandum that was leaked to the press.[a] O'Sullivan concluded that the Commission had basically come out of the marathon negotiations as a loser. QMV was not extended nearly as widely as the Commission had hoped. A new, complex system of QMV was agreed which was likely to make blocking minorities easier to form. A proposal to allow a finite number (probably twenty) of Commissioners' posts to be shared out on the basis of equal rotation between member states, which seemed likely to be approved before the summit, was abandoned. Instead, it was agreed that the size of the college would not be capped until it grew to twenty-seven members, with each member state appointing one. Even after that, the Treaty gave no indication of how big the college should be, other than 'less than 27'. At Nice, both Prodi and O'Sullivan were mercilessly bullied by the summit's chair, Jacques Chirac, with O'Sullivan admitting that 'it was difficult for the Commission to play its normal role of honest broker and guardian of the Treaties'.

Yet, one senior national official argued that, 'the Commission has never contributed very much to previous Treaty revisions'. Against the wishes of the 2000 French Council presidency, QMV *was* extended to trade in services at Nice—a crucial victory for the Commission—despite the retention of unanimity for any issues touching on 'cultural diversity'. It was possible to argue that the new QMV system would rarely produce blocking minorities where they had not existed under the old rules. As for the lament that a twenty-seven-member college would be bloated and ineffective, it is worth considering that 'many national governments (not least the French), function coherently with a larger number of ministers' (Moravcsik and Nicolaïdis 1998: 19). One *cabinet* official—with experience of multiple colleges—insisted that 'the Commission's efficiency is not determined by the number of Commissioners. The key is the President.'

If ratified, the Treaty of Nice will introduce a revised Article 217 TEC entitled 'Organising the Commission and Increasing the President's Powers'. It will give future Presidents explicit authority to reshuffle portfolios, ask for resignations, and 'ensure that [the college] acts consistently, efficiently and on the basis of collective responsibility'. As such, one seasoned observer insists that Nice showed that European leaders 'agree that a more efficient Commission, including in particular a more powerful President, is highly desirable' (Ludlow 2001: 18). Moreover, during the very last minutes of the summit it was agreed that future Commissions, including their Presidents, would be selected on the basis of QMV by the European Council, a move seen as helping to ensure a college of high quality as well as setting a precedent for deciding by QMV at EU summits (Palmer 2000: 3–4). Assuming its ratification (following its rejection in the Irish referendum of June 2001), the Treaty of Nice will pave the way to a dramatically enlarged EU by around 2005, and one with proportionately many more smaller member states. Given that the Commission has always been the natural ally of small EU states, its future might well end up brighter than it first appeared to be after Nice.

[a] 'Brief Summary of the Conclusions of the Nice European Council', Nice, 11 Dec. 2000.

could be made on the first years of the Prodi Commission was that his legacy would be determined by the success of two long-term projects—enlargement and internal reform—more than anything else.

The structure of the college

Assuming its eventual ratification, the Treaty of Nice (see Exhibit 4.2), combined with some elements of the Prodi Commission's administrative reforms, could fundamentally alter the structure of future colleges. Still, basic norms established over fifty years are likely to continue to govern appointments to the college and the relationship between its three basic elements: the President, the college itself, and Commissioners' *cabinets*. This section highlights these norms while focusing on each of these three elements in turn.

The President

A biographer of Roy Jenkins, Commission President from 1977 to 1980, starkly concluded that 'The Presidency of the EEC Commission is an impossible job. Indeed it can hardly be called a job at all—the President has a number of conflicting responsibilities, but no power. By no stretch of the imagination does it resemble the Prime Ministership of Europe' (Campbell 1983: 181).

This claim first seemed anachronistic after Prodi's appointment, but then more like timeless truth. Less than a year after his appointment, Prodi was forced to deny rumours that he was considering leaving the Commission to fight the forthcoming Italian domestic election. The only other Italian to have been Commission President before Prodi, the barely remembered Franco Maria Malfatti, had done precisely the same thing during the 'malaise' period in 1972. Had the Commission gone back to the future?

The legacy of Delors continued to haunt Brussels, both in terms of the political aversion of many member governments to a powerful Commission *and* a desire for Commission activism on issues that required collective—especially rapid—European action. Electronic (or E-) commerce illustrated the axiom that the power of market forces in the world's largest single capitalist market is often so formidable as to overwhelm public power in Europe unless it is wielded collectively, with the Commission in the lead (see Pollack 1997; Peterson and Bomberg 1999: 67). With many firms wishing to sell across the EU, sometimes around the world, from a single web site, the Union faced powerful incentives for policy coordination on issues of taxation, consumer protection, and so on (see Commission 1999a). Moreover, the internal market had given rise over time to a diverse range of 'flanking'

EU policies—research, cohesion, environmental and social plus the euro—designed either to maximize or limit the effects of the internal market, with the Commission playing an important role in each. The freeing of the internal market truly did transform the Commission's institutional position, accentuating its policy role, even if the political lead given by Santer and Prodi never came close to matching that of Delors.

Throughout the Commission's lifespan, during Prodi's as much as Malfatti's tenure, the Commission President remained fundamentally dependent on the political climate in the Union as a whole. In one of the most revealing works ever on the Commission, Ross (1995: 234–7) attributes Delors's success to his ability to take advantage of three contextual variables: national receptivity to European solutions, international changes (especially German unification), and a favourable business cycle from 1985 to 1990. These factors helped Delors exert 'pull' within the European Council, in which the Commission President is the only non-head of state or government who is a full member. Delors (and perhaps Jenkins, at least on issues such as EMS) was viewed as a political equal in the European Council. It is not clear that Santer—although a former Prime Minister himself—ever was.

Prodi's stature was more ambiguous. He was the first Commission President ever to have been Prime Minister of a large EU member state, and was chosen to replace Santer largely on the strength of his experience in wielding 'real power'. Santer's resignation at such a difficult time induced even the UK, never an instinctive supporter of the Commission, to argue that the new President should be a 'political heavyweight'. However, Prodi was treated as more of an underling than an equal at several European summits (see Exhibit 4.2).[6] There was little evidence from the first years of Prodi's tenure to suggest that he had turned the Commission presidency into a front-line, 'first order' political job.

Yet, the College clearly became more *presidential*, with Prodi himself having no specific policy portfolio (unlike Santer, who retained overall responsibility for EMU and external policy) and inserting his 'own people' into key positions of authority within the Commission's services, in a manner that recalled Delors (see Exhibit 4.3). The structure of the college appeared to undergo fundamental change, with Prodi insisting that he would 'offer leadership' to the college, but also declaring, 'I want each Commissioner to be a star, a big star, in his or her own policy area'.[7] But if the policy work of most Commissioners proceeded smoothly and professionally, Prodi himself showed questionable political judgement, proved a poor communicator, and seemed unusually gaffe-prone. European leaders rebuffed him on issues ranging from deadlines for eastern enlargement, tax harmonization, and his invitation to the Libyan leader, Colonel Gaddafi, to visit Brussels. The effect was to fuel arguments that, amidst a 'return to inter-governmental politics' (Wiener and Neunreither 2000: 1), the Commission was in permanent decline.

Exhibit 4.3 Personnel policy under Prodi

Besides decreeing that *cabinets* should be more 'European' (see below), Prodi also insisted that the informal system of 'national flags' on posts in the DGs, whereby senior jobs services were either reserved for a particular member state or shared out between them, had to go. Instead, all vacant posts would be publicly advertised and filled on the basis of merit. Directors-General would also be rotated to new posts periodically, thus ending semi-permanent fiefdoms such as that of Frenchman Guy Legras over the Agriculture Directorate-General.

Yet, evidence soon emerged that old habits in personnel policy had not been broken. In particular, outcry greeted the rapid replacement of Legras with the Spaniard José Manuel Silva Rodríguez after it was promised that the post would be publicly advertised. Rodríguez appeared to imply that the new rules made little difference, as he publicly thanked the Spanish Commission Vice-President, Loyola de Palacio, for her support of his candidacy.

In an atmosphere of considerable disillusion with Prodi's methods, on personnel as well as other matters, a story appeared in May 2000 in the German broadsheet *Frankfurter Allgemeine Zeitung*, alleging that several members of the Commission were plotting to organize a purge of Prodi. The incident was badly handled by Prodi and his spokesman, Ricardo Levi, who insisted that the college take the extraordinary step of meeting without officials or interpreters to discuss the charges. Although it yielded a collective denial of any disunity, the meeting lasted two and half hours, fuelling press speculation about a foiled palace coup. Levi afterwards met the Brussels press corps—by some measures, the largest in the world—but spoke only in Italian, even though most attending journalists neither spoke the language or were provided with interpretation.

Prodi attempted to draw a line under the incident by announcing a reshuffle of top Commission jobs designed to 'make it possible to have very close co-ordination between Commission structures and the President'.[a] However, the impressions given were, first, that he had been forced to purge ineffective associates and, second, that he had shifted hand-picked cronies sideways into top jobs, undermining the new spirit of meritocracy. After Levi was named head of the internal Commission think tank, the Forward Studies Unit, one MEP condemned the Prodi Commission's embrace of '*parachutage* [which] conflicts with its stated intention of reform, openness and promotion on merit'.[b] Moreover, Prodi's 47-year-old head of *cabinet*, David O'Sullivan, was named as only the fourth Secretary-General (top permanent official) in the Commission's history, replacing the Dutchman Carlo Trojan who had been damaged by association with the fall of Santer. The Dutch government fumed that it was 'unpleasantly surprised' at the 'highly regrettable' move.[c] In fact, internal Commission selection procedures *were* undergoing genuine and revolutionary change, with the credentials of candidates being examined far more thoroughly. But if a new breeze was blowing within the Commission, it did not always appear obvious to the world beyond Brussels.

[a] Quoted in *Financial Times*, 4 May 2000.
[b] Lousewies van des Laan, quoted in *European Voice*, 31 May–7 June 2000.
[c] Quoted in *Financial Times*, 4 May 2000.

The college

The appointment of the college has always been one of the most fraught and politicized of all exercises in EU decision-making (see Peterson and Bomberg 1999: 40–1). The Jenkins and Prodi Commissions were both shaped in important ways by the nominee for President himself, with Jenkins (1991: 450) later musing: 'I think I intervened more actively in the process of selection than have either of my successors, Gaston Thorn or Jacques Delors ... Perhaps they learned from my mistakes.' The new Treaty of Amsterdam provisions which lent weight to Prodi's own preferences in 1999 'did not prevent governments from having the upper hand over "their" nomination(s)' (Nugent 2001: 83). The Treaty of Nice, which further empowers the President in choosing the college and mandates selection of the Commission by QMV, could mark a significant change.

The institutional design of the EU is intended to create collective, inter-institutional responsibility for policy initiatives. The logic of the design has given rise to a gradual strengthening of the EP's right to vet member governments' choices as presidential nominee and then the college itself, thus further politicizing the process of making these choices. Armed for the first time with its post-Amsterdam right to veto the Commission, the EP scrutinized Prodi's team closely (as it had done previously, with somewhat weaker powers, with Santer's). Ultimately, however, after some bluster from Christian Democrats—whose gains in the 1999 EP election were not reflected in the political composition of the new Commission—Prodi and his team were comfortably voted in by 414 to 142 (with 35 abstentions). The Santer college was confirmed by an even larger majority of MEPs: 418 votes to 103, with 59 abstentions, although Santer's own appointment as Commission President saw him sneak in with a twenty-two-vote EP majority.

Collective responsibility is not only built into the EU's institutional system generally, it is an absolutely cardinal principle *within* the college, all of whose members must publicly support all decisions and actions of the Commission. The principle is often difficult for the college to uphold. In contrast to cabinet governments, the college is never united by shared party political, national, or ideological affinities. In fact, no one has ever really explained what is meant to hold it together besides a commitment to 'Europe' (see Coombes 1970).

Formally, the college decides by simple majority votes. In a college of twenty as many as nine Commissioners can vote against a motion but then have to support it (with the number rising to as many as thirteen post-Nice). We simply do not know how often the college resorts to formal votes and frequent voting cannot necessarily be equated with more division in the college. However, when the college votes it is usually an admission that the majority view must be forced on at least one or a few Commissioners. By most accounts,[8] voting was more frequent in the Santer Commission than in Delors's, perhaps because the latter was more clearly dominated by its President. In the Prodi Commission, most *cabinet* officials agreed with the assessment of one that there was 'a culture of avoiding votes' in a college whose members were 'very focused on their own responsibilities and relatively unconcerned with some larger "big vision"'.

The single most important factor in determining the unity and cohesiveness of the college is the strength of presidential leadership. Compared to its predecessors, the Prodi Commission was far more ministerial with Commissioners left to get on with their work without much presidential interference. One *cabinet* insider observed: 'the College is only cohesive by default: they don't want to get caught in the same trap as Santer and are united by mutual fear of the Parliament.' One very senior *cabinet* official was more charitable:

There's a b-side to Prodi's leadership style, arising from his general disinterest in details and lack of concern with his own image, and that is that he gives members of the College a lot of rein. But it is a very professional and collegial group . . . there's a lot of mutual accommodation and much less pomposity and sense of individual importance compared to the last [Santer] Commission.

The Prodi Commission was the first in which, according to the Treaty of Amsterdam, the college worked 'under the political direction of the President'. Prodi was forced to prove that the new rules had meaning when the Commissioner for Enlargement, Günter Verheugen, seemed to suggest in a newspaper interview in September 2000 that Germany should hold a referendum on enlargement, a comment which outraged many east European governments. Prodi made it clear before the EP—with Verheugen by his side—that he did not 'lack the means to enforce' the loyal commitment of his college to agreed policies, which he termed 'the hallmark of my presidency'.[9]

One interpretation is that the college has become, over time, a more politically weighty group of individuals, with some Commissioners holding portfolios—especially competition or external trade—that have evolved to the point where whoever holds them enjoys substantial power and autonomy. The Santer Commission certainly reinforced the trend towards the 'increasing politicisation of the College' (MacMullen 2000: 41), with its inclusion of six former prime ministers, foreign ministers, or finance ministers. In a college that includes more numerous and formidable political figures than the colleges of the past, individual Commissioners may well find it more difficulty to convince the college to nod through 'their' policies without scrutiny. This interpretation would generally view the college as increasingly less prone to strong presidential control.

However, since the origins of the EEC, around half of the college has always consisted of former national ministers. The Prodi Commission was broadly in line. What set it apart was, somewhat paradoxically, both how ministerial *and* presidential it was compared to its predecessors.

The *cabinets*

One of the Commission's most vexed problems has always been the proper role of *cabinets* or Commissioners' private offices. In principle, *cabinets* are meant to act as a bridge between the college and the services, and thus between the political and apolitical in the Commission. In practice, *cabinets* are often accused of acting as agents of their member state as much or more than of the Commission as an institution. In the past, *cabinets* were usually (not always[10]) packed with officials— often quite young—who shared their Commissioner's nationality, leaving aside a few token non-nationals (see Peterson 1999). Many were hand-picked by governments in national capitals. Tensions between the *cabinets* and services were rife, especially during the Delors years but also under Santer. In 1998, the Director-General of DG Industry, Stefano Micossi, left the Commission after charging that the *cabinets* engaged in 'political interference unparalleled in member states'.[11] In particular, *cabinets* have always intervened aggressively in personnel decisions, lobbying for the appointment of their own members or 'temporary agents'—civil servants from national capitals seconded to the Commission—to senior posts in the DGs.

Under Prodi, *cabinets* were reduced in size, to six officials instead of as many as nine previously (Prodi's own *cabinet* numbered nine). Each Commissioner was required to appoint a head (*chef*) or deputy head (*adjoint*) who hailed from a member state other than their own. Leading by example, Prodi chose as his own *chef* an Irishman, David O'Sullivan (later to become Secretary-General).

Pre-Prodi, perhaps half of all *cabinet* officials had been reshuffled into their posts from previous *cabinets* (or parachuted into plum jobs in the services). Under Prodi, a significant number of new faces appeared, with only about one-third of *cabinet* officials previously having worked in *cabinets*.[12] The Commission trumpeted the fact that all *cabinets* had officials of at least three different nationalities, and that almost 40 per cent were women (a big increase on past totals). *Cabinets*, along with their Commissioners, were moved out of a central office in Brussels and into the same buildings as the services for which their Commissioner was responsible, thus reinforcing the 'ministerialism' of the Prodi Commission.

One *cabinet* official with experience of both the Santer and Prodi Commissions observed a trend towards 'less contact between *cabinets*. The old system facilitated deals and coalitions.' Another complained 'we are too close to the services. The *cabinets* are there to be hated, to be a shock absorber between the political and technical level. You need a certain fear factor . . . but they don't when they see us all the time.' One senior official opined, 'we were an unhappy family when we were all in one building, but at least we were a family'.

There was growing speculation by 2001 that Commissioners and *cabinets* would be brought back together when the Commission's Berlaymont headquarters were reopened (in 2003 at the earliest) after being refurbished and cleared of asbestos.

As for the suggestion that *cabinets* had ceased to be 'moles' for national capitals, most insiders claimed that little had changed. One concluded that making *cabinets* more multinational 'makes a little bit of a difference and it was worth trying. But the *cabinets* still channel impulses from national capitals, and they probably always will.'

The Commission's powers

The formal, treaty-based powers of the Commission are neither extensive nor spelled out very clearly. Of course, the main source of the Commission's power is its monopoly right to initiate legislation within the first pillar: with few exceptions, nothing can become Community legislation unless the college chooses to propose it. The Commission also has significant independent powers within the CAP and on external trade and (especially) competition policy. In the latter case, the college often acts as judge and prosecuting attorney—and sometimes jury— on cases of state aids to industry, mergers, and anti-competitive practices by firms. Generally, however, the Commission is closely scrutinized by EU member governments.

Two important sources of Commission influence—as opposed to 'power'—are its prerogative (under Article 211 TEC) to deliver opinions on any EU matter, along with its obligation (in Article 212 TEC) to publish an annual report on the activities of the EU. Both give the Commission scope to influence individual policy debates or steer the EU as a whole in specified directions. But the Commission must earn its influence by the quality of its analysis, and particularly its judgement of what will play in national capitals and with relevant policy stakeholders (including industry and non-governmental lobbies).

Over time, the Commission has become increasingly accountable to the EP. Besides its powers to confirm the college (and its President) and to sack the Commission, the EP retains the informal right to scrutinize the activities of the Commission, with individual Commissioners expected to appear regularly before its policy-specialized committees. The emergence of the co-decision procedure (see Chapter 5) as the more or less template decision rule for EU legislation has had the effect of upgrading the institutional position of the EP at the expense of the Commission. When the EP and Council cannot agree, and conciliation must take place, the Commission risks losing its effectiveness as an honest broker unless it remains sensitive to the positions of both the Council and EP, and acknowledges their dominance of the procedure.

The Commission's relationship with the European Court of Justice has traditionally been a close and cooperative one. Much of what became the 1992 project became doctrine as the result of individual ECJ decisions, which the Commission then managed to transform into policy injunctions (see Armstrong and Bulmer 1998). The Court has the formal power under Article 216 TEC to 'compulsorily retire' a Commissioner who 'no longer fulfils the conditions required for the performance of his [or her] duties or if [s]he has been guilty of serious misconduct', providing the Council or Commission applies to the Court. The provision has never been used, although it might have been as a device to rid the Santer Commission of Cresson (see Brittan 2000: 12).

Ultimately, the Commission's most important role is that of a *manager* of policy decided by other institutions, which themselves have more, more explicit, and less challengeable sources of power. The Committee of Independent Experts, whose first report induced the Santer Commission to resign, issued a second report (in September 2000) on the Commission's role as a policy manager, which focused on the distinction between the Commission's roles as direct and shared manager of EU policies. The Commission's direct policy responsibilities had become, according to the Experts, increasingly burdensome even though member governments refused to increase the resources available to the Commission. The result was far too much contracting out of the Commission's work, thus blurring lines of accountability and control.

Meanwhile, the Commission shared responsibility with the member states for most EU policies, acting as a broker and facilitator within organizational networks linking the member states and other EU institutions. For example, the ambitious programmes agreed at the Tampere and Lisbon Summits (1999 and 2000) on justice and home affairs and economic reform (respectively) granted few significant new competences to the Commission, even if both allowed scope for the Commission to catalyse new initiatives or play a steering role. More than ever, the Commission's institutional position seemed dependent on advocacy and persuasion within horizontal policy networks, rather than hierarchical compulsion or coercion.

The college in context

The mass resignation of the Santer Commission was clearly a defining event in the life of the institution. Leaving aside scattered (mostly early) grand declarations by the President himself, the Prodi Commission seemed reluctant to try to take a political lead as a college, with individual Commissioners preferring instead to hunker down to their own portfolios. A member of one *cabinet* lamented that the Commission had become 'like a slightly unattractive girl at a Victorian debutantes' ball: trying a bit too hard to please, and thus reinforcing the weakness of her position'. One former Commissioner lamented the Prodi Commission's 'astonishing weakness . . . it is too deferential, and no one ever gives the Commission credit for acting that way'. Two top Commission officials authored a paper, posted on a web site and then quickly withdrawn, which complained that the Commission was 'overcautious, wrapped up in administrative reforms' and failing to provide 'strategic inspiration and political impulse'.[13] A senior official in the services claimed, 'no one is defending the Commission in any major national capital. The Commission as a whole is losing heart.'

If so, intergovernmentalist accounts of EU politics could be marshalled to explain why. Most make three assumptions about the Commission. First, it makes little difference who is its President. Second, the Commission is only empowered when national preferences converge. Third, the Commission is empowered only to the extent that member governments want to ensure the 'credibility of their commitments' to each other (Moravcsik 1998a: 492). There is little dispute, amongst scholars as well as practitioners, that the Commission has traditionally had little influence over 'history-making' decisions about the broad sweep of European integration, such as treaty revisions. Few advocates of neofunctionalist theories—which hold that integration begets further integration in a unilinear process—argue that the Commission has ever held much sway over decisions to extend the EU's policy competence, even if neofunctionalism offers powerful explanations for the steady advance of legal integration (see Burley and Mattli 1993).

In contrast, institutionalist theories tend to privilege the position of the Commission in day-to-day policy debates (see Pierson 1996). Institutionalism holds that institutions matter and define the parameters of political debates. According to this view, political systems often become locked into existing paths and thus 'path dependency' in actual policy is usually the rule. The Prodi Commission seemed unusually focused on the nitty-gritty of ongoing policy debates, as opposed to defining some grand vision of the EU's future, and offered a genuine policy lead in areas ranging from the liberalization of telecommunications, global trade diplomacy, and reform of the EU's merger control regime. All of these areas revealed continuity with the paths chosen when the internal market was 'freed' in the 1980s.

Some variants of institutionalism combine insights from rational choice and principal-agent theories (see Pollack 1997). They hold that the principal authorities in EU politics—the member governments themselves—delegate tasks to the EU's institutions, which then become their agents in specific policy areas. Member governments retain varying levels of control over their activities, and calculate rationally their own gains or losses when this process occurs. This body of theory sheds particular light on two recent developments.

One is the refusal of the Prodi Commission to accept new tasks delegated to it by member governments on the grounds that it did not have the resources to carry them out effectively. Prodi's refusal to allow the Commission to run a programme to monitor mobility in European higher education in autumn 2000 would have been unthinkable under Delors. In political terms, it sent a signal that the EU cannot work properly when member governments dump a problem on the Commission without giving it adequate resources. In theoretical terms, the Commission seemed not to be a competence maximizer, but rather a 'bureau-shaper' which sought new tasks 'only up to an internal optimum level' at which efficient performance was possible (Dunleavy 1991: 174).

A second development which principal-agent models explain well is the increasing tendency for the EU to make policy by means other than the traditional 'Community method' (see Devuyst 1999). It was difficult to know whether the 2000 Lisbon Summit, at which EU governments unveiled a range of policy commitments designed to give the EU 'the most dynamic economy in the world', was a genuine landmark or not. But it was striking how much of the Lisbon programme eschewed the Community method and EU legislation and instead embraced the so-called 'open method of coordination' (OMC) of national policies through benchmarking, league tabling, and peer pressure (see Hodson and Maher 2001). The Commission's role was confined to that of a scrutinizer of national policies, rather than a proposer of common EU policies. In a sense, EU principals (national governments) were engaging in a new kind of delegation, with the Commission as a different kind of agent.

The new affinity for OMC was also reflected in the creation of a variety of new regulatory agencies, some of which assumed some of the traditional roles of the Commission (see Chapter 14). EU governments seemed to want new kinds of agents—not just the Commission—to whom they could delegate cooperative policy tasks. Usually, however, the Commission retained the job of identifying and seeking to solve coordination problems within networks of (*inter alia*) private actors, consumer and environmental groups, and national and European agencies.

Advocates of multi-level governance as an approach to EU governance have long argued that the Commission enjoys a privileged place at the 'hub of numerous highly specialized policy networks of technical experts' and retains 'virtually a free hand in creating new networks' (Marks *et al.* 1996: 355, 359). In a perceptive analysis of the Prodi era reforms, Metcalfe (2000: 838) concludes that 'the Commission will have to be reinvented as a network organization adept at designing the frameworks of governance and developing the management capacities needed to make them work effectively'. There is little doubt that, in so far as the Commission still provides direction to the EU, it does so mostly through coordinating the actions of a variety of networked, policy-concerned actors to try to make national policies converge (see Héritier 1999; Kohler-Koch and Eising 1999), as opposed to replacing them with EU policies.

Conclusion

Any analysis of the Commission must consider the normative question of what kind of organization the college should be. A policy entrepreneur? An honest broker? A manager of decisions taken by others? Or a proto-government of Europe?

The problem with the last idea is twofold. First, in political terms, Europe is far from ready for a European government. Second, governments—unlike the Commission—are elected. After he was first appointed, Prodi stated that his college would work as a 'European government', with he himself acting as a sort of 'European Prime Minister'.[14] These claims provoked a backlash that lasted well into Prodi's term in office. At the Nice Summit, the UK Prime Minister, Tony Blair, voiced support for the idea of another IGC in 2004 because 'there is much for us to gain from a conference that sets out clearly where it is that the Brussels Commission operates and where it doesn't',[15] as if that was *all* that was needed to reform EU governance. At times, it appeared that EU member governments no longer believed there was a need for a strong Commission which could act as an independent, honest broker between national interests.

One leading commentator argued that '[t]he real question ... is whether the Nice Treaty strengthens or weakens the European Union's capacity to manage a much larger Union' (Palmer 2000: 1). Yet, managing the Union (the focus of Part II of this book) often seemed a less urgent concern than providing political direction to the EU. If the post-Nice Commission seemed unlikely to supply direction to the EU, it was worth recalling that we had been here before: the Commission appeared entirely moribund after Hallstein and before Delors. It then rose from the ashes to give vital direction to the European project in the 1980s.

The initial, high ambitions of the Prodi Commission, and its early disappointments, could be taken as evidence of an inexorable and 'underlying shift of influence away from the Commission towards other EU institutions and the member governments' (H. Wallace 2000: 15). It was possible to argue that the Commission, without some kind of new, democratic underpinning (such as the popular election of its President), was in a permanent state of decline. Yet, in an enlarging EU that also becomes relentlessly more polycentric—with more and more diverse centres of power, development, and control (see Peterson and Bomberg 2000)—the need for a strong, independent, political Commission is unlikely to diminish. In fact, member governments would almost certainly come to regret bitterly its disappearance, if that were ever to occur.

Notes

1 Apparently not satisfied by his political humiliation of Hallstein, de Gaulle (1970: 195–6) later claimed that 'Hallstein may be a sincere European, but this is so because he is German first and foremost whose ambition lies with his country. For within the framework of the Europe he desires, his country could regain . . . dominance through its economic power' (see also Loth 1998*a*).

2 The Luxembourg compromise also placed a range of new restrictions on the Commission, including a bar on making proposals public before the Council could consider them and the requirement that the Commission could only receive the credentials of non-EEC ambassadors to the Community alongside the Council (in a separate ceremony).

3 The Commission's term in office was extended to five years by the Maastricht Treaty so as to align its tenure with that of the EP.

4 Dietrich von Kyaw, quoted in *Financial Times*, 8 May 1999.

5 This quote (and all others not referenced as otherwise in this chapter) is taken from one of eleven interviews conducted as part of the research for this chapter in Nov./Dec. 2000 and Mar. 2001. The interviewees were *cabinet* officials in the Prodi Commission (six, including two *chefs* and two *deputy chefs*), senior officials in the services (two, including a former *cabinet* member), two former Commissioners, and a national ambassador to the EU.

6 The Nice Summit was not the only time when Prodi was roughed up by European leaders (see Chapter 1, n. 5).

7 Quoted in *Financial Times*, 19 July 1999.

8 One former Commissioner interviewed for this chapter insisted that there were 'far more votes under Delors and tight votes'. Another indicated that 'voting wasn't very frequent' in the Delors Commission. Previous interviewees with experience of successive Commissions estimated that there were more votes taken under Santer than Delors (see Peterson 1999: 62). Voting records exist, but are not available to the public.

9 Quoted in *Financial Times*, 7 Sept. 2000.

10 For example, Delors's *cabinets* included German and British officials (see Ross 1995), Santer's *cabinet* was truly polyglot, and (Austrian) Franz Fischler's *chef* for most of his time as Commissioner was an Italian.

11 Quoted in *Financial Times*, 18 Mar. 1999.

12 As is generally the case in the Commission, personnel records on *cabinet* members are incomplete and/or unavailable to the public, thus making precise comparisons impossible. However, using data presented in Hill and Knowlton (2000), a total of thirty-four (out of all 123 *cabinet* officials) had previous experience working in *cabinets*, or 28% of the total, compared to seventy-four with no previous *cabinet* experience, or 60% of the total. The data show no previous information on the former positions held by fifteen *cabinet* officials.

13 See report on the paper, written by two Commission Directors-General, in *European Voice*, 17–22 May 2001.

14 Quoted in *Financial Times*, 12 July 1999.

15 Quoted in *Financial Times*, 8 Dec. 2000.

Further reading

The literature in English on the Commission —surveyed in Peterson (1999)—has exploded in recent years. The single most comprehensive and up-to-date treatment is Nugent (2001), with Ross (1995) Edwards and Spence (1997b), Page (1997b), Nugent (2000), and Stevens (2001) also particularly useful. Coombes (1970) pays dividends to its readers more than thirty years after publication, with Metcalfe (2000) and Hodson and Maher (2001) offering glimpses of possible futures.

Coombes, D. (1970), *Politics and Bureaucracy in the European Community: A Portrait of the Commission of the EEC* (London: George Allen & Unwin).

Edwards, G., and Spence, D. (1997b) (eds.), *The European Commission*, 2nd edn. (London: Cartermill).

Hodson, D., and Maher, I. (2001), 'The Open Method as a New Mode of Governance', *Journal of Common Market Studies*, 39/4: 719–45.

Metcalfe, L. (2000), 'Reforming the Commission: Will Organisational Efficiency Produce Effective Governance?', *Journal of Common Market Studies*, 38/5: 817–41.

Nugent, N. (2000) (ed.), *At the Heart of the Union* (Basingstoke and New York: Palgrave), 2nd edn.

—— (2001), *The European Commission* (Basingstoke and New York: Palgrave).

Page, E. (1997), *People Who Run Europe* (Oxford: Clarendon Press).

Peterson, J. (1999), 'The Santer Era: The European Commission in Normative, Historical and Theoretical Perspective', *Journal of European Public Policy*, 6/1: 46–65.

Ross, G. (1995), *Jacques Delors and European Integration* (New York and London: Polity Press).

Stevens, A., with Stevens, H. (2001), *Brussels Bureaucrats? The Administration of the European Union* (Basingstoke and New York: Palgrave).

Web links

The Commission's own web site— **www.europa.eu.int**—is a treasure trove which handles something like two million 'hits' per month. The sites of the *European Voice* (**www.european-voice.com**) and Belmont Policy Centre (**www.theepc.be**) offer insiders' insights from Brussels. Analyses of the Santer Commission's fall and Prodi Commission's rise are available at **www.palgrave.com/politics/eu/santer.htm** and **www.palgrave.com/politics/eu/ prodi.htm**.

Chapter 5
The European Parliament

Michael Shackleton

Contents

Summary

The European Parliament (EP) is the only directly elected multinational parliament in the world, as well as the only directly elected institution in the European Union. Its actual and potential role is therefore central to arguments about the 'democratic deficit', and whether the EU is democratic and its decisions legitimate. For most of its history, the EP has been a relatively weak institution compared to the Council and the Commission. Since the first direct elections in 1979, and particularly in the 1990s, its powers and status have increased substantially. The EU as an institutional system can no longer be understood without understanding how the Parliament has evolved, how it works and what kind of influence it can exercise now and in a future enlarged Union.

Introduction

On the Ides of March 1999 the European Commission resigned, above all to avoid a vote of censure in the European Parliament which would force it out of office. It was a dramatic moment in the history of the European Union, which underlined the conversion of the European Parliament from a place of discussion and debate to a major political actor involved in determining the overall direction of the European Union. The change had not come overnight. It was the result of developments stretching back over the whole history of the Parliament but especially during the period after the first direct elections in 1979.

This chapter confronts two basic questions. First, what difference has the inclusion of a directly elected institution made to the evolution of the EU? It is argued here that the EP has served to bring into the open a debate about whether EU decisions meet the standards of representative democracy, in terms of enabling the people subject to those decisions the chance to influence them. Second, can the EP help to resolve the so-called 'democratic deficit'? It is claimed here that the answer to this question depends on the kind of political system we want the EU to become as well as our perspective on what is or is not wrong with the present institutional arrangements. The debate about the structure and powers of the EP is therefore about political values.

Historical development

The story of the Parliament has been told as a transition from 'fig-leaf to co-legislature' (Corbett *et al.* 2000: 3–6). In symbolic terms, this change has been reflected in the move from renting premises in Strasbourg that it shared with the Parliamentary Assembly of the Council of Europe to becoming the effective owner of two substantial buildings in Brussels and Strasbourg, both of them with parliamentary chambers (known as 'hemicycles' because of their shape) equipped to seat over 700 members. In terms of formal powers, the EP has undergone much more significant growth than any other institution since the Communities came into existence.

In the early 1950s when the European Coal and Steel Community was created, a parliamentary body was far from the centre of the discussion (Smith 1999: 27–44). The crucial institution was the High Authority, which was given supranational powers in the management of coal and steel. The creation of a parliamentary institution, known as the Common Assembly, alongside the Authority was perceived as the least imperfect way to deal with the issue of accountability of the Authority. The Assembly's only significant power was that of supervising the Authority, with the right to dismiss the entire body by a two-thirds majority of the votes cast, representing an absolute majority of its members (that is, half the total number of members plus one). Member states could choose whether to have direct elections to the Assembly or to allow its national parliament to select members.

The Treaties of Rome saw significant movement in the powers of the Assembly. First, specific provision was made for direct elections: it was no longer to be a matter for each member state to decide. No fixed timetable was agreed for the change, but the commitment to abolish the system of nominated members was made legally binding . Second, the Assembly was given advisory as well as super-visory powers and thus was given its first glimpse of legislative power. These two changes did not have an immediate effect. It took over twenty years for direct elections to be organized and Parliament's formal legislative powers were not altered for nearly thirty years. Nevertheless, the changes were to prove of long-term significance in shaping the institution.

Further changes in the role of the Parliament were closely linked with other modifications to the structure of the EU. Thus treaty revisions introduced in 1970 and 1975 gave the Parliament important budgetary powers, including the right to reject the budget (a right it exercised in 1979 and 1984), to amend it within certain fixed limits, and to approve (or not) the annual accounts. The essential source of these changes was the decision taken at the end of the 1960s to alter the basis for financing the European Community, and to move away from a system of national contributions linked to each country's GNP to a system of 'own resources', whereby the revenue available for financing European policies legally belonged to the Community and could not be withheld. Under these circumstances, there was a strong body of opinion amongst governments, notably the Dutch, that national parliaments could no longer exercise effective control over Community finance and that the task should be passed on to the European Parliament.

As for the question of direct elections, the Parliament found itself in a vicious circle, well described in the independent Vedel report of 1972 on the enlargement of its powers:

[I]f one cannot imagine a Parliament with real powers which does not draw its mandate from direct universal suffrage, it is even more difficult to imagine the election through direct universal suffrage of a Parliament without extended powers. In this way, two equally desir-able objectives are making each other's implementation impossible. The only way to break the vicious circle is to refuse to let one of the two objectives depend on the achievement of the other one first. Neither has priority over the other, nor is their simultaneous achievement necessary (Vedel 1972: 59).

This dilemma persisted until the election of Valéry Giscard d'Estaing as President of France and Helmut Schmidt as West German Chancellor within five days of each other in May 1974. The subsequent Paris Summit agreed to hold direct European elections after 1978. The deadlock of the de Gaulle years was broken.

Direct elections paved the way for a significant extension of the legislative powers of the Parliament. A critical moment was the 1980 *Isoglucose* judgment of the European Court of Justice. This judgment annulled a piece of Community legislation adopted by Council on the grounds that Parliament had not yet given its opinion. The Court made it clear that Council could not adopt Community legislation before receiving Parliament's opinion, where the Treaties require it. Moreover, the Court made a link between the democratic character of the Community and the Parliament's right to be consulted, which the Court described as:

the means which allow the Parliament to play an actual part in the legislative process of the Community. Such a power represents an essential factor in the institutional balance intended by the Treaty. Although limited, it reflects at Community level *the fundamental democratic principle* [emphasis added] that the people should take part in the exercise of power through the intermediary of a representative assembly.

The right to be more than simply consulted over the contents of legislation came about through treaty revisions that were not specifically devoted to the Parliament. In 1987 the Single European Act (SEA) came into force, providing the treaty base for the establishment of a single European market by 1992. It was recognized that achieving a single market would require greater majority voting. In this overall context, member governments were willing to grant the Parliament a new legislative power, known as the cooperation procedure, under which it had the chance to have two readings of proposed legislation, rather than one. Under the procedure, the Council could only overrule the EP by a unanimous vote, providing the Commission was persuaded to back the Parliament's proposed amendments.

The precise form of Parliament's involvement in the legislative procedure was not preordained. In the 1970s the Vedel Report had argued against the idea that the Parliament should be given the right to amend legislation but rather that it should have the right to say yes or no to legislation presented to it by the Council. In fact such a power of 'assent' was granted to the Parliament in the SEA but it was restricted to the accession of new member states (Article 49 TEU) as well as the conclusion of certain agreements with third countries (Article 300 TEC). Some doubted that this right would be used very often but in fact the Parliament was called to vote on relevant international agreements thirty times within the first two years of the SEA being ratified, as well as on new accessions in 1995.

The Maastricht Treaty extended the rights of the Parliament very substantially. It gave the EP the right to vote on the Commission before it took office (Article 214 TEC), extended its formal powers of control by providing for the establishment of committees of inquiry (Article 193 TEC), empowered it to appoint a European

Ombudsman (Article 195 TEC), and made formal provision for the Parliament to invite the Commission to present a legislative proposal, thereby giving it a form of legislative initiative (Article 192 TEC).

Most importantly, Maastricht ushered in a new and transformational procedure, now known as co-decision (though the term is not found in the Treaties), which provides for joint decision-taking and direct negotiations between the Parliament and the Council as well as the possibility for the Parliament to reject draft legislation if such negotiations fail (Article 251 TEC). Under the procedure, the EP and Council are literally and legally equal co-legislators. Supporters of stronger EP powers argued, successfully, that with more majority voting the position of national parliaments was weakened and that a greater role for the EP would improve the democratic legitimacy of EU legislation, by ensuring it has the support of EU citizens as well as EU governments. Moreover, Parliament proved more 'responsible' than some member governments had imagined it would be in the post-SEA period. It respected the commitments imposed by the Treaties and never, for example, sought more time to examine proposals than it was legally permitted. As a result, more reticent member governments became less nervous about extending its prerogatives and accepting the arguments of those, such as Germany, who argued that the powers of the Parliament needed to be extended to increase the democratic legitimacy of the Union as a whole.

The Maastricht Treaty was not an unmitigated success for the Parliament. The role of the Parliament in the second and third pillars (respectively, for the common foreign and security policy and justice and home affairs policies) is limited to consultation: there was and remains no co-decision in these areas. The first pillar's provisions for economic and monetary union offered a variable role to the Parliament: no co-decision but only 'cooperation' on four articles, alongside a consultative role in the appointment of the board of the European Central Bank (ECB). Perhaps most importantly, the Treaty (Article 99 TEC) required the President of the ECB to report to the competent committee of the Parliament. These appearances (four times a year) offer the EP a significant opportunity to raise its public profile.

The Treaty of Amsterdam, though less wide-ranging than Maastricht, again reinforced the position of the Parliament. Co-decision was extended from fifteen to thirty-eight treaty areas and simplified to make it possible to reach agreements more quickly. Parliament was also given the formal right to approve the person proposed by the European Council as President of the Commission. In this way the Treaty legitimized existing practice as well as complementing the right granted at Maastricht to take a vote of confidence to elect or reject the Commission as a whole. The changes were ones of degree, rather than of principle, a pattern that was repeated at Nice in 2000, as we will see below.

Structures of the Parliament

It is one thing to be granted powers, it is another to be able to use them effectively. More than any other EU institution Parliament faces difficulty in aggregating interests in an extraordinarily heterogeneous environment. Before the first direct elections there were 198 MEPs, in six political groups; by 2000 the number of members had more than tripled to 626, split between eight political groups coming from 129 national political parties (see Chapter 12).

How can such a polyglot institution take effective decisions? The European Parliament does not contain a government, and cannot rely on those parliamentarians who belong to the party or parties of government to ensure that a particular political programme is enacted. Yet, the EP is relatively successful in overcoming the clash between efficiency and diversity. Only rarely does it fail to adopt a position for lack of any clear majority.

The key agents in the aggregation of interests are the EP's political groups. Since the beginnings of the Parliament in 1952, members have sat not in national groups, as happens in nearly all international parliamentary assemblies, but in groups created to reflect shared political affiliation (see Chapter 12). The EP's groups have shown themselves capable of considerable collective action. But three other factors—treaty provisions, the committee system, and leadership structures—play a part.

Treaty provisions

The structure of decision-making laid down in the Treaties obliges the Parliament to overcome its internal differences, at least on those issues where its vote is of greatest importance. Simple majorities of all members present are enough for amendments under the consultation procedure or at first reading under co-decision, as well as urgency resolutions or resolutions to wind up debates on topics of current concern. They are not enough to reject or adopt amendments to the Council's draft budget or to its common position at second reading under the co-decision procedure, to give assent, to approve the accession of new member states or to adopt a motion of censure on the Commission. For all of these, an absolute majority (half of all members plus one) has to vote in favour for the Parliament's voice to be heard. These treaty requirements provide a strong incentive for the political groups in the Parliament to come to agreements on the issues that require absolute majorities (see Chapter 12) as well as to encourage members to attend the relevant plenary sessions.

The committee system

Most of the detailed work of the EP is done at the level of seventeen policy-specialized committees, whose political composition broadly reflects that of Parliament as a whole. These committees enjoy a high level of autonomy under the Parliament's rules. All legislative proposals are referred directly, without debate, from the plenary to one of the committees, which then organize the examination of a proposal before it returns to the plenary for a vote. Only one committee can be responsible for a proposal and only its amendments can be considered in plenary; other committees can table amendments that are voted in the responsible committee but do not get a second chance in plenary. The responsible committee appoints a *rapporteur* who follows a legislative proposal from its inception to the conclusion of the procedure. Thus those outside the Parliament who wish to influence the shape of proposals—lobbyists, national governments, or the Council of Ministers—concentrate their efforts on *rapporteurs* and their work in committees, which always meet in public unless a contrary decision is taken at the beginning of the meeting. On the basis of the work of the *rapporteur* the committee comes to adopt a position which will normally prevail in the plenary, unless the members of the committee are unable to overcome their own differences and the vote on a proposal is very close.

The committees are assisted by between three and ten administrative staff. This figure is larger than that found in most national parliaments in Europe, where usually the role of a committee secretariat is essentially restricted to ensuring the smooth functioning of meetings. In the EP administrators play a wider role, both in terms of drafting documents for members and as part of the collective memory of the institution. The relatively significant turnover of members from one parliamentary legislature to the next (nearly 60 per cent in 1999) means that the Parliament Secretariat inevitably plays an important role in the EP's work.

Leadership structures

The Parliament has established leadership structures designed to overcome many of the centrifugal forces at work within it. It elects a President every two and a half years, whose task it is to chair the plenary (with the help of fourteen Vice-Presidents), to represent the institution *vis-à-vis* other institutions and the outside world and to oversee the Parliament's internal functioning. Thus the President has been able since 1988 to speak at the opening of every European Council and to act as a spokesperson for the Parliament as a whole (see also Chapter 2).

The President also chairs two other leadership bodies, the Conference of Presidents and the Bureau. The former is composed of the chairs of all the political groups. It is a relatively new creation, only established in 1993, replacing a body called the Enlarged Bureau, which included all the Vice-Presidents as well as the group chairs and which was seen as unwieldy and inefficient. When consensus cannot be found in the Conference of Presidents, each chair can vote in accordance with a weighting based on the number of members in each group. These rules make it easier to decide on the issues under the Conference's responsibility, including drawing up the draft agenda of plenary sessions, settling conflicts of competence between committees, deciding on inter-institutional issues (such as whether to take a case to the European Court of Justice) and determining whether or not to send delegations outside the EU, for example, to monitor elections.

The role of the Bureau, composed of the Parliament's Vice-Presidents, may appear less politically important as it is geared to internal financial, organizational, and administrative matters. The Bureau draws up the preliminary version of the Parliament's budget, reviews the working of plenary sessions, authorizes meetings of committees away from the usual places of work and appoints senior officials to the administration, including the Secretary-General. Yet the work of the Bureau on internal issues may have an effect outside the institution. In 1999, for example, it established a number of constituency weeks each year where there would be no parliamentary activity in Brussels or Strasbourg. The decision was in part a response to the poor turn-out in the European elections in 1999 (see Table 5.2 below) and the desire to bring members closer to their voters.

Powers of the Parliament

Even if the Parliament can develop coherent positions despite its heterogeneity, what effect do those positions have? How powerful is the European Parliament? These are questions that continue to divide academic, political, and wider opinion, even though the formal position of the institution clearly has been considerably strengthened. In the theoretical literature about the EU, the Parliament's role tends to be downplayed by those who argue that it is essentially member states that determine outcomes. Others, by contrast, point to the way in which the Parliament has used the various powers it has acquired to exercise significant influence over EU decision-making (see, for example, Chapter 11).

To look at what the Parliament is doing on a day-to-day basis is to be confronted with a bewildering array of reports, debates, and questions. To identify where the Parliament does or does not play an important role, it is important to distinguish between the various kinds of decision that are taken in the EU and to recognize that the EP can play a greater role in some than in others (see Peterson and Bomberg 1999).[1] Here we will distinguish between history-making, policy-making, and policy-implementing decisions and suggest that the Parliament is more likely to have an effect at the level of policy-making than history-making decisions and less likely to play a major role at the level of policy implementation. The nature of the EP's powers are such that it is much more difficult for it to influence very major decisions or decisions of detail than it is to influence the content of individual policies.

History-making decisions

The biggest decisions in the European Union are taken at the level of the European Council, after being 'prepared' in prior negotiations between the member states in Intergovernmental Conferences. In this framework the Parliament is an outsider: it is not present in European Council meetings except for the brief appearance of its President at the start of the proceedings and it does not have the formal right to say yes or no to the outcome of an IGC. Despite repeated calls to be given such a right of assent, ratification of the results of an IGC is a purely national affair, through parliamentary vote and/or referendum. On occasions some national parliaments have indicated that they would refuse to ratify a Treaty if the Parliament was against but such a scenario has never become a serious political possibility (Corbett 1993: 64).

The EP has made efforts to reinforce its role in the formation of opinion that leads up to the conclusion of an IGC. Both in the Amsterdam and the Nice negotiations it nominated two members to participate in the preparatory discussions with the member governments, thus giving the Parliament a stronger voice in the intergovernmental negotiations than any institution other than the Commission, though the EP was still excluded from the formal negotiating sessions between the member governments. The success of its efforts to shape IGC debates has varied. The Parliament could not prevent the establishment of the pillar structure at Maastricht, but did succeed at Amsterdam in getting the co-decision procedure simplified (despite opposition from a majority of member governments). The importance of putting such ideas forward can be judged by the consequences of failing to do so. In advance of the Nice European Council the EP was not able to agree on a proposal as to the composition of the Parliament after enlargement. The heads of state and government filled the void with a decision that was not greeted with enthusiasm by MEPs (see below).

Two kinds of decision that can be described as history-making do give the Parliament a formal say after the European Council has taken a decision. As we have seen, the Parliament has the right since Amsterdam to approve the candidate proposed by the European Council as President of the Commission and it also has to give its assent to the accession of new member states. The possibility of the Parliament not approving a Commission President cannot be ignored. In 1994 President Santer was approved by a majority of only twenty-two, despite very heavy lobbying by national governments. After the decision at Nice that the President of the Commission be chosen in the European Council by qualified majority, the involvement of the Parliament would seem likely to be still greater with the possibility that the results of the European elections serve to influence the choice of candidate presented to the EP. As for the accession of new member states, the right of assent is more likely to be relevant in increasing the role of the Parliament in the negotiations than in the final vote. Hence the Parliament can indeed shape some history-making decisions but its role is undoubtedly more restricted than it is on policy-making decisions.

Policy-making decisions

The Maastricht agreement on co-decision procedure established the Parliament as a joint legislator with the Council. The principle has come to be universally accepted by all the institutions, with the argument now revolving around the extent of the procedure. Parliament considers it should apply to all issues decided by qualified majority; member governments continue to be reluctant to accept an automatic link of this kind. The procedure already applies to thirty-eight areas of Community competence with a further five to be added as and when the Treaty of Nice is ratified. Co-decision has thus become the normal, 'template' EU legislative procedure, covering all areas under the first pillar except agriculture, fisheries, taxation, EMU, competition, trade, and most international agreements.

The overall shape of the procedure and the possibilities it offers are presented in Figure 5.1. Two central features should be underlined:

- first, as with the cooperation procedure established under the SEA, the EP and the Council have two readings of legislation. However, under co-decision, if the Council cannot accept the amendments presented by the Parliament at its second reading, the two institutions have to meet in a conciliation committee whose job it is to find an agreement by a process of negotiation. Neither can tell the other one what to do at this stage.

- second, not only are the negotiations subject to a pressure of time—they have to be concluded in a maximum of eight weeks—but without mutual agreement the act is not adopted. Under the Maastricht Treaty the Council could reintroduce its first reading (known as a 'common position') after a breakdown in conciliation talks and challenge the Parliament to find an absolute majority to overturn it. This possibility was eliminated at Amsterdam so that now failure to agree in conciliation brings the procedure to an end. Such a prospect necessarily concentrates the minds of the negotiators.

The behaviour of the two institutions under co-decision is illustrated in Exhibit 5.1, a chronology of the working time directive in conciliation. First, it shows how additional institutional arrangements have been developed to make the procedure work better, including tripartite meetings, known as trialogues, which bring

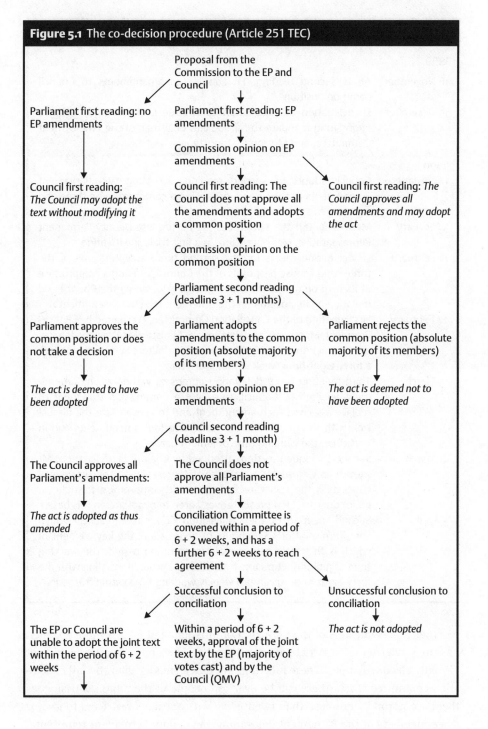

Figure 5.1 The co-decision procedure (Article 251 TEC)

Exhibit 5.1 A chronology of the working time directive under conciliation

1999

16 November	At its second reading, EP adopts ten amendments to Council common position
15 December	EP delegation to conciliation committee is constituted, giving a negotiating mandate to Mr ROCARD, Chairman of the Employment Committee, and Mrs SMET, rapporteur

2000

1 February	Council adopts its second reading, accepting two Parliament amendments as they stand, proposing a compromise on three and rejecting five
3 February	Mr ROCARD and Mrs SMET meet the Portuguese Deputy Permanent Representative, Mrs FIGUEREIDO, in a first trialogue meeting
16 February	EP delegation meets for the second time, accepting one of the three compromise proposals of the Council, offering a compromise of its own on one of the amendments rejected by the Council and maintaining its position on the other four rejected amendments
24 February	First meeting of the Conciliation Committee, co-chaired by EP Vice-President, Mr PROVAN, and Portuguese Minister, Mr PEDROSO, debates the EP amendments intended to enable doctors in training to work a forty-eight-hour week within four years
15 March	Third meeting of EP delegation agrees to withdraw one amendment rejected by Council, to accept a Commission statement to replace a second such amendment and to concentrate the discussion with the Council on the remaining four amendments and in particular, the working time of junior doctors
21 March	Second trialogue meeting, attended by Chair of EP delegation, Mr PROVAN as well as Mr ROCARD and Mrs SMET, with the presidency suggesting the structure for a possible compromise formula on junior doctors. EP representatives agree to negotiate on this basis
3 April	Second meeting of the Conciliation Committee reaches a final compromise after seven hours of negotiation, the key element of which is that after a four-year transposition period, the working time of junior doctors must normally be brought into line with the forty-eight-hour maximum weekly working time within five years.

---

together representatives of the Council, Commission, and EP. Nowhere are such meetings referred to in Article 251 but they have become a regular feature of virtually all conciliations. These meetings are much smaller than the full conciliation committee where there can be over 100 people in the room. At trialogues there are normally no more than twenty-five with speakers restricted to two or three members of the Parliament delegation, the deputy permanent representative of the member state holding the Council presidency (most matters in conciliation fall under the responsibility of Coreper I—see Chapter 13) and a Director or

Director-General of the Commission. Major negotiations on the working time directive took place within trialogues, with the second meeting on 21 March, for example, agreeing a compromise formula that both took as a basis for negotiation.

More generally, this example shows that a real negotiation took place in which both sides gave ground in the interests of moving towards an overall agreement. On the main issue of the junior doctors, the final agreement did see member governments prepared to advance the normal period for implementation of a forty-eight hour week from thirteen to nine years. Thus conciliation made a recognizable difference to the content of Community legislation.

The working time directive is not atypical. Analyses of conciliation tend to concur that a high percentage of parliamentary amendments at second reading are usually either accepted as they stand or in a compromise form more or less favourable to the Parliament. Under the Maastricht Treaty from 1994 to 1999, that percentage was 74 per cent (Shackleton 2000: 328) and for the first year after the Treaty of Amsterdam came into force, it rose to 81 per cent (European Parliament 2000: 19). The important issue is not to establish which institution 'wins' under co-decision but rather to acknowledge that the conciliation procedure has created a new environment within which the views of the Parliament are taken seriously by the Council.

The close relationship between Council and Parliament extends beyond the process of adopting legislation. Each are called upon to act together to defend the results of co-decisions if they are challenged in the ECJ.[2] Defence of the results of acts adopted under co-decision oblige Parliament and Council to cooperate in a way that was unheard of before co-decision was introduced.

The shared interest of Parliament and Council to reach an agreement and, if necessary, to defend it in the Court, has two important consequences. First, it enhances the institutional status of the Parliament. In particular, co-decision reduces the role of the Commission as the privileged interlocutor of the Council: the Commission no longer can withdraw its proposal once conciliation has begun and is restricted to the often vital but nevertheless circumscribed task of seeking to reconcile the positions of the two branches. Second, the Parliament starts to be seen by the public at large as sharing responsibility in changing the shape of laws that affect all European citizens. Slowly it is becoming clearer that legislation is not simply a product of agreement in the Council, but rather that the EP can alter policy outcomes in significant ways.

Finally, the budgetary powers of the Parliament deserve attention as a means of making policy. The Parliament has had the right to modify levels of expenditure in the Community budget within certain defined limits for nearly a quarter of a century. Until the 1990s the exercise of this right saw the EP reshape the budget in areas of 'non-compulsory' expenditure (that is, most categories outside the common agricultural policy), notably the structural funds (Corbett *et al.* 2000: 227–8).

The scope for using the budget in this way has declined over time. Limits on spending have been established through three 'financial perspectives' agreed by Parliament, Council, and Commission in 1988, 1992, and 1999, for the following five, six, and seven years respectively. These agreements set down expenditure limits on different categories of expenditure (agriculture, external policies, and administration, for example) which can only be exceeded by mutual accord and which the annual budget has to respect. Moreover, within these limits, much spending relates to multi-annual programmes, such as the Research Framework Programme, which have been agreed by co-decision. Hence the Parliament now finds itself taking budgetary and legislative decisions at the same time, rather than separately in the annual budgetary procedure. Moreover, the readiness of the Parliament in the 1980s to challenge the Council by calling for extra spending at EU level has declined as the norms of financial rigour have become more firmly established, with all parties committed to the need to respect the limits on public spending provided for in the move to EMU. As a result the budgetary procedure has become a less dramatic affair, more an exercise in joint management than in providing direction for the Union.

Policy-implementing decisions

The implementation of Community policies involves thousands of individual decisions in any one year. No parliamentary body can hope to be able to follow all these decisions in detail but the EP has consistently pressed for scrutiny rights equivalent to those of the Council over the implementing bodies, known as comitology committees, that are chaired by the Commission and bring together representatives of all the member states. It has argued that it should be informed about the work of these committees and should have the opportunity to block draft decisions with which it disagrees.

This argument became even more intense after co-decision was introduced. With the Council able to block draft comitology decisions and take an implementing decision itself, the legislative equality of the two branches that exists in policy-making clearly does not extend to policy implementation. The Council has consistently argued that its role in policy implementation relates to its executive functions and that it therefore is in a different position from the EP. Nevertheless, it was willing to discuss the issue and in 1999 a new comitology decision was adopted, which simplified the procedures, increased the information made available to the Parliament and gave the EP the right to request re-examination of measures adopted under co-decision if the committee is suspected of acting beyond its powers (Corbett et al. 2000: 259–61).

The debate about comitology may seem arcane but it raises essential questions about the openness and accountability of the EU system. The decisions are not simply technical: in the early 1990s, for example, the level of controls needed to stop the spread of BSE was decided in the Veterinary Committee. And yet decisions are taken very far from the public gaze, remaining in the hands of the Commission and national experts. Advocating a more powerful role for the Parliament is implicitly to acknowledge that the existing system is lacking in transparency.

Implementing decisions of this kind often become major political issues. The fall of the Commission in 1999 (see Exhibit 4.1) can be traced back through the work of the EP-appointed Committee of Independent Experts to individual decisions taken inside the Commission. One of these, the so-called Fléchard case, discussed in Chapter 11, saw the Commission deciding not to pursue a claim for full compensation from the French government for EU subsidies that had been obtained fraudulently.

Another example is the work of the first Committee of Inquiry that was set up under the new Maastricht provisions in 1996 (Shackleton 1998). It examined the apparently very technical issue of transit fraud relating to the non-payment of tax on goods coming into the EU and passing through several countries before reaching their final destination. In the course of this inquiry the committee became aware of the growth of tax evasion relating to cigarettes, arising not least from the weakness of the antiquated, national mechanisms in place to control tobacco movements into and around the EU. The EP pressed very hard to encourage closer cooperation between customs authorities in the EU to improve the quality of implementing measures and, at the beginning of 2001, a number of governments joined the Commission in bringing a court action in the United States against the major cigarette manufacturers. Hence the Parliament can respond to and influence the context of implementing measures even if it does not participate directly in the decisions themselves.

The future of the Parliament

The Parliament has gained an important say in the making of policy through the co-decision procedure and can contribute in a more limited way to history-making and policy-implementing decisions. But where does the Parliament go from here? Will its future development follow the trajectory of the last twenty years? These questions cannot be answered in isolation: the future of the EP is intimately linked to the way in which the EU as a whole develops. There is no reason to suppose that the Parliament will necessarily improve its position in some linear way.

This uncertain future was evident in the way in which the Parliament was treated at the European Council in Nice at the end of 2000. In two areas Parliament was successful. First, it was given the right to challenge acts of other institutions in front of the ECJ, even if they do not affect its own prerogatives. Second, in future it will be asked to give its assent to any decision that a member state is in breach of fundamental human rights (Article 7 TEU). In three other areas, the Parliament was less fortunate.

First, the Parliament had called for co-decision to be extended to all areas subject to QMV. In fact, only five new areas will become subject to co-decision (as compared with an increase of twenty-three areas at Amsterdam). For the moment member states have declined to give the fullest expression to the notion of Parliament and Council as two equal branches of the legislative authority.

Second, as indicated earlier, the Parliament had not come up with a formal proposal as to how seats should be distributed in an enlarged EU. The European Council was not so bashful (see Table 5.1). Indeed it used the allocation of seats in the EP to member states as a bargaining chip. It increased the number of seats for Belgium, for example, to offset Belgian opposition to other parts of the deal made, even though the result was to give fewer seats to the more populous Czech Republic. It also agreed to keep the number of MEPs for Germany and Luxembourg the same as before, whilst reducing that of all other states. In this latter case, it combined in a contradictory manner a desire to take greater account of the number of MEPs per head of population and to recognize the particular status of a small founding state of the Community. As a result the Parliament found itself painfully excluded from a history-making decision that will have an important effect on its own internal efficiency (it could find itself with more than 800 members for an interim period!) as well as upon the distribution of national influence.

Third, the member governments agreed that in the next IGC, due to be completed in 2004, the role of national parliaments would be a central point of discussion. No further details were included but it is an issue that could be of the highest relevance for the EP. The decision reflects a growing debate about the possibility of reinforcing the position of national parliaments in the European structure (Raunio 1999).

For many years such ideas were restricted to a very few countries. In France, in particular, there has been consistent support in favour of a more direct role for national parliaments in the EU process. Such support led to the creation in 1989 of a body called COSAC (Conférence des Organes Spécialisés dans les Affaires Communautaires) which brings together MEPs with representatives of the European Affairs Committees within the parliaments of the member states. However, the belief that the twice-yearly meetings of this body are not sufficient to give national parliaments a proper role in the EU has spread beyond France as Exhibit 5.2 shows. Both Tony Blair and Joschka Fischer, German Foreign Minister, have come out in favour, from different perspectives, of a second parliamentary chamber at European level.

As the Exhibit shows, the proposal is not supported by the President of the Commission, Romano Prodi, and the Finnish Prime Minister, Paavo Lipponen, both of whom favour a strengthening of the existing parliamentary structure. The

Table 5.1 Composition of the EP in a Union with twenty-seven member states

A	B	C	D	E	F	G	H
Germany	82,038	17.1	99	99	0	829,000	829,000
United Kingdom	59,247	12.3	87	72	17.2	823,000	681,000
France	58,996	12.3	87	72	17.2	819,000	678,000
Italy	57,612	12.0	87	72	17.2	800,000	662,000
Spain	39,394	8.2	64	50	21.9	788,000	616,000
Poland	38,667	8.0	64	50	21.9	773,000	604,000
Romania	22,489	4.7	44	33	25.0	681,000	511,000
Netherlands	15,760	3.3	31	25	19.4	630,000	508,000
Greece	10,553	2.2	25	22	12.0	479,000	421,000
Czech Republic	10,290	2.1	25	20	20.0	515,000	412,000
Belgium	10,213	2.1	25	22	12.0	464,000	409,000
Hungary	10,092	2.1	25	20	20.0	505,000	404,000
Portugal	9,980	2.1	25	22	12.0	454,000	399,000
Sweden	8,854	1.8	22	18	18.2	492,000	402,000
Bulgaria	8,230	1.7	21	17	19.1	484,000	392,000
Austria	8,082	1.7	21	17	19.1	475,000	385,000
Slovakia	5,393	1.1	16	13	18.8	415,000	337,000
Denmark	5,313	1.1	16	13	18.8	409,000	332,000
Finland	5,160	1.1	16	13	18.8	397,000	323,000
Ireland	3,744	0.8	15	12	20.0	312,000	250,000
Lithuania	3,701	0.8	15	12	20.0	308,000	247,000
Latvia	2,439	0.5	10	8	20.0	305,000	244,000
Slovenia	1,978	0.4	9	7	22.2	283,000	220,000
Estonia	1,446	0.3	7	6	14.3	241,000	207,000
Cyprus	752	0.2	6	6	0	125,000	125,000
Luxembourg	429	0.1	6	6	0	72,000	72,000
Malta	379	0.1	6	5	16.7	76,000	63,000
Total EU 27	481,181	100.0	874	732		657,000	551,000

A: Member states
B: Population (thousands)
C: Population of each member state as a percentage of total EU population
D: Seats per member state under the present Treaty
E: Seats per member state under the Treaty of Nice
F: Reduction as a percentage
G: Number of inhabitants represented by each MEP in each member state under the Treaty of Nice
H: Number of inhabitants represented by each MEP in each member state under the present Treaty.

EP itself has consistently (and not surprisingly) argued against a second Chamber. Its argument is partly based on the fact that national parliamentarians are unlikely ever to have the time to devote to the work of such a new body (this was clearly the case before 1979 when the EP was made up of national parliamentarians) and partly on the assumption that the proper job of national parliaments should be to scrutinize the work of their governments in the EU.

The EP has also made facilities available in its buildings in Brussels to all national parliaments that want to take advantage of them, which five parliaments have

Exhibit 5.2 Four visions of the future of the European Parliament

Joschka Fischer **at Humboldt University, Berlin, 12 May 2000**
'A European Parliament must therefore always represent two things: a Europe of nation-states and a Europe of citizens. This will only be possible if this European Parliament actually brings together the different national political élites and then also the different national publics. In my opinion, this can be done if the European Parliament has two chambers. One will be for elected members who are also members of their national parliaments. Thus there will be no clash between national parliaments and the European Parliament, between the nation state and Europe. For the second chamber a decision will have to be made between the Senate model, with directly-elected senators from the Member States, and a chamber of states along the lines of Germany's Bundesrat.'

Romano Prodi **at the European Parliament on 3 October 2000**
'The European process can only derive its democratic vitality from a dual legitimation; the direct legitimation of the European people, as represented by you, the Members of the European Parliament, and the legitimation of the Member States, which in turn is based on democratic elections. The European Parliament, as the expression of Europe-wide direct universal suffrage, is the institution specifically dedicated to representing the Union of the peoples of Europe. And it is from your endorsement of the Commission that the Commission derives its democratic legitimacy. This then complements the other source of legitimacy, namely the Member States represented in the Council.'

Tony Blair **in Warsaw on 6 October 2000**
'I believe that the time has now come to involve representatives of national parliaments more on such matters, by creating a second chamber of the European Parliament. A second chamber's most important function would be to review the EU's work, in the light of this agreed Statement of Principles (laying down what is best done at European level and what should be done at national level). It would not get involved in the day-to-day negotiation of legislation—which is properly the role of the existing European Parliament. Rather its task would be to help implement the agreed statement of principles, so that we do what we need to do at a European level but also so that we devolve power downwards.'

Paavo Lipponen **at the College of Europe in Bruges on 10 November 2000**
'A constitution for the Union should produce an institutional structure that would permanently secure the equality of Member States by transforming the Council. This would rid us of permanent haggling with the weighting of votes in Council. The Parliament would represent democratic legitimacy from an equally fundamental point of view as a directly elected body with considerable powers. The Commission should enjoy the confidence of the Parliament, with a President with powers to appoint members of the Commission. And in this institutional set-up, just like in national decision-making, all aspects of civil society should be involved.'

done (Danish Folketing, Finnish Eduskunta, British House of Commons, French Senate, and Italian Senate), with a view to improving the ability of national parliaments to scrutinize the EU activity of their governments. In addition, the Parliament has indicated its support for involving national parliaments in new forms of cooperation designed to revise the existing Treaties.

During 2000 a European Charter of Fundamental Rights was prepared by a Convention, composed of fifteen personal representatives of the heads of state and government, sixteen members from the European Parliament, one Commissioner, and thirty representatives of national parliaments. This apparently unwieldy mechanism worked remarkably well, even though consensus was needed to reach agreement: the text it adopted was approved by the European Council in Nice. For the first time national parliaments were given a specific role in defining the shape of the EU. It is a model that the Parliament would like to see used in the work of future intergovernmental conferences, especially in view of the high level of dissatisfaction with the process by which the Treaty of Nice was negotiated.

There remains a strong body of political opinion in favour of giving national parliaments a stronger role than that suggested by the EP. Even after twenty years, the directly elected Parliament is not seen by all as assuring a sufficient link between the European electorate and European institutions. Despite the growth in its powers and its higher public profile since the ejection of the Commission from office in March 1999, interest in the EP's affairs and its broader credibility have not grown sufficiently to convince all of its kind of strategy for developing the EU. Many point to the low level of interest in and the continuing second-order character of European elections. In the 1999 direct elections, as Table 5.2 shows, the

Table 5.2 Turn-out in European Parliament elections

	1979	1981	1984	1987	1989	1994	1995	1996	1999
EU	63.0	—	61.0	—	58.5	56.8	—	—	49.4
Belgium	91.6	—	92.2	—	90.7	90.7	—	—	90.0
Luxembourg	88.9	—	87.0	—	87.4	88.5	—	—	85.8
Italy	85.5	—	83.9	—	81.5	74.8	—	—	70.8
Greece	—	78.6	77.2	—	79.9	71.2	—	—	70.2
Spain	—	—	—	68.9	54.8	59.1	—	—	64.4
Ireland	63.6	—	47.6	—	68.3	44.0	—	—	50.5
Denmark	47.1	—	52.3	—	46.1	52.9	—	—	50.4
Austria	—	—	—	—	—	—	—	67.7	49.0
France	60.7	—	56.7	—	48.7	52.7	—	—	47.0
Germany	65.7	—	56.8	—	62.4	60.0	—	—	45.2
Portugal	—	—	—	72.2	51.1	35.5	—	—	40.4
Sweden	—	—	—	—	—	—	41.6	—	38.3
Finland	—	—	—	—	—	—	—	60.3	30.1
Netherlands	57.8	—	50.5	—	47.2	35.7	—	—	29.9
United Kingdom	31.6	—	32.6	—	36.2	36.4	—	—	24.0

average level of turn-out fell for the fifth time running, with increases in three countries (Spain, Ireland, and Portugal) being more than outweighed by some very big drops in turn-out in other countries, notably Britain and Germany.

The EP may have been a victim of a trend in many western European states for lower election turn-outs. It is also true that the particular character of the EU makes it difficult for voters to see what difference their vote makes. They are not voting for a government nor for a single legislature but rather for an institution where the specific impact of any particular political party is obscured by the need to find consensus amongst political groups as well as with other institutions.

Various solutions have been proposed, all deriving from contrasting views about the future shape of the Union. For some, it is a question of linking the results of European elections with the choice of the President of the Commission. Under such an arrangement, the political affiliation of the Commission President would be determined by which party won the largest number of seats in the elections. The idea here is that the Parliament should become more like national parliaments in Europe, with the executive deriving its support through parliamentary channels. For others, the solution should come from breaking down the national character of the elections by ensuring that some candidates are selected from Europe-wide lists to be found on all ballot papers. From this perspective, the citizen needs to be able to see that the election is about selecting more than national representatives but members with a European outlook on policy issues. Others again consider the way forward is to propose that the Commission President be elected in a separate election, thereby ensuring him or her direct popular legitimacy. This view underlines the separateness of the Commission and seeks to make the EU system resemble more closely the American model.

All these solutions face significant difficulties in that they challenge the existing structure of power and influence. To suggest, for example, that the President of the European Commission should be the head of the list of the political group that gained the most votes in European elections is to challenge the right of member governments to propose a candidate for the EP to approve. To create multinational lists or even to have a fraction of candidates chosen on the basis of such lists might serve to break down the national character of European elections in individual countries. It would also challenge the role of national parties in the selection of candidates, passing some of their control to transnational party organizations (see Chapter 12). And to have direct elections for the President of the European Commission is to create a figure that could pose a major challenge to government leaders.

Moreover, these three solutions assume that the democratic legitimacy of the Union can be significantly reinforced by altering the configuration of the existing European institutions. Not all would agree with such an analysis; indeed many see the need to improve the level of public confidence domestically in the outcomes of what is negotiated in Brussels, as opposed to tinkering with the Brussels mechanisms. From this perspective the 'permissive consensus' amongst EU citizens in favour of what is done in their name in Brussels has broken down. If this is right, the Parliament will have to devote as much effort to proving that it can improve the lot of European citizens as it will to obtaining a stronger role in the institutions of an enlarged European Union.

Conclusions

This chapter has underlined three features of the EP:

- its ability to convince member governments to increase its powers through successive treaty revisions;
- a well-developed internal structure which enables it to overcome internal fragmentation and to take advantage of the possibilities of the Treaties; and
- its relative weakness in history-making and policy implementing decisions compared with a major role in policy-making in the legislative arena.

In theoretical terms, the chapter offers at least three insights from the institutionalist perspective:

- first, it points to the importance of rule changes on the outcome of the policy process. The introduction of the co-decision procedure in particular has not only improved the status of the EP, it has served to alter the shape of the regulations and directives that bind all EU governments and citizens. Process and outcome are intimately linked.
- second, it underlines the role of networks in the policy process. The conversion of the Parliament from an outsider to an insider position has drawn to it an ever wider range of interests. The working time directive example shows how an interest, in this case junior doctors, that has lost out in policy discussions within and between governments in the Council, can turn to the EP to press its case, with a reasonable hope of achieving some success.
- third, it stresses the importance of consensus mechanisms, within the Parliament as well as between it and the other institutions. The result is the spreading of responsibility to ensure that support for policy change is broad. The collective character of decisions in the EU creates a specific tension for the Parliament in that it makes it more difficult for voters to identify who to reward or punish for particular policy outcomes when they participate in European elections.

The chapter also offers a challenge to intergovernmental analysis, which puts the interests of national governments at the centre of explanation of the EU. Why have the member governments been willing, in successive treaty revisions, to reinforce an instititution that challenges their position and influence? In the author's view, it is hard to answer this question without acknowledging the autonomous capacity of the EP to influence the EU process and the way governments perceive it. Now no member state would openly challenge the legitimacy of the institution's role. It remains true that member states are increasingly eager to influence the EP through 'their own' MEPs but such efforts are never guaranteed success, given the heterogeneity of the instititution and its general desire to preserve its independence.

The question now is whether in an enlarged EU the EP will be able to continue to persuade member governments to support an increase in its role, to overcome its growing internal heterogeneity, and to maintain and develop its role in and beyond the policy-making process. The Parliament continues on its 'Journey to an Unknown Destination' (Shonfield 1973).

Notes

1   The categorization used here is slightly different from Peterson and Bomberg's (1999), with 'policy-making' decisions subsuming their two analytical categories of 'policy-setting' and 'policy-shaping' decisions. Peterson and Bomberg (1999: 277) explicitly state that policy implementation is beyond the scope of their study.

2   Two such cases have been brought so far. In October 2000 the Court struck down the directive on the advertising and sponsorship of tobacco that the German government—outvoted in the Council—had challenged (See Chapter 6). In November 2000, the Court rejected a case brought by Luxembourg against the directive designed to facilitate the practice of law in a member state other than that in which the qualification was obtained.

Further reading

There are two main kinds of further reading about the EP. First, there are books and articles that provide more detailed information on how the Parliament works. Corbett, Jacobs, and Shackleton (2000) is now in its fourth edition and provides a highly detailed account of the internal workings of the institution. For those who wish to keep up to date on the details, the best source is the web site of the Parliament at: **www.europarl.eu.int**. Corbett (1998) offers a more historical account of how the institution consciously set out to develop its powers during the 1980s and 1990s. This account is particularly interesting when compared with the Vedel Report (1972) which looked forward to an unknown future for the institution. Second, there is a growing literature about the development of democracy inside the European Union which seeks to place the role of the EP in a wider context. Siedentop (2000) is a good example, considering the conditions necessary for a democratic system at European level from the perspective of political theory. Hoskyns and Newman (2000) and Lord (1998*b*) also provide analyses of the democratic deficit and the role the EP can play in filling it.

Corbett, R. (1998), *The European Parliament's Role in Closer Integration* (Basingstoke: Macmillan).

—— Jacobs, F., and Shackleton, M. (2000), *The European Parliament*, 4th edn. (London: John Harper).

Hoskyns, C., and Newman, M. (2000) (eds.), *Democratizing the European Union* (Manchester: Manchester University Press).

Lord, C. (1998*b*), *Democracy in the European Union* (Sheffield: Sheffield University Press).

Siedentop, L. (2000), *Democracy in Europe* (Harmondsworth: Penguin).

Vedel, G. (1972), *Report of the Working Party Examining the Problem of the Enlargement of the Powers of the European Parliament ('Vedel Report')* (Brussels: *Bulletin of the European Communities*, Supplement 4/72).

Web links

The Parliament web site (**www.europarl.eu.int**) provides up-to-date material on the workings of the institution, including all reports being discussed in committee and plenary, the minutes of the parliamentary session on the day of their adoption, and the full record of the debates. There is information from the President of the Parliament, the political groups, and the EP information offices as well as links to the other EU institutions, national parliaments, and the European Ombudsman. Many individual MEPs have their own web sites which can be accessed through the site of their political group.

Chapter 6
The European Court of Justice

Kieran St Clair Bradley[1]

Summary

The founding Treaties of the European Union lay down an extensive set of legal rules, principles, and procedures for the functioning of the institutions considered in this volume. The legal acts that the institutions adopt, and those of the member states which affect the functioning of the Communities, are subject to judicial review by the European Court of Justice (ECJ). In interpreting treaty and legislative provisions, the Court determines both the meaning and the practical effect of Community law. In a Community so closely bound by the rule of law, it is inevitable that Court judgments can have major political repercussions. The Court's contribution to the political development of the Communities is widely recognized.

Introduction

The European Court of Justice is a different kind of institution from the others discussed in this book. Its home in Luxembourg separates it geographically from the main centres of the other institutions that provide direction to the EU. It is not connected with these institutions in the same way as they are connected with each other. Its members do not attend meetings of the other institutions, nor do those institutions participate in the work of the Court, except through their legal services. Nor is it an arena where power and influence are directly exercised in the pursuit of specific political and policy objectives.

However, the Court plays a central role within the institutional structure of the EU. Its judgments, designed to ensure that the law is observed, form an essential part of the 'rules and practices that influence and constitute behaviour' (see Chapter 1, p. 3). It thereby makes a vital contribution to the institutionalization of the Union. Its work may be less visible to the European citizen but, as this chapter shows, its decisions have played a major part in determining the shape of the Community in which they live.

To understand why, it is important to stress that the European Communities are subject to the rule of law to an extent unparalleled in the history of relations between sovereign states. As the ultimate authority for the interpretation of Community law, the Court of Justice[2] fulfils functions comparable to those vested in the highest national courts. The Court is not the only, or the first, international court. It is occasionally confused with the International Court of Justice (ICJ) or the European Court of Human Rights (ECtHR). Based in The Hague (the Netherlands), the ICJ applies classical international law, and only hears cases referred to it by states which are parties to the ICJ Statute or by organs of the United Nations. The ECtHR, which sits in Strasbourg (France), is exclusively responsible for supervising the application of the 1950 European Convention on Human Rights and Fundamental Freedoms (European Convention), through hearing complaints by individuals or contracting states. By contrast, the Court of Justice may hear cases taken by individuals[3] and Community institutions, as well as by the member states. Furthermore, it applies not only the Community Treaties, but also general principles of law that are recognized in the legal systems of the member states, such as the protection of fundamental rights. In so doing, the Court has developed what it terms 'a new legal order' for the Community, which is quite distinct from either national or international law, comparable in some respects to the constitutional law of a federal polity.

Establishment and structure

The Court was established in 1952 as the Court of Justice of the European Coal and Steel Community. It now exercises the judicial functions for the Communities, and in more limited circumstances, for the third pillar of the Union.

Originally there was a single judicial body for the Community. The Single European Act established a Court of First Instance (CFI), attached to the Court of Justice. Subsequently, the Treaty of Nice has provided for the establishment of 'judicial panels'. As a result, the Community courts will operate on three levels. The composition, structure, and functions of each will be considered in turn.

The Court of Justice

The ECJ comprises one judge per member state, and is planned to continue to do so after the coming accessions. Judges are selected on the basis of their independence and legal stature, and must either have the qualifications to be appointed to the highest court in their home member state, or otherwise have an outstanding academic or professional record; some, but not all, have held high judicial office before joining the ECJ (see Exhibit 6.1). The Court therefore has direct access to authoritative guidance on the law of the individual member states. As a large number of the cases referred to it concern questions of Community law which arise in national legal proceedings, the presence of a judge from each member state assists the Court in understanding the different legal contexts in which such disputes arise, as well as national legal sensibilities. Moreover, when faced with novel legal questions of principle, it can and does draw inspiration from solutions already adopted at the national level.

The ECJ often decides cases in chambers of three or five judges. For particularly difficult cases, or to resolve inconsistencies in the judgments of the chambers, the Court may sit in a plenary formation of eleven or fifteen judges. Whatever the formation, the judgment bears the authority of the Court.

While cases are heard, and judgments published, in all the Community languages, the working language of the ECJ is French. The written submissions are therefore first translated into French before the case can be dealt with, and the judge who is appointed *rapporteur* (effectively, case manager) prepares the draft of the judgment in French. The Court adopts a single judgment to dispose of a case; no separate opinions of the judges, whether dissenting or concurring, are issued, and, indeed, what goes on in the judges' deliberations, which take place in the absence of any officials (except the Court registrar or his representative), may be considered amongst the best-kept secrets in the Community.

Exhibit 6.1 Judicial appointments

Members of both the ECJ and the CFI are appointed by common accord of the member state governments for a renewable six-year term. Though the requirement that all the governments agree to the appointment formally breaks the link between judge and nominating State, judicial appointments are, in effect, in the gift of each individual government.

National practices with regard to the appointment of judges to the highest courts vary considerably (Stone Sweet 2000: 49; Jackson and Tushnet 1999: 490–1). The members may all be elected by the legislature, or some members elected by the judiciary, the government, and the legislature, or by the head of state and by each legislative chamber. Other member states have established judicial appointments boards or other vetting procedures, which allow some form of scrutiny of candidates' suitability for appointment.

The Court is currently the only Community institution whose members are selected without being subject to any direct or indirect scrutiny, though some member states organize their own selection procedure before nominating a candidate to the Community judiciary. The absence of any Community vetting procedure for the Court is widely considered unsatisfactory, and the reasons usually proffered in defence of the status quo, often limited to a disparaging reference to the procedure for appointment of US Supreme Court justices, are unconvincing. One of the principal tasks of the Court is to review the application of Community law by the Member States; judges are thus called upon to review the acts of the governments that appointed them. They also decide disputes between the Council, the Community institution comprising national government representatives, and the other institutions. The personal stature and the quality of the work of the members of the Court have not yet been seriously challenged. However, if they are not seen to be appointed through a procedure that sufficiently guarantees their neutrality *vis-à-vis* governments, at least equivalent to those which apply at the national level, the authority of the institution, and the legitimacy of the Community's legal order, could ultimately suffer.

Apart from the judges, the Court is also 'assisted' by eight advocates-general, whose qualifications for office and appointment procedure are identical to those of the judges. Each of the five largest member states appoints one advocate-general, while the remaining posts are filled by the other member states on a rotation basis. There is no exact equivalent of this office in any of the national legal systems. Advocates-general do not represent any outside body, such as the public prosecutor's or attorney-general's office. As a member of the Court, the advocate-general takes part in the process by which the Court decides the case, by delivering a first opinion on the issues. The Court is not bound to follow the opinion, though in the majority of cases it does so, in some instances simply adopting, or referring to, the opinion as providing the reasons for the result reached. The more extensive treatment of the issues in the opinion provides a useful complement to the understanding of the terser pronouncements of the ECJ.

Where it is not followed, the opinion may partially compensate for the absence of dissenting judgments, by demonstrating potential shortcomings in the Court's reasoning. The very few judgments in which the ECJ has squarely overturned its previous case law have almost all been preceded by an AG's opinion recommending that it do so.

The Court of First Instance

The CFI was established in 1989 to relieve the pressure of work on the Court of Justice by dealing with disputes in which fact-finding plays an important part, such as those on competition law and staff matters. Its principal task is to hear annulment actions and compensation claims by individuals against Community institutions. The losing party may appeal to the ECJ against the legal findings of CFI judgments, though not its findings on the facts. The CFI will be competent to decide appeals from rulings in the judicial panels when these are set up (see below), and it may be vested with competence to provide preliminary rulings in specific areas of Community law.

The CFI currently comprises one judge per member state, though the number may be increased to take account of its workload. The judges must, like ECJ judges, be 'persons whose independence is beyond doubt', and they must have the abilities required to be a national judge. The CFI generally sits in chambers of three, or occasionally five, judges, though a single judge may hear simple routine cases. While there are at present no permanent advocates-general at the CFI, the Treaty of Nice allows for such a possibility. The working methods of the CFI are essentially the same as those of the ECJ. Unlike the higher court, the CFI may not dispense with oral hearings, except where it rules that an action is manifestly inadmissible (for example, if the initiating application was submitted late) or is manifestly unfounded.

Judicial panels

The lowest level of Community court will be the 'judicial panels', which the Council will be empowered to establish by Article 225a TEC, as and when the Treaty of Nice enters into force. Though not expressly so described, it is clear that the panels are to be courts of first instance, each of which will be competent to deal with complaints by individuals in a specific area of Community law, such as disputes concerning the registration of Community trade marks, or staff disputes. Decisions of the judicial panels will be subject to a right of appeal to the CFI. No decision has yet been taken on how many panels will be set up, or their competences, though Article 225a TEC requires that the panel judges be highly qualified, independent, lawyers.

Powers and functions[4]

Unlike the other institutions and bodies considered in this volume, the Court of Justice is an exclusively reactive body. It has no right of political initiative, and can only take decisions on the matters that are brought before it in accordance with the applicable procedures. The Court has few significant informal powers. Its influence in relation to treaty reform[5] or administrative budgetary spending is comparable to that of the ancillary political organs of the Community, such as the Economic and Social Committee.

Where Community law creates obligations for individuals, these are enforced either by the member states or the Commission. Individuals therefore appear in direct actions before the Community courts only as applicants, arguing, for example, that the obligation does not exist, or has not been properly applied, or that its enforcement conflicts with a fundamental right protected under Community law.

There are essentially six categories of legal dispute which the Court of Justice is called upon to resolve. The first two (infringement actions and preliminary rulings) concern principally the respect by the member states of their obligations; the remaining four (annulment proceedings, action for failure to act, action in damages, and rulings on international agreements) concern the obligations of the Community institutions. As the Community relies almost exclusively on the member states for the administration of Community law,[6] the first two are of far greater practical importance. In relation to the four latter categories the Court may be said to rule on the parts of the Community constitution the political institutions cannot reach.

Application of Community law by the member states

The infringement action

Questions concerning the respect by states of their obligations under international agreements are generally left to the states themselves. Where disagreements arise, they may be able to resort to various dispute resolution procedures, such as arbitration, or litigation before the ICJ, or, under the World Trade Organization agreements, to a specially established, and highly judicialized, form of procedure. Under the Community Treaties, however, the Commission is vested with the primary[7] responsibility for ensuring that the member states comply with both the applicable treaty provisions and Community legislation. It carries out this duty mainly through the *infringement action* under Article 226 TEC, which is the most significant manifestation of its duty to act as guardian of the Treaty. The

Commission may pursue a member state before the Court for any breach of Community law, such as failing to apply a treaty rule, a regulation or a decision, or failing to transpose, implement, or apply a directive. Only a small percentage of the cases initiated by the Commission in fact end up in Court, as member states often make a final effort to comply with their obligations during the course of the procedure.

If the Commission wins, the Court will merely declare that the member state has failed to respect the particular legal obligation. Unlike most federal supreme courts, the Court does not have the power to strike down national legislation, though the member state is under an obligation to take the necessary measures to comply with the judgment, and normally does. The finding that the member state has been in default may be relevant in determining its possible liability in damages in national or Community law.

Concerned at the number of infringement judgments that were not being complied with, a follow-up procedure was introduced by the Maastricht Treaty (Article 228 TEC). This allows the Commission to take a recalcitrant member state back to Court, which may impose financial sanctions on the member state until it has complied with the original obligation. The new procedure was applied for the first time in July 2000, when the Court ordered Greece to pay EUR 20,000 per day until it had complied with a 1992 judgment holding that it had failed to apply a number of environmental protection directives (ECJ 2000a).

The preliminary ruling procedure

As Community law is administered primarily by the national authorities, national courts are in a very real sense Community courts. To prevent divergent interpretations of Community rules, the treaty authors devised a procedure to allow the Court of Justice to provide an authoritative ruling on any aspect of Community law submitted to it, and hence guarantee its uniform application. Underlying the preliminary ruling procedure of Article 234 TEC (formerly Article 177) is a dispute before a national court that raises one or several issues of Community law, on the interpretation of the Treaty, or on the interpretation or validity of an act of a Community institution or other body. Where necessary to reach judgment, the national court can obtain a ruling on the Community law question from the Court. Lower courts may choose not to ask for a ruling, whereas national supreme courts are obliged to seek such a ruling where a Community law point arises, except where the answer is obvious or would not influence the outcome of the case.

The Court has interpreted its jurisdiction under this head very widely, both as to the scope of Community acts which can be examined and as to the national bodies which can make such references. It will only refuse to provide a ruling where it is clear that there is no real dispute between the parties to the main action, or that the Community provisions invoked have no connection with the national proceedings. The Court only answers the Community law question, and does not decide the case. In practice, however, the national court will often have little remaining discretion as to the outcome of the proceedings before it.

The significance of the preliminary reference procedure is that the Court's ruling is binding, not only on the referring court, but on all the courts of all the member states faced with the same issue, the so-called 'multiplier effect'. The establishment of this procedure, particularly when combined with the direct effect of many provisions of Community law (see below), obviated the need to create an autonomous system of Community courts, such as the federal courts in the United States. The Community harnesses the authority (and the procedures and infrastructure) of the national courts to apply Community law. While a national government might be tempted for reasons of short-term political gain not to implement a ruling of an international tribunal, it would not usually dare defy its own courts.

As an exercise in judicial cooperation and legal symbiosis, the preliminary ruling procedure has been extremely successful. Notwithstanding occasional bouts of dissent, and subject in some cases to constitutional reservations, the national supreme courts have all come to accept, and apply, the Court of Justice's vision of the Community's legal order (Slaughter *et al.* 1998). It is no accident that all but a handful of the judgments defining this legal order have been pronounced in the context of preliminary rulings (see, for example, *Van Gend en Loos*, below). As it depends on mutual cooperation, the procedure also imposes duties on the national courts, which must formulate the questions properly and supply the necessary information to enable the Court to provide a useful answer. The current overload of the Court's docket (the backlog at the end of 2000 represented over a year's work) may be attributed, at least in part, to an excessive reluctance by some national courts to decide themselves Community law questions which are of no real general significance.

For the most part, the questions referred concern situations where an individual is relying on a provision of Community law to defeat a conflicting national rule, though it is not exclusively concerned with member state respect for their obligations. The procedure also allows individuals a means of challenging indirectly the validity of decisions adopted by the Community institutions, without having to comply with the very stringent conditions for taking an annulment action directly before the Community court.

Respect of Community law by the political institutions

Annulment proceedings

The annulment action is the paradigmatic form of direct judicial proceeding before the Court. It allows the member states and the political institutions and, under certain restrictions, the Court of Auditors and the European Central Bank (ECB), to challenge the validity of a legal act adopted by one or more political institution(s) or the ECB. Individuals may only take annulment proceedings against a decision that is either addressed to them, or that has similar effects to such a decision. As the Court applies this rule restrictively, individuals may not in general challenge the validity of regulations or directives directly, though they may be able to do so indirectly through the preliminary ruling procedure.

The grounds on which an act can be declared void are widely defined in the Treaty, and the Court will in practice examine any argument that an act breaches a legal rule or principle, including rules and principles not formulated explicitly in the Treaty itself. In particular, the annulment action provides member states with a direct means of ensuring the institutions do not encroach on their legislative powers. Where the Court upholds the action, the contested act is declared void, that is, of no legal effect from the moment of its adoption. The defendant institution must take the necessary measures to comply with the Court's judgment. The *Tobacco Advertising* case (ECJ 2000b; see Exhibit 6.2) is a striking example of a successful annulment action.

Action for illegal failure to act

The action for illegal failure to act (often referred to by the French term *recours en carence*) is the other side of the coin to annulment proceedings. It allows the

---

Exhibit 6.2 The *Tobacco Advertising* case

In October 2000, the Court annulled, for the first time, a measure which had been adopted under co-decision. Germany, which had voted against it, had argued that the 1998 directive prohibiting all forms of tobacco advertising was a disguised public health measure, while Parliament and Council contended that the Treaty allowed the Community to adopt any measure to regulate the internal market, not just those that liberalize trade. The Court held that the Community legislator could not rely on other articles to circumvent the express ban in Article 152 TEC on harmonization of health measures. It argued that measures based on Article 95 TEC must have as their object the improvement of the conditions of the internal market, not mere market regulation; any other position would breach the express wording of that provision, undermine the principle of conferred powers, and render nugatory judicial review of the choice of legal basis. After examining the objectives of the directive as stated in the preamble thereto, the Court concluded that the measure neither facilitated trade in advertising products, nor contributed to eliminating appreciable distortions of competition. As the conditions for recourse to Article 95 TEC had not been fulfilled, the directive was annulled. The judgment is particularly noteworthy for two reasons. On the one hand, the Court is sending a signal both to the Community institutions and the member states (and their constitutional courts) that it will enforce the division of material competences reflected in the Treaty. On the other, the judgment illustrates that the enforcement of this division falls ultimately to the judicial, rather than the political, branch of the Community government.

member states, the political institutions, the Court of Auditors, and the ECB to complain that another political institution or the ECB has failed to adopt an act which it is under a legal obligation to adopt. An individual may also take these proceedings, though only to complain that the institution has failed to address a legal act to him. Parliament famously initiated *carence* proceedings in 1983 to force the Council to adopt a common transport policy, while in 1992 the British Liberal Democrats sued Parliament in order to require it to adopt a proposal for a uniform electoral procedure including proportional representation (ECJ 1985, 1993*a*). This type of action is none the less procedurally cumbersome and substantively difficult to apply, and is rarely used.

Action in damages

Where the action or inaction of the Community and/or one of its institutions (or the ECB or, where it is acting on behalf of a Community institution, the European Investment Bank) or officials has caused damage to an individual, he or she may be able to claim compensation before the Court by means of an action in damages. Though the claimant must show that the behaviour of the defendant institution was not merely illegal but that the illegality was 'sufficiently serious', it may be easier to recover damages against the Community than to challenge the validity of legal acts in annulment proceedings (CFI 2000*b*).

Rulings on international agreements

The Community enjoys a wide power to conclude international agreements with third countries and other international organizations. While judicial review *ex post* of such an agreement, through annulment proceedings or the preliminary ruling procedure, is possible, annulment by the Court would leave the Community in a difficult position, in that it would still be bound by the agreement as a matter of international law. To avoid this scenario, the Treaty established a procedure which, under the Treaty of Nice, would allow a political institution or member state to obtain a preventive ruling from the Court on whether an agreement is compatible with the Treaty, before the Community commits itself on the international plane. Though described as an 'opinion', the Court's conclusions are binding; if the opinion is negative, then either the international agreement or the Treaty must be amended to eliminate the incompatibility. The Court's jurisdiction is wide, covering all substantive and procedural issues which could affect the validity of the agreement, and on which it has sufficient information to come to a decision. Until the mid-1980s, such rulings were the only procedural context in which the Court was regularly called upon to rule on the division of competences between the Community and the member states. Its relatively strict approach is illustrated, for example, by Opinion 1/94 on the conclusion of the 1994 World Trade Organization Agreements (ECJ 1994), and Opinion 2/94 (ECJ 1996*a*; see Exhibit 6.3 below).

The range of legal procedures described above allows the Court to resolve the

Exhibit 6.3 Opinion 2/94 on accession to the European Convention

In 1994, the Council requested the Court's opinion on the compatibility with the Treaty of the Community's acceding to the European Convention. As no text of an agreement had yet been drawn up, the Court was unable to rule on its compatibility with the Treaty. It was, however, able to rule on the question of principle whether the Community had decisional competence to accede to the Convention. The Court held that the Community must respect the principle of conferred powers in both its internal and international action, and that no treaty provision conferred on it any general power to enact rules, or to conclude international agreements, on human rights protection. Article 308 TEC (at that time Article 235) could not serve as a basis for widening the scope of the Community's powers beyond the Treaty's general framework, or to amend the Treaty. While respect for fundamental rights is a condition of the lawfulness of Community rules, accession by the Community to the Convention would constitute a constitutionally significant change in the system of protection of such rights, which could only be effected by treaty amendment. The Community therefore had no competence to accede to the European Convention.

The Court's conclusion took some observers by surprise. According to one view, the Court was motivated by judicial pride in refusing to submit its own rulings on fundamental rights matters to a court operating on a higher European level. However the proposition that the Court is vested with exclusive jurisdiction to rule authoritatively on Community law, including that on fundamental rights protection, is clear from both the Treaty and the unchallenged case law of the Court over the previous two decades. The Opinion can more plausibly be seen as an example of judicial deference. In the absence of either an express power or a serious argument for an implied power allowing the Council to contract away part of the Court's functions, the Court had little choice but to leave the matter to the member states. After all, member states were then meeting in an intergovernmental conference and could, if the political will had been present, have amended the Treaty accordingly.

same principal types of dispute—concerning the protection of individual rights and respect for the limits of government—as are faced by a national constitutional court. If direct access to the Court by individuals is rather restricted, the application of Community law in the national courts and the preliminary ruling procedure can usually provide an adequate substitute.

The Court in the political life of the Community[8]

The EC Treaty defines the role of the Court as being to 'ensure that, in the interpretation and application of [the] Treaty, the law is observed' (Article 220 TEC). The

Treaty does not provide any further guidance as to what 'the law' is, apart from the policy objectives, principles, instruments, and procedures it establishes for the Community institutions and the member states. It is clear, however, that 'the law' is something more than the mere provisions of the treaty and Community legislation, and that the intention of the treaty authors was that the Court itself would define 'the law'. Court judgments therefore frequently provide direction for the political institutions in the establishment and the operation of the Community. The Court's contribution to the establishment of the Community constitution can be illustrated by looking at three aspects: the impact of Community law on national law, the Court's role in political disputes, and the scope of judicial review under the Treaty.

The impact of Community law in the member states

Under classical international law, states are free to determine how they fulfil the obligations they assume under international agreements. Some give automatic effect in their national legal system to the rules established by such agreements (Claes and De Witte 1998). This is a constitutional choice, rather than an intrinsic feature of international law. Certain agreements on the protection of fundamental rights, such as the European Convention, do create rights and procedures upon which individuals may rely directly in disputes against government actors. However, unless this is foreseen in the national law of the state concerned, even the European Convention does not have direct effect, in the sense that a conflicting provision of national law may not be applied.

The Treaty lays down a number of legal obligations which are addressed directly to the member states. The nature of the enterprise, to replace the then six national markets by a single 'common market' in which the factors of production were able to circulate freely, at least implied that Community rules should be given the same effect everywhere, as disuniformity in their application would lead to obstacles to trade between member states and distortions of competitive conditions. More pertinently as far as the Court is concerned, the text of the Treaty provides a number of indications that its authors, the member state governments, had intended that Community law obligations should be given full practical effect. Thus the regulation, the basic form of legal instrument for the establishment and functioning of common policies, is expressly stated to be 'binding in its entirety and *directly applicable in all Member States*' (Article 249 TEC, emphasis added). Similarly, Article 81(2) TEC expressly provides that an agreement between companies to restrict or distort competition between them was 'automatically void'; if 'automatic' is not to be redundant, this provision must be taken to mean that the nullity of the agreement may be relied upon in a national court, even in the absence of a Commission decision to this effect. In allowing national courts to submit questions on the interpretation of the treaty, the preliminary ruling procedure assumes that these courts will be called upon to apply Treaty provisions.

The vast majority of treaty articles, including the principal provisions on the common market, do not, however, indicate in such explicit terms the effects they are intended to have in legal relations between individuals and member state authorities. It was inevitable that individuals would seek to rely directly on these provisions, especially where the behaviour of a public authority was at odds with a clear obligation imposed on the member state. The Court of Justice resolved this question of principle in *Van Gend en Loos* (ECJ 1963; see Exhibit 6.4).

It follows from this judgment that, where a legal obligation is imposed by the EC Treaty in sufficiently clear and unconditional terms, on either a member state or another individual, an individual may rely upon that obligation before the

---

Exhibit 6.4 *Van Gend en Loos*

Article 12 of the EEC Treaty (now abolished) prohibited member states from increasing the rate of import duties applicable to trade with other member states. In implementing an international agreement which had entered into force after the Treaty, the Dutch authorities had reclassified a particular product so that the duty payable was 8 per cent; the importer of the product claimed that, when the EEC Treaty had entered into force the applicable rate had been 3 per cent, and that the Netherlands was thus in breach of the Article 12 prohibition. The Dutch court referred to the ECJ the question of whether the importer could rely on this provision.

The Court first set out its approach to the interpretation of Community law, based on an examination of 'the spirit, the general scheme and the wording of the Treaty'. It held that the Treaty was more than an agreement creating mutual obligations between states, relying in particular on the reference to 'peoples' in the preamble, the setting up of autonomous institutions, including two which require popular participation, and the establishment of the preliminary ruling procedure. The Court concluded that, independently of member state implementation, Community law 'not only imposes obligations on individuals but is also intended to confer upon them rights which become part of their legal heritage'.

Van Gend en Loos was a defining moment in the legal history of the Community, comparable to *Marbury* v *Madison* in the constitutional history of the United States (US Supreme Court 1803). At one fell stroke, the Court established that Community law was different from, and more effective in practical terms than, international law. It affirmed that individuals, not the governments, are at the centre of the preoccupations of new Community legal order, and have a role to play in ensuring the correct and uniform application of Community law. Direct effect puts the individual in a direct relationship with the Community in almost every area of economic activity. Moreover, the judgment meant that the establishment of the basic features of the common market—the free movement of persons, goods, and services—were not hostage to delays and difficulties in the political processes.

competent national courts. The provision is said to have 'direct effect'. The Court has also held that where a member state has failed to implement a directive in good time, an individual may rely in proceedings before the national courts against the public authorities upon any of the provisions of the directive which are sufficiently clear and unconditional.

Having ruled that treaty provisions could have direct effect, the Court was soon faced with the logically related issue of whether such provisions had primacy over conflicting national provisions. The outcome, decided in *Costa* v *ENEL* (ECJ 1964), was hardly in doubt. The direct effect of treaty provisions which could be overridden by subsequent national laws was of little practical or legal value, and the Court held that (all) Community provisions had primacy over (all) such laws. In the name of this primacy, and the uniform application of Community law, however, the Court refused to take account of fundamental rights protected in the member states' constitutions, which provoked disquiet in the national constitutional courts. In response to these concerns, the Court ruled that the Treaty required that fundamental rights be protected, as a matter of Community law and in accordance with standards set by the Court itself.

The direct effect of directives had one further indirect effect. Because it was based on the idea that member states could not rely on their own failure to implement the directive, the Court concluded that individuals could only rely on this form of direct effect as against public authorities, but not as against other individuals, such as employers. In practical terms, this meant, for example, that public sector employees could rely on the direct effect of the Community's social protection legislation, and private sector employees could not. To palliate this unsatisfactory situation, the Court held in *Francovich* (ECJ 1991) that, in the absence of direct effect, an individual could sue the member state which had failed to implement a directive giving him or her rights for financial compensation for damage caused by such failure. In subsequent decisions, the Court has extended state liability to all areas of Community activity.

It may at first seem somewhat surprising that the constitutionalization of the Treaty was so readily accepted by those concerned, particularly as the process was mainly carried out at a time (mid-1960s to mid-1980s) when the political processes of the Community were not functioning properly. On the other hand, perhaps the judicially driven constitutionalization was successful precisely because of the political context. The national governments had an interest in the 'strong binding effect' of Community law as 'delicate bargains would be disrupted if member states could disregard and violate them at will', while national courts accepted it for a variety of reasons, including judicial collegiality, empowerment of lower courts as against higher courts, and, more generally, agreement with the 'juridification' of political disputes, that is, their formulation in legal terms and submission to courts of law (Weiler 1999: 192–3 and 201).

The Court and political disputes

The increasing tendency of the member states and Community institutions to resort to legal proceedings to resolve political disputes is strikingly illustrated in the now extensive case law concerning the choice of the legal basis for Community legislation. As the Community does not have plenary decision-making powers, it may only act where it is authorized to do so. The 'legal basis' is the treaty article which grants authority to adopt an act of primary legislation; in particular, it defines the voting requirement in the Council (simple or qualified majority, or unanimity) and the level of participation of the European Parliament (exclusion, consultation, cooperation, co-decision, or assent). It therefore determines precisely the formal degree of influence of each of the political actors over the content of legal acts. The Court displayed a rather relaxed attitude to the question of the choice of legal basis in its early judgments. In *Massey-Ferguson* (ECJ 1973), for example, it upheld the use of what is now Article 308 TEC—which allows the Council, acting unanimously, to legislate in the absence of express treaty powers, where this is necessary to achieve a Community objective—for a customs regulation on the rather dubious ground of 'legal certainty' (Bradley 1988: 390). In fact, the Treaty contained a number of other articles which could plausibly have served as the legal basis of the regulation. For its part, the Council, as the primary legislator, took the view that the choice of legal basis fell within its political discretion which the Court would not review.

For much of the early history of the Community, with the exception of disagreements on the extent of the Community's external relations powers, disputes between the political actors of the Community—that is, the political institutions and the member state governments—were not brought to Court. The Commission, for example, never sought to challenge the compatibility with the Treaty of the practice of unanimity adopted by the Council after the 1966 Luxembourg compromise. Equally, member state challenges to Council acts were almost unheard of, essentially because the same unanimity practice guaranteed the political support of all the member states for such acts; the annulment action by Italy challenging the validity of legislation it had previously approved was the exception that proved the rule (ECJ 1979). During this period, the European Parliament was unable to initiate annulment actions to promote its institutional interests.

The sea-change in this regard was the Single European Act, adopted in 1986. This resulted in the abolition of the practice of unanimity in the Council and, at a stroke, gave both member states and the Commission a direct interest in the legal basis chosen. Under unanimity, individual governments have a veto, and the Commission's room for manœuvre is much less than under qualified majority voting. The Single Act also introduced two new legislative procedures (cooperation and assent), which gave Parliament a direct interest in the choice of the legal basis. The matter came to a head in the *Generalized Tariff Preferences* case (ECJ 1987a; see

---

Exhibit 6.5 Generalized tariff preferences (GTP)

In December 1985, the Council adopted two regulations concerning the generalized system of tariff preferences for 1986. It deleted the legal basis proposed by the Commission (Article 133 TEC on commercial policy, which provides for qualified majority voting). The Council claimed that the correct legal base was Article 308 (then 235) TEC. The Court annulled the regulations, and held as follows:

- the Commission may take an annulment action against a legal act even where it agrees with the content of the act;

- a legal act must indicate its legal basis sufficiently clearly for the parties concerned and the Court to know what it is;

- the adopting institution does not enjoy a discretion as to the choice of legal basis, which must depend on 'objective factors which are amenable to judicial review';

- the Council may only resort to Article 308 TEC where no other treaty provision can be used;

- in this case, Article 133 TEC was available as a legal basis.

The significance of the judgment resides principally in the recognition by the Court that the choice of voting rule and procedure are matters to be determined by the application of legal criteria, rather than political discretion. Procedural due process, already a familiar feature of Community law on the protection of individuals, for example in competition and trade protection, was here applied to the sphere of relations between political actors.

The Court also in effect reversed *Massey-Ferguson* (see above), reflecting the significant change in political conditions since the earlier judgment. In 1973 the use of Article 308 TEC was seen as a daring means of escaping the confines of the Community's express powers; by 1987, the member states were willing to grant the Community new express powers and to extend majority voting in the Council, and Article 308 was thus considered legally retrograde.

Exhibit 6.5), the first occasion for over sixteen years on which the Commission had taken annulment proceedings against the Council in an institutional dispute.

Recourse to the ECJ as a means of clarifying relations within and between the institutions has continued apace since. As regards relations between the majority and the minority in Council, the United Kingdom started annulment proceedings just three weeks after GTP to challenge a directive on which it had been outvoted (ECJ 1988a). Throughout the 1980s, the European Parliament sought to compensate for its institutional weakness through legal proceedings, most successfully in the *Isoglucose* and *Chernobyl* cases (ECJ 1980, 1990a). In the former, the Court recognized that the consultation procedure was legally binding and that the failure to apply it properly justified the annulment of the resulting act, while in the latter, the Court allowed Parliament to initiate annulment proceedings against the Council to promote the correct choice of legal basis for legislation, even though the Treaty did not expressly provide for the possibility of such proceedings at the time. Even relations between the majority and various minorities within Parliament are being subjected to judicial review, though these actions usually do not concern legal basis questions (CFI 2000a, 2001). The Court has also ruled that the Treaty empowers it to decide whether or not an act adopted in one of the outer pillars of Union activity—and not formally subject to judicial review—should have been adopted as a Community act, and hence whether the Council has acted illegally in adopting it (ECJ 1998).

While legal basis disputes are formally between the Community's institutional actors, the subtext is often the extent and distribution of the Community's material competences; the Council acting unanimously with parliamentary consultation will, in principle, produce a rather different, less 'Community-minded', measure than the Council acting by qualified majority in co-decision with Parliament. It is this question which has had more impact in the political life of the Community than the more straighforward issue of whether or not the Community has any such competence. As Weiler (1991: 2451) has remarked, '[language] . . . has never been a serious constraint on a determined political power', which is exactly why the treaty authors put their trust in what may be described as the political safeguards of the competences of the member states, most notably their direct participation in the adoption of legislation and, until the Single Act, the unanimity rule. With the abolition of this rule, the Court of Justice has been required, willy-nilly, to take over the role of defender of states' rights, much as the US Supreme Court has attempted to do at various times during its history.

The scope of the Court's jurisdiction

As noted above, Article 220 TEC requires the Court to ensure that 'the law' is respected. Amongst the most fundamental of legal principles is the requirement that courts not deny justice, by leaving a litigant with no means of legal redress. The fact that the provisions defining its juridiction are drafted in limited terms has meant that the Court has on occasion been obliged to choose between the general principle and the rules of positive law; where the application of the latter would in its view lead to a denial of justice, the Court has, usually, chosen the former. This has, on occasion, led to charges of 'judicial activism', a term so vast and indiscriminate in its usage as to be effectively devoid of meaning (Keeling 1998). The Court's choice may be justified in the framework of legal reasoning, however, by reference to the fundamental character of the requirement not to deny justice. It would not have been sufficient for the Court, on such occasions, simply to rule that the member states can amend the Treaty to fill the procedural lacuna; the possibility of future justice to litigants in similar circumstances would be of little comfort to the litigant denied a hearing for his particular claim.

Exhibit 6.6 *Les Verts* v *European Parliament*

The French ecology party, Les Verts, took annulment proceedings in 1983 to complain that the allocation by Parliament of 'information campaign funds' for the 1984 elections discriminated in favour of other political formations. At the time, Article 173 of the EEC Treaty did not provide for the possibility of legal proceedings against Parliament. The Court admitted the action on the grounds that the Community 'based on the rule of law, inasmuch as neither its Member States nor its institutions can avoid a review of the question whether the measures adopted by them are in conformity with the basis constitutional charter, the Treaty'. As the Treaty intended to allow annulment proceedings against all measures which had legal effects, such proceedings must be available against legal acts of Parliament; otherwise Parliament would be able to encroach with impunity on the rights of the member states, the other institutions and individuals. The Court admitted the action and annulled the contested decision, as the power to allocate election expenses had been retained by the member states.

The judgment in *Les Verts* (see Exhibit 6.6) provides a good example of the Court's acting to ensure protection of individual rights (ECJ 1986a).

Shortly after this case was concluded the Court admitted annulment proceedings by the Council against Parliament's adoption of the 1986 budget (ECJ 1986b). It is clear that the necessity for judicial resolution of this category of dispute was much on the Court's mind in *Les Verts*. The Court sought to ensure the coherence of the system of judicial review of political action, and for this reason subsequently admitted annulment proceedings initiated by Parliament against the Council and the Commission, notably on the choice of legal basis, budgetary matters, and respect of the limitations on implementing powers (ECJ 1992, 1993b, and 1996b). In adopting the Maastricht Treaty, the member states ratified the Court's approach by amending Article 173 EEC (now 230 TEC) expressly to allow such proceedings.

The Court has also adopted a progressive approach to the preliminary ruling procedure. It has held that national courts may not declare Community acts invalid, but must refer the matter to the Court, though Article 234 TEC is silent on the matter (ECJ 1987b). To pre-empt possible misunderstandings of Community provisions, the Court will provide rulings on the interpretation of identically worded national provisions which apply to situations outside the scope of Community law (ECJ 1990c). On one occasion, it responded to a 'request for judicial assistance' from an investigating magistrate who was not obviously a 'court or tribunal' empowered to submit a request for a preliminary ruling (ECJ 1990b).

The Court has not always acted in accordance with this precept. Its interpretation of 'direct and individual concern' for individuals to challenge Community acts other than those which are addressed to them has been criticized as being too restrictive. Its refusal to rule on the 1976 challenge to a Council decision appointing the consultative committee of the Coal and Steel Community (ECJ 1977) looks suspiciously like a denial of justice, while the grounds for its rejection of Parliament's action to contest the first comitology decision in 1988 were recognized to be defective by the Court itself less than two years later (ECJ 1988*b* and 1990*a*). These are, of course, legal criticisms. From the political perspective, the extension by the Court of its jurisdiction is less problematic, as it boosts the protection of the powers of the Council and the member states from European parliamentary encroachment.

Conclusions

The political dimension of the Court's work has attracted a great deal of academic attention. One author has imaginatively suggested, for example, that the Court seeks in its judgments to anticipate, and avoid, possible negative reactions from the most powerful member states, particularly Germany (Garrett 1992). Others have presented the Court as using the law as a mask, camouflaging controversial political decisions in technical legal language (Burley and Mattli 1993). Not all the commentators, however, appear to have heeded the perceptive warning by Weiler that, though the constitutionalization of the Community 'might be read (. . .) as suggesting that the cardinal material locus of change has been the realm of law and that the principal actor has been the European Court . . . this would be deceptive. Legal and constitutional structural change have been crucial, but only in their interaction with the Community political process' (Weiler 1991: 2407; see also Lenaerts 1992).

The warning has become even more pertinent in the years since it was issued. The member states have in effect taken over constitution-making, and even certain aspects of constitutional interpretation, such as the exclusion of harmonizing legislation in certain areas of regulation enforced so dramatically in the *Tobacco Advertising* case, in the ongoing process of treaty revision. In a modern polity which aspires to democracy, this might be considered as a more appropriate division of constitutional roles than that played out in the early years of the Community, when the Court's decisions stood out as monumental legal constructions on the flat and underdeveloped political landscape. From the perspective of the legitimacy of the legal construction, it is important that the Court's case law has been accepted by the Community's political actors, who have regularly built on the Court's rulings in their own constitutional designs.

The Court will of course continue to give direction to the Community in its role as arbiter between the political actors, and in their relations with individuals. It is acutely aware of operating on two planes at once: the horizontal relationship between the judiciary and the other branches of the Community government, and the vertical relationship between the Community and its member states. Where it upholds Community legislation, it may be accused of operating a centralizing, pro-Community policy; if it does not, and strikes down such legislation, it runs the risk of being accused of judicial aggression or 'government by the judges'. Though placing the Court and the law at the centre of the Community's system of governance was a political choice, it does not solve the problem of the Court's legitimacy (Weiler 1998). Public acceptance of the Community's highly developed legal order, with rights and duties for individuals, was less problematic when its judgments concerned the rate of customs duties and trade in alcoholic drinks, and applied directly to a relatively closed community of economic actors who were, or became, familiar with the system and learned how to influence its decisions. The European Union is no longer such a closed system. Court rulings can now affect the deepest concerns of the citizen, and indeed the non-citizen who comes into contact with its legal order. The Court will find itself in new legal terrain, where the guidelines provided by the Treaty are rather more vague than the economic certainties—or, at least, plausibilities—of the EEC, and its judgments are likely to be more politically divisive than anything which has gone before. In this new context, the construction of a complete and well-functioning legal order may prove to be impossible without the establishment of sound political and democratic foundations. In this regard, the Court may not be able to fill in for any failings of the political authorities.

Notes

1 Member of the Legal Service of the European Parliament, and former *référendaire* at the Court of Justice, Luxembourg. The views expressed are personal, and should not be taken as necessarily representing those of any Community institution, member, or department thereof.

2 In this chapter, the term '[European] Court of Justice' (ECJ) refers to the institution, the judicial functions of which may be exercised by the 'ECJ', the Court of First Instance (CFI), and the judicial panels.

3 The term 'individual' is used throughout this chapter to include companies as well as natural persons.

4 For convenience, only actions under the EC Treaty will be considered here, though the rules governing actions under the Euratom Treaty are similar.

5 The ECJ did make a major contribution to the work of the IGC leading up to the Treaty of Nice, working closely with the presidency of the Council on the proposal for reform of the Court system, including the establishment of judicial panels.

6 Competition policy is the only major exception, and even here the Commission has proposed a 'renationalization' of certain aspects of this policy.

7   Member states may also sue each other in infringement proceedings, but the Court has only had to deal with two such cases since 1958.

8   For the sake of brevity, only the Treaty of Rome setting up the European (Economic) Community is here considered.

Further reading

Kennedy (1998) is a good introduction to EC law and the ECJ for the non-specialist. March Hunnings (1996) examines the organization of the ECJ and CFI in detail, while Arnull (1999) provides a comprehensive overview of the material law as it results from the Court's judgments. The most reliable and perspicacious commentator on the Court is Weiler (1991 to 2001); for more sceptical, recent perspectives on the Court's work, see Hartley (1999) and Shapiro (1999). Though not concerned with the European Community, Loughlin (2000) is an excellent general introduction to the relationship between law and politics.

Arnull, A. (1999), *The European Union and its Court of Justice* (Oxford: Oxford University Press).

Hartley, T. (1999), *Constitutional Problems of the European Union* (Oxford: Hart Publishing).

Kennedy, T. (1998), *Learning European Law* (London: Sweet & Maxwell).

Loughlin, M. (2000), *Sword and Scales* (Oxford: Hart Publishing).

March Hunnings, N. (1996), *The European Courts* (London: Cartermill).

Shapiro, M. (1999), 'The European Court of Justice', in P. Craig and G. De Búrca (eds.), *The Evolution of EU Law* (Oxford: Oxford University Press).

Weiler, J. H. H. (1991), 'The Transformation of Europe', *Yale Law Journal*, 100: 2403–2483.

—— (1998), 'Epilogue' in A.-M. Slaughter, A. Stone Sweet, and J. H. H. Weiler (eds.), *The European Courts and the National Courts* (Oxford: Hart Publishing).

—— (1999), *The Constitution of Europe* (Cambridge: Cambridge University Press).

—— (2000), 'IGC 2000: The Constitutional Agenda', in E. Best, M. Gray, and A. Stubb, *Rethinking the European Union* (Maastricht: European Institute of Public Administration).

—— (2001), 'Epilogue: The Judicial Après-Nice', in G. De Búrca and J. H. H. Weiler (eds.), *The European Court of Justice* (Oxford: Oxford University Press).

Web links

The Court's web site, **www.europa.eu.int/cj/index.htm**, contains a considerable amount of information about the workings of the institution, as well as the text of all ECJ and CFI judgments delivered since mid-1997, as well as most of the opinions of the advocates-general.

Part II

Managing the Union

Chapter 7
The Commission's Services

Neill Nugent

Contents

Summary

The European Commission can be thought of as having two arms: a 'political' arm in the form of the college of Commissioners (see Chapter 4) and an 'administrative' arm in the form of the Commission services. Administrative reform under the stewardship of Neil Kinnock in the Prodi Commission has thrown a spotlight on the internal workings of the Commission, and the need to make the services—the permanent bureaucracy of the Commission—work more effectively and efficiently. This chapter focuses on the Commission's services, particularly on recent developments and the prospects for administrative reform. It argues that the Commission's services are highly politicized and have remained remarkably unchanged over the years. However, they now face fundamental—perhaps transformational—change.

Introduction

Academic and journalistic commentaries on the European Commission tend to focus more on the college, the 'political' arm of the Commission, rather than on the services, the Commission's permanent bureaucracy. This concentration is not surprising. Commentaries on national political systems tend to focus more on political executives than on bureaucracies, since the former are more visible and are assumed to exercise more power.

However, just as one must understand governmental bureaucracies to grasp the complexity of national governance, the Commission's services must be explored if the nature of the Commission as an institution is to be understood. The services exercise a central role—sometimes in a leading and sometimes in a supporting capacity—in virtually everything the Commission does. Few Commission initiatives are launched, few Commission proposals are made, and few Commission decisions are taken before they are extensively examined and, ultimately, approved by the services.

Three core themes run through the examination of the services in this chapter. First, whilst the services may be said to constitute the administrative arm of the Commission, they are in important respects highly political and highly politicized. Second, most of the central features of the services are long-standing, with many of them dating back to the 1950s. Third, reform of the services being carried out under the Prodi Commission—the so-called Prodi/Kinnock reform programme (Neil Kinnock being the Commissioner with the reform portfolio)—involves the most far-reaching set of reforms to the services in their history.

The development of the services

The Commission's services have their origins in the High Authority of the European Coal and Steel Community (ECSC). Jean Monnet—the High Authority's first President—wanted the High Authority to be a small and essentially informal institution, engaged primarily in providing policy direction. Shortly after becoming President, Monnet remarked to a fellow member of the High Authority, 'If one day there are more than two hundred of us, we shall have failed' (Monnet 1978: 405).

Monnet's hopes were quickly disappointed. Following its foundation in 1952, the High Authority rapidly assumed a wide range of tasks that required an expansion in staff numbers, a formalization of organizational structures, and a bureaucratization of operations. When, in 1957–8, the Commissions of the European Economic Community (EEC) and the European Atomic Energy Community (Euratom) were established, their administrations were built on the High Authority model—a model which essentially reflected French administrative methods.

With the mergers of the High Authority and the two Commissions in 1967, the single Commission that we now know came into existence. Over the intervening years the policy responsibilities and expertise of the Commission's services have broadened enormously as the Union has become involved in just about every sphere of public policy. Yet, core features of the services have remained remarkably durable throughout the Commission's lifespan:

■ The services have always been expected to be, and in practice generally have been, impartial and independent in their behaviour.[1] The need to be impartial and independent has not prevented the services from working closely with, or being influenced by, a host of governmental and non-governmental representatives on specific policy issues. But considerable care has normally been taken to avoid crossing that thin dividing line between being influenced by outside parties and taking instructions from them.

■ Notwithstanding the attachment to impartiality and independence, the services have consistently been involved in political as well as administrative activities. Many of the functions undertaken mainly by the services—such as preparing policy and legislative proposals, managing (sometimes broadly defined) expenditure programmes, and conducting external trade negotiations—inevitably have had significant political ramifications. More high-profile activities related to these functions, including the taking of final decisions, are exercised formally by the college or by individual Commissioners, but in practice are undertaken in harness with the services.

■ The basic structure of the services has remained largely unchanged, with Directorates-General (DGs) and other services being the main organizational units. The number of DGs and other services has, however, increased considerably since 1958: from only nine DGs and six other services to twenty-four DGs and twenty-one other services by the late 1990s. This expansion was occasioned mainly by the Commission being assigned, or acquiring, increased responsibilities and tasks relating, for example, to environmental policy, regional policy, and fisheries policy in the 1970s. The expansion was also partly the result of political/bureaucratic factors: for instance, the creation in 1993 of a DG to deal with foreign policy was largely a product of the Commission's desire to increase its impact in this area post-Maastricht. The growing number of DGs and services contributed to considerable organizational fragmentation, prompting Romano Prodi, on becoming Commission President in 1999, to announce that the number of subdivisions would be reduced from forty-four to a maximum of thirty-six. At the time of writing (mid-2001) there were, as Table 7.1 shows, twenty-three DGs and eleven other services.

■ The services have always been small compared to national administrations. Commission staff numbers have grown over the years in response to the increased number of member states and Commission tasks, but political resistance to increasing the EU's budget has meant that the growth has not been proportionate, resulting in inadequate staffing levels. In early 1959 there were just over 1,000 full-time staff in the EEC Commission; in 1970 there were close to 5,300 in the merged Commission; by 2001 there were almost 21,500.[2] To these figures must be added temporary and external staff of various kinds, the precise number of whom is unrecorded but who by the 1990s added at least another 30 per cent to overall staffing numbers.

■ Recruitment to the services has been based on competition reflecting meritocratic principles, though this has not always been applied at the most senior levels where some staff have been, in effect, drafted in. The most frequent reason for this practice has been a desire to achieve a broad balance in the 'representation' of member states in the upper reaches of the services.

Organizing the services

The Commission's services are organized into Directorates-General, such as the DGs for Agriculture and Enterprise, and other services, such as the Legal Service and the Translation Service (see Table 7.1). The distinction between DGs and other services is not based on a clear set of rules. DGs are normally concerned with policy sectors (such as trade and environment), while other services are normally concerned with cross-cutting, horizontal tasks (such as interpretation and publications), but there are exceptions, as is demonstrated by the position of Personnel and Administration as a DG and of the Humanitarian Aid Office (ECHO) as an external service. DGs are sometimes seen as being superior to, or more important than, other services, but this can be a misleading view for some of the most important of the Commission's services—including the Secretariat-General and the Legal Service—are not DGs.

The organizational focus of the services naturally reflects, first and foremost, the responsibilities and work of the Commission and, more broadly, of the EU. Thus, DGs exist for agriculture, competition, and economic and financial affairs— areas that have been amongst the Commission's policy responsibilities from the early days of the EC. Similarly, the Secretariat-General, the Legal Service, and the Translation and Interpreting Services have always been vital to the Commission's operation. Other services have been established—sometimes as part of broader

Table 7.1 Directorates-General and other services of the Commission [a]	
Directorates-General	**Other services**
Agriculture	European Anti-Fraud Office
Budget	Eurostat
Competition	Europe Aid–Co-operation Office
Development	Humanitarian Aid Office
Economic and Financial Affairs	Joint Interpreting and Conference Service
Education and Culture	Joint Research Centre
Employment and Social Affairs	Legal Service
Energy and Transport	Press and Communication
Enlargement	Publications Office
Enterprise	Secretariat General
Environment	Translation Service
External Relations	
Financial Control	
Fisheries	
Health and Consumer Protection	
Information Society	
Internal Market	
Justice and Home Affairs	
Personnel and Administration	
Regional Policy	
Research	
Taxation and Customs Union	
Trade	

[a] Situation in April 2001.

reorganizations—as and when they have been seen to be necessary or desirable. So, for example, a new DG for Enterprise was created at the beginning of the Prodi presidency with a mission to promote innovation, a topic that has come to be much discussed at European Council meetings, especially the now annual spring meetings that have as their main focus the modernization of the European economy. DG Enterprise was forged largely out of three DGs that were seen to be too duplicative and not sufficiently focused in their responsibilities: Industry; Telecommunications, Information Market, and Exploitation of Research; and Enterprise Policy, Distributive Trades, Tourism, and Cooperatives.

Services also vary considerably in size, depending on the nature of their responsibilities. Most have between 200 and 500 full-time staff, of whom between about sixty and 120 are in the policy-making A-grade (a full explanation of the staff grading system follows below). Apart from the special case of the Personnel and Administration DG, which has a staff of over 1,500, the largest DG is Agriculture, with a staff of over 800, whilst the smallest is Justice and Home Affairs, with less than 150. As for other services, the Secretariat-General has over 450 staff; the Translation Service has 1,400 translators and 500 clerical staff; and the Joint

Research Centre has just over 2,000, of whom around 1,500 are scientists, most of them on fixed-term contracts.

All services in the Commission, as indeed in other EU institutions, are structured on similar lines. The model is hierarchical and pyramidical, with responsibility ultimately being in the hands of one person at the top and with upwards and downwards lines of internal communications being channelled through specified lines of authority.

The Commission's most senior official is the *Secretary-General*, who is head of the Secretariat-General. There have only been four Secretaries-General in the history of the EC/EU, which helps explain why the decision of Prodi to appoint his own *chef du cabinet* to the job in 2000 was so controversial (see Exhibit 4.3). The Secretariat-General is a key Commission service. It ensures that all parts of the Commission coordinate their activities, act in accordance with laid-down procedures, and liaise properly with other EU institutions—the latter being effected particularly via a network of informal relationships, meetings, and committees which bring together the Commission's services with the secretariats of the Council of Ministers and the EP.

Services are headed by *Directors-General*—or their equivalent—who all enjoy the same formal status. They have senior staff to support them, with the number and status depending on the size, importance, and mission of the service. For example, the External Relations Director-General is supported by three deputy directors-general, one principal adviser and one assistant, whilst the Budget Director-General is supported by one Deputy Director-General, three principal advisers, and one assistant.

The main responsibilities of Directors-General are to oversee the general functioning of their service, to be its principal representative in relations with other services and the outside world, and to be the main line of communication between their service and the Commissioner responsible for the service. Directors-General usually also assume specific policy or task responsibilities within their service, and often have sections of their service reporting directly to them as their line manager.

DGs and other services are divided into *Directorates*, which are headed by Directors. An average sized DG normally has between three and six Directorates, though some of the larger ones have more and some of the smaller ones less. The Agriculture DG, for example, has eleven Directorates whilst the Fisheries DG has four.

Directorates are divided into *units* or divisions headed by heads of unit or division. A typical Directorate contains between three and six units, each of which in turn typically contains between three and seven A-grade staff plus three or four administrative (B-grade) and clerical (C-grade) staff. Figure 7.1 provides an establishment plan of the Health and Consumer Protection DG which, with 530 staff, is slightly larger than an average-sized DG.

Figure 7.1 Organizational plan of the Health and Consumer Protection DG

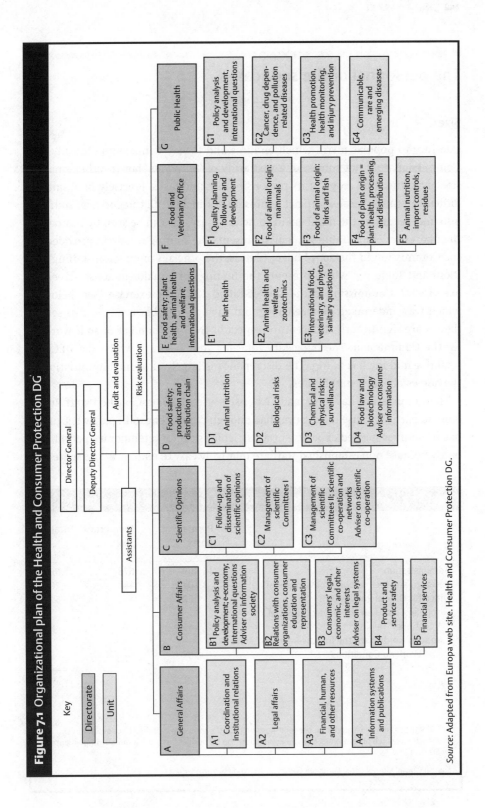

Source: Adapted from Europa web site. Health and Consumer Protection DG.

The personnel of the services

Size

Contrary to popular myth, which endures and is very damaging politically, the Commission does not consist of a vast army of 'Eurocrats' but is rather small in size given the wide scope of its responsibilities and tasks. Precisely how small is difficult to gauge because official figures do not include all categories of staff and also underestimate the numbers in some categories, as can be seen by comparing the figures set out in Table 7.2, which presents the staffing resources provided for the Commission in the 2001 budget (that is, the official Commission staffing position) and Table 7.3, which presents the findings of a major in-house screening exercise of Commission staff—the so-called DECODE exercise (see below)—which was undertaken between 1997 and 1999. As can be seen, the two sets of figures are significantly different in respect of the total number of staff working for the Commission. The budgetary total for 2001 is 21,479 whilst the DECODE total (for mid-1998) is 31,013. The discrepancy is largely explained by variation in the non-established staff figures.

The Commission has long made extensive use of non-established staff. It has done so partly because it has never had enough permanent staff, partly because it has sometimes needed expertise or a particular skill for a temporary period, and partly because non-established staff are relatively easy to employ in the sense that

Table 7.2 Commission staffing resources authorized by the 2001 EU budget

	Permanent posts	Temporary posts	Total
Administration	16,409	678	17,087
Research and technological development[a]	3,704	—	3,704
Office for Official Publications	522	—	522
European Centre for the Development of Vocational Training	45	36	81
European Funding for the Improvement of Living and Working Conditions	85	—	85
Total			21,479

[a] Of which 2,080 are assigned to the Joint Research Centre and 1,624 to indirect action. (Indirect actions are research programmes that are financed by the EU budget but are not directly implemented by EU staff.)

Source: Official Journal of the European Communities, 26 Feb. 2001, L56/137.

Table 7.3 Staffing resources as indicated in the DECODE Report[a]		
Intramural staff[b]		
(a)	Established posts	
	Permanent	16,527
	Temporary	1,520
	TOTAL	18,047
(b)	Local agents (mainly in Commission offices in the member states)	214
(c)	External posts	
	Auxiliaries	1,033
	Seconded national experts	760
	Casual employees	606
	Service providers (in restaurants, crèches, etc.)	1,836
	TOTAL	4,235
Extramural staff[c]		
	Technical assistance offices	863
	Consultants	947
	Man-years for studies	383
	Other man-years	1,572
	TOTAL	3,765
Not covered in DECODE screening		
	Joint Research Centre	1,834
	Cabinets	393
	Commission delegations in non-member states	2,525
	TOTAL	4,752
	GRAND TOTAL	31,013

[a] Information for the Report was collected from Nov. 1997 to May 1999, with the date for figures being conventionally set at May 1998.
[b] Defined as employees working in Commission buildings.
[c] Defined as employees working outside Commission buildings.

Source: Commission (1999d): 9 and 16.

they do not need funding from the Commission budget (seconded national officials receive their salaries from their national employer) or can be funded in ways not requiring authorization by the budgetary authorities (the Council and the EP). Non-established staff are of two main types. First, there are seconded national officials and experts, usually from civil services, who stay with the Commission for between two and three years. There are normally between 700 and 800 national officials working in the Commission at any one time, accounting for just over 10 per cent of total A-grade staff. Second, there are temporary agents, who come in a number of different forms but are normally employed either as in-house 'consultants', 'experts', or 'advisers', or through outside agencies known as technical assistance offices (TAOs). TAOs undertake tasks for the Commission on a contractual basis, and have been the targets of charges that they can easily become unaccountable and subject to fraud (see Committee of Independent Experts 1999*a*, 1999*b*). Over 30 per cent of total Commission human resources are temporary agents, though this number is scheduled to fall as the internal reform programme of the Prodi Commission takes effect (see below).

Personnel policy

The Prodi/Kinnock reform programme on personnel policy means that much is set to change in this area (see below). For now, all EU institutions share the same staff grading structure. The system contains five grades: A-grade is the policy-making and policy management grade; LA-grade is for translators and interpreters; B-grade is for organizational administrative work; C-grade is for clerical and secretarial staff; and D-grade is for manual and service work such as drivers and ushers. Of the approximately 17,500 staff provided for under the administration heading of the Commission's 2001 personnel budget,[3] 35 per cent were A-grade—policy-makers and/or managers.

Most established A-grade staff are recruited to the Commission by written and oral examination—the *concours*—at the lower end of the grade (A7 or A8). Competition is intense, and usually there are well over 100 qualified candidates—that is, people with a good academic qualification and a high proficiency in at least one language in addition to their mother tongue—for each vacancy. Candidates who pass the *concours* are not guaranteed a post, but normally need to make contacts in the Commission so that their names come to mind or someone 'puts in a word' on their behalf when a vacancy arises. There is also some direct entry via competition at middle-ranking A-levels (A4–A6), usually by people who have worked for the Commission as seconded national experts or as temporary officials. Their numbers have, however, been limited, partly because of pressure from existing staff who naturally resist the idea of promotion opportunities being taken by outsiders. At senior levels nationality considerations have been important, with an unofficial national quota system existing for A1–A3 posts and with some particular posts being virtually reserved for certain member states by attaching (informally) 'national flags' to them.

Composition

The services share most of the general characteristics of staff in the public bureaucracies of the member states:

- In terms of gender balance, there is an overall ratio of 56 per cent men to 44 per cent women (Shore 2000: 193). This ratio hides, however, a concentration of men in the higher grades and of women in the lower grades. Men dominate at very senior levels, with only 3 per cent being female at A1 (Page 1997: 70–3).

- Educational attainment varies considerably between grades. Virtually all A-grade staff have a university degree, with most also having a postgraduate degree (Page 1997: 74–9). The pressure for posts has led many graduates to seek employment at B-grade.

- Career structures that give weight to length of service result in strong correlations between age and positions within grades. Amongst the Commission's A-grades this situation applies up to A4 level, but not much beyond because political considerations have figured prominently in the appointment of most officials at A3 and above.

- Information on the ethnic background of its staff is not collected by the Commission, but it is clear from observation that there are relatively few staff of black or Asian origin, and that the few there are occupy mainly clerical and ancillary positions.

The most distinctive feature of the services as compared with national administrations is their multinational and multilingual character. The Commission is thoroughly multinational not only because of the national quota system for A1–A3 posts but also because member states take a close interest in recruitment patterns throughout the A-grade. In the B, C, and D grades, Belgians—with their home advantage—have always been proportionately over-represented. The Commission is truly multilingual not least because there are eleven official EU languages, though the services employ French and English in most everyday work. (For more detailed information on, and for analyses of the implication of, the multinational and multilingual character of the services, see McDonald 2000; Nugent 2001; Shore 2000; and Stevens 2001.)

Functions

The Commission's main functions can be grouped under six headings: policy initiator, legislative functions, executive functions, legal guardian, mediator and broker, and external representative and negotiator.

Policy initiator

Many different actors are involved in EU policy initiation. For example, the European Council and the Council of Ministers regularly request policy papers from the Commission. The EP discusses and approves reports that it hopes will lead to policy action. Member governments, especially when they occupy the Council presidency, table policy documents and proposals at Council meetings. And pressure groups make policy submissions to relevant DGs.

But such initiatives are unlikely to make much progress unless they are supported and developed by the Commission. The Commission is thus centrally involved in initiation of broadly based policy initiatives, such as the highly influential 1997 *Agenda 2000* Paper which made proposals for, *inter alia*, reforming the agricultural and structural policies in advance of EU enlargement to central and eastern Europe. The Commission's services also table proposals on an ongoing basis to develop/revise EU policy in particular sectors and spheres. This range of policy initiating activity involves holding exploratory discussions with potentially interested parties, commissioning reports from outside agencies who can offer a specialism or expertise, and preparing and issuing documents containing policy proposals.

Legislative functions

Save for a few exceptions in justice and home affairs, the Commission has the exclusive right under the EC Treaty to draft legislative proposals. The Council and the EP can request that it submits proposals on specified matters to them, but they cannot undertake the drafting themselves and they cannot direct how the Commission will respond to their requests.

The Commission is also actively involved at later stages of EU law-making. It is so for two main reasons. First, the EC Treaty gives it post-drafting powers. For instance, prior to the conciliation stage of the co-decision procedure, Commission agreement to EP amendments obliges the Council to find unanimity if it wants to take a different position (Article 250 TEC). Up until conciliation the Commission can also withdraw a proposal, though it loses this right once conciliation starts. At that point, the Commission is specifically charged with taking 'all the necessary initiatives with a view to reconciling the positions of the European Parliament and the Council' (Article 251 TEC). Second, the Commission is the only institution that is present throughout the legislative process—at Council, EP, and inter-institutional meetings. These two facts combine to make the Commission an extremely important legislative actor, especially when there are inter-institutional disagreements on legislative content and mediation and brokerage are required.

Executive functions

In a few policy areas, the Commission has direct implementation responsibilities. By far the most important of these is competition, where the Commission has to decide, for instance, whether state aid and certain types of stakeholdings, take-overs, and mergers are permissible under EU law. In most policy areas, however, the Commission does not implement directly. Rather, it seeks to ensure that a proper national implementation framework is in place and then oversees and monitors 'front-line' implementation by outside agencies.

Ensuring a proper implementation framework is in place includes drafting and issuing administrative legislation that sets out detailed rules on such matters as technical standards for marketed goods and price levels of various kinds for products supported under the common agricultural policy (CAP). A draft proposal must normally be channelled through a so-called comitology committee, of which there are approximately 300.[4]

Comitology is truly one of the most arcane institutional features of the EU. Yet, it is important to understand that management and regulatory committees of national officials—one from each member state and voting on the basis of qualified majority—can block Commission decisions or pass issues 'upwards' to the Council (see Nugent 1999: 129–33). The work of the Commission's services is closely scrutinized by comitology committees, often in ways that defy any notion that the Commission is an omnipotent and unaccountable bureaucracy.

As for the overseeing and monitoring of frontline implementation undertaken by outside agencies, this involves almost constant communication between the Commission and a range of (mainly national) bodies, especially where funding programmes are concerned.

Legal guardian

Overlapping and intermingling with its executive responsibilities, the Commission—along with the European Court of Justice (ECJ)—is charged with ensuring that EU law is respected. In essence, this function involves the Commission acting as a watchdog so as to ensure that EU law is applied rigorously and uniformly throughout the member states.

The Commission is highly dependent on 'whistle-blowing' to be made aware of possible breaches of EU law. Even when it is so made aware, its limited resources mean that only a relatively small number of the cases that are referred to it can be properly investigated. Unless major transgressions are involved, or it is decided to use a case to send 'warning signals' to other possible transgressors, the usual approach is to try and persuade national authorities to take up the case or to try to resolve the matter by informal means. However, if a full investigation is launched, rigorous procedures laid down in the EC Treaty must be followed.

Ultimately, an investigation can result in the Commission imposing fines on firms, which are subject to appeal to the ECJ, or, since the Maastricht Treaty, recommending to the ECJ that financial penalties be imposed on member states for failure to comply with previous ECJ judgments. An example of a fine imposed on a firm is the €43 million imposed in September 2000 on Opel Nederland (part of Adam Opel, which is itself the European subsidiary of General Motors) for preventing consumers from other member states buying cars in the Netherlands, where prices are generally cheaper. The first fine to be imposed on a member state was in July 2000 when the ECJ supported the Commission in its claim that Greece was not fully complying with a 1992 Court judgment concerning the disposal of toxic and dangerous waste, and ordered the Greek government to pay a fine of €20,000 for each day of continued breach of obligations.

Mediator and broker

EU decision-making involves a multiplicity of actors, inside and outside the EU institutions, all eager to exercise influence over what the EU does. Within this system there is a strong sense of the need for compromise. In some circumstances, more than one actor formally needs to agree, as happens with the Council and Parliament under co-decision. In other circumstance, there are less formal pressures for compromise, but cooperation by national actors is needed if there is to be proper implementation of decisions.

EU decision-making therefore requires mediation and brokerage, which the Commission is particularly well placed to offer thanks to its excellent knowledge of 'the bottom lines' of the various actors—a knowledge that stems from its many contacts across the EU and its extensive involvement in EU decision-making processes at all stages. The Commission also has the advantage, as compared to, say, the Council presidency, of generally being seen to be independent and non-partisan in its actions. In conciliation, for example, a suggestion is often acceptable to both Council and Parliament if it comes from the Commission, whereas the same suggestion coming from either the Council or Parliament may be unacceptable to the other institution.

External representative and negotiator

The EU is a significant international actor, with a wide range of external policies. The most developed external policy is trade, with the common commercial policy (CCP) requiring all external trade rules to be determined at EU level. Enlargement policy is another external policy area where, necessarily, the member governments must act as one. In other external policy areas—including foreign policy, development policy, and the external dimensions of internal policies such as transport and environment—policy responsibilities are shared between the EU and the member states.

The Commission's external policy functions vary according to the treaty article(s) on which policy areas are based, the amount of policy responsibilities that have been transferred from the member states to the EU, the extent to which policy impinges on political sensitivities, how necessary management by a neutral (not nationally biased) body is deemed to be, and the amount of day-to-day technical work required. In very general terms it can be said that the Commission's functions, and also influence, are greatest in policy areas that display at least one of the following features: fall under the first (EC) pillar, such as trade; have been subject to extensive transfer of competence, such as enlargement; do not normally raise too many political sensitivities, such as development; require neutral policy leadership and management, such as competition; and need extensive technical work to be undertaken, such as agriculture.

Exercising the Commission's functions

If political and administrative tasks could be disentangled, the college would be responsible for the political exercise of the Commission's functions and the services would be responsible for administration. In the wake of the Santer Commission's resignation (see Exhibit 4.1), Romano Prodi (1999a) sought to make the political/administrative distinction clearer, particularly by 'reducing the grey areas which currently tend to blur demarcation lines of autonomy and responsibility between those performing more political tasks and those more involved with administration'. Prodi unveiled a new Code of Conduct for Commissioners and Departments as soon as 'his' college assumed office in September 1999, which mandated that:

Commissioners shall assume full political responsibility. Directors-General shall be answerable to their Commissioner for the sound implementation of the policy guidelines laid down by the Commission and the Commissioner . . .

   Departments shall implement the priorities and policy guidelines set at political level (Commission 1999b: 15–16).

However, in practice, the roles of Commissioners (and *cabinets*) on the one hand and of the services on the other are not as separable or as distinguishable as these provisions of the Code imply. The work of Commissioners and the services overlaps and intertwines for three main reasons. First, it is not always possible to distinguish between what is 'important' and 'political' work and what is 'routine' and 'administrative' work. So, for example, deciding whether a newly marketed product is subject to an existing EU law on product standards may appear to be a routine and administrative matter. But the decision taken may be contested by important economic and social interests and may have significant implications for an industry or for a member state.

   Second, when taking decisions—be they about the policy options to be set out in a discussion paper, the contents and legal bases of draft legislation, or the initiation of action against a member state for infringement of EU law—Commissioners are usually heavily reliant on the services for information, advice, and the preparation of documentation. This reliance is recognized in the Code itself, which includes phrases such as '[departments] shall help to prepare the policy guidelines the Commissioner has to set' and '[departments] shall provide all the information the Commissioner requires in his or her work' (Commission 1999*b*: 16). With most DGs having at least 100 A-grade officials—as compared with the mere six such officials in each *cabinet*—the services are the main repository of accumulated wisdom and specialized knowledge about EU policy activities. They are often the hub of policy networks involving key EU actors, and therefore inevitably influence heavily the direction of political choices.

Third, service officials are not necessarily neutral in their policy views but sometimes have firm policy leanings and preferences and a desire to advance them within the Commission. A considerable body of academic literature on the administrative culture of the Commission testifies to how officials from different DGs often take very different positions on issues. Thus on the question of state aid to industry, the Competition DG is likely to try to keep state intervention to a minimum, whilst DGs such as Employment and Social Affairs and Regional Policy are more willing to allow intervention if it can be shown to promote such economic goals as industrial reconstruction or employment expansion (see, for example, Abélès *et al.* 1993; Cini 1996, 2000). Similarly, the Environment DG is well known for its commitment to the strictest possible standards on, say, auto emissions, whereas DGs with closer ties to manufacturers, such as Enterprise and Trade, seek more flexibility.

So though the roles of the Commissioners and of the services may be theoretically distinct, in practice they are blurred. Somewhat ironically, given Prodi's desire to emphasize the distinction, it is arguably now being even further weakened following his instruction that Commissioners should be based in the same buildings as the service(s) for which they are responsible rather than, as previously, billeted separately in the Commission's 'headquarters'.

The reform of the services

Jacques Santer has complained that the achievements of his Commission (1995–9) have not received the recognition they deserve. His complaints have some justification, not least because it was under his presidency that the first significant attempts were made to tackle long-standing internal problems in the Commission services.

Amongst other things, Santer's pledge to 'do less, but do it better' meant doing something about the inefficiencies and *immobilisme* that plagued the services. Three internal reform programmes were launched. First, *Sound and Efficient Management* (SEM 2000) began in 1995 with the aim of ensuring the Commission used sound financial management practices. Second, *Modernization of Administration and*

Personnel Policy (MAP 2000) was initiated in 1997 with the purpose of simplifying and decentralizing administrative and personnel procedures. Third, *Designing the Commission of Tomorrow* (DECODE, a French acronym) was a major screening exercise of services staff and functions between 1997 and 1999 with the purpose of providing information for a possible major reorganization of resources and methods of operation. By the time of the resignation of the Santer Commission, the SEM 2000 and MAP 2000 programmes were well under way, whilst the DECODE screening had been completed and reform recommendations were being devised. It is thus somewhat ironic that a major reason the Santer Commission was driven from office was that it was seen as not having been sufficiently active in responding to criticisms made—most notably by the European Court of Auditors—of Commission working practices.

The immediate cause of the resignation of the Santer Commission in March 1999 was publication of the first report of the Committee of Independent Experts (1999*a*). Whilst the sections of the report that attracted most attention were those that focused on the college, especially on Santer and Edith Cresson, the report also highlighted numerous performance problems in the services. These problems were subsequently covered at greater length in the second Experts' report, which was published in September 1999 and concentrated primarily on management issues, especially financial management issues, in the services (Committee of Independent Experts 1999*b*). The general conclusion of the second report was that management skills and techniques were poor and that the services needed a thorough overhaul. The report included ninety recommendations for Commission reform, a few of which were directed at the college but the great majority of which were directed at the services.

Santer's successor, Romano Prodi, thus had no option but to make reform of the services one of his major priorities, and indeed it was a condition of his appointment that he would do so. On becoming President-designate, Prodi quickly set to work on Commission reform and within months announced a series of measures that would be introduced when his college assumed office (Prodi 1999*a*, 1999*b*, 1999*c*). Some of these measures were directed at the college, such as streamlining Commissioners' portfolios and making *cabinets* more multinational, whilst others focused on the services. Amongst the latter, the Secretariat-General was given a more pro-active role in ensuring inter-service cooperation and the unofficial national quota system applying to senior posts in the services was abolished.

Prodi further signalled the priority that would be given to reform by creating a college portfolio for reform, assigning the portfolio to the returning UK Commissioner Neil Kinnock, and designating Kinnock as one of the Commission's two Vice-Presidents. Kinnock began working closely with a specially appointed Task Force for Administrative Reform to put the reform programme into operation. First steps included identifying principles that would guide the programme, announcing new rules that would be introduced quickly, and making arrangements for the drafting of detailed proposals in respect of reforms that would need to be phased in gradually (see Kinnock 1999*a*, 1999*b*, 1999*c*). Detailed proposals were issued initially in the form of a consultation paper in January 2000 (Commission 2000*c*) and then in the form of a White Paper in March 2000 (Commission 2000*d*).

The Prodi/Kinnock programme for the reform of the services is designed to ensure that the Commission is 'an international public service of the highest standards and quality' (Commission 1999*c*). This aim is to be achieved by instilling the principles of efficiency, accountability, service, and transparency in the Commission. The specific reform measures of the programme can be grouped under three broad headings.

Organizational restructuring

The number of departments in the Commission's services—that is, DGs and other services—numbered forty-five at the end of the Santer Commission. Very soon after being nominated to be President, Prodi announced that he believed that this was too many and the number should be reduced to no more than thirty-six. Despite the creation of a few new services—such as the Enlargement and Justice and Home Affairs DGs—the thirty-six target was achieved by early 2000 with the dismantling of some services (such as the Information, Communication, Culture, and Audiovisual DG and the Inspectorate-General) and the merger of others (such as the Energy and Transport DGs and parts of three previously separate DGs to create an External Relations DG and a Trade DG).

Whilst President-designate, Prodi also made it clear that he believed the names of many of the Commission's services had become far too long and opaque and the numbering system—by which DGs were commonly referred to by a number rather than their name—was similarly unhelpful to the public at large. Accordingly, the names would be simplified and the numbering system abolished. So, for example, DG XI: Environment, Nuclear Safety, and Civil Protection, became just DG Environment. All new or newly merged services were given simple names such as DG Education and Culture, or DG Health and Consumer Protection (see Table 7.1).

Reforms in personnel policy

The main aims of the reforms in personnel policy are to create a more fluid, meritocratic, and modern staffing system in which the Commission's tasks and human resources match one another and in which the working environment promotes and supports maximum staff performance. The most important amongst the many, interrelated, and overlapping, measures within the reform programme are now outlined.

■ The key aim is to ensure that there are sufficient staff to enable functions to be undertaken properly. This goal is being pursued by a number of means, of which five in particular were identified in a detailed evaluation of Commission activities and human resources carried out by a so-called Peer Group of five Commissioners (Commission 2000e). First, a much stronger priority is being given to moving staff from over-resourced to under-resourced DGs and from low-priority to high-priority areas. The major structural reforms at the beginning of the Prodi Commission led to hundreds of staff being moved to significantly different tasks from those they had previously undertaken. Between September 1999 and July 2000 around 8 per cent of Commission staff, comprising some 1,500 people, were redeployed (Commission, 2000e). The eventual number of staff scheduled to be redeployed is around 2,000. Second, additional staff are being appointed. This requires the budgetary authorities (the Council and the EP) agreeing to the funding of new posts, which they are generally reluctant to do. However, a significant increase was authorized for 2000–2 after the Peer Group Exercise estimated that the Commission was 1,254 posts short of its required strength and that one-third of this shortage would need to be covered by new posts. Third, internal procedures are being simplified, management practices are being strengthened, and organizational arrangements and practices are being made more flexible so as to bring about efficiency gains (see below). Fourth, some non-core activities, such as information provision and participation in exhibitions, are being reduced. Fifth, the Commission is to refuse to accept requests from the Council and the EP to take on extra tasks unless they provide appropriate extra resources.

■ Unofficial national quotas on senior appointments—with more going to bigger member states and fewer to smaller states—have been abolished. Whilst the Commission will, in Neil Kinnock's much repeated words, wish to 'maintain a broad geographical balance' amongst its staff, merit and experience are to be the critical considerations in making appointments. Nationality will no longer matter when a new occupant is appointed to a specific post (see Kinnock, 1999a). By the same token, the practice by which it had become understood, albeit informally, that certain key senior posts would be occupied by a national from a particular member state has been abolished.

■ The appointments system for the most senior of appointments—A1 and A2 posts—has been made more transparent and less vulnerable to interference from Commissioners wishing to press the cases of favoured candidates. Posts should normally be filled 'from among the management grades in the institution or in other institutions' rather than from outside (Commission 1999b). Should posts be filled from outside, it must be only after they have been externally advertised.

■ Buttressing the greater transparency that must be part of the appointments process, the practice of *parachutage* has been abolished. This practice involved filling some senior and middle-ranking posts not by internal promotion but by 'parachuting' candidates in from outside—usually from national civil services or the *cabinets* of departing Commissioners.

■ The understanding that wherever possible Directors-General should not be of the same nationality as the Commissioner responsible for the related portfolio has become a formal requirement. In the event of such clashes occurring after the allocation of portfolios, the Directors-General must move to other posts— as, for example, happened under Prodi with the Directors-General of the Enlargement and Energy DGs.

■ At very senior levels—Directors-General and Directors—officials are 'expected to rotate between functions at regular intervals' (Kinnock 1999a). This 'forced mobility' resulted in the heads of the Agriculture, Economic, and Financial Affairs, and Budget DGs all being moved to other posts in the first few months of the Prodi Commission (the first two posts had also carried 'national flags').

■ The staff grading system, which has long been criticized for being over-protective of 'time-servers', is to be replaced by a more linear system enabling individual abilities and merit to be more easily rewarded through promotion.

■ Much greater attention is to be given in appointments and promotions processes, and also in expanded staff training programmes, to management skills.

■ The reliance on contract staff is being reduced.

Making management more efficient

In addition to the changes in organizational structuring and personnel policy that have just been described, the drive to make the Commission more efficient has two main components. First, a new system of strategic planning is being introduced to enable the Commission to be able to plan and manage in more ordered and measured ways. At the heart of this new system is 'activity-based management', which makes it possible for priorities to be matched more closely to resources. The hope is that the Commission can avoid becoming overloaded with tasks that it does not have the capacity to undertake. The new system is scheduled to be fully operational from 2002 to 2003.

Second, financial management and control arrangements—which had long been criticized by the Court of Auditors and which the Committee of Independent Experts made clear were quite inadequate—are being overhauled. The previous system, in which the Financial Control DG had both authorized and audited expenditure, has been replaced by a more decentralized system. In future, as far as possible, those responsible for authorizing projects will also be responsible for authorizing expenditure on them. The authorization and checking of expenditure will be separate functions exercised by different sets of people.

Prospects for success

The Prodi/Kinnock reform programme is certainly radical by Commission standards, involving the most comprehensive set of internal reforms in the institution's history. It has the potential to revolutionize the operation and efficiency of the Commission. However, judged on a broader canvas, the programme is perhaps not quite as remarkable or innovative as it appears to be, for much of its content is set broadly within the context of new public management (NPM) ideas that, since the early 1980s, have played a significant part in bringing about reforms in many national public administrations, not least in the EU's own member states. At the heart of NPM thinking is a move away from traditional, bureaucratic, and hierarchically based structures to more open and flexible administration. It involves focusing resources on core tasks, decentralizing responsibilities whenever possible, devoting considerable attention to financial control, and establishing modern—incentive driven—personnel systems (see Quinlivan and Schön 2001).

If many of the changes being introduced in the services should have been made long ago, there is no guarantee that they will now be implemented with ease or success. At least three obstacles will have to be overcome if they are to be fully and successfully applied. First, there is considerable cynicism towards the reforms amongst Commission staff, many of whom believe that the reforms are too 'top down' and not sufficiently 'bottom up'. Some very senior appointments in the early months of the Prodi Commission seemed unaffected by the changes, with Director-General and Deputy Director-General positions being seen to be filled largely on a 'being known to be suitable' basis. Prodi's decision (approved by the college) in 2000 to replace the (much criticized) Secretary-General, Carlo Trojan, with his own *chef de cabinet*, David O'Sullivan (see Exhibit 4.3) did not help matters. Second, there is considerable anxiety within the services about the most controversial part of the reform programme—the proposed modernization of the grading and pay systems. Initially, it was hoped that these reforms could begin to be introduced by the end of 2000, but resistance from staff, including the threat of strike action, resulted in detailed proposals being delayed until early 2001. Third, there is the problem of implementing reforms which mainly strive to harmonize, in a highly complex, multicultural, organization.

Fundamental and transformational change of the Commission is, by nature, a long-term process. As Metcalfe (2000: 822) has noted, the fact that the basic design of the Commission has remained largely unchanged since its foundation should 'be a warning against unrealistic expectations of a trouble-free reform process'.

Conclusion

This chapter has introduced and built upon three themes. The first—that the services are not just administrative in character but are also highly political—is reflected most clearly in the services' functions and in personnel policy, both of which have been shown to have clear political dimensions. As part of Prodi's intention to stiffen the distinction between the political and administrative arms of the Commission, an attempt has been made to tighten the description of the roles of the college and the services, and rules have been introduced to de-politicize—or, more accurately, de-nationalize—the appointments process. However, a complete de-politicization of the services is practically impossible, and arguably not even desirable. Political and administrative tasks overlap too much to be completely separable, whilst the services are too important for the governments of the member states to be disinterested in their national composition.

The second theme concerns continuity: how remarkably little the Commission's services have changed in important respects since the 1950s, even though they have naturally developed and evolved to adjust to changing circumstances. In particular, until the Prodi/Kinnock reform programme, personnel policy remained relatively untouched. Even now many of its features—such as aiming for geographical balancing—are not to be completely abandoned.

The third and final theme concerns change, and the far-reaching nature of the Prodi Commission's reform programme. Even though some of the services' core features are being tinkered with rather than being fundamentally disturbed, there is no doubt that major changes are in the offing. In particular, reforms to person-nel policy, structures, and operating practices will make the services more management-focused and, it is hoped, more efficient.

Notes

1 For an official formulation of the services' obligations to be impartial, independent, and never guided 'by personal or national interest or political pressure', see Commission 2000f.

2 These figures are drawn from Cini (1996), Coombes (1970), Hay (1989), Paxton (1981), and the *Official Journal of the European Communities*.

3 *Official Journal*, 26 Feb. 2001, L56/144.

4 Estimates of the number of comitology committees vary according to what are deemed to be the 'qualifying criteria'. The figure cited here, of approximately 300, is taken from the Commission's own 'List of Committees Which Assist the Commission in the Exercise of its Implementing Powers', *Official Journal*,

8 Aug. 2000, C225/2–18. On comitology, see Christiansen and Kirchner (2000), Joerges and Vos (1999), and Nugent (1999).

Further reading

There is an increasing body of academic literature on the Commission. Much of it is, however, not greatly concerned with the distinction between the college and the services within the Commission, but is focused rather on the roles and influence of the Commission as a whole. The list of references provided here concentrates on sources that include extensive discussions and analyses of the services.

Cini, M. (1996), *The European Commission: Leadership, Organisation and Culture in the EU Administration* (Manchester: Manchester University Press).

Edwards, G., and Spence, D. (1997*b*) (eds.), *The European Commission*, 2nd edn. (London: Cartermill).

La Commission Européenne: Cultures, Politiques, Paradigmes (1996), special edition of *Revue Française de Science Politique*, 46/3, June.

Nugent, N. (2000) (ed.), *At the Heart of the Union: Studies of the European Commission*, 2nd edn. (Basingstoke and New York: Palgrave).

—— (2001), *The European Commission* (Basingstoke and New York: Palgrave).

Page, E. (1997), *People Who Run Europe* (Oxford: Clarendon Press).

Shore, C. (2000), *Building Europe: The Cultural Politics of European Integration* (London: Routledge).

Stevens, A. with Stevens, H. (2001), *Brussels Bureaucrats? The Administration of the European Union* (Basingstoke and New York: Palgrave).

Web links

The address of the Commission's web site is **http://europa.eu.int/comm**. The quality of the material on this site varies enormously with, for example, some services giving extensive information about their missions, their personnel, and their organizational structures, and others giving only very sketchy information. The page on Commission reform is extremely useful, providing key documents and much information on the progress of the reform programme.

Chapter 8

Managing the Euro: The European Central Bank

Kathleen R. McNamara

Contents

Summary

This chapter evaluates the economic and political reasons for the creation of the European Central Bank, and describes its structure with particular reference to the balance between the centralization of power within the ECB and ongoing involvement by national policy-makers. The policy areas surveyed include monetary policy, economic policy coordination, and exchange-rate policy, and particular attention is paid to the challenges of delegating monetary policy to the supranational level while maintaining other economic policies at the national level. The chapter concludes with a discussion of democratic accountability and legitimacy, and argues that the ECB's unique degree of institutional independence makes these issues highly salient.

Introduction

On 1 June 1998, the European Central Bank (ECB) began operation. Housed in a gleaming glass and steel office tower in Frankfurt, Germany, the ECB seems a rather prosaic institution, charged with managing Europe's new currency, the euro, making monetary policy for the participating countries, and directing and coordinating the national central banks who together with the ECB make up the European System of Central Banks. On closer reading, however, the ECB is not simply a grey, apolitical organization filled with technocratic central bankers, but rather a unique supranational creation with the potential for deep transformation in the nature of European politics. The ECB's decisions profoundly affect not only the economies of the EU but may also be transforming its politics as critical decisions, formally jealously guarded by states, are transferred to the European level. This chapter will review the theory and history of the euro and the ECB, assess the structure and functioning of the ECB and its linkages to other policy areas in the EU. It also speculates about the pressures which are likely to promote change in the ECB's management of the euro in the next few decades. The chapter begins, however, with a brief discussion of where the ECB fits within the broader set of European banking institutions.

The ECB and the 'other' European banks

The European Central Bank is responsible for formulating and executing monetary policy with the goal of providing a stable economic environment across the EU. While the ECB's interest-rate decisions profoundly shape the economy, the ECB is prohibited from investing money or lending out funds. But two other Euro-banks, established before the ECB, do play an important role in direct financing and granting loans. Their work has stimulated growth and development in regions facing economic hardship, both inside the EU and in neighbouring areas, and is now providing much-needed capital for research and development in emerging sectors of the economy. These institutions are the European Investment Bank (EIB), which was founded by the Treaty of Rome, and the European Bank for Reconstruction and Development (EBRD), founded in 1991 (see Exhibit 8.1).

While these European banks continue to grow in importance, it is the European Central Bank that is the central site of monetary governance and whose authority in setting economic policy represents a key transformative innovation within the institutional landscape of the EU.

Exhibit 8.1 The 'other' European banks

The European Investment Bank

The European Investment Bank (EIB) was created in 1958 by the Treaty of Rome, and is owned by the fifteen states that make up the European Union. The world's largest bank of its kind with loans totalling €29 billion in 2000, the EIB has traditionally financed capital investment in the EU and now does so in central and eastern Europe, often lending support to large infrastructure projects and helping to bind together the single market. The EIB is able to raise funds at very low rates through the capital markets where its bond issues have the highest credit rating. This allows the EIB to lend money at very low rates. In 1999, the European Investment Bank set up the Balkan Task Force, a team of experts who assess the infrastructure needs in post-war south-eastern europe. The EIB then provides long-term finances to the areas the team finds the most needy. The Task Force provides money in many infrastructure project areas, including energy, transportation, communications, and the environment.

In June 1998, the responsibilities of the EIB expanded to include the Amsterdam Special Action Programme. According to this agreement, the EIB is now authorized to lend money for health and education projects and to provide risk capital for small and medium-sized enterprises, especially in the high-tech sector. The idea is to promote job creation and capital investment throughout the EU, and the EIB has been surprisingly nimble in adjusting to its new tasks. Responding to decisions taken at the Lisbon Summit, the EIB has decisively shifted away from the long-term infrastructure emphasis of its earlier years into research and development and has been working with the European Investment Fund (EIF), a previously low-profile subsidiary that now acts as an aggressive venture capital enterprise in partnership with private investment managers in areas such as biotechnology.

The European Bank for Reconstruction and Development

The European Bank for Reconstruction and Development (EBRD) was established in 1991 at the suggestion of François Mitterrand, then President of France. The purpose of the EBRD is to promote economic restructuring and liberalization in the economies of the former communist European states. The EBRD struggled to gain credibility in 1993, after it was discovered that the institution spent more money on its headquarters than on loans to central and eastern Europe in the first two years of its existence. Having gained that credibility, the EBRD now plays a significant role in the redevelopment of the former Soviet states. The loans granted by the EBRD serve to lead these countries towards a market economy, picking up private and entrepreneurial ventures that would fail without its support. According to the EBRD Articles of Agreement however, the bank can only lend to countries that are 'applying the principles of multiparty democracy, pluralism, and market economies'. Thus, the EBRD attempts to promote political change as it assists with economic transformation.

The origins of the ECB

Economic and political rationales

The ECB is the institutional outcome of a process of monetary integration that began early on in the history of the European Union and suffered many set-backs before becoming a reality. Why have the European states had such a long-standing interest in creating a common currency? There are two sets of reasons, economic and political, which are often offered for why nation states might create a single common currency and central bank. The following review of both the theoretical reasoning and the historical evidence on the European case suggests that it is the political rationale that seems more compelling in explaining the creation of the ECB.

The economic benefits from a single currency and monetary institution seem straightforward: the more trade and investment activity there is across an area, the more desirable a single currency should be. A single currency is assumed to ease economic interactions by eliminating the transaction costs of doing business in many different monies, as well as eliminating the risks to business associated with fluctuating currencies (Frieden 1991). The Commission's report *One Market, One Money* stated emphatically that 'Indeed, only a single currency allows the full potential benefits of a single market to be achieved'. (Emerson *et al.* 1992: 20). However, there is surprisingly little empirical evidence or academic agreement on whether exchange-rate uncertainty and currency transaction costs actually do hinder trade flows (Dixit 1989; Chowdhury 1993; Bini-Smaghi 1991; Gagnon 1993). The world's closest trading partners, such as the USA and Canada, have not shared a single currency, yet have seen their trade and investment flows increase dramatically.

The costs of giving up your own currency might indeed be substantially higher than the benefits. First, the new supranational euro eliminates the ability to adjust national exchange rates *vis-à-vis* others within the new monetary union, removing the capacity to reduce the price of your exports abroad. Second, moving monetary policy authority to the ECB means that monetary policy is no longer tailored to fit national conditions but must be collectively decided for the whole of the union. A single currency and central bank makes more sense for an economic region when trade levels are high, when labour is highly mobile, when economic shocks, such as an oil crisis, affect the different geographic parts of currency union in similar ways, and when there are compensating fiscal transfers across the monetary union to make up for uneven economic development.[1] The presence of these elements means that the costs of giving up independent exchange-rate and monetary policy will be minimized, as economic conditions can be adjusted through compensatory actions such as workers moving from depressed areas to areas where jobs are plentiful instead of changes in the exchange rate.

The economic situation of the European Union, however, does not meet these criteria for a healthy single currency and central bank. This does not mean that the ECB will not succeed. On the contrary, the real world of national currencies and sovereign central banks outside the EU also does not match up to these ideal economic conditions. For example, the economic area bounded by the United States does not qualify as a likely candidate for a single currency and central bank, yet few have questioned the appropriateness of the dollar as a single American currency since its introduction during the American Civil War in the 1860s. While a single currency can be argued to be beneficial in an integrated market setting, *politics*, not economic logic, seems to be the overwhelming factor shaping the geography of money, and the success of unified currency standards, throughout history. The EU is no exception.

What is the political logic, then, that has compelled the creation of the euro and the ECB? There are two strands of thinking about the politics of monetary union. For some countries, most importantly France, one key benefit was to move from an informal arrangement in which the French franc was subordinate to the DM (in the earlier European exchange-rate system of the 1980s and 1990s) to a European level institution where the French central bank governor would have a seat at the table of monetary policy-making. More generally, however, the political benefits of a supranational monetary institution revolve around its potential to serve as an engine of political integration and as a tool of policy management. Currencies have a powerful symbolic value to their users, and leaders have promoted the consolidation of monetary authority in the euro and ECB to encourage a sense of collectivity or community within the EU while presenting a more unified face to the international system (Cohen 1998; Helleiner 1998). Some leaders, particularly in France, have long championed the potential for the single European currency to enable Europe to play a larger role in the management of the global economy. Given the size of the single market, the euro, if attractive to investors, has the capacity to rival the dollar as a key international currency.

Finally, the political rationale for a single currency and central bank may also lie in the perception that a European-level monetary institution may be more effective than its national-level predecessors.[2] A new, politically independent central bank might be able to project a more credible image about its policy capabilities to investors, resulting in a more stable currency than those found among states, such as Italy, with historically high levels of inflation and political instability. Academic research is divided about the extent to which making the central bank legally independent from politicians has a positive effect on economic outcomes (Cukierman 1992; Persson and Tabellini 1994; Eijffinger and De Haan 1996; Alesina and Summers 1993; Posen 1993). However, central bank independence has achieved an ideological consensus amongst economists, policy-makers, and business élites that was critical to the decision to delegate monetary authority to the ECB (McNamara forthcoming 2002).

Politics in practice: the long road to EMU

The history of European monetary integration demonstrates that all of the various political objectives of a common central bank were important along the road to the ECB. However, the road was not a smooth one and it was by no means certain that a common currency and central bank would ever be a reality.

Although the original Treaty of Rome did not contain any explicit call for a single currency or central bank, by the 1960s European leaders had begun to discuss the possibility of a monetary union. This early interest was prompted in part by the instability of the international Bretton Woods system, which was no longer effective in smoothing out exchange-rate fluctuations among the major economies. The United States was perceived, by France in particular, as either unable or unwilling to take responsibility for managing the international monetary system.

Dissatisfaction with continued monetary instability and the desire to forge a European response prompted the political leaders of the six member state governments, at The Hague Summit of December 1969, to call for a plan to create a European monetary union. They commissioned a group chaired by the Prime Minister of Luxembourg, Pierre Werner, to report on how to achieve this goal. The Werner Report of 1970 set out a three-stage plan for reaching EMU within the decade. It called for free capital flows across Europe and preferably a single currency, but also noted that irrevocably linked, fixed exchange rates would be sufficient as well. It further called for the creation of a Community system of central banks, modelled on the US Federal Reserve, but left the specifics of the institutional design of the central bank system open, in contrast to the detailed nature of the later Maastricht plan for the ECB. However, the first and only stage of this plan to be implemented was the short-lived currency 'Snake', a fixed exchange-rate regime created in 1972. Movement towards monetary union was hampered by the oil crisis, economic instability, and inflation, and perhaps most importantly, by a political divergence of views across Europe on what would constitute an appropriate policy (McNamara 1998). At this point, it looked like a common European monetary institution would never become a reality.

Creating the ECB

By the second half of the 1980s, European leaders, led by the French in partnership with the Germans, began to consider reviving the monetary union project. The success of the single market programme in moving towards the dismantling of barriers to trade and commerce seemed to forge a logical link with movement forward with a single currency. The success of the single European market also created a sense of excitement and support for bold steps to further Europe's integration. At the June 1988 European Council in Hanover, EU heads of state and government charged the Commission President, Jacques Delors—a key protagonist in the revival of the single currency project—with developing a plan for economic and monetary union. The committee formed to address this goal delivered its 'Delors Report' to the European leaders at a summit in Madrid in 1989. The report's conclusions formed the basis for the subsequent Treaty on European Union, signed in Maastricht in December 1991.

The Maastricht Treaty called for EMU to be achieved in three stages. Stage I, which began immediately, was to be marked by the removal of all capital controls, the reduction of inflation and interest-rate differentials amongst the member states, the increasing stability of exchange rates in the EMS, and more extensive policy coordination. Stage II, begun in January 1994, was to be devoted to the transition to EMU. In this stage, a new body, the European Monetary Institute (EMI) was created to assist in the coordination of national monetary policies and to encourage a convergence in economic fundamentals. The EMI was the precursor to and laid the procedural groundwork for the ECB, which was slated to begin in Stage III—beginning on 1 January 1999—along with a single currency, subsequently named the euro. The national central banks were to continue to exist as members of the European System of Central Banks (ESCB), carrying out the policies of the ECB, somewhat like the US regional Federal Reserve Banks.

The starting date of the final stage of EMU remained subject to a political decision by Europe's leaders taking into account a series of economic criteria as to who could join EMU. The Maastricht Treaty's 'convergence criteria' were a necessary concession to those states, most importantly Germany, that feared EMU would be inflationary if the participating economies were not adequately prepared. The criteria called for member states to achieve low and convergent inflation rates, a budget deficit of 3 per cent of GDP or less, public debt levels of 60 per cent or less, and a stable exchange rate. The rules of Maastricht left substantial room, however, to allow the heads of state to make their own judgement about which states should go ahead into Stage III and on what timetable.

In the end, the decision to begin EMU on 1 January 1999 was effectively made by a special European Council meeting in Brussels in May 1998. While most EU states had made strenuous efforts to meet the convergence criteria by the time of the launch of Stage III, not all conditions were met for all eleven countries slated to participate in the euro. The political desire to continue moving towards a common monetary authority carried the day, and shortly after, the European Central Bank replaced the EMI and began business preparing for the start of EMU at the end of 1998.

The structure of the ECB

The overarching institutional framework for EMU is the European System of Central Banks (ESCB), made up of the national central banks of the participating countries with the ECB itself at the centre. Although the formulation of monetary policy is highly centralized within the ECB, the execution and operation of monetary policy is more broadly decentralized within the ESCB. The basic tasks of the ECB and the ESCB are the formulation and implementation of monetary policy, most prominently through the setting of interest rates; the execution of exchange market operations; the holding and management of official reserves; and the promotion of the smooth operation of payment systems.

The ECB's formal structure was established in the Maastricht Treaty, and it is this structure that has been followed in practice. The ECB is made up of three separate, but closely linked and somewhat overlapping decision-making bodies (see Figure 8.1). The first body, and arguably the most important, is the Executive Board of the ECB. The Executive Board consists of the ECB's President,

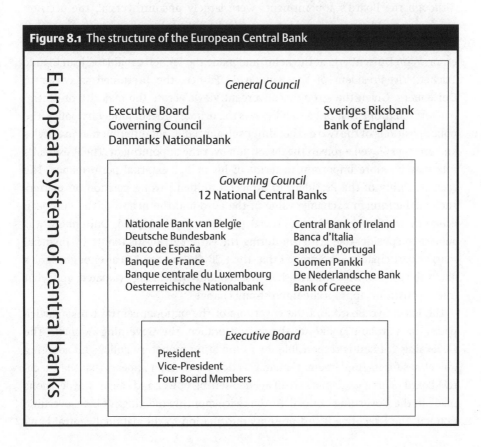

Figure 8.1 The structure of the European Central Bank

European system of central banks

General Council

Executive Board
Governing Council
Danmarks Nationalbank

Sveriges Riksbank
Bank of England

Governing Council
12 National Central Banks

Nationale Bank van Belgïe
Deutsche Bundesbank
Banco de España
Banque de France
Banque centrale du Luxembourg
Oesterreichische Nationalbank

Central Bank of Ireland
Banca d'Italia
Banco de Portugal
Suomen Pankki
De Nederlandsche Bank
Bank of Greece

Executive Board

President
Vice-President
Four Board Members

Vice-President, and four other board members. The Executive Board is responsible
for the day-to-day management of monetary policy, implementing decisions made
by the second body, the Governing Council, and issuing the necessary instructions
to the national banks. Strictly speaking the primary responsibility of this Executive Board is to carry out monetary policy, but, as will be discussed, it is also
heavily involved in the formulation of policy itself.

The six members of the Executive Board are appointed by common accord of the
governments of the member states at the level of heads of state or government, on
a recommendation from the Council and after consulting the European Parliament and the Council. The President is elected for a term of eight years, the Vice-
President for a term of four years, and the remaining members for terms between
five and eight years. The terms of office for the Executive Board members are non-
renewable. None of these individuals is allowed to hold any other position while
on the Governing Council, and all are to be appointed 'from among persons of
recognized standing and professional experience in monetary or banking
matters'.[3]

The first Executive Board of the ECB was indeed chosen from the ranks of highly
respected economists and policy-makers long associated with the EMU project.
Although the Board's appointments were largely uncontroversial, the decision
over who would serve as President provoked a political fight among the member
states. A compromise was reached which put the former Dutch central bank governor, Wim Duisenberg, at the helm, and made the French candidate, Jean Claude
Trichet, Vice-President of the Banque de France, the presumed successor to
Duisenberg. Given the strongly convergent views across the majority of central
bankers in Europe that price stability was the primary goal of monetary policy, the
policy positions of the two did not differ substantially, but different national styles
and prestige played a role in the dissension over the appointment. The President's
role may be more important in terms of his or her external performance. The
relative ability of the President to project a unified, strong position on matters
such as the foreign exchange value of the euro and the health of the European
economy is often viewed as a crucial part of the job. Indeed, Duisenberg was
subject to considerable criticism during the early part of his tenure by financial
market participants, who argued that the ECB did not send clear enough signals
about the state of the economy, how the economy was being evaluated, and what
might constitute appropriate interest-rate changes.

The Executive Board and the governors of the national central banks participating in 'Euroland' make up the second branch, the Governing Council.[4] The
Governing Council is responsible for formulating monetary policy and adopting
guidelines for its implementation. In practice, however, it appears that the Executive Board takes a large measure of agenda-setting power and shapes the decisions
made in the Governing Council. At the twice-monthly meetings of the Governing
Council, the Executive Board presents information to the national central bank

governors on the state of the 'Euroland' economy, provides projections on future developments, and then recommends a specific course of action. Given the large size of the Governing Council and the uniquely European-wide perspective of the Executive Board, the latter's lead role is understandable, and in fact may be more pronounced if EMU grows in terms of the number of participating states. It appears also that decisions in the Governing Council are taken by consensus, not votes, which means that the agenda-setting powers of the Executive Board may be more important than their minority voting position might indicate. However, the national central banks continue to be quite important to the operation of the ECB, as they collect and analyse data crucial to the modelling of the euro zone for monetary policy. The national central banks also are politically important in providing a direct link to the European publics, as they have long-standing relationships with governing bodies in their countries and are an accepted and legitimate part of their national political landscape. As will be discussed in the section below on democratic accountability, some of the national central banks argue that they are uniquely able to provide this legitimating foundation for the ECB.

The third and least powerful branch of the ECB is the General Council, comprising the president, vice-president, and governors of all the EU national central banks, including those not participating in the euro. The remaining four members of the ECB's Executive Board can participate in the meetings of the General Council, but have no voting rights. It is the right of the General Council to be notified before the Governing Council implements most legal acts, so that its members can study and submit observations. However, the General Council's role in practice is very limited, and those members not participating in the euro system are effectively shut out of policy-making.

One of the most notable features of the institutional structure of the ECB is that its statute makes it the most politically independent central bank in the world, even surpassing historically independent entities like the German Bundesbank or the US Federal Reserve. The Maastricht Treaty states that the ECB cannot seek or take instructions from any EU or national entity or any other body. Its independence is arguably more secure than that of any national bank because a modification of its statute would require an amendment to the Treaty, which can only occur with unanimous agreement among the member states. The ECB is linked, but only minimally, to the political bodies of the EU in the following ways (Article 113 TEC). The President of the EU's Council of Ministers may participate in the deliberations of the Governing Council of the ECB and may submit motions for consideration, but cannot vote. A representative of the European Commission may also attend meetings of the Governing Council, but may not vote or present motions. In addition, the ECB must fulfil a number of reporting commitments to European bodies and the public. It must issue retrospective annual reports on its activities. Its President may be required to appear before the relevant committee of the European Parliament, and the President will also be invited to attend meetings of the Council of Ministers when it is discussing matters of relevance to the ESCB. This degree of independence raises many important issues about the desirability and functionality of such a highly delegated institutional structure, issues which will be taken up in the last section of this chapter.

The organizational culture overlaying the ECB's formal institutional structure is still in formation. However, the ECB does seem to have certain distinct qualities that set it apart from the other institutions of the EU. First, the ECB is not subject to the same administrative rules and regulations as the rest of the EU agencies but rather has created its own rules regarding the hiring, promotion, and firing of personnel.[5] The ECB is still a relatively small organization, and staff members pride themselves on being flexible, sensitive to the need for adjustments and change. In interviews, they claim to see themselves as much closer to a private sector firm in organizational culture than what they view as the overly bureaucratized Brussels institutions. In addition, the ECB is not set up on the French-influenced EU Commission *cabinet* system, a fact those working in the ECB see as also quite important in making the dynamics inside the central bank more like a private corporation than the other EU institutions. Neither do they view themselves as just an extension of national-level central banks. While the formal structure of the ECB mimics the German Bundesbank in many ways, there is a conscious effort on the part of some of the highest-level staff to pioneer a truly new institutional culture and identity. However, the ECB's location in Frankfurt has made it easier to attract staff from northern Europe, while making it a less attractive post for other EU nationals, skewing the culture of the ECB towards the Bundesbank model. Asked to draw an analogy between the EU and national banking institutions, some within the ECB approvingly cite the Bank of England, which is viewed as somewhat more 'competitive' and 'market oriented' in its monetary policies, instruments, and organizational rules than the other national central banks. This combination of design and aspiration seems to set the ECB somewhat apart from the national central banks and the other EU institutions, although it remains to be seen to what degree this culture will become more bureaucratized as the ECB ages.

The powers of the ECB: centralization versus national control

The creation of the ECB has had myriad effects on policy-making, moving some policy processes to the European level while leaving other related policy areas in the hands of national governments. These transformations have the potential to ignite serious tensions between centralization and national control in governance and economic policy-making within the EU. The following sections evaluate the likely organization and character of EU policy-making in the key areas of monetary policy, economic policy (particularly fiscal policy), and exchange-rate policy.

Monetary policy

Despite the novelty of the ECB's formal institutional framework, there is significant overall continuity in the substance of European monetary policy-making. In the past two decades, there has been an increasing consensus in Europe on the importance of price stability and central bank independence (McNamara 1998). This consensus has been an important underlying contributor to exchange-rate stability in advance of EMU. The Maastricht Treaty codifies this consensus, stating that the 'primary objective' of the European Central Bank is 'the maintenance of price stability' (Article 105 TEC). The ECB must also 'support the general economic policies in the Community' but 'without prejudice to the objective of price stability'. Price stability is not defined by the Treaty in quantitative terms, but is usually agreed by European central bankers to mean an inflation rate under 2 per cent.

Underlying the emphasis on price stability is the belief that monetary policy cannot have any long-lasting influence on real economic variables such as output growth and employment. European officials have viewed such efforts as producing permanently higher and more variable rates of inflation, which will have negative effects on the real economy. ECB President Wim Duisenberg has stated that 'the monetary authorities can support job creation and the attainment of higher living standards by fostering a stable macroeconomic environment in which business decisions can be made' (Duisenberg 1998b). This monetary policy consensus has not been entirely uncontested. Observers have argued that a strict emphasis on price stability by the ECB may have a deflationary effect, slowing growth within Europe and its trading partners (Eichengreen 1996; Cameron 1998).

To achieve the goal of price stability, the Executive Board early on developed a two-track operational approach. The first strategy is monetary targeting, in which the amount of money flowing through the European economy is measured, and the central bank adjusts its policies to achieve a set money supply goal. The second strategy is inflation targeting, the identification and publication of an inflation target that is used by the bank to guide policy. Both these strategies have their critics and adherents. When these strategies are used together, some critics claim there is a danger that the objectives of policy may be too opaque for observers to determine what they are and if they are being met.

Economic policy coordination

Changes in the process and substance of broader economic policy-making in the EU will be rather subtle, with a much stronger emphasis on the monetary, rather than the economic aspect of economic and monetary union. In the Treaty itself, there is little statutorily to increase the degree of coordination in broader economic policy-making. In practice, what coordination there has been is centred in Ecofin, the EU Council of Ministers for Economic and Financial Affairs, which will continue to be a key locus for general discussions of policy-making, such as the coordination of fiscal policy. National governments are still responsible for the individual development and execution of their economic policies, although they are expected to take account of their EU neighbours and work to coordinate their policies where appropriate. The December 1997 Luxembourg Summit declaration describes this delicate balancing act as follows:

Enhanced economic policy coordination must adhere to the Treaty principle of subsidiarity, respect the prerogatives of national governments in determining their structural and budgetary policies subject to the provisions of the Treaty and the Stability and Growth Pact, respect the independence of the European System of Central Banks in pursuing its primary objective of price stability and the role of the ECOFIN Council as the central decision-making body for economic coordination, and respect national traditions and the competencies and responsibilities of the social partners [business and labour] in the wage formation process.

Indeed, concerns have been raised about whether this policy apparatus will enable member states to coordinate effectively fiscal and monetary policies, and the possible implications of coordination problems for the management of the external value of the euro.

Two political initiatives have addressed this concern by moving beyond the general guidelines for policy coordination established in the Maastricht Treaty. The first important post-Maastricht policy innovation was the Stability and Growth Pact, which builds on language in the Treaty regarding 'excessive government deficits' (Article 104 TEC). The treaty language specifies that a government whose budget deficit exceeds 3 per cent of GDP or whose public debt exceeds 60 per cent of GDP may be required to correct its situation, and may be subject to sanctions and penalties if it fails to do so.

Prompted by the German Finance Minster, Theo Waigel, heads of state and government came to agreement in Dublin in December 1996 on procedures for increased policy surveillance, on the specific penalties to be imposed when countries have excessive deficits, and on the automatic imposition of those penalties. At first, a government will be required to make a non-interest-bearing deposit, and it will be converted into a fine if, after two years, the government continues to run an excessive deficit. The deposit or fine will have a fixed component equal to 0.2 per cent of GDP and a variable component equal to one-tenth of the excess of the deficit over the reference value of 3 per cent of GDP (but the annual deposit cannot exceed 0.5 per cent of GDP). No fine will be imposed if a country is in a severe recession, defined as a fall in GDP of at least 2 per cent over a single year. If output has fallen by an amount between 0.75 per cent and 2 per cent of GDP, Ecofin may exercise discretion in applying the fines if circumstances warrant the deficits. At the insistence of the French President, Jacques Chirac, the agreement was called the Stability and Growth Pact, but its emphasis is overwhelmingly on fiscal recti-tude. The fines themselves may not be economically unbearable, but the political cost will be high and the risk of being fined may thus serve as a deterrent to deficit spending.

Individual governments have pursued the policies they deemed necessary given the Maastricht convergence rules, but there has been little multilateral effort at coordination within this framework. Indeed, there is significant disagreement about the effectiveness of the stability pact for fiscal coordination. ECB President Duisenberg (1998a) has stated that 'The existence of the Stability and Growth Pact leads to the conclusion that EMU does not need a centralized budget. With national budget positions close to balance or in surplus, countries have ample room for manoeuvre to cope with adverse economic developments.' Others, how-ever, have argued that the externalities of a country's policies increase with EMU, requiring closer review of specific policies, not just compliance with general rules and principles.

In this view, it might be necessary to have greater coordination of fiscal policies in a more flexible and interactive policy setting than that prescribed by the Stabil-ity Pact (Begg et al. 1997). Even for those agreeing that fiscal policies are best directed towards rigour (because lax fiscal policies require a tighter monetary policy, which could in turn bring public pressure on the ECB and cause it to retreat to an overly lax policy stance) the Stability Pact is seen as too blunt an instrument. Some long-time official participants in the EMU project have stated privately that some form of fiscal federalism—that is, a more federal European structure with centralized redistributive policies of taxing, borrowing, and spending—is a certainty in the long run.

Concerns such as these have prompted the second important political initiative affecting the character and organization of economic policy-making in EMU, the establishment of a new informal group, the so-called Euro-X or Euro-11 Council (as there were eleven founding members of the euro), now referred to as the Eurogroup, which had its inaugural meeting on 5 June 1998 in Luxembourg. The Eurogroup is a subset of the Ecofin, made up of the ministers of the euro states and acting as a forum for coordination within the euro zone. In a compromise reached between Germany, France, and Britain, the non-EMU member finance ministers are allowed to attend the Eurogroup meetings, but excluded from dis-cussions over issues central to the euro, such as its external value *vis-à-vis* the dollar.

France has been the main proponent of a strong role for this forum. Dominique Strauss-Kahn, the then French Finance Minister, argued at its inauguration that it should form a necessary political counterweight to the highly independent ECB. The Eurogroup has been promoted as a way to coordinate national budgets in an effort to boost growth, plan structural reforms in pensions and labour markets, as well as coordinate tax harmonization in an effort to guard against competition over such policies. Strauss-Kahn also envisioned the Eurogroup playing an international role, representing the EMU countries at the IMF and other international fora.

Strauss-Kahn's departure as Finance Minister (to fight domestic allegations of corruption in France in 1999) did not put an end to discussion over the Eurogroup. Some have noted that the French appear to regard the Eurogroup Council as an 'embryonic economic government for Europe, and a heavy political counter-weight to the ECB' (*The Economist* 1998). Although this ambition has been strongly criticized as a threat to the independence of the ECB, it should not be dismissed. It is instructive to recall that even the very independent Bundesbank is embedded in a framework of political institutions and long participated in an ongoing dialogue with its 'social partners', that is, business and labour (McNamara and Jones 1996; Hall and Franzese 1998). Indeed, support for the development of a EU inter-governmental economic policy council as partner to the ECB has come from former US Federal Reserve Chairman Paul Volcker, who has argued that no central bank 'can long be comfortable as an island unto itself, operating entirely outside a political context' (Volcker 1997: 256).

Germany insists, however, that the Eurogroup should serve merely as an informal body to promote information exchange, and that the Stability and Growth Pact, if adhered to, will produce the appropriate fiscal policies. Britain has been even more resistant to a major role for the Eurogroup, fearing that it will be shut out if the Eurogroup gains real institutional power. Forward movement along these lines among the EMU states may indeed serve to exacerbate the cleavage between the 'ins' and the 'outs', although a widening of this division may be inevitable in any case as EMU progresses.

Exchange-rate policy

While the structure of monetary and fiscal policy decision-making within the ECB is relatively clear, the Treaty on European Union was less clear in the area of exchange-rate policy-making for the euro. Operational responsibility for exchange-rate values, through the conduct of foreign exchange operations (interventions and the daily management of exchange reserves), is the sole responsibility of the ECB. The Treaty is less clear, however, about the locus of responsibility for the formulation or creation of exchange-rate policy. Article 109 TEC treats three aspects of exchange-rate policy, as well as two broader questions of economic governance.

According to the Treaty, the decision to enter into a formal exchange-rate agreement with non-EU countries is the responsibility of Ecofin, and any such agreement would be binding on the ECB. In the absence of such an agreement, the Council, acting on a proposal from the Commission and after consultation with the ECB, may adopt (by a qualified majority vote) 'general orientations' for exchange-rate policy towards non-EU currencies, but only in so far as they do not interfere with the ECB's primary goal of price stability.

As the resurrection of a formal system such as the post-war Bretton Woods international exchange-rate regime is unlikely in the foreseeable future, the vague language regarding 'general orientations' is more likely to govern the informal cooperation that has characterized the international monetary system since the early 1970s. One result is an opening for increasing the Commission's institutional power. The policy discussion about the locus of competence for exchange-rate policy is, in any event, ongoing.

The European Council attempted to resolve some of the ambiguities at its meeting in Luxembourg in December 1997. It adopted a resolution designed to clarify Article 109 TEC, stating that the Ecofin may 'in exceptional circumstances, for example in the case of a clear misalignment, formulate general orientations for exchange-rate policy in relation to non-EC currencies'. An episode such as the attempt to halt the appreciation of the dollar under the 1985 Plaza Accord might be deemed to constitute an 'exceptional' circumstance. At Luxembourg, the heads of state also agreed that the Ecofin Council 'should decide on the position of the Community at international level as regards issues of particular relevance to economic and monetary union'. It interpreted the Council's jurisdiction broadly by including 'bilateral relations between the EU and individual third countries and to proceedings in international organizations or informal international groupings'.

ECB President Wim Duisenberg has stated, however, that an exchange-rate objective is not an appropriate monetary policy strategy for the ECB, 'given that for an area as potentially as large as the Euro area, such an approach might be inconsistent with the internal goal of price stability. The external value of the Euro will thus mainly be an outcome of the ECB's monetary policy.' Formal arrangements with non-EU countries are unlikely, he went on to say, although the ESCB will of course have the technical capacity to 'intervene in order to counteract excessive or erratic fluctuations of the Euro against the major non-EU countries' (Duisenberg 1998a). In contrast, the European Commission and some member states, notably France, have argued that the Treaty does leave the door open for a more activist policy on the part of Ecofin and the Commission. One likely motivation for such a stance is the desire to manage the value of the euro to increase the competitiveness of EU products in world markets.

The initial experience of the euro in exchange-rate markets has been primarily marked by a steep decline in the value of the euro *vis-à-vis* the dollar. The euro began on 1 January 1999 valued at $1.18, but by its first birthday was trading at around €1 to US$1. In its second year, the euro declined to around $0.87. There is disagreement on the implications, economically and politically, of this decline. A good argument can be made that the euro simply began at too high a value, hurting European exporters, and that a certain decline was desirable. However, for those who championed the euro as a way to develop a strong, stable counterpart to rival the dollar internationally, the decline has been disappointing and frustrating. The ECB has sent somewhat mixed signals at times about the desired level of the euro, and a variety of actors have criticized Duisenberg and others for not presenting a more coherent front. There has been an effort at currency intervention coordinated with American officials, but it does not appear that exchange-rate management will dominate the current agenda of the ECB. Fluctuations of the Euro *vis-à-vis* the currencies of EU countries not participating in EMU and those of other states in Europe may be of perhaps greater ultimate concern given the high level of economic and political interaction within Europe.

The uncertainty regarding the legal division of responsibility for exchange-rate policy-making between Ecofin and the ECB is troublesome but not unusual, however, when considered in light of national policy arrangements. Henning (1977: 32) notes that 'In most countries, the relationship between the central bank and finance ministry is treated in legislation only vaguely, if at all'. Historically, the finance ministries have played an active role in exchange-rate management and policy-making throughout the EU. The ECB's view that exchange-rate policy will simply be subordinate to the internal objective of price stability, although enshrined in the Treaty, has already been proved not to be the case in practice. Its doctrine will probably evolve as the ECB matures as an institution. The larger issue raised by exchange-rate policy, however, is one of the relationship of monetary policy to other economic and social goals. Developing the institutional capacity to integrate monetary policy capacity into a broader set of political institutions, at both the EU and national levels, is a challenge that may remain unsolved for some time to come.

Democratic accountability and legitimacy issues

The technical tasks, which the ECB is working to overcome in its first years, are considerable, from developing new European-wide measurements of the economy to the changeover to euro coins and paper currency. However, the political tasks which the ECB faces may in fact be the most difficult to navigate successfully. The main political question confronting Europe's central bankers is how the ECB can maintain independence and profit from the benefits of political autonomy and at the same time be viewed as legitimate and accountable to the European public.

Democratic accountability is not only an ideal that one might be philosophically committed to, but rather is the key to the success of this new EU institution. Concern over the political position of the ECB more broadly is warranted, as independence may end up jeopardizing, not safeguarding the policy effectiveness of the ECB.

The ECB is a unique supranational organization with powers far beyond what we could have imagined sovereign states would delegate to such an institution. But, as argued above, the ECB is also notable for being the most independent central bank in the world. Its statute begins by prohibiting the ECB from seeking or taking any directions from 'Community institutions or bodies, from any government of a Member State or from any other body'. Its personnel rules, the fact that it requires a treaty revision to change its mandate, and the barring of financing of national deficits all contribute to the ECB's independence. But this legal independence is only half the story.

The nature of European Union politics adds to the ECB's independence in more subtle ways because the ECB is not embedded within a larger network of governing institutions. The formal institutions of the EU that might provide accountability, such as the European Parliament, are institutionally weak. However, the parliamentary body charged with oversight of the ECB, the Committee on Economic and Monetary Affairs, is slowly increasing in experience and expertise. The informal political institutions that might provide a legitimating foundation are also tenuous, in that the political loyalties of citizens and sense of connection to the EU level are also limited across the nation states. Any institution needs political friends to help it survive in the advent of difficulties. While a degree of independence is merited, it can be a problem if it means that there is little in the way of substantial dialogue across various groups and only weak legitimating foundations for policy delegation.

In practice, improving accountability may rest on improving communication and transparency, in part by strengthening the institutional linkages with a broad range of interlocutors throughout the EU. The President of the ECB is regularly called before the European Parliament, and although he has no formal obligation to appear, Duisenberg has proven relatively willing to go beyond the confines of the Treaty in interactions with the EP. However, not enough attention is paid by the average citizen in Europe to his testimony. Unlike US Federal Reserve President Alan Greenspan's visits to the US Congress, which are avidly watched on television by millions, Wim Duisenberg's forays in front of the EP receive less attention from the broader public than they do from financial market participants. Unfortunately, the parliamentarians themselves are limited in their resources and capacity to provide comprehensive oversight of the ECB. The ECB Executive Board members often give the impression that communication, for them, is a one-way street, instead of acknowledging that communication can flow both ways, *from* political leaders and their publics about the values and goals of economic policy *to* the ECB. To overcome this lacuna, the role of the Eurogroup in providing a broader context for formulating economic policy could be critical. As the national ministers more directly represent their publics, developing the link-ages between the Eurogroup and the ECB would seem to be an important way forward, without jeopardizing the ECB's independence. More communication with the social partners, particularly EU labour groups, might also strengthen, not erode, the position of the ECB. The most effective national central banks have long had quite close relationships with critical groups that help determine the success of their monetary policies; developing those relationships at the European level will also be a crucial determinant of the ECB's success.

The issue of transparency is contentious, but cannot be separated from the issue of democracy and communication. According to the Treaty, the decision-making branches of the ECB are forbidden to consult any member state governments regarding monetary policy decisions, and the minutes of all proceedings are kept confidential. In a widely read article, Willem Buiter (1999) criticized the ECB for not being sufficiently open, transparent, and accountable and argued that its strategies and objectives need clarifying. To correct this, Buiter argued that the ECB should publish its voting records, minutes, and its inflation forecasts. ECB Executive Board member Otmar Issing (1999) responded that confidentiality is essential for the central bank to fulfill its public mandate of good governance over the euro area by ensuring unbiased voting and discussion among the board mem-bers. If the minutes of General Council meetings are published, Issing (1999: 513) asserts, council members might be inhibited from stating their true opinions, instead worrying how their views will come across to the public in the minutes of the meeting. However, others have argued in contrast that the ECB's lack of trans-parency may result in a lack of credibility and, ultimately, a lack of public support for its policies (Lohmann 1999; Berman and McNamara 1999).

The central bankers inside the ECB are not immune from these debates. Indeed, one key cleavage that has emerged in the first years of the ECB is the ongoing internal discussion over how to ensure that the ECB is indeed politically legitim-ate. Some, such as Issing, believe that performance and policy outputs determine legitimacy, and that independence may improve the chances of price stability, thus allowing the ECB to fulfill its primary mandate. In this view, the performance of the ECB will itself take care of accountability. There are others, however, who believe active communication with the public is crucial, that accountability is a political process, not based solely on economic outcomes. Some in the Governing Council see the national central bank governors as playing a crucial role as chan-nels of 'representation', or communication to their publics, as they are familiar, mostly well regarded, and literally speak the right language. The debates in the Governing Council over the instruments of monetary policy—whether to use monetary targeting or inflation targeting—are, in the view of some, more about accountability than technical merit. Some governors view inflation targeting as more transparent than a monetary target, and want to be sure to include it for that reason. As most central banks use a pragmatic mix of the two policies, it seems likely that different perceptions about the transparency and communicability of each policy may indeed have been a large factor in the intensity of the early debates on this issue. Outside the ECB, transparency remains a concern of financial market actors, who continue to be somewhat dissatisfied with the amount of information volunteered by the ECB about its policies, in publications, press conferences, and appearances before the EP.

In all, it is important to stress that monetary policy, like any other act of governance, requires political constituencies to evaluate and support its actions. While integration in the EU has largely gone forward on the strength of élite bargains and insular policy-making, the prominence and importance of the ECB as an institution makes it less likely to be successful following this model. Research on the Bundesbank and other effective central banks has stressed that channels of political representation have strengthened its abilities to direct the economy, not undermined support for its policies. If the ECB is able to develop in a context of increasing linkages with both national and other EU-level institutions and social groups, it will be to the benefit of the economies and the people of Europe.

Conclusion

The ECB remains a unique and surprising institution. Despite the many odds against monetary union, EMU has now begun and the ECB sits at the helm, presiding over a huge political economy and managing a new global currency. This chapter has outlined the reasons, theoretical and historical, behind the ECB's creation. The challenges it still faces in achieving political accountability and legitimacy while not compromising its independence are formidable. In conclusion, it is worth noting that a further challenge awaits down the road in the area of enlargement as well.

The first issue that needs to be addressed is the timing of entry into EMU on the part of the enlargement member states. While all joining countries are supposed to adopt the euro eventually, there is debate as to how long each new member will wait to join. The Treaties state that countries must wait at least two years after joining the Union before they can join EMU. During those two years, the country must exhibit its ability to keep its own currency stable against the euro. Some applicant countries feel, however, that their past record of stability should be taken into account, thus making them eligible for monetary union before two years, and in some cases, simultaneous with their membership in the European Union. In response, ECB officials express the concern that premature enlargement of the euro zone will weaken their hold on the euro, and thus make it less stable during a time when the original eleven countries might most need support. In the case of most central and eastern European countries, inflation rates are falling, but growth still diverges from the Euroland countries. This disparity would thus make it extremely difficult to predict the outcome of ECB monetary policy.

The decision-making process of the Governing Council of the ECB will also be greatly affected by enlargement, as will all the institutions of the EU. The Governing Council may grow to thirty in number within the next few years. Many believe that this large number of members may make debate more unmanageable, shallow, or encourage national governors to gravitate towards regional blocs. One proposed solution to such a large Governing Council is to appoint governors to represent a cluster of countries, not individual states, but ECB officials believe that this solution would foster regional thinking as well. A second possible solution to EU enlargement is a rotational system in which national governors take turns on the voting panel. In this case, provisions would have to be made so that large countries would not be at a disadvantage in the event that an unusual number of smaller countries wound up on the panel at the same time, or vice versa.

Finally, enlargement also sharpens the issue of the ECB's role in governance more broadly. What should be the linkages between monetary policy and fiscal policy-making at the EU level? How all of the levers of economic policy can be juggled between the national capitals, Brussels, and Frankfurt remains to be seen. We will no doubt be seeing more proposals for increased fiscal policy coordination and perhaps simultaneously a dialogue within the European Parliament and elsewhere on the need for more communication with the citizens of Europe. Managing the euro will continue to be a challenging task. The ECB now joins other critically important EU institutions such as the Commission and the European Court of Justice in formulating policy for Europe, but like them, it also must confront the issue of democratic legitimacy while maintaining its independence.

Notes

1 This analysis rests on the Optimum Currency Area (OCA) theory developed by Mundell (1961), McKinnon (1963), and Kenen (1969).

2 More generally, Oatley (1997) provides a deft account of the variety of distributional and coalitional rationales across the different EU states that contributed to monetary integration.

3 Treaty on European Union, Protocol on the Statute of the European System of Central Banks and of the European Central Bank, chapter 3, Article 11.

4 The ECB board and the twelve national central banks of the euro area also are referred to as the Eurosystem.

5 However, it is still subject to judicial review on the part of the European Court of Justice in regard to its compliance with EU law.

Further reading

For an overview of the history and the rationales behind EMU, see Sandholtz (1993), Dyson and Featherstone (1999), McNamara (1998), and Moravcsik (1998*a*). The emerging literature on the ECB includes Lohmann (1999) and McNamara (2001). See Begg *et al.* (1998) and subsequent volumes of the series *Monitoring the European Central Bank* for excellent economic policy analyses of the ECB.

Begg, D., De Grauwe, P., Giavazzi, F., Uhlig, H., and Wyplosz, C. (1998), 'The ECB: Safe at Any Speed', *Monitoring the European Central Bank* 1 (London: Centre for Economic Policy Research).

Dyson, K., and Featherstone, K. (1999), *The Road to Maastricht* (Oxford: Oxford University Press).

Lohmann, S. (1999), 'The Dark Side of European Monetary Union', in E. Meade (ed.), *The European Central Bank: How Decentralized? How Accountable? Lessons from the Bundesbank and the Federal Reserve System* (Washington: American Institute for Contemporary Germany Studies).

McNamara, K. (1998), *The Currency of Ideas: Monetary Politics in the European Union* (Ithaca, NY: Cornell University Press).

—— (2001), 'Where Do Rules Come From? The Creation of the European Central Bank', in A. Stone Sweet, N. Fligstein and W. Sandholtz (eds.), *The Institutionalization of Europe* (Oxford: Oxford University Press).

Moravcsik, A. (1998*a*), *The Choice for Europe: Social Purpose and State Power from Messina to Maastricht* (Ithaca, NY, and London: Cornell University Press and UCL Press).

Sandholtz, W. (1993), 'Choosing Union: Monetary Politics and Maastricht', *International Organization*, 46/1: 1–39.

Web links

Key official web sites include: the web site of the ECB (**www.ecb.int**); the EU's official euro web site: **www.europa.eu.int/euro/html/ entry.html**; the web site for the European Commission's Directorate on Economic and Financial Affairs: **www.europa.eu.int/ comm/economy_finance/**; and the European Parliament's Committee on Economic and Monetary Affairs: **www.europarl.eu.int/committees/ econ_home.htm**. The web sites of the

Financial Times (**www.ft.com**) and *The Economist* (**www.theeconomist.com**) are the two definitive English language news sources for developments in the euro zone and the ECB. The Centre for European Policy Research (**www.cepr.org**) funds research on a wide range of economic issues, including monetary policy and the ECB, and posts summaries of research publications on its web site.

Chapter 9
Institutionalizing Freedom, Security, and Justice

Jörg Monar

Contents

Summary

Justice and home affairs have been the fastest growing policy-making area of the EU since the mid-1990s. This rapid development and the ambitious political objectives set by the Treaty of Amsterdam and the Tampere summit conclusions of 1999 have forced the EU institutions to embrace major adaptations in an area marked by considerable diversity, a complex hybrid of Communitarized and intergovernmental elements and major differentiation because of the Schengen system and certain member states' opt-outs from it. The European Council has gained a major leadership role and the Council of Ministers has gone through two major reforms of its working structures. The Commission has only recently developed a more active role while undertaking significant internal changes as well. Some progress has been made on democratic and judicial control, but major deficits persist. A special feature has been the emergence of a number of special agencies such as Europol.

Introduction

Justice and home affairs (JHA), now regrouped under the ambitious title of the 'area of freedom, security, and justice', constitute in many respects a special area of EU policy-making. Its peculiar origins, its extremely rapid development since 1993, the variety of the issues it covers—asylum, immigration, border controls, judicial cooperation, drugs, organized crime, and police cooperation—and the complexity generated by differentiated integration in this area have made it a formidable challenge for the EU institutions.

The institutional origins of EU justice and home cooperation can be traced back to three different structures. The first intergovernmental cooperation mechanism, the Trevi framework,[1] focused on the fight against international terrorism and was set up in the mid-1970s in the context of European Political Cooperation (EPC); that is, outside the EC (see Chapter 10). In 1985, when the Schengen system on the abolition of controls at internal borders was launched (see Exhibit 9.1), it established another intergovernmental cooperation framework which was linked to neither EPC nor the EC, and was initially limited to five member states. Additionally, a number of working parties were set up in the context of the EC Council in the second half of the 1980s to deal with issues arising from the completion of the internal market (particularly cross-border crime). Thus, at the beginning of the 1990s justice and home affairs cooperation took place in three different contexts: Trevi as part of EPC, Schengen, and the EC. At that time the term 'management' of justice and home affairs would have looked slightly out of place. Cooperation in this area had not yet gone beyond a range of poorly coordinated intergovernmental groups without decision-making powers, legal instruments, and clear objectives.

Both external challenges (such as illegal immigration and organized crime) and internal factors (the completion of the internal market) then led the member states to create, for the first time, a policy-making basis for JHA in the context of the Treaties. This was done through the introduction of the 'third pillar' (Title VI TEU) with the Maastricht Treaty in 1993. Despite a lack of adequate legal instruments or clear objectives, the third pillar led to a first rapid extension of EU activities in JHA, parallelled by substantial progress in the Schengen system, which itself more than doubled its membership to thirteen member states (see Exhibit 9.1).

With the entry into force of the Treaty of Amsterdam in May 1999, the development of EU policies in JHA was transformed into a fundamental treaty objective. Article 2 TEU provided for the maintenance and the development of the European Union as an 'area of freedom, security, and justice' (AFSJ). This new integration objective was at the same time reinforced by the introduction of a range of new

Exhibit 9.1 The Schengen system

The Schengen agreement is an unusual case of selected EU member states developing intergovernmental cooperation outside the EU's Treaties, achieving success (in the lifting of border controls between its signatories), expanding its membership, but then deciding to give intergovernmental cooperation a treaty base and 'home' in the EU's institutional system. The system is named after the small town of Schengen in Luxembourg, which is close to both Germany and France. The first Schengen agreement was signed by the governments of five EU member states (Germany, France, and the Benelux states) in 1985. By the end of 1998 the Schengen system had built up a legal *acquis* of several hundred pages and the EU had adopted a number of important conventions and over one hundred (mainly non-binding) texts. In 1999, Schengen was given a treaty base via the Amsterdam Treaty, but not all of it and with opt-outs for certain member states.

Only twelve EU member states currently participate fully in the Schengen system. Denmark, according to the Treaty of Amsterdam, is a signatory of the Schengen convention but secured an opt-out possibility from any Council decision building on the Schengen *acquis* in the context of Title IV TEC.[a] The United Kingdom and Ireland, tied by their own 'Free Travel Area', negotiated at Amsterdam a full opt-out from both Schengen and measures adopted under Title IV TEC, yet kept an opt-in possibility. That option was then used by the British government in May 2000 to secure Council agreement to participate in substantial parts of the Schengen *acquis*, particularly the ensemble of the provisions regarding the establishment and operation of the Schengen Information System (SIS). A similar move was made on the Irish side, and both governments have already opted into a number of individual EC acts under Title IV TEC which are linked to the Schengen *acquis*. As a result both Ireland and the United Kingdom are now both partial Schengen members and partial participants in measures under Title IV TEC.

To complicate matters even further two non-member states, Norway and Iceland, sought and managed to be closely 'associated' with the incorporated Schengen *acquis* because of the 1957 Nordic Passport Union (which mandates free movement of persons across the borders of its members[b]) and, more practically, because of the largely uncontrolled 1,650 kilometre land border between Norway and Sweden. Since the EU insisted on complete institutional autonomy as regards the further development of the Schengen *acquis*, the solution agreed was that Norway and Iceland would apply most of the operational parts of the Schengen *acquis* but content themselves with 'decision-shaping' instead of 'decision-making' in the context of a special Mixed Committee (see below, p. 194).

[a] Article 5 of the Protocol on Denmark (Protocol No. 5).
[b] The members of the Nordic Passport Union are Denmark, Finland, Iceland, Norway, and Sweden.

policy objectives, the Communitarization of asylum, immigration, and other issues of the former 'third pillar', the incorporation of the Schengen *acquis*, new and more appropriate legal instruments and improved judicial control. This, and the results of the Tampere European Council of October 1999, led to a further expansion of the scope of policy-making in justice and home affairs, with dozens of new legislative acts being adopted, a considerable number of new legislative initiatives and even the establishment of new bodies—such as a prosecution agency, known as Eurojust, and a European Police College. There is no other example in the history of the integration of an area of loose intergovernmental cooperation having made its way so quickly to the top of the Union's political and legislative agenda.

Yet this rapid development has come with—and to some extent at the price of—an unprecedented degree of legal complexity. The Treaty of Amsterdam has split up JHA policy between a group of newly Communitarized areas under Title IV TEC (asylum, immigration, external border controls, and judicial cooperation in civil matters) and another group which remains within the intergovernmental context of Title VI TEU (police and judicial cooperation in criminal matters). From an operational point of view, this legal borderline between EC and intergovernmental areas causes many problems because the different strings of decision-making, procedures, and legal instruments which are applicable make any more comprehensive 'cross-pillar' action more difficult and cumbersome. For instance, whereas measures against trafficking in persons and illicit drug and arms trafficking have to be adopted on the basis of Articles 29 and 30 TEU, external border control and customs cooperation measures, which are essential elements of any effective action to deal with such trafficking, are now covered by TEC provisions. A further element of complexity has been added by the incorporation into the Treaties of the Schengen *acquis* (see Exhibit 9.1).

All these different and special elements in the development of JHA policy have had—and still have—their impact on the role and interaction of the EU institutions in this area of policy-making. They also explain why the institutions have had to go through multiple rounds of institutional adaptation.

The European Council

Because of both its political importance and its hierarchical position, the European Council could have played a key role in developing JHA cooperation right from its beginnings in the mid-1970s. Yet it was only after the revolutionary transformation in central and eastern Europe, which increased the permeability of borders, that JHA started to make their way up towards the top of the European

Council's agenda. Since the mid-1990s JHA issues have figured more or less regularly in its presidency conclusions, although not necessarily as major items on the agenda.

As in other areas of EU policy-making, the prominence given to JHA issues largely depends on whether or not at least one head of state or government takes a strong interest in it and/or whether the issue figures high on the agenda of a presidency. For instance, German Chancellor Helmut Kohl's insistence on the rapid establishment of Europol during the German presidency at the Essen European Council of December 1994, led to the inclusion of a forceful statement on this subject in the presidency conclusions. It set an effective deadline for the conclusion of the negotiations on the Europol Convention for the Cannes European Council of June 1995. Although the substance of major new initiatives is normally agreed on in the framework of the Justice and Home Affairs Council (of Ministers), the formal adoption of the resulting texts by the heads of state and government can significantly increase the political importance attached to new initiatives. As a result there will be more pressure on the Council of Ministers and its bodies to reach an early agreement on the necessary implementing measures. An example for this sort of impetus provided by the European Council was the 1997 'Action Plan to Combat Organized Crime'.[2] Following the decision of the Dublin European Council of December 1996 to set up a High Level Group on organized crime, this Group submitted a comprehensive draft action plan which—after having been endorsed by the Council of Ministers in April 1997—was formally approved at the Amsterdam European Council in June 1997. The Action Plan provided a substantial programme for the Council of Ministers which was largely, though not completely implemented by the end of 1999. It in turn provided the basis for the new 'Millennium Strategy' on the fight against organized crime adopted in March 2000.

For a long time the European Council did not bother to provide the Union with any special impetus in the JHA areas as Article 4 TEU would suggest. Even after Maastricht most of the issues were still regarded as rather technical and a matter for specialized ministers who anyway were keen to keep developments in this field under their own control. This changed with the Treaty of Amsterdam. The extent of the treaty changes affecting JHA exceeded not only the expectations (or fears) of most observers but even those of some ministers, possibly even of some of the heads of state or government themselves. There can be little doubt, for instance, that the Danish Prime Minister, Pol Nyrup Rasmussen, who had become used to hiding behind British obstructionism in this area, was taken somewhat by surprise by the increased flexibility of the new British Labour government which made many of the final compromises possible in June 1997.

Once Amsterdam had created a huge new potential for EU action on JHA matters, the heads of state or government had to consider how to use it. Not only had Amsterdam created new expectations for this area, but most of the heads of state or government had by then also become aware that issues such as illegal immigration, drugs, and crime were of major concern to EU citizens and had at least in this sense actually become 'high politics', requiring more visible action by the European Council. There may also have been an increasing feeling during 1998 that the JHA ministers—often under the influence of conservatively minded senior officials—were slow in taking up the challenge of implementing the Amsterdam provisions and were proceeding on a business-as-usual basis. The December 1998 Vienna Action Plan on priorities and measures regarding the implementation of the Treaty of Amsterdam provisions on JHA,[3] whose second, operational part hardly went beyond the pre-Amsterdam agenda, could only confirm this impression. The subsequent decision to hold a special European Council on JHA matters in the Finnish city of Tampere (1999) can therefore be seen as an attempt by heads of state or government to assert both their leadership role in what had now become a major EU policy-making area and to avoid the Amsterdam impetus being lost (see Exhibit 9.2)

Tampere certainly did not mean that AFSJ was subsequently taken over by the European Council. The Tampere Summit was a 'special session', and subsequent European Councils gave less prominence to JHA. Yet Tampere meant that JHA had made it to the top of the agenda of heads of state or government and that their

---

Exhibit 9.2 The Tampere European Council: a landmark for JHA

The Tampere European Council of October 1999 proved to be a landmark for both the political and the institutional development of EU JHA. Launched in March 1999 by a joint letter of German Chancellor Gerhard Schröder and Finnish Prime Minister Paavo Lipponen, the preparations carried out under both the German and the Finnish presidencies were among the most careful and extensive of recent European Councils. At a fairly early stage broad agreement was reached that the heads of state or government would focus on three areas, asylum and immigration policy, the creation of a European area of justice, and the fight against transnational crime. Contrary to some predictions that the heads of state or government would spend most of the actual meeting on burning international (non-JHA) problems and unresolved EU business, the Tampere Summit did focus on progress towards building up the AFSJ. Not only did heads of state or government agree on the introduction of a 'common asylum system' and a range of precise targets in order to meet this objective, they also covered at least partially new ground as regards future EU action on access to justice and mutual recognition of judicial decisions. Moreover, they agreed to create two new institutions, a cross-border prosecution agency Eurojust and a European Police College, and set target dates for Commission and Council to implement the Tampere agenda, providing both with a strong mandate for exploiting the potential created by the Treaty of Amsterdam. The new impetus provided by Tampere was felt almost immediately. By the end of 2000, key compromises had been achieved on the establishment of a European Refugee Fund and the creation of Eurojust and the European Police College.

intervention could make a difference. The experience of moving into a still relatively new area of policy-making, not yet encumbered by firmly entrenched compromises and several layers of existing EC legislation and offering considerable new possibilities of major and potentially popular action, was not lost on the heads of state or government. Indeed, they have covered at least some JHA issues in all of their meetings since Tampere.

The Council of the EU

During the more than two decades of purely intergovernmental cooperation in JHA, the General Affairs Council (of foreign ministers) was by far the most important institution in this area of policy-making, not only in taking formal decisions, but also as regards the initiation of policies and their implementation. The Commission's weak position under the Treaties, its initially non-existent and then (until Amsterdam) only limited right of initiative, the unanimity requirement, and the member states' exclusive right of implementation meant that the Council was—whenever and wherever it wanted—the master of the whole policy-making process from initiation to implementation. Its dominance was challenged only when Amsterdam brought partial Communitarization and the extension of the Commission's shared right of initiative to all JHA areas.

After Maastricht the ministers started to meet formally as the 'Justice and Home Affairs Council', regrouping representatives at ministerial level from the ministries of both interior and of justice. The formal establishment of the JHA Council meant that the foreign ministries lost the important role they had formerly played in this domain because Trevi had been part of 'their' European Political Cooperation structure. During the mid-1990s some foreign ministries struggled to retain at least a limited control over JHA through their role of 'coordinating' the positions of the various national ministries involved in JHA, ultimately in vain.

In accordance with the Council's Rules of Procedure, representation in Council sessions has to be at ministerial level. Since the definition of this 'level' is left to the member states, junior ministers such as British Ministers of State or the German Staatssekretäre can take the place of their respective cabinet ministers. Yet this happens less frequently in the JHA Council than in some of the other Council formations. Most of the time the member states send to the JHA Councils not only their cabinet ministers of interior but also their counterparts from ministries of justice. The fact that two senior ministers from each member state are attending testifies to the political importance which national governments and the ministers themselves now attach to JHA. The ministers are assisted during the meetings by their permanent representatives, officials from their own ministries and from other ministries which might be concerned by some of the points on the agenda. The Commission is normally represented by the Commissioner with responsibility for JHA, assisted by the Director-General of the Commission's new DG Justice and Home Affairs.

The double representation at the ministerial level makes sense because many JHA issues concern the domains of both ministers of justice and ministers of interior. As in the case of the Ecofin Council, the representation of two ministries helps the Council develop more comprehensive approaches and strategies and reduces coordination problems between the national ministries involved. The presence of two national cabinet ministers, however, can lead to problems of coherence in national delegations. For example, the French position under the first Jospin government was occasionally affected by differences between the Minister of Interior, Jean-Pierre Chevènement, and the more pro-European Minister of Justice, Elisabeth Guigou. Because of their larger remit and (generally) more important political role at the national level, ministers of interior tend to carry slightly more weight in the Council meetings, although the ministers of justice play an uncontested lead role in areas of their primary competence, especially as regards judicial cooperation.

Since 1994 the Justice and Home Affairs Council has met in formal sessions three to four times each year. It has become customary to hold one additional informal Council meeting during each presidency. These informal sessions allow for the discussion of strategic issues outside the constraints posed by the Council's procedures and the large numbers of advisers involved in formal sessions. The informal sessions can sometimes lead to more substantial results than their formal counterparts. A good example is the informal session held in Vienna in October 1998 when the ministers were able to achieve substantial progress on the fight against corruption in the private sector, mutual legal assistance in criminal matters, and on the action plan for the 'area of freedom, justice and security'. While no formal decisions can be adopted during informal sessions, the progress achieved can be formalized in binding or non-binding texts afterwards. The total number of texts adopted by the JHA Council has only grown slightly from fifty-four in 1994 to seventy-five in 2000, but since Amsterdam a much larger percentage of them have been legally binding. The predominance of the unanimity requirement means, however, that most of the adopted texts continue to be least common denominator agreements.

Another unusual feature of JHA policy-making is joint Council meetings. These are convoked if comprehensive policy approaches or measures extending beyond the sphere of responsibility of the JHA ministers are on the agenda. An example is the joint Ecofin/JHA Council meeting which was held in October 2000 for a policy debate on how to make the fight against financial crime more effective.[4]

The incorporation of the Schengen *acquis* has had a major impact on the format and procedures of JHA Council meetings. One issue to be settled was the participation of the ministers of the non-Schengen EU member states, such as Ireland and the United Kingdom, in deliberations on measures applying only to the Schengen countries. Since the establishment of any form of 'restricted' Council would not only have been highly divisive but also contrary to the Treaties, it was decided that the ministers of Ireland and the United Kingdom would have full rights of participation in these deliberations but—for obvious reasons—no right to vote. This peculiar situation became further complicated with the formal accession in 2000 of the United Kingdom to substantial parts of the Schengen *acquis*. Quite naturally the British government claimed a right to vote on those Schengen matters (such as the Schengen Information System) it had opted into, whereas it was not granted a right to vote on the others (such as controls at borders).

The participation of the two non-EU countries associated with the Schengen system, Norway and Iceland, also required a creative institutional solution. The association agreement of May 1999 has given them the right to express their views on proposed new Schengen measures which are of concern to them through a 'Mixed Committee' at ministerial level, which regroups the members of the EU Council and the ministers of Norway and Iceland. For obvious practical reasons the member states agreed to hold these Mixed Committee meetings in connection with the JHA Council meetings. They are now regularly held 'in the margins' of the JHA Council. This means that the ministers representing Norway and Iceland join their EU colleagues at a pre-agreed time in the meeting room (before or after the normal Council meeting) to deal with any Schengen aspects concerning all of them (see Exhibit 9.3). Unsurprisingly the Schengen members (plus the United Kingdom and Ireland where applicable) have normally already 'pre-agreed' on the issues at stake and in practice the representatives of Norway and Iceland have little scope for effective influence on the final shape of the decisions adopted by the Council. Nevertheless this additional feature of post-Amsterdam 'flexibility' further complicates the Council's proceedings, reduces transparency, and increases the difficulties of effective parliamentary control at both the national and the European levels.

The Senior Council committees

As in other areas of EU policy-making, the decisions taken on JHA at the ministerial level are prepared, and in most cases predetermined, by the work of a considerable number of bodies which operate within the Council framework below the ministerial level. From a hierarchical point of view the most important of these is Coreper, whose central role in preparing the Council's work was formally extended to JHA by the Maastricht Treaty. Yet, at least initially, Coreper's position

Exhibit 9.3 A JHA Council and 'Mixed Committee' agenda

AGENDA for the 2237th meeting of the COUNCIL OF THE EUROPEAN UNION
(Justice, Home Affairs and Civil Protection)

Brussels, Thursday 15 (09.30) and Friday 16 March 2001

1. Adoption of the provisional agenda
2. Approval of the list of 'A' items
3. Proposal for a Council Directive on minimum standards for giving temporary protection in the event of mass influx of displaced persons and on measures promoting a balance of efforts between Member States in receiving such persons and bearing the consequences thereof
4. Council Regulation reserving to the Council implementing powers with regard to certain detailed provisions and practical procedures for examining visa applications
5. Council Regulation reserving to the Council implementing powers with regard to certain detailed provisions and practical procedures for carrying out border checks and surveillance
6. Preparations of the meeting with JHA ministers of the candidate countries
7. Civil crisis management
8. Fight against drugs by law enforcement (open debate)
9. Crime prevention towards an European Crime Prevention Policy
10. Draft Framework Decision on the protection of the environment through criminal law
11. Fight against cybercrime
12. Any other business

In the margins of the Council:

A. MIXED COMMITTEE AT MINISTERIAL LEVEL
(THURSDAY, 15 MARCH 2001 at 09 h.30)

1. Adoption of the provisional agenda
2. Illegal Immigration via the Western Balkans
3. Draft Council Framework Decision on the strengthening of the penal framework to prevent the facilitation of unauthorised entry and residence and Draft Council Directive defining the facilitation of unauthorised entry, movement and residence
4. Information on the Application of the Schengen *acquis* in the Nordic States as from 25 March 2001
5. Any other business

B. MEETING WITH CANDIDATE COUNTRIES
(FRIDAY, 16 MARCH 2001 at 10 h.00)

1. Possible measures to improve preaccession cooperation in combating organized crime
2. Asylum, protection and preventive measures against illegal immigration

in the JHA context was somewhat less clear than its traditionally very powerful position within the EC framework. One reason for this was that the Maastricht Treaty's introduction of JHA in the form of a separate intergovernmental 'pillar' outside the EC framework, with a 'coordinating committee' of its own—the so-called Article 36 Committee (before Amsterdam, the K.4 Committee)—made it subject to different decision-making procedures. With its traditional focus on Community policies and procedures, Coreper not only appeared slightly out-of-area in JHA but also saw its role challenged by the 'expert' Article 36 Committee.

Not all of the ministries responsible for JHA at the national level readily relinquished control over their domain to Coreper which was—and still is—widely seen as a coordinating instrument primarily controlled by the ministries of foreign affairs, economics, and finance. As a result 1993–4 saw some friction between Coreper and the Article 36 Committee, with the latter trying to bypass Coreper by forwarding texts directly to the ministerial level. Yet, it did not take long for Coreper to establish its hierarchical superiority over the Article 36 Committee. The permanent representatives argued successfully that they were in the best position to ensure the coherence of the different strings of decision-making in the 'first' (EC) and 'third' (JHA) pillars, and their initial lack of expertise was compensated by the attachment of special 'JHA Advisers' from the relevant national ministries to the permanent representations. By giving to the national ministries a powerful voice within the permanent representations, the JHA Advisers reduced those ministries' initial resistance to Coreper's central role.

The permanent representations' JHA Advisers now often meet as a group which prepares discussions in the Coreper. Occasionally this group can even be more influential on decision-making than the Article 36 Committee, which meets less frequently. All texts coming up for formal ministerial decision have to pass through Coreper. It is indicative of the political importance attached to JHA that all matters are dealt with by the Permanent Representatives themselves (that is, Coreper II) and not their deputies (see Chapter 13). As such, ministers in the EC context deliberate only on points on which no agreement has been reached in Coreper. All other points are normally adopted without discussion (as 'A points').

As a result of the Communitarization of a major part of the JHA by the Treaty of Amsterdam, substantial changes had to be made to the Council working structures. One predictable effect of the Amsterdam reforms was the limitation of the remit of the Article 36 Committee to the few areas still covered by the 'third pillar' (Title VI TEU). One might also have expected that as a result of this Communitarization, the working structures of the areas now falling under Title IV TEC would be organized in accordance with the usual three-level system (working groups–Coreper–Council) existing in other areas of EC policy-making. Yet several member states insisted on retaining a special coordinating body for matters of asylum, immigration, and external border controls. When the new working structures of the Council were drawn up during spring 1999 it was decided that this coordinating body should take the form of a 'Strategic Committee' working directly under the authority of Coreper. This leaves the newly Communitarized areas of asylum and immigration with a four-level structure similar to that in the remaining intergovernmental areas within the remit of the Article 36 Committee (see Figure 9.1). A further 'intergovernmental' feature in the revised working

Figure 9.1 The post-Amsterdam working structure of the Council in the JHA area

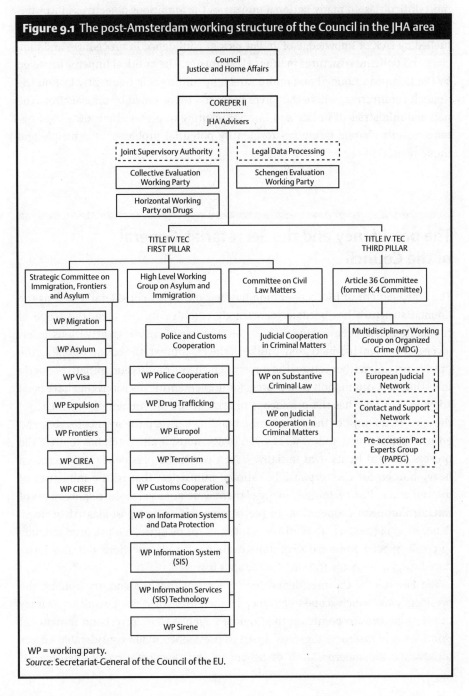

WP = working party.
Source: Secretariat-General of the Council of the EU.

structure of the Council is that the working parties dealing with the functioning of the SIS have all been included in the police and customs cooperation part of the working structure, despite the SIS functions in the Communitarized areas of external border controls, asylum, and immigration.

It is often at the committee level that decision-making on JHA encounters the most difficulties. In many national ministries the ambitious objectives of Amsterdam and Tampere have been received with a scepticism that has been further fuelled by lack of knowledge of and/or lack of confidence in procedures and judiciary and policing structures in other EU countries. The political impetus provided by the European Council and (more rarely) by ministers is frequently lost on the Council committees, where the forces of inertia represented by officials from the national ministries of justice and interior wanting to protect their own legal systems against change rarely fail to identify potential problems of principle and implementation.

The presidency and the Secretariat-General of the Council

The management of JHA cooperation has become a very considerable task as the Council structure has become increasingly complex in this area, the scope of cooperation has been extended, and the number of meetings at various levels (over 400 in 1999) has increased. Unlike in the EC context, the country holding the presidency can neither rely on the impetus given by Commission initiatives nor on investing the Commission with powers for implementing decisions that have been adopted. Not only has the presidency to arrange for the numerous meetings, set the agenda, do most of the compromise building between the member states, and ensure that adequate follow-up is given to decisions, it also often has to drive the process forward by its own initiatives. As a result the presidency has become a heavy burden for the responsible national ministries; that is, the ministries of interior and of justice. Initially many of them were not used to the requirements of intense European cooperation. In preparation for its first post-Maastricht presidency in 1994 the German Ministry of Interior, for instance, felt the need not only to create special administrative units dealing with EU questions but also introduced special language training for the staff involved.

The key role of the presidency does not mean that the country holding the presidency has much scope to advance its own priorities. The presidency can try to prioritize certain points on the Council's agenda that correspond to national priorities. For instance, the 1998 Austrian presidency made considerable efforts to advance the incorporation of Schengen and develop a comprehensive EU migration strategy. Both were in line with Austria's interests as a Schengen member and its exposure to migratory flows from eastern Europe.

Yet—as in other EU policy-making areas—the presidency must avoid the impression of pushing a particular national agenda if it wishes to act as an honest broker. Because of the unanimity requirement the presidency's margin of manœuvre in making proposals and building up compromises is even further reduced. Bold initiatives launched without extensive preparatory efforts to build consensus have little chance of succeeding and can even reduce the overall influence of the presidency. The 1998 Austrian presidency ran into major difficulties in the Council when it submitted a Strategy Paper on migration and asylum which suggested, *inter alia*, moving away from asylum as an individual right to asylum as a 'political offer on the part of the host country' and adopting measures against illegal entrants which ensured that 'the individual is put back on the other side of the border' before the start of an asylum procedure.[5] The Strategy Paper had clearly not been based on sufficient consultation with the other capitals, and had to be withdrawn, thus weakening the presidency's position.

The administrative burden for a country holding the presidency is to some extent reduced by the Council's Secretariat-General, which started to build up a new administration for Justice and Home Affairs, Directorate-General 'H', as early as 1992. Under the guidance of its first Director-General, Charles Elsen (a Luxembourg national), DG H quickly developed into an efficient, though discrete, administrative unit. It now not only ensures the smooth preparation of hundreds of meetings and the transaction of Council JHA business according to the rules of procedure, it also ensures continuity of business from one presidency to the next and often helps to iron out difficulties between the member states or between presidency, Commission, and European Parliament.

The European Commission

The European Commission's position in the development of JHA in the EU was—at least initially—not an easy one. On one hand the Commission was driven to play an active and even prominent role. The abolition of controls at internal borders was both a central element of the internal market project and a major political objective in view of the creation of a Europe of the citizens. Thus, the Commission clearly had a political responsibility to push for the adoption of adequate compensatory measures in the JHA sphere. On the other hand, until well into the 1990s, the Commission faced major opposition by several member states to any move towards a Communitarization of JHA.

Initially the Commission took the view that it had both the necessary legal competence and the responsibility to deal with the necessary JHA compensatory measures within the Community sphere. Lord Cockfield's White Paper on the completion of the Internal market (1985) included not only proposals on the abolition of internal border controls but also on harmonization in areas such as asylum, immigration, visas, and rules on drugs. Yet as early as 1985 the Commission saw one of its decisions—regarding rules dealing with immigration for employment purposes—challenged before the ECJ by Denmark, France, Germany, and the United Kingdom. Also, the setting up of an increasing number of inter-governmental groups dealing with the JHA compensatory measures, starting with the Ad Hoc Group on Immigration in 1986, made it clear that the Commission faced fierce opposition and major competence battles in the drive towards com-munitarization. As a result, the Commission changed its line of action from 1988 on, preferring to associate itself on a pragmatic basis with intergovernmental cooperation on JHA rather than to continue with its former 'doctrinaire' approach, a change of strategy that was made public in a Communication adopted in December 1998.[6]

The Commission's change of approach at the end of the 1980s led to scathing attacks by the European Parliament, which criticized it as a capitulation to inter-governmental cooperation. Indeed, one can hardly avoid the impression that in order to avoid protracted confrontation with the member states and to secure a place at the table of intergovernmental cooperation, the Commission adopted a rather subdued and low-profile role. Yet, at the same time, one has to see that confrontation would probably only have led to a stalemate in the EC sphere, additional obstacles to progress in the intergovernmental sphere, and probably a complete marginalization of the Commission. What the member states regarded as the Commission's 'constructive' strategy may have contributed to their agree-ment on granting the Commission a formal right of initiative within the third pillar in the Maastricht Treaty in 1993. Yet this right was only of a non-exclusive nature and did not extend to judicial cooperation in criminal matters, customs cooperation, or police cooperation. In spite of this slight strengthening of its pos-ition, the Commission continued even after Maastricht to play a rather discrete, though by no means negligible role in JHA matters. It introduced only a few major formal initiatives, although some of these—such as the 1993 initiative on a Draft External Frontiers Convention[7]—were of considerable political importance.

The Commission's powers in JHA were slightly strengthened by the Treaty of Amsterdam. According to Article 67 TEC the Commission still has to share the right of initiative with the member states in all the Communitarized areas under Title IV during a transitional period of five years, and only after this period will its right of initiative become exclusive. This restriction is made worse by the limita-tion of the Commission's margin to manœuvre resulting from the maintenance of unanimity in the same areas during the transitional period. Under Title VI TEU the Commission still has to share its right of initiative with the member states, but by virtue of amended Article 34 TEU it now extends also to matters of police and judicial cooperation in criminal matters.

The Commission's extended right of initiative and the Communitarization of the areas now under Title IV TEC made evident the case for a reform of the Commission's until then rather small 'Task Force Justice and Home Affairs'. In 1999 the new Prodi Commission took the decision to establish a new DG Justice and Home Affairs to be headed by Adrian Fortescue (a UK national), the experienced head of the old Task Force. This new DG was built up during 2000 and now consists of two Directorates, one for the Communitarized areas and the coordination of measures in the fight against drugs, and one for the remaining areas under Title VI TEU and external relations (including enlargement questions). Despite this build-up of the new DG which has significantly strengthened the Commission's administrative and policy formulation capacity in the JHA area, its in-house expertise on many JHA issues is still limited and it has to rely to a considerable extent on experts 'on loan' from national ministries.

Since the entry into force of the Treaty of Amsterdam (May 1999) the Commission has started to play a more active role in the JHA area. It has submitted a range of legislative proposals—especially on asylum, immigration, and judicial cooperation issues—and has adopted a number of Communications outlining the main challenges facing the EU in these areas. This increase in activity can be partially ascribed to the obvious upgrading of the importance of JHA by the Treaty of Amsterdam, which was reconfirmed by the Tampere European Council in October 1999. Having become an area of 'high politics' for the member states, the Commission could hardly afford to continue its previous low-profile role in the area. Right from the outset the new Prodi Commission placed JHA much higher on its agenda, as demonstrated in its 2000–5 legislative programme.[8] Yet personalities matter, too, as the Portuguese Commissioner, Antonio Vitorino, who took over responsibility for JHA from Anita Gradin, had far greater expertise in the area and adopted a much more ambitious and dynamic approach.

The Prodi Commission has also made greater efforts than its predecessor to act as a policy initiator. A major example is the Commission's 2000 Communication on a European migration policy[9] which, rejecting the 'zero immigration' principle traditionally adopted by the Council, suggested a 'new approach' with a more flexible and proactive immigration policy. The Commission emphasized that channels for immigration for economic purposes are needed to meet urgent needs for both skilled and unskilled workers, and that a more open and transparent policy on migration movements with a more effective coordination of national policies could help to reduce illegal immigration, irregular work, and the economic exploitation of migrants. This initiative was well timed in the sense that the previous months had seen a growing debate in some member states on immigration in the light of specific skill shortages and the problem of ageing EU populations. The Commission was also able to provide an additional impetus to the 'access to justice' element of the construction of a European area of justice through the presentation in February 2000 of its Green Paper on legal aid.[10] It effectively highlighted the many practical—and all too often costly—problems encountered by EU citizens in cases of cross-border litigation and contained a number of proposals in areas such as the conditions of eligibility for financial aid, effective access to a qualified lawyer, and the production and distribution of information on cross-border access to justice issues.

It should be noted that the Commission is facing competition as regards its initiative role in JHA matters. Since 1999 member states have made increasing use of their own (shared) right of initiative. As this comes in addition to the substantial use of the right of initiative by the presidency—a tradition 'inherited' from the old third pillar—the Commission often finds its potential field for initiatives partially pre-empted. In some cases the Commission has little option but to base its own proposals or general ideas on previous member states initiatives, as in the case of the negotiations during 2000 on the establishment of Eurojust (see Exhibit 9.4).

The non-exclusivity of the Commission's right of initiative may be justified in the light of the still much greater expertise of national administrations in the JHA

Exhibit 9.4 Establishing Eurojust: an initiative of the member states

In June 2000 Germany submitted a first formal initiative on the composition and tasks of the unit.[a] It was followed in July by a joint initiative—a quite innovative feature—of the 'four presidencies' (the current French one plus the preceding Portuguese and the two succeeding Swedish and Belgian).[b] There were significant differences between the two texts. The German initiative, to avoid delays in setting up the unit, proposed a very light structure with liaison officers from the member states which would primarily serve as information exchange agents. The 'four presidencies' initiative, however, not only gave the central role to the institution as such rather than to the liaison officers, it also envisaged certain operational functions for Eurojust such as the power to ask a member state to undertake an investigation or to prosecute specific acts. Moreover, it granted Eurojust an assessment function as regards cooperation between the member states with the possibility of asking member states' authorities to engage in specific coordinating action. In its own Communication on Eurojust of November 2000,[c] the Commission could only build upon these two initiatives by backing—as a compromise—a two-stage approach with a lighter provisional unit in the first stage and a fully fledged Eurojust with tasks of its own, a legal personality, and an appropriate infrastructure to follow in the second stage. Although the Commission came out firmly in favour of Eurojust becoming more than just a documentation and information centre, it acted in this case as hardly more than a follow-on initiator to the member states.

[a] Council document 8938/00.
[b] Council document 10356/00.
[c] COM(2000) 746.

area and the fact that the implementation of JHA decisions continues to be largely in the hands of the Council and the national governments. Some element of competition may also be good in the sense that it forces the Commission to come up with potentially better ideas than the member states. The Commission has also a chance to make its proposals prevail through more extensive previous consultation with member states and the high legal quality of its proposals. Yet the presence of partially overlapping proposals in the Council obviously complicates the Commission's task in the Council and reduces its possibilities to steer negotiations towards an outcome which represents more than the least common denominator of member states' interests.

Democratic and judicial control

Decisions on JHA—especially concerning immigration, the fight against drugs, and internal security—can have major and direct implications for citizens. Certain measures such as those aimed at limiting abuses of the asylum system, the transfer of personal data, and money laundering can potentially infringe the rights of individuals. Adequate democratic and judicial control of JHA activities thus should be a priority issue for institutional development in the JHA field. Yet the intergovernmental origins and culture prevailing in this field means that both the European Parliament (EP) and the Court of Justice are largely marginalized in the context of the old third pillar and were totally excluded from the Schengen system before its incorporation. Ministers and senior officials were quite happy to deal with the many sensitive JHA issues behind closed doors, arguing that adequate control was provided by national parliaments and courts. However, the increasing number of EU measures agreed after the mid-1990s, repeated attacks by the EP on what it regards as one of the most glaring aspects of the Union's democratic deficit, and complaints about the lack of adequate information provided to national parliaments forced member states to act. The Amsterdam reforms changed the situation of both the European Parliament and the Court of Justice quite significantly.

The European Parliament

The European Parliament's position was strengthened through the introduction of a formal right to be consulted on all legally binding acts both under Title IV TEC and Title VI TEU. This marked a big improvement on the previous situation under which the Council had only a vaguely phrased obligation to consult Parliament on the 'principal aspects' of JHA cooperation. By virtue of Article 67 TEC, co-decision could be introduced on all the 'Communitarized' matters under Title IV TEC after the end of the transitional period in 2004, though still subject to a unanimous decision by Council. Since 1998 (before the entry into force of the Treaty of Amsterdam) the Parliament has adopted full legislative reports with a corresponding resolution on all legally binding Council acts. The Parliament's 'Committee on Citizens' Freedoms and Rights, Justice and Home Affairs' has (in spite of its cumbersome title) become a quite effective body of scrutiny. The Committee's reports normally provide a detailed critical evaluation of the proposed acts with a range of suggested amendments and a presentation of broader political points of view.

Major problems of democratic control persist, however. One is the simple fact that the EP's powers are currently limited to legislative consultation only. Whatever amendments the Parliament suggests, the Council is in no way forced to take them into consideration. In practice the impact of the Parliament's opinions on the Council's final decisions tends to be very limited, although the Commission increasingly refers to positions adopted by the Parliament in its own proposals.

A further problem is that the Council continues to adopt documents on strategy on which the Parliament is not consulted. As these are not legally binding the Council is not forced to do so but the Parliament resents this practice as these strategy documents often predetermine future EU action. Examples include the Action Plans on Afghanistan, Iraq, Morocco, Somalia, and Sri Lanka as major countries of origin and transit which were adopted by the Council in October 1999 and implemented during 2000. These Action Plans were sharply criticized by the European Parliament because of what it regarded as an imbalance between the provisions on punitive action and those concerning integration and the absence of an adequate distinction between immigration and asylum issues. But the Parliament was not consulted in advance of their adoption.[11] Effective scrutiny is also made more difficult by the increasing number of legislative initiatives from member states, which often lack the legal clarity of Commission initiatives and create confusion as to which proposals are going to be the basis for final decision in the Council.

Despite a remarkable internal adaptation to the challenges of a relatively new policy area, the Parliament is clearly struggling, both at the plenary and the committee level, with the enormous workload resulting from the rapid development of the AFSJ. The Parliament's task is not made easier by post-Amsterdam 'flexibility' which makes it often less than clear to which member states and when a proposed measure is going to apply.

The European Court of Justice

The role of the Court of Justice was much strengthened by the Amsterdam Treaty. The newly Communitarized first pillar areas came automatically under the Court's jurisdiction, and in the remaining 'intergovernmental' areas of police and judicial cooperation in criminal matters the possibility of judicial review by the Court was introduced. Yet the Court's role remains subject to a number of restrictions, some of which are substantial. As regards the first pillar, the Court has no jurisdiction on measures regarding controls on persons at internal borders which relate to the maintenance of law and order and the safeguarding of internal security. The Court's competence does not extend to judgments of national courts. These restrictions are new in the Community legal order. Several restrictions were also introduced in the third pillar context. The most substantial one is that of Article 35 TEU which provides that the Court has no jurisdiction as regards the exercise of the responsibilities of member states with regard to the maintenance of law and order and the safeguarding of internal security. It explicitly precludes the Court from reviewing the validity or proportionality of operations carried out by the police or other law-enforcement agencies of a member state. Taken together these restrictions mean that the scope of the ECJ's powers in the JHA field is clearly more limited than in traditional EC policy areas. Although significant case law has not yet emerged since the entry into force of the Treaty of Amsterdam, there can be little doubt that this will make it more difficult for the Court to ensure legal unity, coherence, and certainty in the development of the JHA *acquis*.

Europol and other special agencies

This chapter would be incomplete without mentioning the tendency of the Council to set up more and more bodies, outside the main institutions and designed to fulfil specific tasks. The most notable are the European police organization, Europol, in The Hague, the European Monitoring Centre for Drugs and Drug Addiction in Lisbon, the European Monitoring Centre on Racism and Xenophobia in Vienna, the European Police College and the cross-border prosecution unit Eurojust (provisionally based in Brussels). These specialized agencies have in common the facilitation of cross-border cooperation between national authorities and the provision of a central point for the collection and analysis of data that can be used for problem assessment and policy development. Through their statutes and management structures these bodies are primarily under the control of the member states, although the Commission is to a varying degree involved in and associated with their work. Their position outside the traditional institutional context and policy circuit and their limited tasks give these bodies a politically neutral position. The example of Europol (Exhibit 9.5) shows, however, that these special agencies can acquire considerable importance, and also become controversial.

Exhibit 9.5 Europol

Europol was formally established in October 1998, taking the place of the provisional Europol Drugs Unit that had been in existence since 1993. It is not a Community institution but an international organization with legal personality. The Management Board is composed of representatives from the member states and its core staff—now over 300—consists of senior national police officers normally delegated for a number of years from their national forces.

Although Europol was not granted any operational powers—Helmut Kohl's idea of making it a sort of European FBI was rejected by other member states in the early 1990s—it has become the central point for police cooperation within the EU through its extensive tasks of information exchange and analysis. These include not only obtaining, collating, and analysing information and intelligence, and facilitating the exchange of information between member states; Europol also supports investigations in the member states, provides 'strategic intelligence' for operational activities at the national level, and assists member states in areas such as training of officers and research into crime-prevention methods. Its formal remit has been repeatedly extended to new areas such as terrorism, child pornography, and the fight against money forgery and laundering.

Europol is in the process of gaining an even more active role. The Treaty of Amsterdam makes it possible for Europol to address requests to member states regarding the conduct and the coordination of their investigations in specific areas. In 2000 the Council adopted a 'Recommendation' to that effect.[a]

The establishment of Europol provoked a number of controversies over adequate data-protection rules, the privileges and immunities of Europol officers, and the absence of effective parliamentary control. Europol has proved its usefulness at the centre of EU police cooperation. Yet, there is undeniably a certain risk of the proliferation of such special agencies leading to a 'grey area' of institutionalized JHA cooperation without effective democratic control.

[a] OJ C 289, 12.11.2000.

Conclusions

Given the extraordinary growth of the JHA agenda during the 1990s, the challenge of institutional adaptation and management was certainly greater here than in any other EU policy-making area. Overall it would seem that the institutions have responded well. The European Council has shown real political leadership, which it certainly did not exercise in this area before. The Council of Ministers has gone through two major changes of its working structures (after Maastricht and Amsterdam) which have led to a complex but comprehensive and (after initial problems) effective committee system. Pragmatic solutions have been found to the problems generated for Council by Schengen-related differentiation and the various opt-outs, and the administrative capacity and support for the presidency has been strengthened. The Council's output has increasingly shifted from non-binding to binding texts, and the number of legislative initiatives has significantly grown after the Amsterdam reforms. The Commission has moved from a tactically motivated low profile in JHA to a more active role in policy initiation, making full use of the new potential provided by the Treaty of Amsterdam and building up its in-house expertise in an area which does not belong to its traditional domains of competence. The European Parliament has also been able—especially through its Committee on Citizens' Freedoms—to develop scrutiny procedures which can keep pace with the large number of Council acts, thus reducing to some extent the glaring democratic deficit of JHA under the old third pillar. The establishment of a range of special agencies—most prominently Europol—has facilitated cross-border cooperation between national authorities and has provided a valuable data-collection and analysis base for policy development at EU level.

Yet there are also a number of management problems. The political guidance provided by the European Council in the JHA area tends to lose much of its impetus at the level of the Council committees, where doubts and objections from national ministries slow down the decision-making process. The predominance of unanimity encourages least-common-denominator agreements. Negotiations in the Council are made more complex by increasing the number of initiatives from member states, some of which have been of low quality. The Commission still lacks adequate, across-the-board, in-house expertise on policy formulation in JHA matters, often making it very dependent on the input of national experts. The European Parliament's powers of democratic control continue to be limited to consultation, the weakest form of parliamentary participation in the legislative process, and often do not extend to important strategy documents. At the committee level its scrutiny capacity is often stretched to its limits because of the large number of new initiatives coming up in the Council and the often very limited time for consideration of Council texts, especially if these emanate from member states. Although the role of the Court of Justice has been drastically expanded by the Amsterdam reforms, a number of serious restrictions apply to judicial control in the JHA domain. The position of the special agencies, finally, has given rise to concerns about adequate political and democratic control.

Some of these management problems can be reduced or eliminated through further institutional adaptation. Others—especially those in the areas of democratic and judicial control—will require further treaty reforms. Further 'flexibility' in JHA, for instance through new forms of 'enhanced cooperation', could increase the complexity of the decision-making process, reduce transparency, add to democratic scrutiny problems and lead to legal fragmentation. The institutionalization of JHA is an ongoing process. In the interest of effective management, further differentiation—as was done with Schengen and the opt-outs—

seems fundamentally undesirable. Institutional differentiation in the AFSJ is already rather daunting, and more so than in any other area of EU policy.

Notes

1 According to den Boer and Wallace (2000: 494), 'Trevi was a network of national officials, from ministries of justice and the interior, cryptically named after its first chairman, A. R. Fonteijn [that is, the Dutch word for 'fountain'], and the Trevi Fountain in Rome, where the first meeting was convened.'

2 *OJ* C 251, 15 Aug. 1997.

3 *OJ* C 19, 23 Jan.1999.

4 Council document 12205/00.

5 Council document 9809/98.

6 COM(88) 640.

7 COM(93) 694.

8 COM(2000) 154.

9 COM(2000) 757.

10 COM(2000) 51.

11 Bull. EU 3–2000, 1.4.3.

Further reading

General works on JHA policy include Barrett (1997), Peers (2000) and den Boer and Wallace (2000). The annual review of the activities of the EU, published by the *Journal of Common Market Studies*, provides updates on developments (see Edwards and Wiessala (1998; 1999; 2000; 2001). Monar (2001) offers an analysis of JHA policy in the context of the changing politics of the EU more generally. On asylum and immigration policy, see Guiraudon (2001), Kostakopoulou (2000), and Lavenex (2001*a*, 2001*b*).

Barrett, G. (1997) (ed.), *Justice Cooperation in the European Union* (Dublin: Institute of European Affairs).

den Boer, M., and Wallace, W. (2000), 'Justice and Home Affairs', in H. Wallace and W. Wallace (eds.), *Policy-Making in the European Union*, 4th edn. (Oxford and New York: Oxford University Press).

Edwards, G., and Wiessala, G. (1998) (eds.), *The European Union 1997: Annual Review of Activities* (Oxford: Blackwell).

—— (1999) (eds.), *The European Union: Annual Review 1998/1999* (Oxford: Blackwell).

—— (2000) (eds.), *The European Union: Annual Review 1999/2000* (Oxford: Blackwell).

—— (2001) (eds.), *The European Union: Annual Review 2000/2001* (Oxford: Blackwell).

Guiraudon, V. (2000), 'European Integration and Migration Policy: Vertical Policy-Making as Venue Shopping', *Journal of Common Market Studies*, 38/2: 251–71.

Kostakopoulou, T. (2000), 'The "Protective Union": Change and Continuity in Migration Law and Policy in Post-Amsterdam Europe', *Journal of Common Market Studies*, 38/3: 497–518.

Lavenex, S. (2001*a*) 'Migration and the EU's New Eastern Border: Between Realism and Liberalism', *Journal of European Public Policy*, 8/1: 24–42.

—— (2001*b*), 'The Europeanisation of Refugee Policy: Normative Challenges and Institutional Legacies', *Journal of Common Market Studies*, 39/5: forthcoming.

Monar, J. (2001), 'The Dynamics of Justice
and Home Affairs: Laboratories, Driving
Factors and Costs', *Journal of Common
Market Studies*, 39/4: 747–64.

Peers, S. (2000), *EU Justice and Home Affairs*,
(Harlow: Longman).

Web links

The best places to start to look for web-based information on JHA policy are the site of Directorate-General H of the Council (**www.europa.eu.int/comm/dgs/ justice_home/index_en.htm**) and that of the Commission's DG Justice and Home Affairs (**www.europa.eu.int/comm/dgs/ justice_home/index_en.htm**). The EP's Committee on Citizens' Freedoms and Rights, Justice and Home Affairs has its own web site: **www.europarl.eu.int/ committees/libe_home.htm**. For information on Europol, go to **www.europol.eu.int**.

Chapter 10

Making the CFSP Work

Knud Erik Jørgensen

Contents

Summary

This chapter portrays the Common Foreign and Security Policy (CFSP) as both an institution and a policy. First, the origins of the CFSP are explored. This section makes clear the dynamics of legal, organizational, normative, and policy institutionalization, and highlights patterns of continuity and change between the CFSP and its forerunner, European Political Cooperation (EPC). Second, the chapter describes the institutional structure of the CFSP as it fits into the larger system of EU governance. The institutions of the CFSP are shown to be politically contested: far from reflecting any master plan, they are the result of political compromises, incremental changes, and processes of collective identity formation. Third, the powers of the CFSP are examined, particularly the differences between formal and informal powers. Finally, leading theories of European integration are 'mined' for explanations of the CFSP's evolution, and three scenarios of future CFSP development are presented.

Introduction

David Owen's (1996) book, *Balkan Odyssey*, gives one of the most vivid and illuminating accounts of the CFSP at work. Owen describes his experiences as an EU mediator during the Bosnian war, explaining how the EU got involved in the conflict, how his work was undermined by the United States and other actors, and why the EU opted for a policy that did not result in a peaceful resolution of the conflict. In fact, Bosnia became one the worst policy failures in the history of the EU. The Bosnian case painfully illustrated the (limited) powers and policy instruments of the CFSP. Moreover, it demonstrated how the wider institutional environment influences choices made by member states concerning whether—or not—to conduct foreign policy by means of the CFSP. Thus organizations like the United Nations (UN), Nato (the North Atlantic Treaty Organization) and the Organization for Security and Cooperation in Europe (OSCE) all played a role, sometimes working at cross-purposes and occasionally acting contrary to EU efforts to take a lead in crisis management. Finally, though a tragic imbroglio, the Bosnian case prompted a learning process for European foreign policy-makers, changing their mentalities, preferences, and policies concerning international crisis management.

Unfortunately, insider accounts like those of Owen's are rare. Nevertheless, several studies by 'outsider' analysts provide excellent insights into the CFSP at work as a *policy* (Smith 1995; Torreblanca 2000; Smith 1999, Ginsberg 2001), or describe the *legal-institutional* evolution of the CFSP (Wessel 1999). The emergence of these two approaches reflects the fact that the acronym CFSP, ambiguously, designates two different things: a set of institutions and a policy. Thus the CFSP is the product of specific kinds of European institutions, established by the (Maastricht) Treaty on European Union. As such the CFSP is a favourite hunting ground for analysts who have a strong preference for understanding the legal-institutional dimension (and sometimes reducing the CFSP to that very dimension). Yet, the CFSP is far more than an institutional machinery: it also has an output dimension. Policy-making processes within the CFSP institutions produce policy or, rather, a range of policies. Political ideas and interests are translated into political action, specifying political goals and means to reach them. While this chapter approaches the CFSP as both a set of institutions *and* a set of policies, it is written mostly from an institutionalist perspective. In line both with recent neoinstitutionalist and constructivist scholarship on the EU, it embraces a broad definition of institutions, which extends beyond formal organizations to include rules, norms, and practices.[1] Its central argument is that the CFSP is very much a work in progress, whose failures thus far have been rooted partly—but only partly—in its institutional weakness. The obvious difficulties of creating a truly common foreign policy by 'Brusselizing' national foreign policy institutions have proved a formidable barrier to progress. There are signs that the CFSP is beginning to mature institutionally, but the idea that foreign policy remains a national prerogative, which touches directly upon national sovereignty, remains a very powerfully entrenched norm in Europe.

The origins of the CFSP

The CFSP was formally established by the (Maastricht) treaty on European Union, which came into force in November 1993. Since then the Treaty provisions have been amended at Amsterdam and in Nice. No single master variable can explain the emergence of the CFSP. It is more fruitful to regard the CFSP as the outcome of a historical process in which actors, institutions, and developments in the international and European system have mingled in often unpredictable ways. To understand why the CFSP exists, and takes the peculiar institutional form that it does, it is therefore useful first to look back at its forerunner.

European Political Cooperation

The precursor to the CFSP was European Political Cooperation (EPC), which existed from 1970 to 1993, and was far less institutionalized than its successor. During its first fifteen years of existence, EPC was based on informal international agreements—the Luxembourg (1970), Copenhagen (1973), and London (1981) Reports. In 1986, the European Council adopted the Single European Act and thereby gave the EPC a treaty base. Voting procedures continued to be very simple: decisions were taken unanimously, a procedure known historically to be among the best means to avoid both dynamism and efficiency.

EPC was also less institutionalized in terms of organization. It existed parallel to the Council of Ministers and the Council Secretariat-General, meaning that when foreign ministers met to discuss foreign affairs, it was not in the General Affairs Council (GAC) but in a separate forum. During its first years, foreign ministers even met at different places depending on whether it was convening as the GAC or in the context of EPC. In one famous instance, foreign ministers met in Copenhagen in the morning to discuss EPC business, then flew to Brussels to reconvene as the GAC on the afternoon of the same day (see Allen 1998: 53).

EPC ministerials were not prepared by the permanent representatives (Coreper) but by national foreign ministries' political directors, or very senior officials for political affairs, meeting as the Political Committee (PoCo). EPC expert working groups were separate from the expert working groups within the Council Secretariat-General which managed external relations. The EPC Secretariat functioned outside the Council Secretariat, on a rotation basis and staffed with officials from national foreign ministries. The institution responsible for initiatives, chairing meetings, and implementing decisions was the presidency, rotating between member states. Apart from the tiny EPC Secretariat, no permanent organizational structures existed to facilitate policy-making. Indeed the prime aim of EPC was consultation and coordination of national foreign policies rather than common European policy-making.

In so far as the EPC was institutionalized, it was definitely not at the level of European institutions but rather as a very decentralized, yet increasingly integrated system of national foreign ministries. It featured a high density of interaction, not least through the secure telex network, Coreu. Still today, examination of the CFSP reveals that foreign ministries are permanent, institutional structures, embedded in long-established practices. They remain the cornerstones of the emerging European foreign policy-making system.

Similarly, the institutionalization of EPC was mostly in terms of establishing norms and rules, so-called soft law, for ever closer consultation and coordination. It fostered an ethos of 'if not sharing then understanding' the foreign policy horizons of national representatives. Norms were established on the appropriate behaviour of member state governments holding the presidency, the need for consultation to precede individual foreign policy initiatives, and generally on the desirability of European solidarity whenever it was possible. Ways of thinking about foreign policy gradually changed from individual to collective intentionality; that is, from a predominantly 'I intend' mode to a more 'we intend' mode. With new ways of thinking, foreign policy practices changed, a phenomenon reflected in numerous book and article titles on the transformation of European foreign policy. Early accounts of EPC pointed to processes of socialization, the creation of habits, and the development of an *esprit de corps* among key decision-makers. The result was what was termed a consultation reflex, leading eventually and gradually to the 'Europeanization' or 'Brusselization' of national foreign policies (de Schoutheete 1986; Nuttall 1992, 2000; Jørgensen 1997a; Allen 1998).

Norms, however, are double-edged. They do not lead automatically to a common European policy. It took more than two decades before the EPC really began to touch upon, even challenge or threaten, well-established norms and rules embedded in national foreign policy establishments and practices. At this point, it became clear that hegemonic forms of thinking about foreign policy in Europe privileged national sovereignty, independent decision-making, the notion of *domaine reservé*, and, in essence, treated the EU as a foreign policy area among other areas, such as the Middle East or Asia.

While EPC in its formative years was very narrow in terms of areas covered—the OSCE (then called the 'Conference' on Security and Cooperation in Europe) and the Middle East were among the first—it gradually expanded and became a rather full house just before the change to CFSP. The scope of EPC became ever wider as it was deepened. At the beginning the emphasis was on rhetorical or symbolic politics. Gradually, more and more substance was injected into EPC policy-making, beginning with modest examples of sanctions politics and ending with policies of conditionality designed for Third World countries and eastern Europe. EPC eventually extended to programmes to promote reform in central and eastern Europe, and the development of a policy to cope with the breakup of Yugoslavia. A European mainstream position on an increasing number of foreign policy issues was developed to the point where it made sense to employ the term, *acquis politique*.

In summary, the institutionalization of EPC in both legal-formal and organizational terms was very modest. The creation of collective norms and rules became increasingly important, yet against a background of predominantly traditional forms of national foreign policy. William Wallace (1977) famously and rightly described the early phases of EPC as 'procedure as substitute for policy'. However, to properly understand the launch of the CFSP in the early 1990s, it is important to realize that the EPC was, inadvertently, a long-term exercise in *institutionalizing*, in a highly incremental (and slow) fashion, collective foreign policy-making in both a legal, organizational, and sociological sense. Almost every instance of formal agreement was practice-driven; that is, legal institutionalization (codification) was preceded by norm-governed practices, with organizational institutionalization often a response to practical problems rather than the outcome of any grand design.

From EPC to CFSP

The move from EPC to CFSP under the Maastricht Treaty was characterized by both continuity and change. In terms of organization, major changes were introduced. Among the most important was the elimination of the essentially parallel structure of EPC and the embedding of the CFSP within a 'single institutional framework'. The EPC Secretariat was merged into the Council Secretariat-General and at the political level, foreign ministers now met in the General Affairs Council (GAC) only. Meetings in the General Affairs Council were prepared by Coreper, albeit with input (and plenty of turf-battling) from PoCo. In short, common European foreign policy-making became part of the wider EU institutional structure rather than being developed in splendid isolation.

In terms of norms and rules, foreign ministers probably did not feel revolutionary changes in moving from an EPC to a CFSP mode. However, at the administrative level, big changes were felt and occasionally caused tensions. Well-established practices and perspectives—Coreper working in Brussels and political directors working mainly in national capitals—predictably caused problems. Similarly, the Council Secretariat takeover of the EPC Secretariat brought clashes between different administrative cultures. Well-established EPC norms and rules were losing some of their rationale or being profoundly shaken.

Finally, the policy dimension was clearly upgraded. For the first time ever, the explicit aim was to develop a common European foreign policy. Thus, the CFSP not only was given a new institutional structure but also aimed to become a comprehensive policy. Certainly it was possible to build on experiences gained under the EPC regime and developed during the previous two decades. But launching the CFSP was not just about continuity, and decision-makers clearly felt it necessary to go beyond the very significant limits of EPC. The fact that designers of the Treaty on European Union included, at least hypothetically, the introduction of defence matters is one example. At the same time, different EU external policy modes were reconciled with one another or brought closer together, partly through an upgrade of the role of the European Commission's role in CFSP matters, and partly through an upgrade of the Council's role in Communitarian matters like trade policy, development aid, and policies of reform assistance.

The wider international environment

The international environment has always shaped the development of the EC/EU. From the signing of the Treaty of Rome in 1957 until just before the Maastricht Treaty was negotiated, the EU confronted at its eastern boundary the communist bloc in eastern Europe and the Soviet Union. Indeed, this confrontation was part of the rationale for creating the EC. In western Europe, the EC had to face counter-projects like the British-inspired European Free Trade Association (EFTA), built around the promotion of free trade of selected goods and not much more (see Curzon 1974). Meanwhile, in southern Europe, Spain, Portugal, and Greece were ruled by authoritarian regimes. Finally, across the Atlantic, the USA—*primus inter pares* of the transatlantic community and Nato—preferred low-key European foreign policies that were obediently supportive of US objectives. Following the traumatic collapse of the European Defence Community initiative in 1954 (see Piening 1997: 32), the Americans were consistently opposed to independent, common European military experiments.

Surrounded by three counter-projects in Europe, a hegemonic leader of the 'West' and with failed political projects of its own, it is hardly surprising that the EC was politically introverted. With the enormous political will of the French President, Charles de Gaulle, directed against supranational modes of European integration, EC 'domestic affairs' proved sufficiently troublesome to distract attention from any serious experimentation with a common European foreign policy. The fall of de Gaulle, the new West German foreign policy—*Ostpolitik*[2]—and a rough nuclear parity between the superpowers were required to prompt the EPC experiment, and put the EU on the long and winding road of mounting a 'common' foreign policy.

The establishment of the CFSP took place against the background of a distinct and very unusual phase of international affairs. The fall of the Berlin Wall symbolized the end of bipolarity, including the military-political division of Europe. Furthermore, the EU's foreign policy establishment concluded that Europe's contribution to the Gulf war was little short of embarrassing. Finally, with the collapse of the German Democratic Republic, Yugoslavia, Czechoslovakia, and the Soviet Union, the EC experienced high-level instability at its boundaries and was forced to develop policies that sought to promote geopolitical stability. Decision-makers realized that 'hot' policy-making was required instead of just EPC-style declaratory diplomacy (Guehenno 1992). In other words, given the new context, policy-makers realized that the EPC was fatally insufficient, too slow and short on impact.

Institutionally, it was most unhelpful to have the EPC outside the proper European institutions, particularly when reform-promoting policies towards central and eastern Europe—with their distinct blend of economic and political instruments—were catapulted into high-priority status on the European agenda. Furthermore, the emergence of 'hot' crises in the heart of Europe led, step by step, to the conclusion that purely civilian means were inadequate for crisis management and that the disposal of military means was a precondition for any successful involvement in coercive diplomacy. The question became: how to go beyond civilian means and apply military force? While the USA temporarily solved the problem by once again accepting the burden of leadership (especially in the Gulf war), European decision-makers used the Western European Union (WEU), the exclusively European defence alliance which had lain mostly dormant and in Nato's shadow (see Deighton 1997), as a laboratory for what could, perhaps, eventually become a European defence policy. Provisions concerning crisis management, the so-called Petersberg[3] tasks (humanitarian and rescue tasks, peacekeeping tasks, and combat-force tasks in crisis management, including peacemaking), were introduced in the Treaty of Amsterdam on European Union. Yet, it proved politically impossible for the EU to agree to take over the WEU and incorporate it into the Union itself. Only a subsequent consensus among the larger member state governments—particularly after the experience of the Balkans— paved the way for the launch of what was billed as a 'European Security and Defence Policy' (ESDP), including the merger of the WEU with the European Union in 2001.

The structure of the CFSP

Paradoxically, the institutional structure of the CFSP is at the same time very centralized and very decentralized. It is centralized in the sense that most policy-making is carried out within the Council, including its various agencies, and decentralized in the sense that member state governments play a crucial role. This section describes the key elements of this peculiar construction, how they have evolved over the years and, finally, how the CFSP fits into the larger EU system but also into the web of international institutions.

How do the parts of the CFSP fit together?

Formally, CFSP is handled in an intergovernmental mode, implying that member states are more directly involved than in any policy area handled in a Communitarian mode of governance. Thus member states—or more precisely the foreign ministries of member states—are directly involved in making the CFSP work. Each member state has the right to influence each phase during the policy life cycle: agenda-setting, policy-making, decision-making, and implementation. By signing the (Maastricht) Treaty on European Union, each member state became legally committed to 'give active and unconditional support to the implementation' of the common policy; to 'ensure that their national policies conform to the common positions'; and to 'undertake to uphold the joint actions' (see Exhibit 10.1) launched by the EU as a whole.

These provisions signify above all political commitments even if they have been given a legal form. A crucial precondition for any CFSP that the rest of the world views as truly alive and 'kicking' is therefore that member states comply with these commitments.

In some respects, the CFSP remains not a lot more than the member states that constitute it. National political representatives make up the European Council and the Council of Ministers, just as member states' senior officials constitute key institutions like Coreper and the Political Committee. The epicentre of CFSP decision-making is indisputably the General Affairs Council (GAC), chaired by the (rotating) presidency. Decision-making is prepared by the Council Secretariat-General, together with Coreper, the Political Committee, and expert working groups of national officials. From these key institutions links radiate to other European institutions.

However, CFSP policy-making is not purely intergovernmental: not only member state governments and the Council machinery are active. Since the Maastricht Treaty came into force, the European Commission has been 'fully associated' with CFSP policy-making, not only formally but also in practice. Moreover, the Treaty of

---

Exhibit 10.1 CFSP common positions and joint actions

These Euro-speak terms refer to legally binding instruments introduced in the Maastricht Treaty. They specify decision-making procedures, allowing in some cases—usually following a unanimous vote on the Council—for qualified majority voting.

More than 100 *common positions* have been adopted since the Maastricht Treaty was ratified. A major share of the first wave of common positions concerned the western Balkans but they have since been applied more widely. For example, in June 2000 a common position was adopted concerning EU support of the peace process between Ethiopia and Eritrea sponsored by the Organization of African Unity (OAU). Generally, common positions are declaratory statements—saying something as opposed to doing something—directed towards the areas of the world where Europe has 'special interests'. Nevertheless, when the Council adopts common positions, member states are formally more committed to the Euro-level policy and, hence, more constrained in national policy-making, than they ever were under EPC.

Joint actions are operational actions with financial means. Since 1993, the Council has adopted more than 100 joint actions. An example is the joint action of April 2000 on the European Union assistance programme to support the Palestinian Authority in its efforts to counter terrorist activities emanating from the territories under its control.

Amsterdam introduced a number of institutional innovations, the full effects of which will not be clear for years but which do give the CFSP more ballast in Brussels. The CFSP was given its own source of policy advice, in the form of a Policy Planning and Early Warning Unit, which offers EU policy-makers an alternative source of advice to the analyses of national foreign ministries. The rotating Council presidency retains the responsibility for CFSP affairs but it is now assisted by the Secretary-General of the Council, who was designated at Amsterdam as the 'High Representative for the CFSP', as well as by the European Commission. Together, the Council presidency, High Representative, and Commissioner for External Affairs form a 'troika' which represents the EU as a whole in international diplomacy. Thus during the 2000 French presidency, this troika was made up of the French Minister for Foreign Affairs, Hubert Vedrine, the High Representative, Javier Solana, and the Commissioner for External Relations, Chris Patten.

Contested development

The CFSP has developed incrementally and has essentially been practice-driven. It has also been politically contested, as its development since 1993 shows. The Maastricht Treaty introduced new policy instruments and member states committed themselves to a common policy more than ever before. Many of the preconditions for a more ambitious European role in foreign affairs were put in place. Yet, many of the new instruments had birthmarks from the political compromises that had created them. For example, the inability of member governments to agree on the means for financing the CFSP at Maastricht meant that each joint action had to be funded on a case-by-case basis, leading to endless wrangling over the balance between the Community budget and national contributions, and which member state would pay how much, in paying for relatively small humanitarian actions in the Balkans.

The adoption of the Treaty of Amsterdam did not have a revolutionary impact on the development of the CFSP, primarily because major contested issues proved impossible to solve. Minor changes were introduced, such as delegating legal competence to Coreper to respond urgently to acute international crises. The new Council unit for Policy Planning and Early Warning was also established, although its design and size remained contested. Some (smaller) member states preferred a unit sufficiently large to allow for staff from all member states, while other (larger) member states pleaded for a relatively small unit. The result was a unit of origin-ally around thirty (now over 100) members staffed by personnel (mostly) from the member states, but also including officials from the Council Secretariat, the Euro-pean Commission, and the Western European Union, the latter until its activities were terminated as a result of the EU/WEU merger.

After 1998, some of the most contested features of the CFSP, including the development of an ESDP, the merger of the EU and WEU, and the creation of operational European military forces suddenly became feasible. An insightful observer, Nicole Gnesotto (2000), argues that the fact 'that all countries of the Union ... now subscribe to the political and operational aims set out at Cologne and Helsinki', at which the so-called 'headline goals' for creating a military Rapid Reaction Force were agreed, constitutes 'a major political revolution'. However, it remains to be seen whether the political goal of being able to deploy, by 2003, a Rapid Reaction Force of 60,000 troops within sixty days and sustain it for at least one year can be met.

A European State Department in the making?

Is it naïve to think that the High Representative and the Council institutional structures are, respectively, a nascent European foreign minister and a European Foreign Ministry? From one perspective, the appointment of a Secretary-General for CFSP only implies that the EU has accomplished what in Nato has been daily practice for decades. Yet nobody ever expected the Secretary-General of Nato to become a transatlantic foreign minister or the Nato Secretariat in Brussels to become a transatlantic foreign ministry. In other words, the EU is merely catching up. Furthermore, the CFSP Directorate-General of the Council Secretariat-General

(DG E) is a tiny structure that is hard to view as a foreign ministry about to be born. The arrival of an even smaller unit for policy planning does not really undermine this argument. In any case, if something like a European foreign ministry is ever to appear, it is more likely to emerge within the European Commission, an institution that already has the task of handling crucial aspects of European foreign policy and running a very large network of delegations (embassies) in foreign capitals.

Another perspective would view the choice of Javier Solana as what the media now routinely calls 'the EU's foreign policy chief' as proof that all the talk about appointing a political heavyweight to the post of High Representative for the CFSP was serious. Moreover, the dynamism of the CFSP after his appointment was simply unparalleled in the entire history of European foreign policy, suggesting that something truly novel was under way. A historical example may be helpful to put contemporary developments into perspective. What has historically happened to diplomatic services when nations have been unified? Adam Watson (1982: 147) speculates that '[a]mbassadors within the European Community could become like the envoys of German princes to each other after 1871; symbols of sovereignty and part of the dignified rather than the efficient side of "international" life'.

How does the CFSP fit into the EU system?

Just as the CFSP—as a set of institutions—has become the epicentre of policy-making, the CFSP—as a policy—has become the *primus inter pares* of EU foreign policies. Thus, when sanctions *vis-à-vis* a third country are introduced or cancelled, they are considered a means to support wider political ends; equally so when a policy of conditionality is applied, or when the freezing of funds or a ban on flights is decided. Many of these measures cannot be implemented by the CFSP itself but require the involvement of other institutions, most often the European Commission, for instance when decisions call for instruments outside the direct reach of CFSP decision-making to be used.

The CFSP is clearly 'at home' in the Council and has well-established organizational links with most other EU institutions. Thus key aspects of the CFSP have been integrated into the work of the European Council, which is the highest decision-making body of the EU. The European Council decides on the principles and general guidelines and adopts common strategies, implying that both Communitarian and intergovernmental instruments of foreign policy are subsumed within a single strategy (see Exhibit 10.2). CFSP joint actions, common positions, and other decisions derived from a common strategy are adopted by qualified majority. Depending on how widespread common strategies become, this is

Exhibit 10.2 CFSP common strategies

The 'common strategy' is one of the new foreign policy instruments introduced by the Treaty of Amsterdam. Common strategies are adopted unanimously by the European Council 'in areas where member states have major common interests'. They are at the top of the hierarchy of instruments in the sense that, once the European Council has adopted a common strategy, the Council can adopt decisions, common actions, or common positions by means of qualified majority voting. By mid-2001, three common strategies had been adopted by the European Council, all covering areas in the EU's 'near abroad':

- Russia
- Ukraine
- The Mediterranean—with a special emphasis on the so-called Barcelona process (see Gomez 1998).

The western Balkans has been contemplated as the target of a fourth common strategy.

The EU's experience so far with common strategies has been mixed. What in principle looks like a good idea and an instance of strategic thinking in the EU, seems in practice to be a rather difficult exercise. In 2001, the EU's High Representative for the CFSP, Javier Solana, voiced harsh criticism of the politics of adopting common strategies in a leaked report.[a] High-profile areas in which the EU has a certain *acquis politique* have been chosen instead of less ambitious and 'under-developed' policy areas. Furthermore, Solana criticized the member states' practice of regarding a common strategy as a Christmas tree on which they could hang all sorts of 'national interest glitter', resulting in something less than a strategy. In summary, Solana prefers less comprehensive and narrowly defined common strategies with verifiable objectives, and not just broad statements of intent for public consumption.

[a] See reports in *Financial Times* and *Le Monde*, 23 Jan. 2001.

potentially a very significant development. Finally, the European Council is responsible for the EU's takeover of the WEU.

The European Commission has developed into a key partner in CFSP policy-making. Being 'fully associated' with the CFSP means that the Commission has a right of initiative but not the exclusive right it enjoys in the first pillar. The Commission participates at all levels, from the European Council to the Council, and at various administrative levels. While the Commission's approach to the development of a common European foreign policy has been both defensive and offensive, depending on the political climate, a working relationship seems to have been established for day-to-day policy-making.

At the same time, the future design of the Euro-polity remains politically contested (see Exhibit 10.3). On the one hand, the President of the Commission, Romano Prodi (2000) has proposed to integrate the function of the High

Exhibit 10.3 'Towards a common European foreign policy: how are we doing?'

This exhibit reproduces text from a particularly thoughtful speech delivered by Chris Patten, Commissioner for External Affairs at the Winston Churchill Memorial Lecture in Luxembourg on 10 October 2000.

'But what do we actually want to achieve as a European Union? I suggest two key goals:

'First, to manage more effectively our relationships with our nearest neighbours. The Member States' ability to do that effectively is plainly less than that of the EU acting as a whole, deploying to the full extent the full range of policies over which the Community has competence, from trade to external assistance, from environmental cooperation to competition policy, as well as some aspects of justice and home affairs. Our aim: the projection of stability . . .

'Second, we should try to bring our experience of multilateral co-operation to a wider stage. The EU has been a tremendous force for stability and prosperity on this continent. It has reconciled long-standing enemies and helped make further wars between them unthinkable.

'Europe had a mixed record in the last century; our continent spawned two world wars and the Holocaust. But we also showed a happier face to the world, becoming a powerful example of how intractable problems can be overcome by nation states working together, given the political will and the right framework.

'Our first priority must be to help to ensure that Europe has a strong economy capable of upholding a strong foreign policy. As Ernie Bevin, the first postwar British Foreign Secretary said: "Give me the coal, and I'll give you the policy".

'So we must promote a competitive European economy. The Commission's external trade policy is a central component of European foreign policy. The EU must contribute to open, rule-based international trade. We should champion globalisation, which I strongly believe to be a force for good, not only because of the economic benefits of trade that it can bring to the poorest countries, but because it promotes open societies and liberal ideas. But we must also address the risk of polarisation between the connected and the isolated. Liberal trade and advanced technology are making people better off but not everywhere and not in every country.'

Representative into the Commission. On the other, the external Commissioner, Chris Patten, emphasizes that 'the Commission has . . . an important role to play not, let me stress, carving out new responsibilities for itself, but exercising those it has already, in the service of CFSP'. The prime reason for the Commission's key role is that it handles some of the crucial aspects of common European foreign policy. In Patten's words, 'The Commission . . . bears responsibility for some of the most valuable tools for implementing any European foreign policy. Those include external trade questions, including sanctions, for example; responsibility for European external assistance (worth some €12 billion [in 1999]); or for many of the external aspects of Justice and Home Affairs' (Patten 2000).

The European Parliament (EP) is also involved in the CFSP, but to a rather limited degree. It has never played a key role in European foreign policy in the sense of being a decision-making body, or in preparing the general guidelines for the CFSP. Instead, it has had to settle for being kept informed or at best consulted in foreign affairs. The European Parliament does, by means of the assent procedure, enjoy direct participation in foreign policy areas beyond the narrowly conceived CFSP that are handled in the first pillar: notably certain categories of international agreement (Article 300 TEC) as well as accession treaties (Article 49 TEU). From time to time, the European Parliament has tried to make full use of its rather limited scope for influencing the development of EU foreign policy. For example, it has wielded its budgetary powers, not so much to try to shape the CFSP, but rather to exert pressure on the Commission to reform the operation of its external delegations.

Clearly, the CFSP does not comprise everything that could be called 'foreign policy' or even 'EU foreign policy', which includes trade policy, development aid policy, and—most recently—European security and defence policy (ESDP). With the establishment of ESDP, the CFSP is being equipped with a dimension that for decades had been totally unthinkable (see Exhibit 10.4). The arrival of ESDP means military staff working in the Council Secretariat, meetings of the chiefs of military staff and of defence ministers, with issues being discussed including the creation of a European expeditionary corps and military capabilities.

A final yet crucial point to make is that the CFSP is not only compatible with the larger EU system, but also with organizations outside the EU. In particular, the development of ESDP has implied significant changes in the relationship between the EU and Nato. Joint meetings are now organized, information shared, and Nato officers in military attire can be spotted in the Council building. An encounter between different organizational cultures is taking place and new norms concerning the classification of sensitive military documents, and the rules of access applying to them, are having to be introduced in the Council Secretariat. Clashes have been inevitable, with the European Parliament in particular accusing the Council of obsessive secrecy. Yet, it mattered that Javier Solana had been both Nato Secretary-General (1995–9) and foreign minister of Spain (and thus a key player within the CFSP from 1993–5), and hence was eminently well suited to introduce a military dimension to the 'civilian' EU.

Exhibit 10.4 Creating the ESDP

In 2000 Javier Solana (Solana 2000b), the High Representative for the Common Foreign and Security Policy, insisted that 'A more effective foreign and security policy begins with the political will to use all the available existing instruments in a more co-ordinated and coherent way . . . until now we have been unable to add military means to the measures available. This is now changing.'

The change was gradual, as the first steps towards creating the ESDP were taken as early as 1998 (interestingly, under the presidency of Austria, which remained neutral and outside Nato). But the change was dramatically reflected in the Treaty of Nice. Mostly at Dutch insistence (see Ludlow 2001: 21), Nice paved the way for the incorporation of the WEU into the Union by drastically downgrading the status of the former (Article 17 TEU). The Treaty of Nice also transformed PoCo into a Political and Security Committee and gave it an explicit role in crisis management (Article 25 TEU).

The government of Ireland (another neutral, non-Nato member) feared—with good reason, as it turned out—that the ESDP provisions of Nice would make it more difficult to win the Irish referendum needed to ratify the Treaty. The Irish accepted the changes at Nice because they did little more than codify what already had been agreed elsewhere. The staunchly pro-ESDP French presidency, wishing to take no chances, argued successfully for a political declaration, attached to Article 25 TEU, which explicitly recognized the need for the ESDP 'to become operational quickly' and designated the Laeken European Council of December 2001 as the latest it should happen. The upshot was that the momentum to create the ESDP was by this point so unstoppable that there was not even any need for the Treaty of Nice to be ratified before its launch.

Powers of the CFSP

The formal powers of the CFSP are established by the Treaty on European Union, as well as certain declarations or protocols annexed to the Treaty. These formal powers regulate aspects of policy-making, including agenda-setting, decision-making, and implementation. Until the adoption of the Treaty of Amsterdam, member states enjoyed an exclusive right of agenda-setting, whereas now they share this right with the European Commission. This distinct phase of policy-making is less distinct in terms of who is actually influencing policy-making. For decades, the Commission has been formally 'associated' with the work carried out in the field of foreign policy. Whether or not the Commission has decided to deploy its informal powers has depended on such factors as the 'political climate' and the clout or interests of the persons serving as President of the Commission or as Commissioner for External Relations. Formal powers have evolved in an incremental fashion. Most of the time they have been predominantly Franco-German driven, meaning that French-German partnership has provided the leadership necessary for codifying already existing practices or providing visions for the future.

Foreign policy touches the core of national sovereignty. As such, the powers of member states and the intergovernmental dimension of the European Union have been privileged in the field of CFSP. By contrast, the powers of the European Commission, European Parliament, and the European Court of Justice have deliberately been limited, resulting in a very asymmetrical institutional balance of power. To the degree the Commission has a role in CFSP, it is primarily because it has been assigned a treaty-based and powerful role in the conduct of the Union's external economic relations and development policies—important aspects of any common European foreign policy. When it comes to informal powers, the Commission's room for manœuvre is considerably larger. Drawing on its unique technical knowledge of some areas, the Commission can yield more influence on decision-making than its formal powers would suggest. These informal powers may even be strengthened in the future. However, in the foreseeable future such a development is constrained by the administrative culture of the Commission, which has focused for years predominantly on the EU's domestic scene, and when focused on foreign policy then almost exclusively on the first pillar. Recently, the Commission started to expand its expertise, for instance by hiring experts on security and defence. To the degree that the European Parliament plays a role, it is either because the Treaty assigns it such a role or acts in the hope—perhaps a vain one—that the EP can provide the CFSP with a degree of democratic legitimacy. The ECJ has been kept away from the CFSP, demonstrating that if legal norms and rules are at play in regulating the CFSP, they are not the law rules of the EC but rather part of international law.

Do we have a problem of accountability?

This issue is hotly contested, in part because the question—to whom is the CFSP accountable?—is so delicate. In order to address the issue, it is necessary first to investigate the cornerstones on which it is constructed; that is, before providing answers or jumping to conclusions let us try to make sense of the question. The issue is clearly more complex than it appears to be, touching upon issues like transparency and legitimacy. Can decision-makers be held accountable if there is no transparency? Is it desirable that all aspects of decision-making be transparent? In national polities, designers of constitutions have solved this problem by creating institutions for confidential consultation or deliberation. Furthermore, constitutions often specify that the conduct of foreign policy is the government's prerogative. Yet similar solutions have not been introduced at the European level. Confidential institutions have not been created and because there is 'governance without government', no EU government can have the CFSP as its own prerogative.

One school argues that accountability is far too limited, and that solutions to the problem are urgently needed. According to this view, the Council and the Council Secretariat, being the 'home' of the CFSP, are far from being the most transparent or accountable institutions among EU institutions. As the European Commission fares only slightly better, the predictable solution is to propose an increased role for the European Parliament. Confronted with this solution, some argue that the EP has demonstrated its lack of skill in foreign affairs, frequently promulgating moral principles or absolutes which are divorced from political reality.[4] Others respond that as soon as the European Parliament is delegated more power, it automatically will become more responsible and competent in its dealings with foreign affairs.

A second school denies that accountability constitutes a problem. It claims that the CFSP apparatus is clearly accountable to member states. Furthermore, members of working groups, Coreper and PoCo are formally accountable to their administrative or political bosses in European institutions or in national foreign ministries. Thus, officials in the Council Secretariat are accountable to heads of Directorates-General who again are accountable to their ministers. Thus, according to this school of thought decision-making in the field of common European foreign policy is characterized by a surprisingly high degree of accountability.

Problems of the CFSP

The CFSP's alleged problems are often deeply embedded in institutional power politics. Thus, representatives of the European Commission or EP tend to magnify problems, while representatives of the Council Secretariat or member state governments tend to downplay them (see Burghardt 1993). Promoters of a Communitarian common foreign policy are eager to point out that the problems of the CFSP are rooted in its intergovernmental character, leading them quite predictably to propose solutions implying a more influential role for the Commission. Yet, for the independent analyst, it seems to be futile always to search for institutional solutions to problems that may have other sources. Thus, while there is no lack of analyses pointing out various problems of the CFSP, there is a considerable lack of studies investigating possible sources of the problem and pointing out potential solutions.

The distinction between the CFSP as an institution and as a policy shows its worth in the following illustrative examples. In terms of organization, an outsider may wonder if using three different decision-making modes—that is, common strategies, common positions, and joint actions—including three major European institutions and the foreign ministries of currently fifteen member states (to be joined by fifteen ministries of defence) really is the optimal organization for the making of a common European foreign policy. Perhaps for good reason, the former President of the European Commission, Jacques Delors, characterized the Maastricht Treaty as 'organized schizophrenia' and the CFSP as a 'Maserati with the engine of a lawn mower'. The preferred decision-making modes make it difficult in the first place to reach consensus—make policies—and once made, policies tend to be preserved beyond their time, precisely because consensus was so difficult to reach. In other words, modes of decision-making tend to make the EU a relatively slow decision-maker, hardly capable of tactical moves or swift policy reviews. From this perspective, the EU is not eminently well prepared to engage in international crisis management.

Moreover, the CFSP is perfectly capable of suffering from all the problems that are endemic to public policy more generally. Thus there may be problems of inertia—compare CFSP policy-making concerning the Palestinian-Israeli conflict or the EU's development aid policy with the common agricultural policy or the common fisheries policy. Furthermore, CFSP policy-making may suffer from bad judgements concerning likely cause and effect, for instance by threatening a disintegrating Yugoslavia with economic sanctions or promising future financial support, only to find that the conflicting parties already had too many stakes in their conflict to find the threats really threatening or the carrots of any interest. In short, the failures of the CFSP are often better explained by factors associated with the policy in question, rather than the institutional setting in which the CFSP is made.

Theorizing the evolution of the CFSP

Theorizing about the CFSP is not easy. Most leading theories of European integration aim to explain integration generally, and are therefore not particularly well suited to explain a specific and distinct instance of integration such as the CFSP. Explaining the making of specific policies within the CFSP 'umbrella' requires theories or approaches developed with that purpose in mind, for instance public policy analysis or theories of foreign policy-making. However, neither foreign policy nor defence policy are generally considered part of the portfolio of European public policies, which includes well-known domestic policies such as agriculture, environment, or competition policy but not 'un-civilian' foreign or defence policies. As a consequence, analysts interested in applying theories of European public policy-making have a hard time finding illustrative examples. That said, great potential exists in applying, for instance, the analytical framework developed by Adrienne Héritier (1999), which aims to explain how the EU 'escapes from deadlock', particularly because deadlock has significantly characterized CFSP policy-making.

When we turn to theories of foreign policy, we face the problem of either neglecting or overemphasizing national foreign policies. Most theories have been developed in order to explain national foreign policy and are thus ill-suited to explain the CFSP. In contrast most studies of the CFSP are either atheoretical or explain the CFSP without considering the crucial context of national foreign policies. Very few take both levels of policy-making into account (for a beginning, see White 2001).

Considering the CFSP as a set of institutions, it is worth recalling that institutions may be conceived as comprising dimensions like practices, norms, and rules; that is, more than organizational dynamics narrowly conceived. From such a starting-point, we find that three particularly urgent theoretical questions arise:

- Why did cooperation in the field of foreign policy change from an informal to a formal mode? Most authors agree that governments opt for informal agreements when they want to preserve maximum flexibility, while at the same time aiming to regulate future foreign relations. The move from informal to formal agreements is a means to change the balance between self-determined action and instances of European order (Lipson 1991; Kratochwil 1993).

- Why were further changes introduced, particularly in the Maastricht and Amsterdam Treaties? These changes seem to be explicable by factors such as institutional learning (Haas 1990), dynamics of Treaty reform (Moravcsik 1998a; Christiansen and Jørgensen 1999), external shocks, spill-over effects, and sequences of interaction, norm-creation, and codification, respectively.

- What has the impact of the CFSP been on national institutions and actors? Most studies investigating the relationship between national foreign policies and European foreign policy focus—for good reasons—on the flow of influence from member states to European policy-making (Hill 1983, 1995; Manners and Whitman 2001). Thinner on the ground—and increasingly urgently needed—are studies of the impact of the CFSP on national institutions, actors, and policies (exceptions include Tonra 1997; Soetendorp and Hanf 1998).

Conclusion: scenarios for the future

We conclude by sketching three different possible scenarios for the future development of the CFSP.

Scenario 1: enhanced status quo

Here we play it safe, noting that the development of the CFSP so far has been a peculiar blend of pragmatic and principled thinking and incremental change.

Dynamics of legal-institutional design have proved to be largely practice-driven. In terms of norms and rules, actors have traditionally kept a finely tuned balance between collective and national policy-making. Should we expect these dynamics to be significantly different in the future? The ESDP has been launched, informed observers report on progress towards stated goals, whereas other observers express significant scepticism as to whether or not the immense problems on the horizon will end up slowing down the process (see Howarth 2001). In contrast, policy-makers may get used to working with the policy planning unit, resulting in joint decision-making on a higher level than previously. Finally, policy-makers may begin actually to use the instruments available, and apply more widely common European policy instruments.

With the upcoming eastern enlargement—which seems 'always five years from now'—it is tempting to predict that for the foreseeable future the process of enlargement will have a rather limited impact on the development of the CFSP. Yet such an assessment would be slightly misleading, in part because the enlargement process already has an impact on the applicant states, all of which are trying as hard as they can to be in line with EU mainstream positions. Compared to the socio-economic and symbolic dimensions of membership, CFSP matters are of minor importance and are generally not allowed to disturb the negotiation process on enlargement. As such the present round of enlargement follows the pattern of previous enlargements in which, with the possible exception of Greece, foreign policy has been a non-issue. However, the logic of the telos of membership does not last for ever. Once in, the central European states with stakes in the first round of enlargement—Estonia, Poland, the Czech Republic, Hungary, and Slovenia—will predictably try to influence the *Ostpolitik* of the EU, and Hungary and Slovenia will additionally demonstrate a pronounced interest in the EU's policy on the Balkans. The CFSP, like international relations generally, will always be shaped by modern geopolitics.

Scenario 2: the EU becomes a truly international player

This scenario is based on the observation that a gradual process of slow change sometimes suddenly transforms into a dynamic process, a so-called 'system transformation' (Lindberg and Scheingold 1979). Perhaps the evolution of the European integration process has reached a phase when it will transform itself from being a primarily inward-looking 'domestic' process to make external relations a new high priority on its political agenda. After all, at the turn of the millennium the EU is 'running' countries (Bosnia, Kosovo, and Somalia), and planning a joint 60,000 troop expeditionary force. Furthermore, some of the key preconditions have been fulfilled, as the EU and member states in statistical terms constitute a global player, providing a major or significant part of world development aid, humanitarian assistance, or troops to UN peacekeeping operations. A remaining key issue is whether the EU and its members states are capable of transforming their combined economic clout into political power, enabling leadership. Joint initiatives between the external Commissioner, Chris Patten, and the High Representative, Javier Solana, concerning the Balkans may well indicate a new stage in inter-pillar coordination. Similarly, Patten's (2000) very frank analysis of the EPC and early years of CFSP combined with his ambitious plans for reforming the European Commission's involvement in external relations may indicate both a new level of consciousness about preconditions for elevating the EU and a new level of ambition. Finally, with a flash of humour, Solana has asked whether 'the EU's original DNA is being genetically modified'.

Scenario 3: institutional decay

Signs of potential institutional decay have always, like a shadow, followed the development of the CFSP. Thus policy-makers decided to include new instruments in the Maastricht Treaty, yet have been very reluctant actually to apply them. Similarly, the Commission became 'fully associated' yet has not really been encouraged to play such a role. While the UK and France embarked on collective policy-making *vis-à-vis* the breakup of Yugoslavia, they did not hesitate much, when they later deemed it necessary, to join the so-called Contact Group: an exclusive club of great powers (with the USA, Germany, and Russia—later to include Italy) which often acted to undermine the CFSP. In the context of the Treaty of Amsterdam, the decision to establish a unit for policy planning was accompanied by a comprehensive list of tasks for the new unit. Yet, the unit has been staffed in the spirit of minimalism, hardly indicating a serious interest in common policy planning among member states. The future may be no different or, precisely very different in the sense that decay may spread and become unstoppable. Note that institutional decay hardly ever shows at a formal level, indeed the formal wording of treaties may continue to emphasize strengthening and consistency, just as aspirations may continue to be expressed as bullet points in speeches. Yet implementation may become increasingly difficult; degrees of non-compliance may rise ever higher; and member states may begin to emphasize national interests more than European interests. Instances of minilateralism—such as the Contact Group—may not necessarily qualify as institutional decay. But still more examples of 'enhanced cooperation' groupings may indicate that commonality in European foreign policy is declining.

All three scenarios have their subscribers, indicating that the nature of the CFSP is and probably will remain deeply contested. Each scenario is based on a considerable amount of evidence and, crucially, the 'weighing' of evidence differs widely among analysts. The main argument of this chapter is that the CFSP—as an institution *and* a policy—has developed further than many are ready to accept. Nevertheless, national foreign policies of member states have not withered away, meaning that both these policies and the CFSP are best understood if seen as two sides of the same coin.

Notes

1 In particular, this chapter draws on theoretical elements from the historical and sociological schools of institutionalism. For excellent introductions, see Hall and Taylor (1996) and Peters (1999). Both schools have been applied in studies of the EU (see Armstrong and Bulmer 1998). Recent constructivist scholarship on European integration is collected in Christiansen *et al* (2001).

2 *Ostpolitik* was the West German government's policy of developing closer relations with its eastern neighbours, particularly the German Democratic Republic (East Germany), begun by Chancellor Willy Brandt during the 1970s. The policy put the Brandt government at odds with its American ally.

3 The Petersberg tasks were first defined at a WEU summit held in Petersberg, near Bonn in Germany, in June 1992.

4 The European Parliament has not been the only target of such criticism, yet the EP's strong emphasis on moral principles is likely to continue to produce mistrust among national foreign policy-makers, making them disinclined to upgrade the EP's role. Furthermore, national parliaments in many EU member states do not play a significant role in the field of foreign policy. For better or worse, it is to some degree a European tradition. Why not expect this tradition to be present at the European level of policy-making?

Further reading

CFSP practices tend to run ahead of analytical and theoretical reflection. Nevertheless, the literature on the CFSP is significant and covers most aspects. Broad insider perspectives can be found in Nuttall (2000), Cameron (1999), and Piening (1997). The relationship between the conduct of national and common European foreign policy is described in Hill (1996) and Manners and Whitman (2001). Both Allen (2000) and White (2001) discuss theoretical issues. The *European Foreign Affairs Review* is exclusively devoted to

publishing articles on the CFSP and related matters.

Allen, D. (1998), 'Who speaks for Europe?', in John Peterson and Helene Sjursen (eds.), *A Common Foreign Policy for Europe?* (London and New York: Routledge).

Cameron, F. (1999), *Foreign and Security Policy of the European Union* (Sheffield: Sheffield Academic Press).

Hill, C. (1996) (ed.), *The Actors in Europe's Foreign Policy* (London and New York: Routledge).

Manners I. and Whitman R. (2001) (eds.), *The Foreign Policy of the EU Member States* (Manchester: Manchester University Press).

Nuttall, S. (2000), *European Foreign Policy* (Oxford: Oxford University Press).

Piening, C. (1997), *Global Europe: The European Union in World Affairs* (Boulder, Colo.: Lynne Rienner).

White, B. (2001), *Understanding European Foreign Policy* (Basingstoke and New York: Palgrave).

Web links

CFSP declarations and statements are well documented in the *European Foreign Policy Bulletin*, available online at **www.iue.it/ EFPB**. The fact that the CFSP is at home in the Council of the EU means that the Council's web site **www.ue.eu.int/pesc** is the site to go for. However, the EU's general web site (**www.europa.eu.int**) run by the Commission, also contains very valuable information. The ESDP is well documented at **www.europeansecurity.net** and **www.weu.int/institute**.

Chapter 11

Financial Control: The Court of Auditors and OLAF

Brigid Laffan

Contents

Summary

This chapter analyses the evolution of two of the Union's institutions designed to protect the financial interests of the Union: the Court of Auditors, a full EU institution since the Treaty on European Union (1993) and OLAF, the EU's Fraud Prevention Office. The chapter examines the origins of the institutions, how their internal structures have evolved, their powers and their place in the institutional landscape of the Union. Their growing importance arises from the expansion of the EU budget, the growth of 'net contributors', the emergence of an accountability culture in the EU and the proliferation of EU specific rules in the area of financial management.

Introduction

The focus in this chapter is on the EU's institutions with responsibility for a particular aspect of management, namely, financial control and anti-fraud activities. Those institutions are the European Court of Auditors (ECA) and OLAF (Office de la Lutte Anti-fraude), known in English as the European Fraud Prevention Office. The Court of Auditors, based in Luxembourg, is already more than twenty years old, dating back to 1977. In contrast, OLAF is a much newer body, only created in June 1999. The European Parliament, exercising its role of fostering political accountability, played an important part in the establishment of both institutions. The member states were persuaded that an independent audit body was warranted, given the emergence of an EU budget with supranational characteristics. The fight against fraud assumed greater salience as the size and reach of the EU budget expanded. Peterson highlights the challenge facing the EU arising from the coexistence of pooled sovereignty and divided accountability (Peterson 1997: 559–78). These institutions are part of an attempt to reconfigure systems of accountability to take account of pooled sovereignty.

Financial management, and in fact management more generally, tends to be marginalized in scholarly discussions of the European Union. We should not forget, however, that it was a failure of management that led to the first resignation of an entire Commission in the history of the Union. The political crisis that culminated in March 1999 with the departure of the Santer Commission had its origins in the deep-rooted and perennial problems of financial management in the European Union. Moreover, a continuing stream of sensational newspaper headlines highlighting the smuggling of animals, cigarettes, or liquor act to undermine public confidence in the effectiveness of EU institutions and its policy regimes.

Effective management of the EU budget poses a considerable challenge to the EU and the member states. The annual budget amounting to some €92 billion in 2001 is largely managed by the member states, with only some 12 per cent managed directly by the Commission and an additional 6 per cent spent on the administrative costs of running the institutions. The effective management and control of the budget is not just, or even primarily, a task for the EU's institutions but can occur only if member states have the capacity and willingness to protect the financial interests of the Union. Combating fraud, corruption, and waste— much of it transnational—is a formidable task. The Court of Auditors and OLAF operate in a challenging environment given the complexity and reach of the EU budget.

The origins of the institutions

The Court and OLAF evolved from pre-existing bodies with responsibility for financial control and fighting fraud. The Court of Auditors replaced two mechanisms of independent financial control, the European Communities Audit Office and the Auditor of the European Coal and Steel Community (ECSC); OLAF evolved from the Commission's internal anti-fraud unit known as UCLAF (Unité de Co-ordination de la Lutte Anti-fraude), established in 1988 by the Delors Commission. Both were created as a response to the perceived weakness of their precursors as well as broader changes in the EU as a whole. The provision for a Court of Auditors in the 1975 Budget Treaty was directly related to the transition from national contributions to a system based on 'own resources', an independent revenue base. In addition, the granting of the power of the purse to the European Parliament was seen to require a related shift in the locus of financial auditing. The political argument in favour of a Court of Auditors was made in 1973 by the President of the EP's Budgetary Committee, Heinrich Aigner, who argued that a more supra-national EU budget necessitated an independent EU audit body that would supply the EP with the information necessary for it to exercise the powers it had acquired to vet the annual budget. His case was reinforced by a series of well-publicized frauds against the EU budget and the limited and patchy nature of the financial investigation undertaken by the Audit Board and the ECSC Auditor (H. Wallace 1980: 101–2; Strasser 1992).

The establishment of OLAF in 1999 can be traced back to 1988 when the Delors Commission felt compelled to establish UCLAF in response, notably, to repeated requests from the European Parliament to the Commission to enhance its fight against fraud. UCLAF was part of the Commission's Secretariat-General rather than the Directorate-General for Financial Control. For many years, it was a largely symbolic response to the problem of fraud, rather than a serious anti-fraud unit. With an initial staff of ten in addition to temporary agents from the member states, UCLAF could do little more than coordinate the anti-fraud units in the big spending DGs—Agriculture, Customs Union, and Structural Funds. The need to go beyond a symbolic response was heightened by repeated reports of fraud against the EU budget in the media, in reports from the UK's House of Lords, in the Court of Auditors reports, and in UCLAF's own annual reports (Laffan 1997a; see Exhibit 11.1).

In 1993, Commissioner Peter Schmidhuber was given direct responsibility for combating fraud and a new director, Per Brix Knudsen, was appointed to UCLAF. The European Parliament insisted in that same year that all anti-fraud divisions in the Commission should be integrated into UCLAF rather than dispersed throughout the organization. After 1994, consolidation took place alongside an increase in

> **Exhibit 11.1** Fraud against the EU budget
>
> The annual reports of the Commission on *The Fight Against Fraud* provide considerable insight into the manner in which the EU budget is de-frauded. There is no agreement on just how much fraud is perpetuated against the EU budget. The official figure puts it at 1.4 per cent of the budget whereas others have estimated up to 10 per cent. The following examples are illustrative of the scams that can take place.
>
> **Frauds against the revenue side of the budget**
> Frauds of this nature usually consist of deliberate mis-statements on customs declarations. The aim is to minimize duties or in other cases to maximize refunds, particularly from the Common Agricultural Policy. Some prominent examples include:
>
> *Cigarettes*: 92 million cigarettes were illegally diverted during the transit process from Denmark to Portugal. The procedure involved the forging of customs stamps. A total of some €15 million in customs duties were evaded.
>
> *Meat Carousel*: This scam involved importing live cattle into Italy from eastern Europe. The animals were then resold on the Italian market without an invoice and re-exported to non-member countries to obtain a refund.
>
> *Fraud against the payments side of the budget*: A type of fraud that usually involves the embezzlement of money from the structural funds or getting aid on a false basis from the CAP. One example is money claimed from the European Social Fund for retraining courses that were never taught.

the number of staff in UCLAF (sixty permanent staff and sixty-two contract staff by 1997), with the effect that all those with responsibility for combating fraud in the Commission were finally within one chain of command.

In 1998, in anticipation of the coming into force of Article 280 of the Treaty of Amsterdam on protecting the EU's financial interests, the Commission proposed that an independent anti-fraud office should replace UCLAF. However, the real impetus for creating OLAF came from continuing criticisms of the Commission's financial management and a very critical report by the Court of Auditors of UCLAF itself (see COA 1998*b*). The Court's report acknowledged that the Commission had made a major effort in its fight against fraud, but concluded that 'the organizational arrangements, including those in relation to the member states, are not always clear and are often complicated and cumbersome'. Among the problems identified were:

- over 50 per cent of the UCLAF staff were on temporary contract with a consequent lack of continuity;
- its databases were not fully operational or effective;
- monies that were fraudulently paid were not being recovered;
- procedures and responsibilities concerning the fight against internal corruption and breaches of discipline were unclear and incomplete. (COA 1998*b*: 1, 2)

The subsequent decision to create OLAF was taken as the relationship between the Commission and the European Parliament worsened on the whole question of the Commission's management capacity. The prospect of a new body failed to ward off attacks on the Commission in the EP and from the Committee of Independent Experts it established in January 1999 (see Exhibit 4.1). After the Santer Commission resigned in March 1999, the Prodi Commission immediately identified OLAF as a central plank in its response to the criticisms of the Commission's ability to combat fraud. The Committee of Independent Experts was critical of UCLAF, finding that 'its intervention sometimes slows the procedures down, without improving the end result' (Committee of Independent Experts 1999*b*).

The remit of OLAF may appear more functional than that of the European Court of Auditors with the emphasis on protecting the financial interests of the Union and combating fraud. However, like the Court of Auditors—whose web page slogan is 'Helping the European Union achieve better value for your money'— OLAF claims a normative purpose, suggesting that it is the engine of a 'Europe of legality' against international crime (OLAF 2000).

Structure of the institutions

European Court of Auditors

The Court of Auditors consists of fifteen members, one per member state, the members' *cabinets* (two staff per member) and about 550 staff, who form the operating core of the organization. Just under half are professional auditors. As in other institutions, the top official is the Secretary-General who is responsible for the functioning of the administration.

The members elect a President for a three-year renewable term (see Figure 11.1). The Council appoints the members of the Court for a six-year renewable term after consultation with the European Parliament. The Parliament's Budgetary Control Committee holds formal hearings on appointments to the Court, which have led on one occasion to a candidate being replaced. In 1989, when the Parliament issued an opinion objecting to two nominees from a total of six, France agreed to nominate another candidate (the other, Greece, did not; see Strasser 1992: 271). According to the Treaty, the members of the Court must be from the national external audit bodies or have 'special qualifications' for the office (Article 247 TEC). The stipulation that those 'who are especially qualified' may serve means that the Court of Auditors consists of a mixture of professional senior auditors, finance officials, and former politicians. Unlike the European Central Bank, its members do not necessarily constitute a cohesive professional college.

Figure 11.1 Distribution of responsibilities in the European Court of Auditors (March 2000)

Presidency
Coordination and follow-up of the Court, Legal Service, Institutional external relations and public relations

Audit Group I (3 members)
European Agricultural Guidance and Guarantee Fund

Audit Group II (4 members)
Structural funds, Employment and social affairs, Internal policies, Rural development

Audit Group III (3 members)
Third countries, CEECs, European Development Funds

Audit Group IV (3 members)
Administrative expenditure of the institutions, External offices, Agencies, Own resources, Banking

ADAR Group (6 members)
Annual Report, Contradictory Procedure, Work Programme, Training, Audit Procedures, Audit Manual, Relations with OLAF

DAS Group (6 members)
Statement of Assurance

Secretariat-General

The President of the Court is essentially *primus inter pares*: his/her authority rests on the fact that fellow members of the Court elect him or her. The President oversees the operation of the Court and is the public face of the institution, presenting the COA's Annual Report to the European Parliament and to the Ecofin Council and representing the Court *vis-à-vis* national audit offices. The role of the President has been enhanced by the growing importance of financial control in the Union. Since its inception, the Court has had eight Presidents (see Table 11.1). One of the most outspoken was André Middelhoek, who served until 1995. As a member of the Court from the outset, Middelhoek was very committed to the idea that the Court should be an EU institution, formally and legally (as it was so designated by the Maastricht Treaty), and was also determined to heighten the profile of the Court and to give greater salience to the issue of financial management. In particular, Middelhoek was eager to increase the Court's authority over the financial operations of the Commission and the member states and to show to European citizens that someone was looking after their money. Middelhoek had an especially difficult relationship with Jacques Delors, and went on to play a major role in the 1999 Commission resignation crisis when he chaired the Committee of Independent Experts in a particularly muscular fashion.

Table 11.1 Presidents of the European Court of Auditors	
Sir Norman Price (UK)	1977
Michael Murphy (IRL)	1977–81
Pierre Lelong (F)	1981–4
Marcel Mart (Lux)	1984–90
Aldo Angioi (I)	1990–2
André Middelhoek (NL)	1992–5
Bernhard Friedmann (G)	1996–8
Jan O. Karlsson (S)	1999–

Regardless of the personality of its President, the Court is a collegiate body characterized by a vertical hierarchy between the auditing staff and the college of members, and a horizontal division between the sectoral auditing areas. From the outset, the Court had organizational autonomy and exercised sole responsibility for the organization of its work and rules of procedure.

The court is divided into eight units—four audit groups, two horizontal groups responsible for Audit Development and Reports (ADAR) and the Statement of Assurance (SOA), and the offices of the presidency and the Secretariat-General. The four audit groups are responsible for the different areas of EC expenditure, with each headed by a member who is known as the Doyen—the senior member in charge of the area. Audit Groups I and II are responsible for the internal policies of the Union with one whole group devoted to agricultural policy. The third group audits the Union's external financial instruments including the European Development Fund. The fourth audit group takes care of the administrative expenditure of the institutions and the revenue side of the budget—that is, the EU's own resources. Each group is responsible for the cycle of audits and for preparing for the deliberations of the Court in full session.

The Court as a college meets approximately every two weeks and is attended only by the members and the Secretary-General. Decisions are taken as in the Court of Justice by a simple majority vote. The members' *cabinets*, unlike their counterparts in the Commission, do not prepare the meetings of the Court of Auditors. In fact, the *cabinets* (two staff per member) exercise an ambiguous role in the internal work of the Court. There is clearly some resentment of the *cabinets* among the auditing staff, but members have not wished to modify a system that gives them a support structure at the apex of the institution.

The structure of the Court has developed on the basis of one member per state, thus giving it an increasingly top-heavy structure over time. The size of the Court has grown from nine to fifteen as the number of member states has expanded. Under the Treaty of Nice, this number will expand again as more members join the

Union, with the Treaty making explicit provision for 'one national from each member State' (Article 247 TEC).

The Treaty of Nice also contains a potentially important provision that gives the Court authority to establish 'internal chambers' for the adoption of certain categories of reports (Article 248 TEC). The provision on internal chambers is seen as one way of streamlining the operation of the Court after enlargement. Given the disparate backgrounds of the members of the Court, which will become even more marked in an enlarged EU, ensuring that the college works effectively and to the highest professional standards required in an auditing institution is a genuine challenge.

OLAF

OLAF's structure grew out of UCLAF, the office that it replaced in 1999. The key difference between UCLAF and OLAF is that the latter was given a special independent status in the regulations that led to its establishment. It remains, however, a part of the Commission under the responsibility of the Commissioner in charge of the budget. Its independence is clear in its investigative powers and OLAF's Director-General (Franz-Hermann Bruener at the time of writing) is independently responsible for its investigations. (S)he is appointed by the Commission for a five-year period, renewable once following a favourable opinion from the Supervisory Committee of OLAF, the Council, and the EP. The Director-General of OLAF may neither seek nor take instructions from any government or EU institution, including the Commission, and may uphold its prerogatives before the European Court of Justice. The management of the Office is under the guidance of a Supervisory Committee of five persons who have no links to EU institutions and are specialists in its area of work.

After its creation, OLAF underwent a process of rapid expansion as its staffing levels more than doubled in eighteen months, to an anticipated 300 by the end of 2001. OLAF inherited its internal structure from UCLAF but adopted a new organizational structure in 2000. This restructuring served to make a clear distinction between a Directorate for Policy, Legislation, and Legal Affairs, on the one hand, and a Directorate for Investigations and Operations, on the other. The policy directorate is very similar in purpose and practice to a traditional Commission service, whereas the latter is operational in character and deals specifically with investigations. The Directorate for Investigations has two pools of investigators that are multi-disciplinary in character and consist of former members of national police forces, anti-fraud-units, customs services, and lawyers, instead of the sectoral teams that characterized UCLAF.

Powers of the institutions

European Court of Auditors

Formal powers

Notwithstanding its title, the Court of Auditors does not have any judicial functions. It deals exclusively with financial auditing, even though its remit has been expanded in the Treaty on European Union (TEU), the Treaty of Amsterdam, and the Nice Treaty. Article 248 TEC specifies that the Court is required to 'examine whether all revenue has been received and all expenditure incurred in a lawful and regular manner and whether the financial management has been sound'. In other words, the Court was given responsibility for three different facets of financial auditing: notably, legality, regularity, and sound financial management or value for money. The stipulation that it audit 'all' revenue and expenditure meant that its remit included the budgets of the three European Communities, the European Development Fund, the Communities' borrowing and lending activity, and all satellite bodies established by the Union. Its task is a vast one given that the EC's financial instruments are deployed in the member states and in third countries throughout the world. The Commission estimates that in any one budgetary year, it engages in 400,000 budgetary transactions (Laffan 1997*a*).

The formal powers of the Court were significantly expanded by the Maastricht Treaty in 1993 when it was given responsibility for providing the Council and the European Parliament with what is known as a *Statement of Assurance* concerning the reliability of the accounts and the legality and regularity of the underlying transactions. This power implied a major expansion in the reach of external auditing in the Union. The Treaty of Amsterdam in 1997 made a number of minor changes to the mandate and working methods of the Court, but made provision for the publication of the Statement of Assurance in the EU's *Official Journal*. The Treaty of Nice mandated the Court to supplement the Statement of Assurance with specific assessments of 'each major area of Community activity' and also paved the way for the eventual establishment of internal chambers in the Court.

The Court has developed a number of non-treaty based practices. The President of the Court may issue what is known as a presidential letter to any of the institutions to raise important issues arising from an audit. The presidential letter summarized here (see Exhibit 11.2) provides a chilling account of challenges of financial management in the European Union and of the politicized nature of the Commission when faced with high-level national intervention.

Output of the Court

The Court is a prolific producer of reports. The core of its work is to undertake

Exhibit 11.2 The Fléchard Case[a]

This letter was sent to the Commission by the President of the Court, Jan Karlsson. It provides a detailed 12-page analysis of a case of fraud against the EC budget and the manner in which the Commission handled it. It draws particular attention to the role of OLAF.

Facts of the case
A French company, Fléchard won a tender to supply butter to the Soviet Union. The company bought 58.645 tonnes of butter including 6,750 tonnes of Irish inter-vention butter from the Department of Agriculture (DAF) in Dublin. The Irish butter was exported in December 1991 by the French company with the declared destination of the Soviet Union but it was diverted to the Polish market. A joint investigation carried out by the DAF and DG Agriculture of the Commission concluded that the 'transaction had been orchestrated as a fraud from the outset'.

Involvement of the Court and OLAF
The Court received two anonymous letters of complaint concerning the Commission's management of the case in 1998–9 and a further letter was received by the Parliament's Budgetary Control Committee. The Court informed UCLAF which immediately began an investigation.

Findings concerning the case
Regulation 863/91 provided that a security would be forfeited if a product did not reach its destination. In this case the security, lodged by Fléchard, amounted to €17.6 million. In March 1992, DG Agriculture of the Commission requested that the Irish authorities demand the full payment of €17.6 million. But between May 1992 and September 1993, the French authorities intervened on behalf of the French company on four occasions to try to reduce the amount of the forfeit that would have to be paid by Fléchard. During 1993, there was considerable attention given to the case in the Commission with the involvement of the Legal Service, Financial Control, the President of the Commission's Cabinet, and DG Agriculture. The Commission eventually agreed to a settlement of €3 million, or less than 20 per cent of the total of €17.6 million. (The settlement was a source of difficulty for Pascal Lamy, who had served as Delors's *chef du cabinet* during the Fléchard affair, when he was vetted by the EP after being nominated for the Prodi Commission.)

Conclusions of the Court
The Court was clearly uneasy about the Commission's management of this case. It felt that the terms of the settlement had no legal basis, that Fléchard had acted in bad faith from the outset, that the administrative arrangements in DG Agriculture were breaking down, and that the Commission needed to strengthen its arrangements for high risk subsidized exports.

[a] Presidential letter from President Jan Karlsson to the Commission President, 11 May 2000.

audits and to publish the results of such audits in the form of reports. Between 1989 and 1995, it produced ninety-six reports including five annual reports (Laffan 1997a: 197). The tempo has increased since then (see Table 11.2 for a summary). The

Table 11.2 Reports of the Court of Auditors 1993–1998

Annual Reports/Statements of Assurance	6
Special Annual Reports	76
Special Reports	46
Opinions/Observations	38
Total	166

Source: Annex 3, 1998 Annual Report of the Court of Auditors.

Court's work programme and auditing cycle enters the policy process in the form of the Court's Annual Report, published in the autumn of each year for the preceding year, the Statement of Assurance, which has been drafted since 1994, a myriad of special reports on particular institutions, policy programmes, or financial processes, and Opinions when requested by the Council or Observations on the initiative of the Court.

The Annual Report used to be a very large document running to some 450 pages each year. The massive tome consisted of detailed observations of different spending programmes and the replies of the Commission and other EU institutions on its observations. The length of the report and the level of detail it contained was a deterrent to all but the most eager followers of EU finances. To give greater salience to individual issues that might not emerge fully from the Annual Report, the Court established a new policy in 1997 of publishing in special reports the results of audits that dealt with specific sectors. One upshot is a shorter and sharper Annual Report, which allows the Court to draw attention to the Special Reports.

A 2001 report on the COA by the British House of Lords found 'the Special Reports of generally greater value than the Annual Report, although variations in the quality of the former were recognised' (House of Lords 2001). The Special Reports can be quite long documents. For example, the Special Report on UCLAF in 1998 (Court of Auditors 1998b), which had a direct bearing on the decision of the Commission to establish OLAF, was fifty pages long. The growing emphasis on Special Reports can be gleaned from Table 11.3, which outlines the focus of the Special Reports in 1998.

The majority of the COA's reports involve audits of the Union's internal policies with a particular emphasis on the CAP and structural expenditure. In addition there were six reports in 1998 on the Union's external expenditure, a growing proportion of the Union budget. The reports on UCLAF and on allowances paid to MEPs were designed to audit practices in the Union's institutions. Two years later in 2000, the Court audited the expenditure of the European Parliament's political groups (Court of Auditors 2000). The Special Report on the political groups made trenchant criticisms of the management of their budgetary resources (see Exhibit 11.3 for a summary). It was particularly critical of the manner in which the groups

Table 11.3 Focus of Court of Auditors' Special Reports in 1998

External Expenditure
Special Report 1/98 Cooperation with non-member Mediterranean states
Special Report 5/98 Reconstruction in former Yugoslavia
Special Report 7/98 on development aid to South Africa
Special Report 11/98 on Phare and Tacis
Special Report 24/98 European Development Funds
Special Report 25/98 on nuclear safety measures in the CEECs and NIS

Internal Programme Expenditure
Special Report 2/98 on clearance of EAGGF accounts
Special Report 4/98 on EU action as regards water pollution
Special Report 12/98 Rural Development 2
Special Report 14/98 ERDF assistance
Special Report 15/98 Structural fund interventions
Special Report 16/98 Structural operations
Special Report 17/98 Energy programmes
Special Report 18/98 Fisheries sector
Special Report 19/98 BSE crisis measures
Special Report 21/98 EAGGF clearance of accounts
Special Report 22/98 Equality programmes
Special Report 23/98 Information and communications measures managed by the
Commission

Customs Union/Revenue Base
Special Report 4/98 on reduced rate of levy on New Zealand milk and Swiss cheese
Special Report 6/98 on assessment of VAT and GNP
Special Report 9/98 Protection of EC financial interests in VAT on intra-Community Trade
Special Report 13/98 Risk analysis in customs control
Special Report 20/98 Audit checks on agricultural products receiving export refunds

EU Institutions
Special Report 8/98 on UCLAF
Special Report 10/98 Allowances of MEPs

employed staff, uncovering a multiplicity of contractual arrangements that contained clauses concerning labour and tax law of doubtful validity. In its replies to the findings of the Court, the EP provided details of the measures it was putting in place to ensure that there was improved management of the finances deployed by the political groups.

From the outset, there has been considerable consistency in the findings of the Court. In 1981, its benchmark study of the financial systems of the European Communities, included the following key findings:

- limited staff resources devoted to financial management;
- serious delays in the clearance of European Agricultural Guidance and Guarantee Fund accounts;

> **Exhibit 11.3** The Court of Auditors' report on EP political groups
>
> **Overall conclusion**
> The lack of clarity in the rules and procedures applicable to the groups in respect of the eligibility of their expenditure, the frequent absence of any satisfactory system of internal control, and the weaknesses of the present external audit system have contributed to the considerable problems discovered by the Court in respect of the legality/regularity of the transactions. There is no guarantee that the funds were always used in accordance with the principles of sound financial management.
>
> **Specific recommendations**
> - Clarification of the criteria concerning the eligibility of expenditure
> - Need for transparent rules for financing European political parties
> - Centralization of the disbursement of and accounting for expenditure in the Parliament's administrative departments
> - Clear rules for property and the inventory of goods
> - Publication of certified accounts
> - One external auditor selected by tender
> - Clarification of the contractual relationship between the groups and their employees

- financial accounts hardly intelligible to users;
- insufficient emphasis placed on the evaluation of results by the Commission;
- problems in the definition of the tasks of the Commission's internal controller;
- no comprehensive strategy for computer software, hardware, and operating staff resources (Court of Auditors, C342, 31 Dec. 1981).

These criticisms have been repeated regularly in the Annual Report, the Special Reports, and since 1994, in the Statement of Assurance.

The Court's institutional position

In analysing the Court's position in the Union's institutional landscape, it is important to distinguish between its relationship with its auditees, on the one hand, and its place in the Union's system of financial control, on the other. Inevitably, tensions exist between the Court as an audit institution and the other EU institutions that are subject to its audits. Although the work of the Court covers all EU institutions and bodies, the most critical relationship is the one with the Commission as the institution that manages, at least formally, the bulk of EU expenditure. The relationship with the Commission was very difficult for many years as the young Court strove to find its niche in the Union's institutional landscape. One of the first controversial issues with the Commission related to the issue of a 'right of reply' to the Court's observations. The Court conceded that the

Commission and the other institutions could reply and that these replies would be published in conjunction with the main text of the Court's reports. In 1981, in evidence to the European Parliament, a Commissioner claimed that 'the Court evaluates the Commission's activities from a negative point of view rather than from a positive one, and in consequence finishes up with an assessment which does a disservice to Community integration'.[1] In the early years, the Commission never fully reconciled itself to the role of the Court in 'value for money' auditing, and clearly felt that the Court was straying from its audit function into policy or political judgements. Auditing remains a contested area between the Commission and the Court. Gradually, however, in the 1980s, the Court and the Commission developed a working relationship as the latter came to accept that the audit body was a permanent feature of the Union.

Relations deteriorated again during Jacques Delors's term as President of the Commission. During the negotiations of the Delors II budgetary package (covering 1993–9), the Commission was furious at a report from the Court to the Council on management problems in the structural funds. Delors complained that the report made it more difficult for him to get the member states to agree to a larger budget.

The Santer Commission made improving relations with the Court one of its main objectives. Santer had had considerable contact with the Court during his time as Prime Minister of Luxembourg. The Santer Commission attempted to upgrade its relationship with the Court by ensuring that individual Commissioners and Directors-General attended meetings with the Court (Laffan 1997a). It is paradoxical, then, that the Court contributed to the resignation of the entire Santer Commission in March 1999 when the 1996 discharge procedure became embroiled in a wider debate on management problems in the Commission (see below).

The Court is not the only cog in the wheel of financial management in the Union. Such management is also the responsibility of the Financial Controllers in all of the EU institutions, OLAF, the national authorities that manage EU finances, and the national audit offices. Given the extent and range of the Union's budgetary activities, the Court needs to work in partnership with national audit offices. Court audits in the member states are carried out in liaison with the national audit authorities, all of which have appointed a liaison official with the Court. In the period since the ratification of the Maastricht Treaty in 1993, the Court has devoted considerable energy to improving its links to the national audit offices, especially given the latter's staffing resources and responsibility for national financial interests. The Treaty of Amsterdam stipulated that 'The Court of Auditors and the national audit bodies of the member states shall co-operate in a spirit of trust while maintaining their independence' (Article 248 TEC).

The Court's formal relations with the Council and the European Parliament take place within the so-called discharge procedure. Under this procedure the EP has the power to grant or withhold approval for the Commission's implementation of the annual budget. The Council also offers a recommendation but the Parliament takes this decision alone. The Commission is legally bound to take the EP's discharge resolutions into account. The procedure is based on the analysis by the EP's Budgetary Control Committee of the Court's Annual Report, its Statement of Assurance, and any special reports published during the budgetary year in question. The EP drafts a discharge report largely based on the work of the Court. Because of the discharge procedure, contact is continuous between the Court and the EP's Budgetary Control Committee. The Parliament refused to grant a discharge in 1984 with respect to the 1982 budget and has delayed the discharge on a number of occasions since then.

However in spring 1998 the most politically charged discharge process in the history of the EU began. In March, the EP Budgetary Control Committee recommended that the EP delay giving the Commission a discharge for the 1996 budget following one more critical report from the Court of Auditors. The issue then became entangled with additional allegations of mismanagement involving Commissioner Cresson and later the European Community Humanitarian Office (ECHO). An internal Commission whistle-blower added to the politically charged atmosphere (see Van Buitenan 2000 and Chapter 4).

The Commission survived a motion of censure but only because a special Committee of Independent Experts was appointed to investigate the charges of mismanagement. The ultimate result was the resignation of the entire Santer Commission. In an indirect way the Court's highly technical work of auditing therefore contributed to what was a history-making event in the politics of the Union. Most of its activity, however, is directed towards the less dramatic but still crucial task of improving the financial control procedures of EU institutions and protecting the financial interests of the Union.

OLAF

OLAF exercises the following tasks in the fight against fraud, corruption, or any other activity affecting the financial interests of the EU:

- it conducts all the investigations conferred on the Commission by Community legislation and in third countries through agreements;
- it safeguards the Community against behaviour that might lead to administrative or penal proceedings;
- it exercises a coordinating role *vis-à-vis* the national auditing authorities in the fight against fraud;
- it contributes to the development of methods for combating fraud.

In order to carry out these tasks, OLAF conducts external audits in the member states and where permissible in third countries and has the power to conduct internal investigations in the EU institutions when fraud or corruption is suspected.

OLAF (2000) issued its first annual report in June 2000. The report underlined the continuity between OLAF and UCLAF in terms of investigations but also highlighted the changes that will flow from the establishment of a new institution with a tighter set of regulatory procedures, clearer independence, more investigators, and the development of a new operational approach. When presenting the report, the new Director of OLAF was quick to point out that the Office needed more teeth to investigate value-added tax fraud and better access to the member states' files. He drew attention to the continuing problems arising from the differences in national legal systems which prevent the emergence of EU-wide anti-fraud rules and common penalties for offenders.[2]

OLAF, like all EU institutions, operates in an institutional environment that is multi-levelled, cross-national, and very diverse. It has to develop strategies for managing diversity and for dealing with the multiple anti-fraud agencies in Europe. It seeks to work closely with national authorities not as a substitute for national action but as a means of more effectively fighting fraud that is transnational in nature. As much crime and fraud in Europe today has a transnational dimension, OLAF itself is partly a response to transnational pressures. In short, legal Europe is attempting to catch up with criminal Europe. OLAF has developed a clear strategy about how it intends to position itself in the institutional landscape, seeing its role as a 'platform' for anti-fraud activities in Europe. It wishes to 'add value' to the fight against fraud and sees itself as doing so through intelligence gathering and sharing with the member states, through building bridges among the anti-fraud agencies at national level and through coordination of cross-national investigations.

The institutions in context

Financial control and the larger 'EU' system

The evolution of the Court of Auditors and OLAF in the EU system illustrates how institutions and their external environments interact. These institutions were established at different times, more than twenty years apart, in response to changes in the salience of financial management, control, and accountability in the EU system. The establishment of the Court was recognition of the supranational nature of the EU budget and OLAF of the failure of self-regulation within the Commission. Both institutions represented a strengthening of the relatively weak organizations that preceded them. The Court of Auditors had to devote considerable organizational energy to becoming a 'living institution'—to becoming embedded in the EU system. The Court had to evolve a culture of auditing that was suitable to the extended scale and reach of the Union's financial activities. Like all EU institutions it had to work with diversity—auditing cultures, attitudes to financial management, diversity of professional background, legal arrangements in the member states, and multiple languages. No less important than its internal structures are its relationships with other parts of the EU system. The Court is part of the system of financial audit and control that exists in the EU involving internal financial control, external audit, and measures to combat fraud. It is part of the Union's accountability structures in that the Parliament's Budgetary Control Committee relies on reports of the Court for its annual discharge process. The Court has played its part, albeit a secondary one, in the unfolding drama of EP–Commission relations. The Court has gradually established working relationships with all EU institutions and its institutional status gives it the same legal status as the institutions that it audits. Its stronger, formal status in treaty terms matters in the day-to-day politics of auditing in the Union. As the salience of good financial governance has gained prominence in the Union and received the backing of the Council and the European Council, the Court has turned its attention to enhancing its relationship with national auditing authorities.

OLAF is a very young organization, which is in the process of establishing its internal structures, procedures, and processes and is expanding its human resources. Like the Court of Auditors, it is part of the Union's accountability structure with a specific remit to combat fraud and crime. Its remit is based on the clear recognition that there is an important transnational dimension to budgetary fraud in the EU. The establishment of OLAF as an independent unit attached to the Commission but with a separate chain of command was a response to the problems the Commission had in conducting internal investigations when there were allegations of fraud by individuals in the Commission's services. The tardiness with which fraud in the tourism directorate in particular was investigated in the early 1990s undermined the credibility of the Commission's internal processes. Like the Court of Auditors, there is a clear recognition in OLAF that it must work with and through national investigative channels.

Theories of integration and institutional development

From the outset, scholars of integration paid considerable attention to what they saw as the novel characteristics of the Union's institutional architecture. In fact, institutions were central to neofunctionalist analysis, as well as early volumes on the EU's policy process. Not unexpectedly, the growing volume of literature on the factors driving integration—liberal intergovernmentalism, supranational governance/new institutionalism, and social constructivism—all address different dimensions of institutionalization and institutional evolution in the EU.

How well do these theories of European integration explain the establishment and evolution of the European Court of Auditors and OLAF? Both institutions are non-majoritarian institutions with a role as guardians of the EU purse. All political systems have institutions whose *raison d'être* is supervision and control. Social constructivism draws our attention to the importance of ideas and discourse in shaping political action and structures. In the case of the two institutions analysed in this chapter, established concepts of democratic government, and accountability, shaped the institutions from the outset. The fact that external audit was a well-established norm and practice in domestic government would have made it very difficult for any member state to argue against the establishment of the Court of Auditors. By conducting audits and reporting on the findings of such audits the Court of Auditors contributed to the diffusion of democratic practices of governance in the EU. In particular, social constructivism provides a useful lens for analysing the normative dimension of institution-building and related processes of learning and socialization (Checkel 1999: 548). The Court of Auditors, together with other actors in the system, had a responsibility to strengthen the norms of sound financial management, legality, and regularity in relation to the EU budget, and did so through its recommendations and opinions concerning the Financial Regulation. In an effort to enhance its effectiveness, the Court of Auditors and more recently OLAF have promoted learning and socialization on issues of financial management and fraud in the EU system.

The literature on institutionalization and supranational governance provides a lens with which to analyse the development of these institutions over time (Sandholtz and Stone Sweet 1998a: 16–20; Pierson 1996; Pollack 1998). The processes highlighted in this literature, such as rule-making and institutionalization, are clearly evident in the evolution of the Court of Auditors and OLAF. The member states may have established the Court of Auditors to oversee their agent, the Commission, in its management of EU monies but over time the Court, because of its audit remit, has had to follow the audit trail into the member states. One of the unintended consequences of the establishment of the Court was the manner in which national financial management came under increasing scrutiny. Treaty revision and changes in the Financial Regulation all contributed to an enhancement of the norm of sound financial management in the EU and to creating a web of rules around the control of EU expenditure. The Court and OLAF are but part of the wider development of an institutionalized control/accountability culture in the Union.

Liberal intergovernmentalism is more concerned with why institutional delegation takes place rather than the consequences of such delegation. A liberal-intergovernmental analysis of the development of the Court of Auditors and OLAF would privilege an explanation based on the need for credible commitments. From this perspective, the role of both these institutions is to assure predictable, fair, and transparent compliance with the rules. However, the credibility of the commitment is bolstered by both of these institutions not by limiting democratic involvement, a key argument in liberal intergovernmentalism, but by reinforcing democratic control, because both institutions are part of the democratic fabric of the EU polity (Moravcsik 1998*a*).

The impact of the institutions

Given the perennial problems associated with the management of EU finances in successive reports of the Court of Auditors and in the Commission's Annual Reports on *The Fight Against Fraud*, it would be tempting to dismiss the work of the COA and OLAF as very inadequate. Such a conclusion would, however, be premature. The reports of the Court since the end of the 1970s did much to highlight management inadequacies in the first place, and the COA's constant pressure on the Commission led to an acceptance—however tardy—that there were very real problems of financial management in the Union. The Commission responded by strengthening formal systems for overseeing the implementation of the budget, but as Levy (2000: 187) has concluded: 'moving beyond formal change is a general problem that bedevils most aspects of EU programme management.' The Commission struggled throughout the 1990s to enhance its internal management processes and to strengthen its links to the member states. This effort has borne some fruit but the continuing evidence of weak management and fraud contained in the reports of the independent experts on the Commission in 1999 underlined just how chronic the problems are.

The Court of Auditors played a particularly important role in EU institutional politics by altering the balance in relations between the EP and the Commission. Its reports provided the Budgetary Control Committee with the raw material to exercise the discharge procedure in a manner that strengthened parliamentary control over the Commission. The resignation of the Santer Commission was the most dramatic event to result from the problems of self-regulation in the Commission. Without the slow drip feed of COA reports, it is unlikely that it would have happened. It is more difficult to draw conclusions about the impact of OLAF given its short time in existence. Its increased staffing and independent investigative powers suggest that it will have more teeth in the fight against fraud than UCLAF but the challenges it faces remain formidable.

Conclusions

The establishment of the Court of Auditors in 1977 was dependent on the changing nature and funding of the EC budget. In turn, once the Court found an institutional identity and established its approach to auditing, it began to highlight the problems of financial management in the Union. Its effectiveness improved with the internal development of an agreed audit culture and growing human resources. For well over ten years, the Court had to fight to ensure that its findings were taken on board in the Commission, the Council, and at national level. With the major expansion of the Union's budgetary resources after 1988 and a growing net contributors club, financial management found its way from the margins of the agenda to centre stage. Gradually the rules surrounding financial management were strengthened and the member states were forced to accept a tighter regime of financial control. The Court of Auditors, whose institutional position was strengthened in this period, contributed to but also benefited from the growing salience of financial management in the Union. The establishment of OLAF in 1999 was a response to the problems of fraud against the financial interests of the Union and more specifically to the problems of self-regulation in the Commission. The Court of Auditors and OLAF represent institutional innovation in the EU system. They were established in response to changes in the dynamic of the EU budget and to changes in relations between the Union's institutions. The depth of the management problems identified in relation to the EU budget in 1999 demonstrates the extent of the challenge facing these two institutions both now and in future as the Union enlarges.

Notes

1 *OJ* (1981), C344/8, para. 21.

2 See *European Voice*, 27 June 2000.

Further reading

For an overview of the EU budget see Laffan (1997*a*), which contains a chapter (7) devoted to the management of EU monies. Laffan (1999) analyses the Court's relationship with other EU institutions and charts how it became embedded in the Union's institutional system. Levy (1996) highlights the difficulty of diverse national auditing traditions for external auditing in the Union, while Levy (2000) is the most in-depth analysis available of financial management in the EU, based largely on reports of the Court of Auditors. House of Lords (2001) provides fascinating material garnered from expert witnesses on the role of the Court.

House of Lords (2001), *The European Court of Auditors: The Case for Reform*, 12th Report, 3 April, **www.publications.pariamen98/99/Idselect/Ideucom/63/6302.htm**.

Laffan, B. (1997*a*), *The Finances of the Union* (London: Macmillan).

—— (1999), 'Becoming a "Living Institution": The Evolution of the European Court of

Auditors', *Journal of Common Market Studies*, 37/2: 251–68.

Levy R. (1996), 'Managing Value for Money Audit in the European Union: The

Challenge of Diversity', *Journal of Common Market Studies*, 43/4: 509–29.

—— (2000), *Implementing European Union Public Policy* (Edward Elgar: Cheltenham).

Web links

The most important web-link is to the **www.europa.eu.int** site which provides access to all of the EU institutions. Once you access the main server, the link to the individual institutions is direct. The link to the Commission provides access to the Budget Directorate and the Financial Control Directorate in addition to OLAF which is found at **www.europa.eu.int/** **comm/dgs/anti_fraud/mission**. Europa provides access to the Court of Auditors' extensive site which gives access to the Annual Reports, Special Reports, and a bibliography on the Court of Auditors. The link to the European Parliament provides access to the work of the Budgetary Control Committee which is central to the annual discharge of the budget.

Part III

Integrating Interests

Chapter 12
Political Interests: The EP's Party Groups

Tapio Raunio[1]

Contents

Summary

The party system of the European Parliament (EP) is dominated by the two main party families: social democrats on one hand (PES), and centre-right conservatives and Christian democrats on the other (EPP). In the early 1950s, members of the EP (MEPs) decided to form ideological groups instead of national blocs in order to counterbalance the dominance of national interests in the Council. Nevertheless, national parties remain influential within party groups, not least through their control of candidate selection. In comparison with parties in national legislatures, the EP party groups are non-hierarchical, with emphasis on legislative work done in the committees. Without any EU executive office at stake in European elections, the vertical linkage function of the party groups—that of connecting voters to public policy-making—will remain poorly developed without changes in the balance of power between the EU institutions. However, in horizontal terms, the EP party groups and the parties at the European level perform an important function by integrating political interests across the Union.

Introduction

Compared with parties in EU member state legislatures, the party groups of the European Parliament operate in a very different institutional environment. There is no EU government accountable to the Parliament. There are no coherent and hierarchically organized European-level parties. Instead, MEPs are elected from lists drawn up by national parties and on the basis of national electoral campaigns. The social and cultural heterogeneity of the EU is reflected in the internal diversity of the groups, with a total of 129 national parties winning seats in the Parliament in the 1999 elections. The party groups are thus structurally and firmly embedded in the political systems of the EU member states.

The chapter begins by examining the shape of the EP party system. It then analyses the structure of the party groups and the role of national parties within them, before exploring the relationship between the groups and committees. It argues that the delegation of authority downwards to committees and individual MEPs is essential to the Parliament's policy success. Next, it examines parties at the European level and argues that, without any executive office at stake in European elections, the vertical linkage function of the party groups—that of connecting voters to the EU policy process—will remain poorly developed. However, in horizontal terms, the EP party groups and the Europarties perform an important function by integrating political interests across the Union. Finally, the concluding discussion summarizes the key points of the chapter.

The shape of the EP party system

The Common Assembly of the European Coal and Steel Community (ECSC), the predecessor of the Parliament, held its inaugural session in September 1952. In the first important vote held in the Assembly, to elect its President, the members split along group lines instead of voting as national blocs. The party groups were officially recognized in the standing orders of the Assembly in June 1953. The decision to form party groups crossing national lines was motivated by the desire to avoid the dominance of national viewpoints, and needs to be understood in the light of the developments in the early 1950s. First, the creation of the High Authority (predecessor of the Commission) and the Assembly marked the emergence of truly supranational institutions, in contrast to those of the inter-governmental Council of Europe (particularly its Consultative Assembly). Second,

national interests in the ECSC were already represented in the Council of Ministers, and the Assembly sought to counterbalance this through its ideologically
based group structure.

Throughout its history up to the present day (Exhibit 12.1 summarizes the
parties in the EP in 2001) the EP party system has been based on the left–right
dimension, the main cleavage in all European countries despite the gradual
erosion of traditional class ties and the entry of new issues, such as environmental
concerns, onto the political agenda (Huber and Inglehart 1995). The seating order
in the chamber reflects this, with the social democrats and former communists on
the left side of the hemicycle, the liberals in the middle, and Christian democrats
and conservatives on the right. Table 12.1 shows the distribution of seats in
the Parliament between 1979 (the date of the first direct elections to the EP) and
2001. Initially the party system consisted of only three groups: socialists/social
democrats (PES), Christian democrats/conservatives (EPP), and liberals (ELDR), the
three main party families in EU member states.[2] The Christian Democratic group
was the largest group until 1975 when the British Labour Party joined the Socialist
group.[3]

The shape of the EP party system depends on developments in the national
politics of the EU member states. Particularly the electoral volatility and high
degree of party system fragmentation in France and Italy have destabilized the EP
group structure. The existence of the smaller groups is under threat in each con-
secutive election (Bardi 1996). For example, the survival of the radical left EUL–NGL
and the Green group depend on the electoral fortunes of a handful of national
parties. While the national character of Euroelections thus undermines the institutionalization of the EP groups, the quest for power within the Parliament, on the
other hand, consolidates the position of the larger groups.

Table 12.2 demonstrates the strengths of the party families in the 1979–2001
Parliaments. The PES and EPP have dominated the chamber throughout this
period, controlling more than half of the seats. After the 1999 election, they
retained control of approximately two-thirds of the seats.

For the first time since the introduction of direct elections, the EPP in 1999
became the largest group with 233 members. However, the entry of primarily
conservative parties has undermined the Christian democratic profile of the group.
Forza Italia has travelled a particularly tortuous journey to arrive in the EPP. Having first been rejected by both the EPP and ELDR after the 1994 elections, it formed
a group of its own (FE), then merged in 1995 with the Gaullist European Democratic Alliance (EDA) to form the Union for Europe (UPE). Finally, after protracted
negotiations, it ended up in the EPP in 1998. The British Conservatives may fit into
the EPP even less comfortably, and it was at their insistence that the title European
Democrats was added to the EPP's group name after Tory MEPs decided to become
part of the group (to maximize their influence and office benefits).

Exhibit 12.1 Party groups in the 1999–2004 European Parliament

European People's Party and European Democrats **(EPP–ED, 232 seats)**
For the first time since the 1979 elections, the EPP–ED is the largest group in the Parliament. The group is a mix of Christian democrats and conservatives with parties from all EU member states. The largest national party is the German Christian Democratic Union/Christian Social Union (CDU/CSU). The conservative wing of the group has strengthened over the years with the entry of parties like the Spanish Partido Popular, Forza Italia, the French (Gaullist) Rassemblement pour la République and the British Conservatives. Still, EPP has traditionally and consistently been strongly in favour of closer European integration.

Party of European Socialists **(PES, 181)**
This group brings together social democratic and socialist parties from all EU countries. The largest party delegations are the German Social Democrats (SPD) and the British Labour Party. The PES supports further integration, primarily because with EMU the defence of traditional goals of the left—such as social and environmental legislation and employment policies—require European-level action to complement national measures.

European Liberal, Democrat, and Reform Party **(ELDR, 52)**
The ELDR consists of various liberal and centrist parties and has traditionally occupied a pivotal role between the two large groups. While the accommodation of Nordic centre parties has increased group heterogeneity, the ELDR remains committed to further European integration.

Greens/European Free Alliance **(G/EFA, 46)**
This group is an alliance between green parties and various regionalist parties. The regionalist parties of EFA—such as the Scottish National Party and (Spanish) Catalan 'Convergence and Unity' party—did not win enough seats to form a group of their own and thus chose to sit with the Greens. The Greens have in recent years become strongly pro-EU, largely due to similar reasons as the PES.

Confederal Group of the European United Left / Nordic Green Left **(EUL–NGL, 42)**
The EUL–NGL brings together a variety of left-socialist and former communist parties. The title NGL was added to the group name after the 1995 enlargement as the Finnish and Swedish left parties wanted to emphasize their separate identity within the otherwise largely Mediterranean group. EUL is divided over the desirability of further integration.

Union for Europe of the Nations **(UEN, 21)**
The UEN is primarily a conservative grouping. However, its main national parties— the Pasqua-Villiers list from France, Irish Fianna Fail, and Italian Allianza Nazionale— are also opposed to or, at least, critical of further integration.

Europe of Democracies and Diversities **(EDD, 19)**
This group is the only real anti-integrationist group in the Parliament, uniting MEPs from the French pro-hunting/defence of rural traditions group, the UK Independence Party, anti-EU Danes, and Dutch Calvinists.

Technical Group of Independent Members **(TGI, 19)**
This group is not a 'party group' *per se*, but it brings together the Italian Bonino list and Lega Nord and the far-right French Front National and Belgian Vlaams Blok delegations. As its name implies, the group is a technical coalition formed to reap the material and procedural benefits that groups enjoy in the Parliament.

Note: The seat shares are from April 2001.

Table 12.1 Party groups in the European Parliament, 1979–2001[a]

Groups	1979	1981	1984	1987	1989	1993	1994	1995	1997	1999	2001
PES	113	123	130	165	180	198	198	221	214	180	181
EPP	107	117	110	115	121	162	157	173	181	233	232
ELDR	40	39	31	44	49	46	43	52	41	50	52
EDG	64	63	50	66	34						
EDA	22	22	29	29	20	20	26	26			
COM	44	48	41	48							
CDI	11	11									
RB			20	20	13	16					
ER			16	16	17	14					
Greens					30	28	23	25	28	48	46
EUL					28						
LU					14	13					
EUL–NGL							28	31	33	42	42
EN							19	19			
FE							27	29			
ERA							19	19	20		
UPE									55		
UEN										21	21
TGI										20	19
EDD										16	19
NA	9	11	7	15	12	21	27	31	54	16	14
Total	410	434	434	518	518	518	567	626	626	626	626

Abbreviations: PES = Party of European Socialists; EPP = European People's Party, European People's Party and European Democrats (EPP–ED) since the 1999 elections; ELDR = European Liberal, Democrat and Reform Party; EDG = European Democratic Group; EDA = European Democratic Alliance, European Progressive Democrats until the 1989 elections; COM = Communist and Allies Group; CDI = Technical Group of Co-ordination and Defence of Independent MEPs; RB = Rainbow Group; ER = European Right; Greens = The Green Group, Greens/European Free Alliance since the 1999 elections; EUL = European United Left; LU = Left Unity; EUL–NGL = Confederal Group of the European United Left, since 1995 the group has included the sub-group Nordic Green Left; EN = Europe of Nations; ERA = European Radical Alliance; FE = Forza Europa; UPE = Union for Europe; UEN = Union for Europe of the Nations; TGI = Technical Group of Independent Members; EDD = Europe of Democracies and Diversities; NA = Non-attached.

[a] Date: 1979 = after the European elections (EE); 1981 = following the first EE in Greece in Oct. 1981; 1984 = after the second EE; 1987 = after the first EE in Spain in June and in Portugal in July; 1989 = after the third EE; 1993 = situation in January following the mergers between EPP and EDG in May 1992 and between EUL and PES in Jan. 1993; 1994 = after the fourth EE; 1995 = situation in January after the latest EU enlargement; 1997 = mid-term of the fourth Parliament; 1999 = after the fifth EE; 2001 = Apr. 2001.

The formation of the PES presents far fewer problems, as each member state has a centre-left, social democratic party. Both the EPP and PES—alone amongst EP party groups—include parties from all member states.

The Liberals played a key role in the early stages of the Parliament, but since the first direct elections their seat share has remained below 10 per cent. The enlargement of the Union, and the change of electoral system in the UK from single-member plurality districts to proportional representation prior to the 1999

Table 12.2 Party families in the directly elected European Parliament[a]

Party family	Radical left	Greens and regionalists[b]	Social democrats	Liberals	Christian democrats and conservatives	Extreme right	Anti-EU parties
1979–84	COM (44)		PES (113)	ELDR (40)	EPP (107) EDG (46) EDA (22)		
1984–9	COM (41)	RB	PES (130)	ELDR (31)	EPP (110) EDG (50) EDA (29)	ER (16)	
1989–94	EUL (28)[c] LU (14)	Greens (30) RB	PES (180)	ELDR (49)	EPP (121) EDG (34)[d] EDA (20)	ER (17)	
1994–9	EUL–NGL (28)	Greens (23)	PES (198) ERA (19)	ELDR (43)	EPP (157) EDA (26) FE (27)[e]		EN (19)
1999–2004	EUL–NGL (42)	G/EFA (48)	PES (180)	ELDR (50)	EPP (233) UEN (21)		EDD (16)

[a] Technical groups are excluded as they are not based on ideological affiliation. The seat figures refer to the beginning of each Parliament.
[b] Regionalists were a sub-group of the Rainbow Group in 1984–94 and EFA member parties sat in CDI in 1979–84 and in the social democratic ERA group in 1994–9.
[c] Disbanded in January 1993. The majority of the group joined PES.
[d] Joined EPP in May 1992.
[e] EDA and FE merged in July 1995 to form UPE (55).

elections, have numerically benefited ELDR. Simultaneously, however, the group has become ideologically more heterogeneous. The accommodation of Nordic centre parties has proven problematic, especially on integration matters in which the Danish, Finnish, and Swedish parties are considerably more Eurosceptical than the group majority.

The smaller groups, too, are often rather mixed bags. The communists, or the radical left, have formed a group under various labels since 1973. The title Nordic Green Left was added to the group name, Confederal Group of the European United Left (EUL–NGL) after the 1995 enlargement. Entry to a group can be vetoed by a party from the same country. For example, when forming EUL–NGL after the 1999 elections, there was a real question mark about the entry of the French Trotskyite Lutte Ouvrière, but in the end the French Communist Party accepted it into the group.

The Greens achieved an electoral breakthrough in 1989, and have since then strengthened their position. They benefit more than most groups from the second-order logic of Euroelections, which favours small parties at the expense of larger mainstream parties. The Green group in the fifth Parliament is an alliance between representatives from green parties and MEPs from Basque, Flemish, Scottish, Spanish, and Welsh regionalist parties.

The conservative party family has been represented by the European Democratic Group (EDG), a group formed around the British Conservatives in 1973, as well as the EDA. The former joined the EPP in 1992 and the latter established the Union for Europe of the Nations (UEN) in 1999. The extreme right parties formed a group after the 1984 and 1989 elections. The regionalist parties of the European Free Alliance (EFA) have never mustered enough seats to form their own group, and their MEPs have instead sat as sub-groups in the Technical Group of Co-ordination and Defence of Independent MEPs (CDI) (1979–84), Rainbow Group (1984–94), ERA (1994–99), and the Green group in the 1999–2004 Parliament (Lynch 1998). Finally, the anti-EU parties—who are very much in the minority in the EP—formed the Europe of Nations group after the 1994 elections and Europe of Democracies and Diversities (EDD) after the 1999 elections. Most non-attached MEPs are members of extreme right-wing parties or are independents.

Internal organization

In the context of national legislatures a parliamentary party group is defined as 'an organized group of members of a representative body who were elected either under the same party label or under the label of different parties that do not compete against each other in elections, and who do not explicitly create a group for technical reasons only' (Heidar and Koole 2000*a*: 249). Applying this definition to the Parliament, we note the features that distinguish the EP groups from national legislative parties. First, most—but not all—of the national parties in the EPP and PES groups were elected under the same label (EPP or PES), but these labels were hardly used in the campaigns and remain largely unknown among the voters.[4] Moreover, the EPP and PES contain often more than one party per member state, and therefore these parties compete against each other in the elections.

The EP's Rules of Procedure, the standing orders of the Parliament, set numerical criteria for group formation. Since the 1999 elections the minimum number of MEPs required for group formation is twenty-three if they come from two member states, eighteen if they come from three member states, and fourteen if they come from four or more countries. From the 1999 elections onwards mononational groups, with the groups comprising MEPs from only one country, were no longer permitted. The availability of considerable material and procedural benefits explains the emergence of technical groups, like CDI in 1979–84, the Rainbow Group in 1984–94, and the Technical Group of Independent Members (TGI) after the 1999 elections. While the money from the Parliament may appear inconsequential in absolute terms, it has nevertheless been crucial for certain smaller regionalist and green parties that have not enjoyed similar access to comparable resources at the national level. Material benefits include, for example, office space, staff, and money for distributing information. The sum each group receives depends on the number of MEPs and working languages in the group. In 2000 the groups were directly allocated about €34 million, and financial support for them accounted for about 15 per cent of the EP budget.

While the number of staff employed by the groups has risen in absolute terms (532 posts in 2000 compared with 285 in 1982), the ratio of group staff per member has improved only moderately (0.85 in 2000, up from 0.66 in 1982). In addition, each MEP has one to three personal assistants (financed from the EP budget) and both the committee and the EP staff assist groups and MEPs. Group staff perform a variety of duties, ranging from administrative routines to drafting background memos, following developments in committees and drawing up whips in plenaries (Corbett *et al.* 2000: 82–6). Turning to procedural rights, appointments to committees and intra-parliamentary leadership positions, and the allocation of reports and plenary speaking time are based on the rule of proportionality between the groups. Certain plenary actions, such as tabling amendments or oral questions, require the backing of a committee, a party group, or at least thirty-two MEPs. Non-attached representatives are thus also procedurally marginalized in the chamber (Williams 1995).

Three factors work against cohesive party groups in the Parliament: the balance of power between the EU institutions, the rules for candidate selection, and the internal heterogeneity of the groups. A key element in producing unitary group action in national legislatures is the fact that governments depend on the support of the parliamentary majority. Especially when the government enjoys only a small majority, both the government and the opposition groups have strong incentives to act cohesively. The EP party groups lack this motive. While the Commission is appointed by the Parliament and can be brought down by it (as happened indirectly in 1999), the composition of the Commission is not based on the outcome of the Euroelections.[5]

Second, 'centralized nomination procedures should lead to greater party cohesion' (Bowler *et al.* 1999a: 8). National parties, and not EP groups or Europarties, control candidate selection. Therefore national parties possess the ultimate sanction against MEPs. This applies particularly to countries using closed lists (France, Germany, UK, Greece, Portugal, Spain) or mixed systems, where parties present pre-ordered lists and the electors vote either for a party or an individual candidate (Austria, Belgium, the Netherlands, Sweden). In the past national parties have often adopted a lacklustre approach to their MEPs, leaving them relatively free to do what they please 'far away' in Brussels. However, the vote on appointing Jacques Santer as the Commission President in 1994 indicated that when receiving conflicting voting instructions from national parties and their EP groups, national party guidelines can override EP party group positions (Hix and Lord 1996). In particular, we can expect MEPs seeking re-election to be very reluctant to ignore national party guidelines. Finally, of all the legislatures, the heterogeneity of the Parliament is probably matched only by that of the Indian Congress. No less than 129 national parties from fifteen member states won seats in the 1999 elections. The largest group, EPP, consisted of thirty-five national party delegations. Such a high level of heterogeneity, not to mention the problems involved in communicating in eleven official languages, presents a formidable challenge for the groups.

However, roll call analyses (see Table 12.3) indicate that the groups do achieve rather high levels of cohesion (Attinà 1990, Hix and Lord 1997, Raunio 1997, Hix 2001). Reflecting its disagreements over European integration, the PES was prone to internal splits until the early 1990s, but has since become much more cohesive. The EPP, in turn, has become less cohesive since the mid-1990s as the group membership has been widened to include several conservative parties. Groups dominated by a single party have often reached very high levels of cohesion, while technical groups and the radical left groups have seldom made attempts to build common positions. In comparative terms, the EP groups are less cohesive than party groups in the EU member state legislatures, but more cohesive than parties in the US Congress and at least on a par with party groups in the Swiss federal parliament (Hix 1998, Lanfranchi and Lüthi 1999).

What accounts for this relatively unitary behaviour? Until the Treaties of Maastricht and Amsterdam one could argue that as most votes in the Parliament had little if any impact, it did not really matter how MEPs voted. According to this line of reasoning the fragile foundations of group cohesion would be put to test once the Parliament acquired real legislative powers (Bardi 1994). Indeed, there are signs that group cohesion has declined as the EP has gained new powers.

An alternative explanation focuses on how group organization is tailored to face the twin challenge of internal heterogeneity and the strong position of national parties. Decision-making within groups is primarily consensual, with groups putting much effort into building positions that are acceptable to all or nearly all parties in the group. Unlike national party leaders, EP group chairs do not control or even influence candidate selection, nor can they promise lucrative ministerial portfolios or well-paid civil service jobs.[6] Groups have whips, but they basically just remind MEPs of group positions and indicate which votes are important. While the groups have fairly similar organizational structures, with leaders, executive committees, and working parties, the groups can nevertheless be characterized as non-hierarchical and non-centralized.

Table 12.3 Group cohesion in the Parliament

Group	Parliament 1979–84	1984–9	1989–94	1994–9	1999–
PES	65.8	62.2	78.6	89.0	84.8
EPP	83.2	84.1	88.2	90.2	81.1
ELDR	77.2	69.5	85.7	80.1	87.8
EDG	77.3	82.9	92.2		
COM	71.9	71.2			
EDA	75.7	70.8		93.2	
Greens			87.5	85.2	75.4
EUL			92.3		
RB		67.8	69.5		
ER		96.1	88.9		
EUL–NGL				83.8	61.4
LU			93.8		
FE				81.3	
ERA			100.0		
EN				70.7	
UEN					58.3
EDD					40.5

Note: The index of agreement (IA) developed by Fulvio Attinà is a variant of the Rice index typically used to measure group cohesion in legislatures. 'The index is a measure of the relation that exists between the three modalities of votes—in favour, against and abstention—cast by the members of a group; more exactly, it is the percentage measure of the relation between (*a*) the difference between the highest numbering modality and the sum of the other two modalities in a vote by the MEPs of a group, and (*b*) the total number of the votes cast by the group:

$$IA = \frac{highest\ modality - sum\ of\ the\ other\ two\ modalities}{total\ number\ of\ votes} \times 100$$

The index is equal to + 100 when all the deputies belonging to a group vote in the same way. Between + 99.9 and + 0.1, agreement decreases, but more than half of the voters express the same voting modality. At 0 we have a split in half of the votes in two modalities or, with three modalities, one of these is exactly equal to the sum of the other two. When the index has a negative value, the votes break down into three modalities, and even the highest number of votes in one modality is less than half of the total group vote (Attinà 1990: 564).

Sources: 1979–84 and 1984–9, Attinà (1990: 574); 1989–94, Raunio (1997: 95); 1994–9, Hix and Lord (1997: 142); 1999–2004, data provided by Simon Hix.

At the start of the five-year legislative term the groups elect their leaders (chair/president), who usually occupy the post until the next elections or even longer. The chairs represent their group in the Conference of Presidents, the body responsible for setting the Parliament's agenda and for organizational decisions. The number of vice-chairs varies between the groups. For example, in 2000 PES had fourteen and EPP six vice-presidents. The Green group uses two co-chairs, one of whom is a woman.

The executive committee of the group is the Bureau, composed of the chairman, vice-chairs, heads, and possible additional members of national party delegations, and the treasurer. The Bureau is responsible for organizational and administrative issues, and prepares policy decisions for group meetings. The Bureau plays a key role in facilitating group consensus. In their discussion on factionalism within national parties, Bowler *et al.* (1999a: 15) argue that

> there are reasons for thinking that factions can help rank-and-file members discipline their leadership, either by providing faction leaders to take part in policy discussions (reporting back to their members) or by making it clear to party leaders that a block of votes will desert if some policy line is crossed. In this sense, factions help party leaders understand where their support or opposition lies within the party and the levels of this support or opposition.

The same dynamic is at work in the EP groups. When one replaces factions with national party delegations, we see that by guaranteeing all national delegations representation in the executive committee, the group leadership learns about the positions of national parties and the intensity of their preferences. The groups convene regularly in Brussels prior to the plenary week as well as during Strasbourg plenaries. The meetings in Brussels constitute a 'Group week', usually lasting two to three days. When MEPs feel they cannot follow the group position, they are expected to make this clear in the group meetings (Bay Brzinski 1995). Party groups have also established working groups for examining specific policy areas and for coordinating group policy on those issues (Hix and Lord 1997: 77–166, Raunio 2000b).

National party delegations are the cornerstones upon which the groups are based. Some groups are indeed no more than loose coalitions of national parties, while even in the oldest and most organized groups—EPP and PES—one can occasionally see divisions along national lines. Most national delegations have their own staff, elect their chairs, and convene prior to group meetings. However, the impact of national parties is mitigated by three factors.

First, national parties are seldom unitary actors themselves. National parties throughout the Union are, to a varying extent, internally divided over integration, and these divisions are reproduced in the Parliament. Perhaps the best examples are the British Conservative and Labour delegations (Westlake 1994). Second, the EP is a committee-based legislature, with emphasis on building issue-specific majorities in the committees. Third, the majority of bills and resolutions do not produce divisions along national lines. Much of the Parliament's agenda is taken up by internal market legislation, not by constitutional matters or redistributive decisions like the allocation of structural funds.

Why do MEPs and national party delegations vote with their group most of the time? The most important reason is policy influence. Cohesive group action is essential for achieving the group's objectives, while cooperative behaviour within groups helps MEPs in pursuing their own policy goals. Considering that national parties control candidate selection, part of the answer lies in the fact that national parties have by and large refrained from intervening in the EP's work. Were the party leaders to begin monitoring MEP behaviour on a more regular basis, through increased policy coordination or even voting instructions, group cohesion would be seriously threatened (Raunio 2000a). Third, considering the huge number of amendments and final resolutions voted upon in each plenary, the voting cues provided by group whips are an essential source of guidance for MEPs.

To summarize, the non-hierarchical group structure, based on institutionalized interaction between the leadership, the committees, and the national delegations, facilitates group cohesion. On the other hand, the accommodation of national viewpoints leads arguably to lowest common denominator decisions. However, these policy compromises are a prerequisite for the Parliament to influence EU legislation. The next section examines coalition dynamics in the chamber, focusing on the role of party groups in the EP's committees.

Coalition politics and parliamentary committees

Committees are established to make parliaments more efficient. They facilitate specialization and thereby enhance parliaments' ability to influence legislation and to hold the government accountable. While there is much variation among European legislatures, most parliaments have strengthened the role of committees in order to reduce the informational advantage of the executive (Mattson and Strøm 1995, Longley and Davidson 1998, Norton 1998). In a comparative study of west European legislatures, Damgaard (1995) found that in twelve out of eighteen parliaments, committee members had 'medium' or 'high' influence on party positions. The same applies to the European Parliament.

The Parliament has proven successful in using its legislative and appointment powers (see Chapter 5). When explaining this success, scholars have emphasized the interaction between party groups and committees. More specifically, the rapporteurship system, with parliamentary resolutions based on reports drafted by individual members, is identified as crucial (Bowler and Farrell 1995, Tsebelis 1995, Earnshaw and Judge 1997, Lord 1998a, Hix 1999b: 74–98, Wurzel 1999). Committees enjoy extensive procedural rights in processing legislation and in shaping the EP's agenda. The key question for the party groups is therefore how and to what extent they influence committee proceedings.

Representation on committees is roughly proportional to group size, with committee memberships and chairs reallocated at mid-term (after two and a half years). Research on committee appointments by Bowler and Farrell (1995: 227) showed that 'the share of committee places is proportional by both nationality and ideological bloc. Within these limits, set by allocations along ideological or national lines, there is scope for the kinds of specialized membership and recruitment made in the US Congress.' Within committees are four positions of authority: chair, vice-chair, party group coordinators, and *rapporteurs*. Committee chairs are highly prestigious positions. Committees elect their own chairs, but in practice party groups decide the allocation of chairs and vice-chairs, with the d'Hondt method[7] used for distributing the chairs. Chair allocation is thus proportional, again reflecting procedures used in most European parliaments (Mattson and Strøm 1995). Party group coordinators are responsible for coordinating the work of their groups in the committees. Together with the committee chair, the coordinators negotiate the distribution of rapporteurships between the groups.

Turning to the passage of legislation, when the bill arrives in the Parliament from the Commission, a committee is designated as responsible for producing a report on the issue, with one or more committees assigned as opinion-giving committees.[8] Committees use an auction-like points system for distributing reports to the groups, with group coordinators making bids on behalf of their groups. The allocation of reports is roughly proportional to group strength in the Parliament. However, as the points total of each group is proportional to its seat share in the chamber, the most expensive reports (those that 'cost' the most points), such as those on the EU budget or on important pieces of co-decision legislation, are largely monopolized by EPP and PES.

The *rapporteur* must be prepared to make compromises. Majority-building as early as the stage at which reports are drafted helps facilitate the smooth passage of the report in the committee and in the plenary. The draft report, together with amendments (tabled by any member), is then voted upon in the committee. Before the plenary the groups decide their positions: what amendments to propose, and whether to support the report or not. National party delegations often hold their own meetings prior to the group meetings. Finally, the report and amendments (by the responsible committee, a party group, or at least thirty-two members) are voted upon in the plenary.

Throughout the processing of the bill, party groups monitor the proceedings in the committees, with working parties and coordinators playing key roles. However, the technicality of much Community legislation strengthens the informational advantage and autonomy of the committees. With the exception of the assignment process, party group influence within committees is therefore modest, with groups having coordinating mechanisms for overseeing committee work instead of hierarchical structures for controlling MEP behaviour in the committees.

The 'partyness' of committee work may be relatively low, but coalition-building at the plenary stage is driven by partisan concerns. The EP party system is based on the left–right dimension, but the left–right cleavage is less important than in European national legislatures. This results from three factors: there is no government and opposition in the chamber, the Parliament (or the EU) does not have competence on many traditional left–right matters such as health care, taxation, or social policy, and the anti/pro-integration dimension constitutes the second main structure of competition in the Parliament (see Hix 2001).

Coalition formation depends both on the issue voted upon and on the voting rules. While the primary decision rule is simple majority (50 per cent + 1 of those voting), for certain issues specified in the Treaty (mainly budget amendments and second reading legislative amendments adopted under co-decision) the Parliament needs to muster absolute majorities (50 per cent + 1 *all* of its members, 314/626 MEPs). Until the 1999 elections the formation of majorities was primarily based on cooperation between PES and EPP. After the 1999 elections this cooperation has played a lesser role than before, with EPP and PES opposing each other more often regardless of the voting rule. Still, these two large groups voted together on approximately 60 per cent of all votes (Hix 2001).

Figure 12.1 displays potential winning coalitions in the 1999–2004 Parliament under both simple and absolute majority voting rules. Attendance in plenaries had often been notoriously low (Scully 1997, Raunio 1997, Kreppel 2000), but average attendance during the first six months of the 1999–2004 legislature was 74 per cent, equating to 461 MEPs (Hix 2000). Therefore Figure 12.1 depicts the realistic threshold for achieving a simple majority, 232 MEPs. Taking this into consideration, the EPP–PES alliance ('grand coalition') is still the safest option for building majorities. Numerically broader is the 'super majority', bringing together all main party groups. Both the right-wing 'free market' coalition (EPP, ELDR, UEN) and the 'social EU' coalition (PES, Greens, EUL–NGL) are fragile and need additional members. PES, Greens, and EUL–NGL control between them 270 seats, and therefore

Figure 12.1 Coalitions in the Parliament in 1999–2004

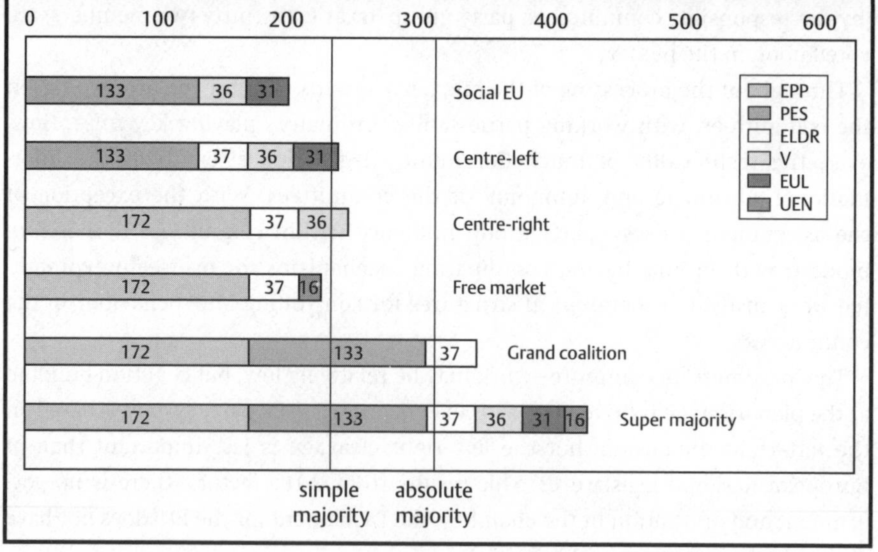

need very high attendance rates for forming winning coalitions under simple majority rule. This explains the strength of the ELDR, and increasingly also the Greens, in the Parliament. The Liberals, situated ideologically between EPP and PES, are often in a 'pivotal' position, that is, their inclusion can turn a losing coalition into a winning combination. The Green group, which sits physically in the middle of the hemicycle, between PES and ELDR, has become more pro-integrationist and market-friendly in recent years. Their ideological moderation facilitates cooperation with EPP and PES.

The first half of the 1999–2004 EP indicates that the bargaining power of the groups has changed to the advantage of the centre-right groups. However, the success of non-left alliances depends on ideological cohesion (notably within the EPP) and on attendance rates. For example, while the centre-right groups may be able to agree on internal market legislation, their ideological unity is likely to break down on libertarian questions and in constitutional matters. The EP party system in the 1999–2004 legislature is more competitive than before, but from the point of view of the elections this hardly matters, as is argued in the next section.

Electoral accountability

Voting decisions in Euroelections are heavily influenced by domestic political allegiances and by the national party-political environment. The primacy of domestic factors results from the strategies of national parties that control candidate selection and carry out electoral campaigns and from the institutional context in which EP elections are conducted.

Most national parties in most EU countries fight Euroelections on domestic issues. National parties have good reason to avoid competing with each other on issues concerning the broad sweep of European integration. The overwhelming majority of national parties were established before European integration, and are therefore based on the traditional social cleavages recognized in the political science literature. As the anti/pro-integration dimension cross-cuts these cleavages, parties tend to experience internal fragmentation on EU questions (Hix and Lord 1997: 21–53, Marks and Wilson 2000). Survey data shows that both MEPs and MPs are on average more representative of their voters on traditional left–right matters than on issues related to European integration (Thomassen and Schmitt 1999a). Such electoral considerations aside, it appears that there has been relatively little genuine interest in European elections within national parties, especially among party leaders. This is again natural, for the primary channel for influencing EU policy is by holding executive office at the national level, not through winning seats in the Parliament. Elections to the Parliament are therefore scarcely 'European'. The elections are held during the same week, and the candidates compete for seats in an EU institution, but there is no common electoral system, constituency boundaries do not cross national borders, and campaigning is conducted by national parties on the basis of national agendas. Therefore the Parliament's agenda and the electoral campaigns bear little if any relation to each other.

Moreover, the lack of competing alternatives tends to deaden election campaigns. In most member states the main parties are in broad agreement over integration (see van der Eijk and Franklin 1996, Blondel *et al.* 1998: 164–92, Ray 1999, Thomassen and Schmitt 1999*b*). Parties classified as 'Eurosceptical' are normally either former communist parties (Germany, Greece, Portugal, Sweden) or extreme right-wing parties (Austria, Belgium, France, Germany, Italy) (Taggart 1998). The majority of Europeans are not willing to support such radical parties. At the European level the policy profiles of the Europarties—Party of European Socialists (PES), European People's Party (EPP), European Liberal, Democrat, and Reform Party (ELDR), European Federation of Green Parties (EFGP)—have become increasingly similar, especially after PES and EFGP changed their attitudes to European integration (Hix 1999*a*). This reflects overall policy convergence, especially in economic policy, between national parties belonging to the Europarties. With the exception of marginal fringe parties, basically all parties are considered fit to govern, with national coalition cabinets often including parties across the ideological spectrum (Mair 1997).

The main EP party groups are organs of their Europarties. The EPP was established as early as 1976. However, it was not until the inclusion of the 'Party Article' in the Maastricht Treaty that the socialists, liberals, and greens turned their federations into parties: PES was established in 1992, EFGP and ELDR in 1993.[9] Following the Treaty of Nice, the Party Article (Article 191 TEC) reads

1. Political parties at the European level are important as a factor for integration within the Union. They contribute to forming a European awareness and to expressing the political will of the citizens of the Union.

2. The Council, acting in accordance with the procedure referred to in Article 251 [co-decision procedure], shall lay down the regulations governing political parties at European level and in particular the rules regarding their funding.[10]

EP groups are represented in the party congresses and executive committees of the Europarties. The group chair reports to the congress on the work of the group, and sits in the Europarty's executive committee. While the Europarties apply qualified and simple majority voting in their internal decision-making, they are still better understood as forums of cooperation and policy coordination between national parties. The exact policy influence of Europarties is practically impossible to measure, and depends primarily on the willingness of national member parties to pursue and implement the agreed policy objectives. However, the Europarties serve as important arenas for the diffusion of ideas and policy coordination. Particularly the meetings of party leaders, held usually at the same venue as the summits of the European Council, enable national parties to coordinate their actions prior to the summits (see Hix and Lord 1997, Johansson 1999, Ladrech 2000). Moreover, Europarties prepare the ground for future enlargements by integrating interests from the prospective central and eastern European member states. Through their membership in the Europarties, parties from the applicant countries engage in partisan cooperation that is important in nurturing wider, pan-European political allegiances.

Considering the shape of the EU political system, the Europarties are likely to remain primarily as networks of national parties, even with public funding of Europarties from the EU budget. However, there is a potential solution for enhancing the position of the Europarties and their EP party groups without altering the balance of power between the EU institutions: changing the rules of the electoral game by giving the Europarties the right to influence candidate selection. For example, the Europarties could be responsible for deciding the names and order of the candidates elected from EU-wide lists. The Parliament has called for the adoption of supranational lists starting from the elections scheduled for 2009. According to this scenario a share of MEPs would be elected from a single Union-wide constituency, with the remaining representatives elected from member states. For this move to have its intended effect, the share of MEPs elected from the EU-constituency would have to be sufficiently high to have an impact on seat distribution in the chamber, say at least 15–20 per cent of the MEPs. This would probably be sufficient for motivating national parties to use Europarties' manifestos and for stimulating EU-wide campaigns.

Conclusions

The Parliament has structured its internal organization so as to maximize its influence in the EU political system. The thrust of legislative work is done in the committees, where individual rapporteurs draft reports that form the basis for parliamentary resolutions. Also the internal organization of the party groups is non-centralized, with emphasis on building consensus among national party delegations. The core of the EP party system is formed by conservatives and Christian democrats (EPP), social democrats (PES), and the smaller liberal (ELDR), green (G/EFA), and radical left (EUL–NGL) groups. The party system is relatively unstable, with each Euroelection leading to the emergence and disappearance of smaller groups. Therefore the EP party group structure is weakly institutionalized.

The forthcoming enlargements may further destabilize the group structure as the party systems of the central and eastern European countries remain fragmented. However, the heterogeneity of the groups resulting from enlargements (with over forty parties in the largest groups!) will probably make the groups more hierarchical. As the number of national parties within a group increases, the weight of individual party delegations declines, and investing the group leadership with stronger powers may be the only way to produce unified group action, or even to maintain current levels of group cohesion.

The biggest, and most demanding, challenge for the party groups is to command loyalty and support among EU citizens. Without any European government to hold accountable, and without any 'real' European elections conducted by European-level parties, the party groups are bound to remain unknown among the majority of Europeans. The EU resembles in many ways the US pluralist political system, with multiple veto-players, power-sharing, and policy coordination between state and federal levels, and strong interest groups (Coultrap 1999)—but also weak and internally divided parties (or party groups in the EU's case). Indeed, the EP's party groups make the American Democrats and Republicans seem comparatively cohesive and single-minded, and the latter are certainly far better known to average citizens. To put it simply, Europeans do not yet know how and to what extent the EP party groups influence EU policies.

Notes

1 I am grateful to Simon Hix, Roger Scully, and the editors for their insightful comments.

2 For a brief history of the groups, see Corbett *et al.* (2000: 59–82). Group names and abbreviations used in this chapter are based on the 1999–2004 Parliament. Following the 1999 elections, the EPP is called EPP–ED, but I will use the acronym EPP.

3 For analyses of party groups in the pre-1979 Parliament, see van Oudenhove (1965), Fitzmaurice (1975), and Pridham and Pridham (1981).

4 In fact, Europarty labels can be counter-productive for national parties. In their discussion on parties in the US House of Representatives, Cox and McCubbins (1993) argue that congressmen have an incentive to be loyal to their party groups, as the reputation of their groups is important in terms of re-election. Distancing oneself or the party from the Europarty can actually be a safer electoral strategy for MEPs, especially in member states whose publics are less supportive of European integration.

5 After the 1999 elections there is a kind of government and opposition divide in the Parliament, with PES, often backed by ELDR and Greens, supporting the Commission and EPP criticizing Prodi's team. This results from three factors: (1) following the resignation of Santer's Commission, the Parliament is more eager to attack the Commission, (2) despite the emergence of the EPP as the biggest group in the Parliament, the

partisan composition of the Commission leans towards centre-left, and (3) opposition from the German Christian Democrats, with no commissioner of their own, and the British Conservatives, eager to criticize most things the Commission does.

6 The party groups have very limited means to influence appointments in the Commission. In fact, groups have probably less influence regarding appointments than before as the Commission has introduced stricter criteria for filling positions (see Chapters 4 and 7). When there is party influence, it occurs via national governments, not through EP groups.

7 Named after its inventor, the Belgian mathematician Victor d'Hondt, the method is used for allocating seats in electoral systems based on proportional representation. The party group winning most seats in the Parliament gets the first committee chair, and the number of seats held by that group is then divided by two and compared with the seat shares of the other groups. The group with most seats at this point receives the second committee chair. The process continues until all committee chairs have been allocated.

8 For detailed information on the processing of legislation in the Parliament, see Corbett *et al.* (2000: 105–29, 176–215).

9 For comparative analyses of Europarties, see Hix and Lord (1997), Bell and Lord (1998), and Johansson and Zervakis (2001). For case-studies of party families, see Ladrech (2000), Jansen (1998), and Dietz (2000).

10 The second paragraph was added by the Treaty of Nice. In addition, the Treaty contained the following declaration on the Party Article: 'The Conference recalls that the provisions of Article 191 do not imply any transfer of powers to the European Community and do not affect the application of the relevant national constitutional rules. The funding for political parties at European level provided out of the budget of the European Communities may not be used to fund, either directly or indirectly, political parties at national level. The provisions on the funding for political parties shall apply, on the same basis, to all the political forces represented in the European Parliament.'

Further reading

The volume edited by van der Eijk and Franklin (1996) is an essential guide to understanding voter and party behaviour in Euroelections. Pridham and Pridham (1981) provides a detailed account of the emergence of European party federations in the 1970s, while the volume edited by Johansson and Zervakis (2001) explores their subsequent development and functions in the EU political system. Hix and Lord (1997) analyses the role of parties in the EU policy process, with chapters on national parties, EP party groups, and party federations. Kreppel (2001) provides a data-rich account of how the Parliament and its party groups influence EU legislation.

Hix, S., and Lord, C. (1997), *Political Parties in the European Union* (Basingstoke: Macmillan).

Johansson, K. M., and Zervakis, P. (2001) (eds.), *European Political Parties between Cooperation and Integration* (Baden-Baden: Nomos).

Kreppel, A. (2001), *The European Parliament and the Supranational Party System: A Study of Institutional Development* (Cambridge: Cambridge University Press).

Pridham, G., and Pridham, P. (1981), *Transnational Party Co-operation and European Integration: The Process towards Direct Elections* (London: George Allen & Unwin).

van der Eijk, C., and Franklin, M. N. (1996) (eds.), *Choosing Europe? The European Electorate and National Politics in the Face of Union* (Ann Arbor: University of Michigan Press).

Web links

Basic information on the European Parliament and its party groups may be found at: **www.europarl.eu.int/groups/**

The web sites of the Parliament's party groups provide information on the members and national parties in the groups, the internal organization of the groups, together with policy statements, press releases, and latest news regarding the groups.

European People's Party: **www.eppe.org**
Party of European Socialists: **www.eurosocialists.org**
European Liberal, Democrat and Reform Party: **www.eldr.org**
European Federation of Green Parties: **www.europeangreens.org**

The home pages of the four Europarties provide a brief history of the parties, their election and policy programmes, and links to national member parties, the EP party group, affiliated organizations, and even their 'own' commissioners.

Chapter 13
National Interests: Coreper

Jeffrey Lewis

Contents

Summary

The Committee of Permanent Representatives (Coreper) originated as an iterative diplomatic forum to prepare meetings of the Council of Ministers. It quickly and quietly evolved into a locus of continuous negotiation and *de facto* decision-making, gaining a reputation as 'the place to do the deal'. This reputation is based largely on the degree of insulation from domestic audiences and an unrivalled ability to 'make deals stick' across a range of issue areas and policy subjects. Most importantly, as this chapter will show, Coreper spotlights the process of integrating interests in a collective decision-making system with its own organizational culture, norms, rationality, and style of discourse. The result is an institutional context where international and transgovernmental interaction effects cannot be considered exogenous to the process whereby national interests are formed.

Introduction

This chapter addresses the role of the Committee of Permanent Representatives (Coreper) in the EU.[1] According to one analyst, 'the caliber and effectiveness of permanent representative officials determines to a great extent how countries fare in the EU' (Dinan 1999: 260). Another claims that the members of Coreper are 'among the great unsung heroes' of European integration (Westlake 1995: p. xxiv). Both observations offer a useful entry-point to understanding Coreper and how it functions. First, it is a pivotal actor in 'everyday' EU decision-making and for this reason, member states consider Coreper one of the most important postings in Brussels. Second, and what may seem counter-intuitive to the first point, Coreper is less visible than other institutional sites in the EU. As this chapter will clarify, Coreper's importance as an institutional actor is related to its ability over the years to avoid the limelight and to work behind the scenes at finding agreements and forging compromise.

Coreper is the site in EU decision-making where national interests and European solutions interact and commingle more frequently, more intensively, and across more issue areas than any other. Coreper is also something of a chimera: to some, it resembles a bastion of intergovernmentalism; to others, it appears less like interstate bargaining than a haven for Eurocrats to 'go native'. Neither view, in such stark terms, is accurate. Nor is either view entirely wrong. As Hayes-Renshaw and Wallace (1995: 563) found in their study of the Council's institutional form, 'it is both representative and collective'. Under the lens of the 'new institutionalism' (NI), this dialectical tension is precisely what makes Coreper so interesting to study.

Coreper is 'responsible for preparing the work of the Council and for carrying out the tasks assigned to it by the Council' (Article 207 TEC). From this austere mandate, Coreper has developed into a major player in the EU system. Among its 'assigned tasks' is the remit to 'coordinate the work of the various Council meetings and to endeavour to reach agreement at its level' (Council of the European Union, 1996: 39). In essence, this means that Coreper holds responsibility for the performance of Council as a whole. In NI terms, there is an obligation of result, which the permanent representatives find is an unwritten part of the job description. As one ambassador explained, 'there is a high collective interest in getting results and reaching solutions. This is in addition to representing the national interest.' Another claimed to have an unwritten, global, permanent instruction to 'find solutions'. A third said, 'if we have to take it to the Council, there is a sense that we have failed.' Signs of this responsibility and the mandate that it rests on can be traced back to the dog days of Eurosclerosis, and the heads of state and government who innovated European Council summitry. In particular, the communiqué of the 1974 Paris summit holds: 'Greater latitude will be given to the permanent representatives so that only the most important political problems need be discussed in the Council.'[2] It was during this same period that integration researchers began to observe that Coreper resembled 'a Council of Ministers in permanent session' (Busch and Puchala 1976: 240).

In many ways, Coreper is the ideal institutional site to examine national interests in the context of everyday EU decision-making because Coreper is the needle's eye through which the legislative output of the Council flows. Because a defining trait of the Council is its sectoral differentiation, pursuing the 'national interest' across its operating formations requires national systems of interest intermediation and interministerial coordination that are exceptionally complex even for the smallest member states or those with the most centralized EU affairs machinery.[3] It is here that permanent representatives, with their cross-Council negotiating mandates and intersectoral policy responsibilities, practice an essential aggregation function, which runs the gamut of EU affairs. The EU ambassadors and deputies are thus critical interlocutors in the ability of a member state to pursue what Anderson (1999: 6) calls a 'milieu goal' in Brussels, which is the ability to 'ensure that government policy objectives are consistent, both within Europe and across the national and supranational levels'.

In the next section, we examine how the permanent representatives acquired such a central position in the EU system. We then sketch out the structure of Coreper, including how it works and has changed over time. Next, the Committee's main powers, namely *de facto* decision-making and an institutional capacity for integrating interests, are examined. Coreper is then placed into the broader context of the EU and theories of European integration. Finally, a brief concluding section will summarize these themes and hypothesize whether a decision-making system such as the EU needs an institution like Coreper to operate effectively.

Coreper's origins

Although no mention was made in the Treaty of Paris for the creation of a preparatory body, it was less than six months after the Treaty entered into force on 23 July 1952 that the need for such a body was apparent. At the first meeting of the Special Council of Ministers (8–10 September 1952), the *ad hoc* group on the organization of the Council's work was instructed to come up with a proposal for a preparatory committee. The Coordinating Commission, or Cocor (Commission de Coordination du Conseil des Ministres), was the result. The formal decision to create Cocor was taken by the Special Council of Ministers, but it was only with the Treaty of Rome that the legal basis for a preparatory committee was established (Article 151 EEC).

The first Cocor meeting was held on 5 March 1953. Cocor began to meet monthly in Luxembourg, with representatives travelling back and forth from their national capitals. Cocor diplomacy was premissed on mutual trust, a spirit of accommodation, and an equality of voice between big and small states. Ernst Haas, writing in the late 1950s, drew a sharp distinction between Cocor and the brand of diplomacy found at the Council of Europe, for example, equating the former with the 'principle of a novel community-type organ' (1958: 491; 1960).

From the earliest proposals to set up a permanent preparatory body, the issue of delegating formal decision-making authority was allowed to remain

---

Exhibit 13.1 Constitutive politics and the Spaak Committee

The creation of a permanent Brussels-based body composed of high-ranking civil servants was based on a proposal from the Committee of the Heads of Delegations, chaired by the industrious Belgian Foreign Minister, Paul-Henri Spaak (more popularly known as the Spaak Committee). The Spaak Committee, set up by the foreign ministers at Messina (June 1955) to discuss future steps in European integration, began meeting intensively at the Château de Val Duchesse outside Brussels in July 1955. Eight months of talks produced the Spaak Report (April 1956). The recommendations of the Spaak Report were approved by the foreign ministers meeting in Venice (May 1956) and, after further IGC negotiations (again led by the Spaak Committee), culminated in the Treaty of Rome (March 1957). In one of the less well-known political coups in the history of the EU, it was the Spaak Committee that strongly endorsed a permanent negotiating body and, for the most part, its members were the same individuals who would become the first permanent representatives.

As Noël (1967: 219) recounts, Article 151 EEC became a 'means of prolonging and perpetuating . . . that rather extraordinary "club",' (that is, the Spaak Committee) which was 'both a meeting place of authorized and faithful spokesmen of the six Governments and a group of militants (even of "accomplices") dedicated to a vast and noble political undertaking' (see also Lindberg and Scheingold 1970: 242). Noël (1966: 88) hints at the novelty of this, whereby the Spaak Committee morphed into what would become Coreper, since the Interim Committee set up in March 1957 contained many of the same personnel and 'preserved the same atmosphere and spirit'. Except for France and Italy, the Interim Committee delegates would also become the first permanent representatives in early 1958. In short, the Spaak Committee and the creation of Coreper is a striking example of 'constitutive politics' in the institutional history of European integration.[a]

---

[a] Anderson (1997: 81) defines 'constitutive politics' as the 'processes and outcomes that establish or amend EU rules of the game', as distinct from 'regulative politics' which are the 'processes and outcomes that take place within established routinized areas of EU activity'.

ambiguous. Such a non-debate is evident at the 1956 Intergovernmental Conference (IGC) where the design of a new permanent, Brussels-based committee was negotiated (see Exhibit 13.1). In the course of discussions it became clear that there was agreement among the foreign ministers *not* to create a Brussels-based body composed of deputy ministers. Instead, they agreed that high-ranking diplomats should head the permanent delegations. But there was little talk on what substantive form the permanent representatives' role should take and the issue was left open. Articles 151 EEC and 121 Euratom reflected this ambiguity. They allowed simply for the Council's rules of procedure to 'provide for the establishment of a committee composed of representatives of member states. The Council shall determine the task and competence of that committee.'

Early on, the open-ended nature of Coreper's authority set off alarm bells at the Commission. Following the January 1958 decision to begin the work of the Committee without precisely defining its tasks and powers, the Commission asked for clarification of Coreper's role (de Zwaan 1995: 75). In March 1958, Belgian Foreign Minister Larock, acting as Council President, defended the Council's provisional rules of procedure and assured Commission President Hallstein that they ruled out the possibility of delegating decisional authority to Coreper (Noël 1967: 228–9). There were similar questions raised in the European Parliament, with some MEPs concerned the Committee could usurp the Commission's right of initiative (de Zwaan 1995: 75). After these early years, the Commission, and in particular the Secretary-General's office with Emile Noël at the helm from 1958 to 1987, would come to view the permanent representatives as potential allies in a common cause. As one Commission participant stated, 'We consider Coreper more as an ally than something we have to fight with.' Coreper is often the strategic point of inroad to the Council, since the Commission prefers to have detailed, substantive discussions with the permanent representatives who (unlike many ministers) are also well versed in the legal intricacies of the Treaty. Jacques Delors, while Commission President, often personally appeared in Coreper to explain and 'sell' key Single Market proposals to the permanent representatives before they were presented at the ministerial level.[4]

From the late 1950s, Coreper, quietly and often unnoticed, acquired a reputation for forging compromise and finding solutions across an ever-growing range of issues. This was contrary to their reputation in academic circles, as integration researchers typically characterized Coreper as an exemplar of intergovernmentalism and hardball bargaining.[5] As the EC 'deepened', Coreper acquired new responsibilities and general policy competencies (Noël and Étienne 1971). Agricultural policy was an exception to this, and in 1960, the Special Committee on Agriculture (SCA) was set up to take over the specialized and technical aspects of administering the CAP. The deepening process created exponential pressures for Coreper to develop *de facto* legislative competencies in order to minimize policy-making bottlenecks and impart coherence to the segmentation of the Council's work. The bifurcation of Coreper in 1962 into parts I and II (discussed below) was an acknowledgement of this burgeoning workload. But contrary to conventional accounts, such as Weiler's (1981: 285) claim that 'decisional supranationalism' was weakened by the addition of Coreper to the EC system, the permanent representatives exemplified a brand of diplomacy based on thick bonds of mutual trust, understanding, responsiveness, and a willingness to compromise. The ability to serve as a gatekeeper for the Council's work was not simply about paving the way for ministers to find agreements, but, increasingly, the ability to dispose of large quantities of business by forging consensus out of seemingly irreconcilable national positions. In this respect, Coreper can be viewed as a source of institutional innovation, what Peterson and Bomberg (1999: 254) refer to as the ability to offer 'new supranational solutions to national problems' by encouraging 'new types of agency in what is perceived as a positive sum game'.

Structure of the institution

In terms of structural location, Coreper occupies a unique institutional vantage point in the EU system. Vertically placed between the experts and the ministers and horizontally situated with cross-sectoral and inter-pillar policy responsibilities, the permanent representatives have a general overview of the Council's work. Relative to the experts meeting in the working groups, they are political heavyweights; but compared to the ministers, they are both policy generalists and experts in the substantive questions of a file. In his classic study of Coreper, Joseph Salmon referred to this unique perspective as the *vue d'ensemble* (1971: 642). The institutional perspective of the *vue d'ensemble* is a qualitative feature of Coreper, part of the organizational culture and a kind of cognitive map.

Defined in the narrowest sense, Coreper consists of thirty 'members', who are jointly referred to as the permanent representatives.[6] This includes fifteen EU ambassadors and fifteen deputies. The Committee meets in two formats: I (deputies) and II (ambassadors). The Commission is always represented in both Committee formats. But Coreper is embedded in a much more extensive network of national delegations in Brussels, known as the EU permanent representations (Permreps). At a glance, the Permreps look like embassies, but as the EC/EU has deepened they have grown in size and coverage to become microcosms of the national governments and 'veritable administrative melting-pots' (Hayes-Renshaw *et al*. 1989: 128). Permreps also serve as a nerve centre for managing the presidency, and a delegation will often increase by up to 25 per cent to handle the workload.

Table 13.1 Growth in the size of EU permanent representations, 1965–2000

Member states	2000	1995	1993	1991	1986	1969	1965
Belgium	46	36	34	31	26	18	18
Denmark	46	38	38	35	31	—	—
Germany	79	62	55	47	41	28	21
Greece	55	66	73	62	48	—	—
Spain	58	54	51	50	31	—	—
France	70	50	45	41	29	19	18
Ireland	37	37	24	26	24	—	—
Italy	49	42	44	44	40	29	22
Luxembourg	13	14	7	13	6	8	4
Netherlands	47	45	34	30	24	21	19
Austria	68	65	—	—	—	—	—
Portugal	55	48	47	44	36	—	—
Finland	60	37	—	—	—	—	—
Sweden	50	52	—	—	—	—	—
United Kingdom	55	50	45	39	45	—	—

Sources: For 2000, IDEA online (**www.ue.eu.int**); Guide to the Council of the European Communities, various years.

This can be seen in Table 13.1, where the size of the French delegation in 2000 reflects their presidency rotation.

Since 1975, a group of assistants to the ambassadors, known as the Antici counsellors, finalize and prepare the agendas for weekly Coreper II meetings. The Anticis also act as advisers to their ambassadors, minimizing the element of surprise by floating ideas and testing arguments before or at the margins of meetings, drafting reports to send back home, and attending European Council summits as note-takers. In 1993, the deputies formalized a similar group of assistants, known as the Mertens counsellors. The Antici and Mertens counsellors are emblematic of the array of dense transgovernmental networking which takes place among national administrations through the EU delegations. Other close groupings that meet regularly and work on substantive policy matters include the CFSP counsellors and the CEEC enlargement counsellors. In general, the permanent representations are a mechanism for socialization to the EU, training new generations of diplomats and policy specialists, orchestrating presidencies, and 'educating' national administrations to 'open their minds to a new EU reality'.

Coreper I and II

Coreper is split into two formations based on a functional division of labour. Both meet weekly and each have their own Councils to prepare (see Table 13.2). Coreper II is composed of the ambassadors and responsible for the monthly General Affairs Council (GAC) as well as issues with horizontal (especially inter-pillar), institutional, and financial implications. The lion's share of weekly Coreper II agendas deal with EU external relations (that is trade, aid, foreign policy). What is more, discussions range widely, for example, shifting from Polish potato imports to future relations with China. Coreper II is also closely implicated in multi-annual budget negotiations (Delors I and II, Agenda 2000), and historically, with IGCs (often serving as a delegation's personal representative).

Coreper I is made up of the deputies and is responsible for the misleadingly labelled 'technical' Councils such as the Internal Market, Environment, Social Affairs, Transport, and Fisheries. While this work is labelled 'technical'—take, for example, setting fish support prices for the CFP—it is also often intensely political. Since the introduction of the co-decision procedure, a new Coreper I task is representing the Council side at conciliation committee meetings with the EP.[7] Conciliation preparations, and the search for pre-conciliation ('first and second reading') compromises with the EP, now account for a large share of Coreper I business, perhaps as much as 50 per cent of the deputies' time.

Table 13.2 Responsibilities of Coreper I and II

Coreper II – Permanent representatives

General Affairs Council
Justice, Home Affairs and Civil Protection Council
Development Council
Budget Council
Multi-annual budget negotiations (Delors I and II, Agenda 2000)
Structural and cohesion funds
Institutional and horizontal questions
Association agreements
Accession
IGC personal representatives[a]

Coreper I – Deputy permanent representatives

Single European Market (Internal Market, Consumer Affairs, and Tourism Council)
Conciliation in areas of co-decision
Environment Council
Employment and Social Policy Council
Transport and Telecommunications Council
Industry and Energy Council
Fisheries Council
Research Council
Culture Council
Education and Youth Affairs Council
Health Council
Agricultural Council (veterinary and plant-health questions)

[a] Varies by member state and IGC

As a general rule, the division of labour between Coreper I and II functions smoothly. Occasionally, a file that comes under Coreper I's remit is co-opted by the ambassadors. This occurred in 1997 with the EU embargo on fur imports from countries using leghold traps, which began as an animal rights issue for the Environmental Council and Coreper I, but was turned over to Coreper II when broader trade interests were entangled in a dispute with the United States. Finally, there are intangible differences in status and ego between the ambassadors and deputies, with the former exuding almost limitless self-confidence to get the job done. 'We are mere mortals compared to the ambassadors,' one deputy joked.

Who are the EU permanent representatives? Ambassadors are almost invariably senior-ranking diplomats from the ministries of foreign affairs. For most member states, the deputy is also recruited from foreign affairs; exceptions include Germany, where the deputy has always come from economic affairs, and the UK, where the deputy frequently comes from the Department of Trade and Industry (DTI). The permanent representatives are selected from the highest tier of career diplomats and senior civil servants, usually with a considerable background in European affairs. The member states control appointments, and there is no approval process in Brussels. Appointments are typically made after a recommendation or at least tacit approval from the head of state or government. Such high-level political selection contributes enormously to the credibility (and confidence) of the permanent representatives to negotiate in Brussels. 'We don't care if he wears a nice suit,' one participant explained, 'we want to know: can he deliver?' In European diplomatic circles, Coreper is considered a top posting. EU permanent representatives rank the position on a par or slightly above postings to Washington, New York, and Paris.

Coreper appointments are also noteworthy for the length of tenure and absence of partisan politics. The average appointment is five years, slightly longer than the typical three- or four-year diplomatic rotation. But some permanent representatives remain in Brussels for much longer, upwards of a decade or beyond. For example, since 1958, Belgium has had five ambassadors; Germany only four deputies. Longer appointments provide 'continuity in the representation of interests' (de Zwaan 1995: 17). Perhaps a more surprising finding is that permanent representatives are fairly insulated from electoral politics and shifts in government (Portugal and Greece are the exceptions).[8] A good example was British Prime Minister Tony Blair's decision to keep Ambassador Stephen Wall in Brussels despite his close affiliation with the previous Conservative government.[9]

Contestation

Since 1958, Coreper has been the senior preparatory forum of the Council. The vertical channels of coordination placed the permanent representatives in clear command of how files were routed to the ministers. They were undisputed gatekeepers. Since the early 1990s, this role has been contested. While on paper both the Maastricht and Amsterdam Treaties acknowledge and reconfirm Coreper's senior preparatory status, two developments are undermining this in practice.

First, there has been an intensification in the rivalries between preparatory committees (Lewis 2000). There are nagging turf battles over CFSP competencies with the Political Committee. The political directors even attempt to short-circuit Coreper by meeting the morning of the GAC to present updates and recommendations directly and without input from the ambassadors. The creation of a Political and Security Committee (PSC) in 2000 signals a potential new source of preparatory fragmentation as the PSC ambassadors will hold responsibility for the fledgling European Security and Defence Policy (ESDP) (assisted by the new Military Committee and Military Staff). And Coreper II has effectively conceded responsibility for the Ecofin Council (and the 'Eurogroup' of euro zone finance ministers) to the Economic and Finance Committee (EFC). EFC reports are not even seen by the permanent representatives; they are sent directly to the finance ministers.

A second source of contestation is the relative decline of the GAC. For the first several decades of the EU's development, the GAC was *primus inter pares*. But the process of deepening has effectively raised the status of many other sectoral Councils. The GAC has lost its claim to providing leadership or acting as an overall coordinator of EU affairs (Gomez and Peterson 2001). Today many in Brussels believe Ecofin has supplanted the GAC as the senior formation of the Council. For most member states, this is a reflection of the domestic inter-ministerial balance of power, which has witnessed a relative eclipse of foreign affairs (Hocking 1999). The weakening of the GAC is slowly having effects on Coreper as well. This is already evident in the EFC–Ecofin (and 'Eurogroup') linkages that bypass Coreper. Another indicator is the Primenet system that connects prime ministers and their sherpas into a direct transgovernmental network. In this case, links to Coreper are bypassed by horizontal linkages at the level of the prime ministers' offices (see Chapter 2). Some at the permanent representations perceive this general pattern of contestation as weakening Coreper's institutional role.

Powers of the institution

By focusing on Coreper, we are essentially looking at what Peterson (1995) has termed the 'systemic' level of 'policy-setting' decisions. But EU decision-making is also 'heavily nuanced, constantly changing, and even kaleidoscopic' (Peterson and Bomberg 1999: 9) with significant variation by policy sector and issue area. Within this complex and multi-dimensional setting, two formal and informal powers stand out at Coreper level: *de facto* decision-making and the institutional capacities to integrate interests.

De facto decision-makers

Coreper is a continuous negotiation chamber where, in reality, many decisions are made. But the permanent representatives have no formal decision-making authority. Juridical decision-making authority is a power exclusively reserved for the ministers, and formal voting is expressly prohibited at any other level of the Council.[10] But in practice, Coreper has evolved into a veritable decision-making factory. There are subtle ways around the formality of *de jure* voting, such as the 'indicative vote' of how a delegation would vote if the matter was put before the ministers. More common is the tactful packaging of a discussion by the presidency, where the chair will ask 'I assume no one else requests the floor?' or state 'a sufficient majority exists'. No vote is taken. There is no raising of the hands. But many agreements are reached in this manner and many decisions are thus made.

Although we lack systematic empirical data because of the confidentiality of negotiations, participants claim that the overwhelming bulk of decisions are made consensually. Even under conditions of QMV, permanent representatives often spend extra time to 'bring everyone on board'. Pushing for a vote is considered inappropriate in most cases, and the 'consensus assumption' is a reflexive habit. A clear example of this consensus reflex can be seen in the legislative record of the 1992 Project. Out of the 260 Single Market measures subject to QMV, approximately 220 of them were adopted unanimously, without a vote at all (de Schoutheete 2000: 9–10).

The single best empirical indicator of the weight of Coreper's decision-making role is the prolific 'A-point' procedure. A-points are 'agreed points' which are passed *en bloc* and without discussion by the ministers at the beginning of each Council session. B-points are those issues sent to the ministers that do require further discussion. This corresponds to the agenda of each Council meeting that is divided into parts A and B. The A-point procedure leads to situations where ministers are formally adopting EU legislation in areas where they have no policy expertise. Two representative examples, both involving the Transport ministers, include adoption of a 1992 directive on the safety and health at work of pregnant workers, and in 1990, the raft of legislative acts that enlarged the EU to include the five East German Länder (Peterson and Bomberg 1999: 291, n. 6). In his study of the twenty Agricultural Councils from 1992 and 1993, van Schendelen (1996: 540) calculates that 65 per cent of all agenda items were adopted as A-points.

But quantifying what is settled in Coreper relative to the ministerial level is no easy task. For starters, any given proposal will have different components (definitions, scope, derogations, and so on) agreed at different levels (working group,

Coreper, Council), some of which may be significant, some purely technical. Sometimes, in a kind of role reversal, it even appears that the ministers prepare discussions over substance for Coreper (a pattern Noël recognized in the 1960s).

Even more of a challenge for researchers, quantifying A- and B-points requires extensive interpretation. In addition to 'genuine' A- and B-points, there are a number of other unofficial types, including 'false' B-points, which is really an A-point, since agreement has been reached in Coreper. But it is placed on the Council agenda as a B-point so the ministers can be seen, for political reasons, to have discussed the issue or to have statements read into the official minutes. Another practice that defies simple categorization is a political agreement at the level of the ministers, sometimes as vague as signalling that a 'political green light' for agreement exists, which is sent back to Coreper for finalizing and submission as an A-point.

Despite these measurement problems, it can be clearly established that Coreper's stamp weighs heavily in the Council's legislative output. The most striking feature of all is *not* that civil servants have been delegated *de facto* decisional authority, but the effectiveness of this mechanism in maintaining the output and performance across so many sectoral formations of the Council. Whether this role can be sustained in an enlarged and increasingly polycentric EU is a question considered in the concluding section. We turn now to *how* Coreper is able to reach so many decisions, and what is potentially the group's most valuable institutional contribution to EU decision-making, its capacity in integrating interests.

Integrating interests

Continuous negotiation

Coreper's structural placement imparts a coherence and continuity in the representation of interests that would otherwise be difficult to match. Not only is Coreper distinguishable by the intensity of negotiations, but the permanent representatives' involvement across the different domains of EU decision-making is pervasive as well. In addition to preparing upcoming Councils in the regular cycle of weekly meetings, the permanent representatives sit beside their ministers during Council sessions, briefing them beforehand and offering tactical suggestions. They attend European Council summits and can serve as behind-the-scenes consultants. They monitor the proceedings of the working groups and offer specific points of strategy or emphasis. The ambassadors are also closely involved in monitoring cooperation and association agreements, cooperation councils (including Euro-Med conferences and Euro-Asian summits), and accession negotiations.

Finally, from the beginnings of the Lomé Convention with ACP states, the ambassadors have prepared ACP–EC Councils through the ACP–EC Committee of Ambassadors which precede each yearly meeting (Council of the European Union 1996: 53). And while the links between the EP and Coreper II remain weak, conciliation has created an intense negotiation forum between MEPs and the deputies.

All this creates a dynamic of ongoingness in Coreper's work, reinforced through weekly meetings. Add to this the regular cycle of Coreper luncheons, held by Coreper II before the monthly GAC and sometimes on a more topical, *ad hoc* basis.[11] Lunches sometimes function as long-term strategic planning sessions, often with a European Commissioner invited as a guest. More frequently, and because attendance is so tightly restricted, lunches are used to tackle the thorniest of problems (Butler 1986: 30). Then there are the informal Coreper trips hosted by the presidency which precede European Council summits.[12] Trips are long weekends of socializing 'rich in food and culture', used to reinforce interpersonal relations and the bonds of thick trust, a kind of 'oiling of the mechanism'. This ongoingness of negotiation builds an institutional memory in Coreper from which the permanent representatives learn to draw (Lewis 1998*a*: 485).

Instruction and voice

Permanent representatives are under 'instruction' from their national capitals. In principle, for every agenda item there is an instruction, setting, at a minimum, what is and is not acceptable as an outcome. Again in principle, this instruction is arrived at after domestic coordination through the relevant line ministries and often through an inter-ministerial coordination mechanism.[13] In practice, the instruction process is much more complex, especially in temporal sequence. For starters, most instructions have in-built flexibility. Of course, there are certain taboo areas (institutional reform, fiscal policy) and national sensitivities—but here permanent representatives claim not even to need instructions because they already know what positions to take.

Much more fundamental to this story is the degree to which permanent representatives have an institutionalized voice in the instruction process itself. Some generic patterns of this include, first, departing from instructions and making recommendations back to the capital for changes. The power of recommendations obviously varies by issue area and the personal authority of a permanent representative, but they are most effective in areas where there is a risk of becoming isolated or, under the shadow of the vote, disregarded in a possible compromise. Second, the capitals often signal that a margin of manœuvre exists. Sometimes, permanent representatives are told not to take an instruction seriously, or that the position in the printed instruction can be disregarded. 'Instructions are a way for [the capital] to say they have done their job,' one ambassador explained. Third, when there is a political need to avoid confrontation or politicization at the level of the ministers, permanent representatives (sometimes even told: 'avoid Council') will have a freer hand in making deals and selling success at home. Fourth, there are times when the capital does not know or cannot decide (or does not want to decide, see below). Here the permanent representatives are causally contributing to the definition of what national interests in the EU context are. As one Antici counsellor explained, 'Instructions already contain a big Brussels element in them, and sometimes they are Brussels instructions, because the first ten lines of our report imply an instruction ... sometimes they just copy our reports into instructions.' A different pattern emerges when the capital does not want to decide. According to a large member state ambassador, 'Sometimes they don't give an instruction because sometimes the ministers don't want to be pinned down. The result of this is that we make policy often from here.'

The degree of voice that the permanent representatives can obtain is derivative of Coreper's basic mission: to find solutions. Finding collective solutions and 'getting on with it' is an unspoken job requirement that gives Coreper its reputation for being results-oriented. It can even happen that permanent representatives disregard their instructions. As one ambassador detailed:

It [disregarding instructions] happens. The first time it feels like a big deal. The second time, it's easy. The problem is to know what are the interests of your country ... Now sometimes the capital gets nervous, they have various lobbies behind it usually. We also have to keep in mind that what has been built up over the last forty years is important. [The ethos is] that a file should go. That we should proceed forward. This is constantly a factor in what we do. Often we have much more at stake than the dossier.

While it is important to avoid an over-socialized view of the permanent representatives, one should not underestimate the relative autonomy that Coreper as a collective decision-making forum can obtain. The instruction process is often a two-way street, with permanent representatives able to insert a high degree of voice in their construction. And as a group, the Committee can engage in transgovernmental bargaining tactics such as the 'plotting' of a compromise in the collective interest of finding solutions (see below).

Insulation

One of the really distinctive features of Coreper diplomacy is the degree of insulation from the normal currents of domestic constituent pressures. The meetings themselves are treated with an air of confidentiality, and many sensitive national positions are ironed out in restricted sessions where the permanent representatives can speak frankly and in confidence that what is said will not be reported to the capitals or the media. This can even include group discussion on how an agreement will be packaged and sold to the authorities back home. 'At our level, publicity does not exist,' an ambassador explained, 'Our body is absolutely black; we can do deals.' Another stated, 'We are better placed than the capitals to know what are the real interests of our countries. We are less exposed to the pressures, the short term problems of the time. This affects us much less.'

A structural feature of Coreper that often goes unnoticed is that insulation affords member states the capacity to reshape domestic constraints. As an ambassador put it, 'Coreper is the only forum in the EU where representatives don't have a domestic turf to defend.' Because of this, he went on to add, 'it is often politically necessary to present a position knowing it is unrealistic. My minister of finance needs certain arguments to be presented. He has certain pressures from his constituencies. We have to make it look like we fought for this even though we both know it will lead nowhere. I will present it, and if it receives no support, I will drop it.'

A dense normative environment

Coreper's institutional capacity to aggregate interests across such an array of issue areas and under such a steady workload is lubricated by a dense normative environment. There are a number of mutually reinforcing norms found in Coreper that contribute to everyday decision-making and the output of the Council. Five stand out in particular. First, there is a norm of diffuse reciprocity, or the balancing of concessions over an extended shadow of the future. 'We do keep a sense in an unspecific way of obligations to another member state,' one ambassador remarked. Diffuse reciprocity can take many forms, including concessions and derogations, or 'going out on a limb' to persuade the capital for changes or a compromise. Dropping reserves or abstaining (rather than a 'no' vote) are also political gestures which can be filed away and later returned in kind.

Second, there is a norm of thick trust and the ability to speak frankly, reconfirmed weekly through the normal cycle of meetings, trips, and lunches. Thick trust is especially important during endgame negotiations and restricted sessions when the 'real knives come out on the table'. Third, there is a norm of mutual responsiveness that is best described as a shared purpose to understand each other's problems. Mutual responsiveness is a form of collective legitimation, where arguments or pleas for special consideration are collectively accepted or rejected by the group. The fourth norm is a consensus-reflex. This is what Hayes-Renshaw and Wallace (1995: 465) refer to as 'the instinctive recourse to behave consensually'. Even under conditions of QMV, permanent representatives often spend extra time to 'bring everyone on board'. Finally, there is a culture of compromise that is premised on a basic willingness to accommodate divergent interests and is reinforced by the other norms listed above. The normative effects of this culture include a self-restraint in the calculations and defence of interests, seen for example when delegations quietly drop reserves after failing to convince the others of their arguments (Lewis 1998*a*).

EU norms are internalized through a multi-levelled process of socialization. At the micro-level, new participants in Coreper go through a process of adaptation and learning. One Mertens counsellor claimed that it takes newcomers at least six months to 'find their way', since, 'They stick close to their instructions. They don't yet have all the technical knowledge of the dossiers. They cannot gauge what is whispered in their ears.' And, finally, a dense normative environment should not be confused with idyllic cooperation. At times, Coreper negotiations are heated battles. An ambassador explained: 'Sometimes we fight. This happens on something difficult if we know we are in the best position to make a deal at our level . . . Sometimes we know the deal will be better at our level . . . If it goes to the ministers, we sense that the result will probably be blockage.'

Plotting

Plotting is a negotiation pattern found in Coreper that demonstrates how a collective rationality can reformulate individual, instrumental rationality. The basic function of plotting is using the group to redefine a national position or to reshape domestic constraints.[14] 'To get new instructions we have to show [the capital] we have a black eye,' an ambassador explained, 'We can ask Coreper for help with this; it is one of our standard practices.' According to another, 'Sometimes I will deal with impossible instructions, by saying, "Mr. Chairman, can I report back the fierce opposition to this by the fourteen others?" And sometimes fierceness is exaggerated for effect.' An excellent illustration of plotting occurred with Coreper II negotiations to reduce the number of Council formations (following the conclusions of the December 1999 Helsinki Summit). In this case, as a participant explained:

All fifteen [ambassadors] had negative instructions. They all had their own lists of what to keep, what to cut. This is because each has its own lobbies, you know, on gender questions, and so on. We all have our own [national] coordination problems. So we met in a luncheon. I told them, 'You understand this is pointless.' And I asked them, 'Will you report back that you were totally isolated?' So each has reported home that the other fourteen are more or less in agreement.

In general, plotting and underlining opposition is a tool to deal with recalcitrant bargaining positions. Exaggerating the fierceness of opposition is also a group strategy to collectively legitimate or reject arguments.

Style of discourse

Coreper even has its own locution. There is a shared discourse with its own key phrases, such as when a delegation is signalling a willingness to compromise.

There is a style of presenting arguments. There is also the art of derogation, where permanent representatives ask for help or special consideration. Learning the discourse is an important socialization mechanism. As Peterson and Jones (1999: 34) point out, new members to Coreper 'must learn to use the language (even rhetoric) of appeals to the "European project"'.

There is a discourse to reveal who is behind their instructions and who is not. 'I can tell', a deputy explained, 'when someone wants to distance themselves from their instructions.' Some tactics are less subtle than others. One strategy is to just read them. They may say, 'Mr. Chairman, I'd like to read you something that I myself do not understand,' or 'unfortunately I have to bore you with the following . . .'. Some claim to be able to tell if a colleague agrees with their instructions by body language alone.

Discourse is also used to signal when something is important or to request mutual understanding in more subtle ways. According to one ambassador: 'There is a Coreper language with its own code words and code phrases. When used, this language is clearly understood by everyone. For instance, if I have bad instructions that I'm against, I can say, "but of course the presidency has to take its responsibilities," which means put it to a vote and I'll lose, I accept this.'

Most importantly, arguments matter. The power of a good argument can be as compelling as a blocking minority or the shadow of the veto. The possibility for persuasion and the norm of mutual responsiveness works as a great equalizer in Coreper negotiations. As a result, smaller member states who articulate clear, sound arguments can often punch above their weight. A financial counsellor from a large member state drew the following contrast: 'Sweden, who is always taking part in the debate, has influence far beyond their votes. Germany, is the opposite; they have less influence than votes.' An Antici echoed this sentiment, 'If you convince others, it's with good arguments. Big or small makes no difference. In fact, the big member states often have higher burdens of proof in order to convince the others.'

Accountability

There is a growing perception that decision-making in Brussels is remote, opaque, and even undemocratic. Given Coreper's role in everyday decision-making, it is somewhat surprising that in all the discussions to address the EU's 'democratic deficit' during the 1996–7 IGC its name was nearly completely absent. But given Coreper's problem-solving functions and the need for insulation from politicization effects discussed above, it is clear why member states would be reluctant to tinker with such finely tuned mechanisms. There are occasional suggestions which emanate from a capital that perhaps a new Coreper III of ministers or deputy prime ministers would work to democratize the system, but support for such ideas has never gained much momentum.

It is also easy to push the image of an all-powerful, unaccountable group of backroom decision-makers too far. Committee members are accountable to their ministers for the positions taken in negotiations and it is always a possibility (though specific examples are extremely hard to come by) that a minister can undo a deal done at Coreper-level. Permanent representatives who strayed too far or were overruled by their ministers would quickly lose credibility in Coreper and in the home capital. But whether such an indirect system of accountability is a sustainable form of governance remains an open question.

The institution in context

Blurring the national and the European

Coreper's institutional architecture challenges the conventional dichotomy that sharply demarcates the national and European levels. As a collectivity, Coreper exemplifies the claim that national and European levels of governance have become amalgamated in the EU system (H. Wallace 2000: 7; Wessels 1997). Accordingly, Coreper is an anomaly for theorists who draw rigid distinctions between 'national' and 'supranational' agents and agency. For example, in one prominent account of European integration, 'supranational entrepreneurs' are effectively limited to mean European Commissioners (Moravcsik 1998a: 54–60; 479–85). The cost of this assumption is a rather narrow view of how the complex constructs of the national and European levels fit together. As William Wallace (2000: 529–30) has argued, 'It would be a caricature of this intricate policy process to counterpose national actors and supranational entrepreneurs as separate elites, promoting opposed interests.' The EU permanent representatives clearly illustrate how national and supranational roles and identities can become nested and coexist. The most robust finding from the interview data compiled for this chapter is that permanent representatives hold a primary national identity with a distinct secondary allegiance to collective, EU decision-making. What is more, permanent representatives do not self-reflectively see these as competitive or contradictory identities. They are not 'different hats' worn at different times or held in juxtaposition to each other. Most importantly, national and supranational identities are not zero-sum or antithetical. Some theorists apparently still think otherwise, such as Sandholtz and Stone Sweet (1998a: 6) who claim, 'we leave as an open question the extent to which the loyalties and identities of actors will shift from the national to the European level. There is substantial room for supranational governance without an ultimate shift in identification.'

Instead of this limited notion of shifts and transfers of identity, what we see in

Coreper is a cognitive blurring of the boundaries between the national and the European. In describing his role as both representative of a member state to the EU and representative of the EU to his member state, a deputy claimed, 'I wear a Janus face.' The metaphor of the Janus face can be detected throughout the interview data in how permanent representatives perceive their institutional roles and multiple allegiances to represent national interests and participate in making collective decisions. None of this suggests that national identities and interests become marginalized or blended together; rather, what stands out is the interpenetration of the national with the European and vice versa.[15]

However, it is also important to point out that the future appears more uncertain for the permanent representatives than at any point in the past. Will Coreper continue to maintain such a role in EU decision-making? Two developments serve to challenge Coreper in new and perhaps unpredictable ways. First, enlargement. Will Coreper continue to function the same in an EU of twenty-seven or more? There are opposing bets here. Some believe Coreper will lose its ability to synthesize the national and the European in such an unwieldy and heterogeneous grouping. Others see Coreper as growing in importance since the comparative dysfunctions at the level of the ministers, which can act more as a 'talking shop' than a chamber of substantive negotiation, are much worse. Much will depend on how quickly and extensively new EU members become socialized to Coreper's normative environment. According to Peterson and Jones (1999: 38), 'an effective and respected EU ambassador may be the most important single asset any new member state can have'. Finland, already considered as one of the most communitarian EU members, shows that internalizing the habits of cooperation and culture of compromise can happen fairly quickly. But in the case of the CEEC applicants, there is reason to suspect that learning curves will be much steeper (Ungerer 1993: 82).

Second, differentiation and variable geometry. Can Coreper remain the spine of the inter-institutional framework as the EU becomes more polycentric and differentiated? The challenge here is that differentiation is a stress on Coreper's horizontal, inter-pillar competencies. We can see this already in euro-zone policy-making, with the fragmentation of preparatory authority between Coreper II and the EFC. 'Enhanced' forms of cooperation also risk altering the finely tuned mechanisms of consensus-seeking which has become a reflexive habit among the permanent representatives. While some may see differentiation as a 'structured and organized form of diversity' (de Schoutheete 2000: 68), others point out more perverse effects whereby 'Member governments are no longer as willing as they once were to accept all EU obligations, to permit other governments equal participation in all decisions, or to grant the same benefits' (Moravcsik 1998b: 5). Very simply, as the EU becomes more polycentric and differentiated, Coreper's role as the guardian of the single institutional framework may become less and less meaningful. As a collective decision-making body based on principles of 'collective governance' and as a place where even the smallest member states can be heard,

Coreper stands much to lose by differentiation. As one ambassador put it, 'the danger is that you end up with a monetary Europe, and a budgetary Europe, a defence Europe'.

Conclusions

This chapter has focused on integrating interests in the context of the EU and in particular, the systemic, policy-setting level at which Coreper operates. How are interests *defined* and how are interests *defended* in the EU system? Many integration theorists take interests as predetermined by a variety of domestic political and socio-economic forces. The result is that interests are assumed as exogenous to interaction at the EU level. But a closer examination of Coreper reveals that maintaining this starting assumption requires a rather 'thin' theory of international interactions. What is more, the 'alternative argument' tests used by intergovernmentalists are often temporally and conceptually limited. If interests are endogenous, they argue, we should expect to see autonomous 'Eurocrats' going against objective, material national interests, or changes in national interests which otherwise would not have occurred.[16] In short, if the intergovernmentalist image is off the mark, we should expect to see systematic evidence of officials who 'go native'. But is this the only test that would falsify the intergovernmentalist story? From the lens of the 'new institutionalism', a series of alternative questions come into focus. What if governments bargain in Brussels without clearly defined, ordered, and ranked national preferences? What if the national capital and interministerial coordination process could not 'make up their mind?' What if national preferences are not as tightly coupled with the demands of dominant domestic groups as intergovernmentalists steadfastly hold? Or, what if the decision-making machinery of the Council was purposely designed to allow for a certain degree of insulation—precisely to escape the kinds of domestic political pressures which figure so prominently in the intergovernmental image of interest formation? Even more unthinkable in traditional dichotomous terms—what if the distinctions between the national and supranational become blurred? What if the interpenetration of politics in Brussels and the national capitals became 'fused' (to borrow Wessels's term) to the point where it no longer makes sense to think of separate, autonomous domains but rather a 'multiperspectival' space (Ruggie 1993: 172)?

Rather than offer definitive answers to these important theoretical questions, the modest aim of this chapter has been to show the utility in asking them in the first place. The complexity of national interest representation in the EU calls for models of integration that can handle multiple causality, where the constitutive processes of interest formation are hypothesized to include independent causal mechanisms at both the national and European levels. Rather than privileging either the domestic or international level as 'primordial', this argument makes a straightforward, epistemological set of claims. Interests are not reducible to domestic politics. Interaction in the EU system matters. As this chapter has shown, the institutional context and normative environment found in Coreper offers empirical support for these claims.

Notes

1 This study is based on 102 semi-structured interviews conducted at the permanent representations and with regular Coreper participants from the Commission and the Council General Secretariat between Feb.–July 1996, Feb.–Apr. 1997, and May 2000. The sample includes: 20 permanent representatives (10 ambassadors, 10 deputies), 31 Antici and Mertens counsellors, 28 policy specialists, 8 legal advisers, 10 officials in national capitals, and 5 others. All interview quotes come from this field research unless otherwise noted.

2 *Bulletin of the EC*, 12–1974, point 1104.7.

3 For comparative studies of national coordination systems, see Kassim *et al.* (2000); Rometsch and Wessels (1996); Spence (1995); Hayes-Renshaw and Wallace (1997: 211–43).

4 Interview, Brussels, 15 May 2000.

5 See Webb (1977: 18–19) for instance.

6 Many refer to the permanent representatives as solely the group of EU ambassadors. For convenience, I refer to both sets of officials (ambassadors and deputies) as the permanent representatives.

7 The member state holding the presidency is represented by a minister.

8 For a more detailed examination of this pattern, see Lewis (1998*b*: 111–13).

9 Ambassador Wall did receive some laughs when he began showing up at the 1997 IGC negotiations with newly reversed positions (interview, Brussels, 26 May 2000).

10 Article 7(1) of the Council's Rules of Procedure state that the 'delegation of the right to vote may only be made to another member of the Council' (that is, another minister).

11 Coreper I also convenes working lunches, usually two or three per presidency.

12 Trips are restricted to the ambassadors, the Anticis, and spouses.

13 Examples include the Cabinet Office in Britain or the SGCI (Secrétariat général du Comité inter-ministériel pour les questions de coopération économique européenne) in France.

14 This is known as 'COG collusion' in two-level games research. See Evans (1993: 406–7).

15 For a conceptualization of how 'the European dimension is included in national self-conceptions', see Wæver (1995: 412, 430). See also Hayes-Renshaw and Wallace (1997: 278–89). For a detailed case-study on Germany, see Katzenstein (1997).

16 For a representative claim to this effect, see Moravcsik (1991: 70–1).

Further reading

For an excellent treatment of Coreper's role in EU decision-making, see Hayes-Renshaw and Wallace (1997) and Westlake (1995). De Zwaan (1995) offers perhaps the most comprehensive treatment available in English, although it tends towards the descriptive and legalistic. Hayes-Renshaw *et al.* (1989) and Noël (1967) are both classics. See also Lequesne (1993) and Mentler (1996). For a testimonial of the EU system from the former doyen of Coreper, see de Schoutheete (2000). Finally, for more on the Spaak Committee, see Mayne (1962) and Willis (1965).

De Zwaan, J. (1995), *The Permanent Representatives Committee: Its Role in European Union Decision-Making* (Amsterdam: Elsevier).

Hayes-Renshaw, F., Lequesne, C., and Mayor Lopez, P. (1989), 'The Permanent Representations of the Member States to the European Communities', *Journal of Common Market Studies*, 28/2 119–37.

—— and Wallace, H. (1997), *The Council of Ministers* (London and New York: Macmillan and St Martin's Press).

Lequesne, C. (1993), *Paris–Bruxelles: Comment se fait la politique européenne de la France* (Paris: Presses Universitaires de la Fondation Nationale des Sciences Politiques).

Mayne, R. (1962), *The Community of Europe* (New York: W.W. Norton).

Mentler, M. (1996), *Der Auschuss der Ständigen Vertreter bei den Europäischen Gemeinschaften* (Baden-Baden: Nomos).

Noël, E. (1967), 'The Committee of Permanent Representatives', *Journal of Common Market Studies*, 5/3 219–51.

Schoutheete, P. de (2000) *The Case for Europe: Unity, Diversity, and Democracy in the European Union* (Boulder, Colo., and London: Lynne Rienner).

Westlake, M. (1995), *The Council of the European Union* (London: Cartermill).

Willis, F. R. (1965), *France, Germany, and the New Europe, 1945–1963* (Stanford, Calif: Stanford University Press).

Web links

The most useful online resource to monitor Coreper's work is the Council's web site—**www.ue.eu.int/en/summ.htm**—although details on Coreper I and II meetings remain hard to come by. Increasingly, links to the EU presidency offer basic information such as dates, agendas, and so on. For an online database of Coreper personnel (including valuable contact information for arranging interviews at the permanent representations), select 'Who's who in the Council' (and then choose the link 'Permanent Representatives Committee').

Chapter 14

Functional Interests: European Agencies

Giandomenico Majone

Contents

Summary

This chapter analyses the rise of the new ('second generation') European agencies created in the 1990s, as well as the debate about 'third generation' agencies in such areas as telecommunications and food safety. These developments demonstrate the existence of functional needs which are not satisfied by the present institutional structure of the Community. What has been achieved so far does not yet amount to a stable solution, but is more in the nature of stop-gap measures, or even symbolic politics. However, recurring credibility crises of national and European regulatory systems, a growing conviction that traditional views on delegation are by now completely outdated and, not least, a new configuration of functional interests, increase the likelihood of far-reaching institutional reforms in the near future.

Introduction

'Agency' is not a technical term, but rather an omnibus label to describe a variety of organizations—commissions, boards, authorities, offices, and so on—which perform functions of a governmental nature, and which often exist outside the normal departmental framework of government. The most comprehensive definition of the term is probably provided by the United States Administrative Procedure Act (APA). According to this important statute, which regulates the decision-making processes of all agencies of the federal government, an agency is a part of government that is generally independent in the exercise of its functions and that by law has authority to take a final and binding action affecting the rights and obligations of individuals.

All the agencies that have proliferated in Europe at the national level over the last three decades—Regulatory Offices and 'Next Step' Agencies in Britain, Autorités Administratives Indépendantes in France, Regulierungsbehörde in Germany, Autorità Indipendenti in Italy, among others—are agencies in the sense of the APA. For reasons to be discussed below, the same is not true at the European level. In fact, most European agencies of the first and second generation (see Table 14.1), as well as the EU statistical office, Eurostat, are agencies only *de facto*. The European Central Bank, on the other hand, is an independent agency both *de facto* and *de jure*. With few exceptions, all European agencies, or quasi-agencies, of the second generation have been established to deal, directly or indirectly, with regulatory issues. For this reason, and because of the central importance of regulatory policy-making in the EU, we shall consider only regulatory agencies.

This chapter discusses the present and future role of regulatory agencies, and networks of such agencies, in EU governance. In particular, it explores the political, legal, and normative issues raised by the delegation of regulatory functions to bodies operating at arm's length from the institutions of the EU.

Why regulatory agencies?

The current popularity of the agency model at national, European, and even international levels should not obscure the fact that there are alternative ways of making and implementing regulatory policies. The main institutional alternatives to
regulatory agencies are government departments (or the Directorates-General of
the European Commission), control by courts, or self-regulation.

A number of factors may influence the placing of new regulatory tasks on agencies, rather than allocating them to existing departments, or giving more work to
courts (Baldwin and McCrudden 1987). In some cases, functions are thought likely
to be better managed if they are the sole or main interest of a specialized agency,
rather than a peripheral matter dealt with by an organization whose attentions
are primarily directed elsewhere. The increasing technical and scientific complexity of many regulatory issues has also led to the establishment of agencies that are
seen as experts in these substantive matters. A government department is often
seen as not being able to provide the independence needed in some of the applications of expertise, while courts lack the requisite scientific, technical, or economic
knowledge. Moreover, delegation of rule-making powers may be needed when
constant fine-tuning of the rules or standards, and quick adaptation to technical
progress, are required. As shown by the early experience of technical standardization in the European Community, a collegial body such as the Council of Ministers
often cannot devote the time needed to these matters, or else they simply cannot
act quickly enough (Majone 1996). Agencies' separateness from government may
also make them a preferred mechanism for co-opting certain groups into the
policy-making process. This seems to have been an important consideration in the
creation of such agencies as the European Foundation for the Improvement of
Living and Working Conditions, and the European Agency for Health and Safety at
Work.

When regulatory responsibilities are delegated not to public agencies but to
private or semi-private bodies, one speaks of self-regulation. Self-regulation plays a
significant role in highly technical areas such as industrial standardization, and
wherever product or service quality is an important consideration. A self-
regulatory organization (SRO) can normally command a greater degree of expertise and detailed knowledge of practices within the relevant area than a public
agency. A second advantage is that the rules issued by a private body are less
formalized than those of public regulatory regimes. This informality reduces the
cost of rule-making, and facilitates quick adaptation of the rules to new technical
knowledge and changing conditions.

A problem of self-regulation is the risk of capture of the SROs by the regulated
interests. Capture is a problem also for agencies, but with self-regulation,

regulatory capture is there from the outset, since the members of the SROs come from the same groups or organizations they regulate. For this reason, a public agency may provide better protection of such interests than an SRO.

Monitoring is another potential problem since the willingness of a SRO to publicize and punish wrong-doers is likely to be less than that of a public regulator. One possible solution is a two-tiered system where a public agency acts chiefly as a regulator of regulators, with the SROs handling day-to-day rule-making and enforcement.

In sum, at both national and European levels, self-regulation may be a useful adjunct to statutory regulation administered by a public agency, but cannot replace it.

The new European agencies

The agencies created in the 1990s do not have the power of rule-making, enforcement, and adjudication normally granted to American regulatory bodies, and even lack the more limited powers enjoyed, for instance, by Britain's Regulatory Offices or France's Autorités Administratives Indépendantes. Thus, the Council Regulation which set up the European Environment Agency (EEA),[1] specifies the tasks of the agency as follows:

- to provide the Member States and the Community with information;
- to collect, record, and assess data on the state of the environment;
- to encourage harmonization of the methods of measurement;
- to promote the incorporation of European environmental information into international monitoring programmes;
- to ensure data dissemination; and
- to cooperate with other Community bodies and with international institutions.

It will be noticed that regulatory functions are not included in the agency's mandate. Even the European Agency for the Evaluation of Medicinal Products (EMEA), which comes closest to being a fully fledged regulatory body, does not take decisions concerning the safety and efficacy of new medical drugs, but submits opinions concerning the approval of such products to the European Commission.[2]

There are several reasons why the European agencies have not been granted broader powers. A significant factor is the traditional emphasis on an essentially legislative approach to market integration. The Community adopts a legislative act (a directive) which is subsequently transposed by the member states into their own legal order, and implemented by the national administrations. Hence the delegation of regulatory powers to autonomous European bodies was always resented by the member states as too intrusive, since it alters the delicate balance of power which has made possible the growth of Community competences. The traditional separation of rule-making and enforcement was also convenient for the Commission, which was more interested in the rewarding task of developing new rules than in the thankless and politically costly task of implementing existing ones.

Again, the lack of a significant European tradition of statutory regulation by means of independent agencies certainly contributed to the reluctance of member states to accept the establishment of such bodies at Community level (Majone, 1996). For its part, the Commission has always opposed the delegation of some of its powers to autonomous institutions. This is shown, for example, by its firm rejection of recurrent proposals, made by Germany and other member states, for the creation of an independent European Cartel Office in order to reduce political influences on competition and merger decisions. Table 14.1 lists first- and second-generation agencies.

The Meroni doctrine and delegation

The politically motivated opposition of the Commission and the member states to fully fledged regulatory agencies at European level receives some legal support from a narrow reading of Article 7 TEC, which states: 'The tasks entrusted to the Community shall be carried out by the following institutions: a European Parliament, a Council, a Commission, a Court of Justice, a Court of Auditors. Each institution shall act within the limits of the powers conferred upon it by this Treaty.' This has been interpreted as a general prohibition on the establishment of additional bodies, so that nothing short of treaty revision would allow for the creation of truly independent agencies.

As early as 1958, the European Court of Justice with its 'Meroni Doctrine'[3] (see Chapter 6), slightly eased the consequences of such a narrow reading of the Treaty, thus allowing the Commission to delegate certain of its executive functions to bodies not named in the Treaty. However, such delegation is subject to strict constraints (Lenaerts 1993):

- delegation can only relate to powers which the Commission itself possesses;
- such assignment must relate to the preparation and performance of executive acts alone;
- as a consequence of this, independent bodies must not be given any discretionary powers;
- hence the Commission must retain oversight over the delegated competence and will be held responsible for the manner in which it is performed;

Table 14.1 European agencies of first and second generation

	Start of activities	Primary objective	Location	Official web site
European Centre for the Development of Vocational Training	1975	To assist the Commission in promoting and developing vocational training	Until 1994 Berlin, since 1994 Thessaloniki	www.cedefop.gr/
European Foundation for the Improvement of Living and Working Conditions	1975	To contribute to the planning and establishment of better living and working conditions	Dublin	www.eurofound.ie/
European Environment Agency	1994	To set up and manage a European information and observation network and ensure the dissemination of comparable information	Copenhagen	www.eea.eu.int/
Office for Harmonization in the Internal Market	1994	To contribute to harmonization in the domain of intellectual property, and, in particular, the domain of trade marks	Alicante	www.oami.eu.int/
Translation Centre for Bodies in the European Union	1994	To provide translation services for the bodies and agencies set up by the Council	Luxembourg	www.cdt.eu.int/
European Training Foundation	1995	To contribute to the development of vocational training systems in central and eastern European countries	Turin	www.etf.eu.int/
Community Plant Variety Office	1995	To implement the new regime of Community plant variety rights, like patents and copyrights	Angers	www.cpvo.fr/

European Agency for Safety and Health at Work	1995	To provide the Community bodies, the member states and those involved with all relevant technical, scientific, and economic information; to create a network linking up national information networks and facilitate the provision of information in the field of safety and health at work	Bilbao	europe.osha.eu.int/
European Agency for the Evaluation of Medicinal Products	1995	To coordinate the existing network of experts for the evaluation and supervision of medical products; to provide scientific advice on any question relating to the evaluation of medical products for human and veterinary use	London	www.eudra.org/ emea.html
European Monitoring Centre for Drugs and Drug Addiction	1995	To provide objective, reliable, and comparable information at European level concerning drugs, drug addiction, and their consequences	Lisbon	www.emcdda.org/
European Monitoring Centre on Racism and Xenophobia	1998	To provide the Community and its member states with objective, reliable, and comparable data at European level on the phenomena of racism, xenophobia, and anti-Semitism	Vienna	www.eumc.at/

Source: Official home page of the Agencies, Offices, Foundations, and Centres of the European Union, **www.europa.eu.int/agencies/carter_en.htm.**

■ finally, such a delegation must not disturb the balance of power among Community institutions.

This reasoning is reflected in the current status of the European agencies, which are subject to direct Commission oversight and largely engage only in preparatory administrative acts. Certain agencies such as the Community Plant Variety Office, the Trade Mark Office (official title: Office for Harmonization in the Internal Market), and the EMEA, have as their main task the implementation of a Community regime which has been established by the Community institutions. For this reason they have been given more extensive powers.

At any rate, the principle of delegation expressed by the old Meroni doctrine is totally out of step with the development of social scientific knowledge about means of controlling agency discretion without excessively intruding upon the delegated authority implicit in an enabling statute. This doctrine is also out of step with the development of European regulatory policies over the last three decades. Lip-service notwithstanding, it has *de facto* been repealed. It is true that the new European agencies have not been granted formal independence and decision-making authority. However, their very existence confirms that the Commission as well as the member states are becoming increasingly aware of the severe mismatch between the increasingly specialized functions of the Community and the administrative instruments at its disposal.

The politics of institutional choice: the birth of the EEA

The emergence of much-needed institutional innovations is impeded not only by outdated doctrines but even more by the clash of conflicting interests at national and European levels. Political actors and interest groups are well aware that institutional choices have significant consequences for the context and direction of policy. They are prepared to invest resources in order to influence such choices in their favour, so that issues of institutional design are caught up in politics as much as issues of policy. As Terry Moe (1990: 27) writes: 'However grand and lofty the policies that emerge from the political process, it is virtually guaranteed that the bureaucratic arrangements that go with them are the product of compromise and thus, in part, are designed by opponents to ensure that policies are not achieved.'

In the context of institutional choice, political compromise means that opposing groups have a direct say in how an agency and its mandate are constructed. Political compromise offers a chance for the opponents of a policy to have a say in the design of the implementing agency and thus, as Moe argues, to impose structures that make effective performance difficult to achieve. This simple model of

Figure 14.1 Organization of the European Environment Agency

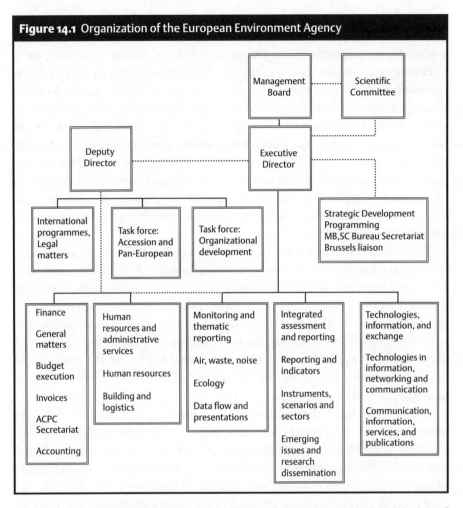

institutional choice helps us to understand the origin and organizational design of a body like the European Environment Agency (see Figure 14.1).

The Council Regulation which establishes the agency states: 'No longer than two years after entry into force of this Regulation ... the Council shall decide on further tasks for the Agency.'[4] The possible new tasks include:

■ associating the EEA in the monitoring of the implementation of Community environmental legislation;

■ awarding environmental labels to environmentally friendly products, services, and technologies;

■ and establishing criteria for assessing environmental impacts.

These three tasks reflected the demands of advocates for a more powerful environmental agency than either the member states or the Commission envisaged. Their inclusion in the revision clause of the enabling statute was an important part of the political compromise that made the creation of the EEA possible. All member states, political parties, and European institutions voiced support for the proposal of an environmental agency at the European level, made by Commission President Delors in January 1989. However, this general agreement concealed deep divisions concerning specific structural choices, especially those concerning the regulatory powers and effective independence of the new agency.

The European Parliament (EP), green parties, and some top Commission officials (such as Ripa di Meana, the Environment Commissioner) wanted a body with regulatory 'teeth'. In varying degrees all member states opposed the idea that the agency could monitor the implementation of European environmental legislation by national regulators, preferring to restrict its task to the collection of environmental information, and to networking with national, European, and international research institutions.

The position of the majority of the Commission officials was rather ambivalent. On the one hand, executives of the Directorate-General for the Environment were concerned about the criticism of industry and of some member states, especially the UK, that the Commission's environmental proposals were not grounded in 'good science'. They were even more concerned by the poor implementation of environmental directives. Hence, the idea that the EEA could become a sort of inspectorate of national environmental inspectorates, along the lines of the existing Fisheries Inspectorate, had a number of influential supporters in the Commission, as well as the EP.

On the other hand, the Commission was reluctant to surrender regulatory powers to an agency operating at arm's length. Commissioner Ripa di Meana, initially a supporter of an independent EEA, realized that the Treaty of Rome, interpreted in the light of the Meroni doctrine, probably prevented the delegation of rule-making powers to a new body, and called the attention of the EP to this legal obstacle. The Commission proposal of June 1989 outlined four functions for the new agency: (*a*) to coordinate the enactment of EC and national environmental policies; (*b*) to evaluate the results of the environmental measures; (*c*) to provide modelling and forecasting techniques; (*d*) to harmonize processing of environmental data to facilitate information exchanges with international organizations. Being aware of the opposition of the member states to the inspectorate model, the Commission did not propose any inspection tasks for the EEA.

The position of the EP

The Commission's proposal was quite distant from the EP's 'ideal point'. The fact that Beate Weber, the *rapporteur* of the Parliament's Environment Committee, travelled to Washington DC to gain first-hand knowledge of the US Environmental Protection Agency, suggests the model of regulatory agency that European parliamentarians had in mind. Between November 1989 and February 1990 Frau

Weber drafted an opinion which sought to extend the role of the agency beyond that envisaged by the Commission and the Council. The Environment Committee maintained that the EEA should be given power to police environmental abuses, and to supervise national enforcement of EC environmental regulations. The Committee also argued that the agency should carry out environmental impact assessments on certain projects funded by the EC both inside the Community and in non-EC countries, and that it should be given the task of developing a Community green label for environmentally friendly products (Brown 1995).

The EP believed that the agency should be independent from the Commission. Also the composition of the management board of the EEA—the body which sets priorities for the work of the agency—became a point of contention. According to the EP, environmentalist groups should be represented in the board, along with representatives from the member states, the Commission, and the EP itself, and the board should be allowed to take decisions by majority vote.

The outcome

Comparing the preferences of the main political actors—member states, Commission, EP—with the provisions of the EEA Council Regulation, one sees that the member states clearly won the contest over institutional choice. As already mentioned, the main task assigned to the agency is to provide the Community and the member states with the information needed for framing and implementing sound and effective environmental policies and, in particular, 'to provide the Commission with the information that it needs to be able to carry out successfully its tasks of identifying, preparing, and evaluating measures and legislation in the field of environment' (Article 2 of the Regulation). The wording is sufficiently vague, however, that it is not clear whether the agency would be allowed directly to influence policy formulation, for example by evaluating alternative proposals for regulatory measures. In fact, until now the EEA has not been allowed to carry out research that is directly policy relevant (see Exhibit 14.1).

Furthermore, the Regulation fails to clarify the relationship between the agency and the Commission, on the one hand, and the national environmental regulators, on the other. The decisive influence of the national governments is also revealed by the composition of the management board. It consists of one representative of each member state and of the three EFTA countries—Iceland, Liechtenstein, and Norway—that have joined the agency as full members (hence eighteen national representatives in all); two Commission representatives; and two scientific personalities designated by the European Parliament.

As we saw, the main concession to the advocates of an agency with regulatory powers is contained in Article 20 of the enabling regulation, but this is simply a promise to reconsider certain competences of the EEA in the future. So far, the agency has not been given any significant role in the EC regulatory process. It does

---

Exhibit 14.1 European Environment Agency (EEA) mission statement

To deliver timely, targeted, relevant and reliable information to policy-makers and the public for the development and implementation of sound environmental policies in the European Union and other EEA member countries.
   The agency carries out its mission by:

- Making use of the capacities of the European Environment Information and Observation Network (EIONET), a network of environmental bodies and institutions active in the member countries:
- Cooperating with other international environmental agencies and organizations;
- Bringing together, in compatible formats, the best available environmental data from the individual countries.

Source: EEA, *An Introduction to the European Environment Agency*, 1999

---

not monitor the implementation of Community environmental legislation; it does not assess environmental impact statements; and eco-labels for environmentally friendly products are still awarded by the national regulators, not by the EEA.

Political compromise has produced an institutional design characterized by uncertain competences, unresolved conflicts, and failure to deal with the serious implementation problem of EC environmental policy.

While it is difficult to see how the EEA could some day become an actual regulatory agency, the path of development of another agency, the EMEA, suggests the possibility of interesting institutional innovations in the future.

From committee to agency: the road to the EMEA

A closer examination of the European Medicines Evaluation Agency provides valuable insights into how the present comitology system for implementing EU legislation may evolve into a system where committees become the operational arm of European agencies, and link up with national authorities to form transnational regulatory networks. To understand the logic of this transformation it is necessary to recall the main stages in the development of pharmaceutical regulation in the EC.

The first attempt by the European Community to regulate the testing and marketing of pharmaceutical products is Directive 65/65 on the authorization of medicines, introduced in 1965 with the dual objective of protecting human health and eliminating obstacles to intra-Community trade. The member states were deeply divided about the best strategy to achieve these goals. Countries with a strong pharmaceutical industry, such as Germany, lobbied for a decentralized system of mutual recognition of national authorizations. Other member states supported a centralized authorization procedure at European level, arguing that a system based on mutual recognition would allow firms to apply for an authorization in countries with low safety standards, leading to a regulatory 'race to the bottom'.

Faced with this disagreement, the Community adopted a compromise solution entailing a gradual approach to the mutual recognition of national market authorizations. Thus the 1965 directive only established the principle that no medical drug should be placed on the market without prior authorization, and defined the essential criteria of quality, safety, and efficacy for drug approval.

The multi-state procedure

The second phase of regulatory developments began in 1975, with Directive 75/319 setting up the 'multi-state drug application procedure', and establishing the Committee for Proprietary Medicinal Products (CPMP). This Committee composed of national experts has played, and continues to play, a key role in the Community approach to the regulation of pharmaceuticals.

Under the multi-state procedure, a firm that had received a marketing authorization from the regulatory agency of a member state (called the *rapporteur* country) could ask for the recognition of that approval by at least five other member states. The agencies of these countries had to approve or raise objections within 120 days. In case of objections the CPMP had to be notified. The Committee would express its non-binding opinion within sixty days.

The procedure did not work well. Actual decision times were much longer than those prescribed by the 1975 directive, and the national agencies did not appear to be bound either by the decisions of other regulatory bodies or by the opinion of

Table 14.2 Frequency of systematic objections raised by the member states as a percentage of received applications

Objecting state	Frequency of objections
Belgium	88
Denmark	83
France	74
Greece	48
Ireland	55
Italy	93
Luxembourg	0
Netherlands	92
Spain	67
United Kingdom	86

Source: COM (91) 39 final, p. 17.

the CPMP. Because of these disappointing results the procedure was simplified eight years later,[5] but even this new procedure did not succeed in streamlining the approval process since national regulators continued to raise objections against each other almost routinely (see Table 14.2). In 1994, the final year of the multi-state procedure, objections were raised in every one of the authorization procedures. This explains why firms generally chose to continue to seek authorization from each national agency separately.

The concertation procedure

A different procedure was introduced in 1987 for biotechnology and other high-technology products. This new 'concertation procedure' was in effect the first EC-wide licensing procedure. It required that the application for the authorization be filed both with the national authorities and with the Committee for Proprietary Medicinal Products (CPMP). As with the multi-state procedure, the country where the authorization had been filed acted as *rapporteur*, but unlike the older procedure, no decision on the application was to be made by any member state before the CPMP had expressed its opinion. The final decision remained with the member states, however. The evaluation of the application, led by the *rapporteur* country, was carried out at the same time in all the member states—hence the name 'concertation procedure'.

The new procedure was an advance with respect to the old process, but was nevertheless problematic for firms. As with the previous procedure, there was a tendency for delays in the notification of decisions following the CPMP opinion. Waiting for all countries to notify their decisions following the Committee's opinion could result in serious delays in a firm's ability to start marketing a new drug (Matthews 1998).

The centralized procedure and the establishment of the EMEA

On 1 January 1995, the problematic multi-state and concertation procedures were replaced by three new approaches and a new agency (see Table 14.3).

The multi-state procedure was replaced by a decentralized procedure that continues and reinforces the principle of mutual recognition introduced in 1975. Marketing authorizations can also be granted on a country-by-country basis via national registration procedures. Finally, the concertation procedure was replaced by the centralized procedure,[6] which also established the European Agency for the Evaluation of Medicinal Products.

Under the centralized procedure, applications are made directly to the agency, leading to the granting of a European marketing authorization. Use of this procedure is compulsory for products derived from biotechnology and optional for other innovative medicinal products. EMEA is also called on to arbitrate in disputes arising under the decentralized (mutual recognition) procedure. Opinions adopted by the EMEA in either the centralized procedure or following arbitrations lead to binding decisions formally adopted by the Commission.

As the establishment plan of the EMEA shows (see Figure 14.2), all the technical work of the agency is carried out by the Committee for Proprietary Medicinal Products (CPMP) and the parallel Committee for Veterinary Medicine (CVMP)—and by the working and expert groups established by the two Committees.

Before the creation of the agency these two Committees were composed of representatives of the member states and of the Commission. Today the CPMP (here we concentrate on this body, but similar rules apply to the Veterinary

---

Table 14.3 An overview of the European authorization system

Human and animal health

The European system for the authorization of medicinal products for human and veterinary use has been in place since 1995. It is designed to promote both public health and the free circulation of pharmaceuticals. Access to the European market is facilitated for new and better medicines—benefiting users and European pharmaceutical research.

In the case of veterinary medicinal products, consumer and animal health is protected through the fixing of maximum residue limits in food-producing animals.

EMEA: a network agency

The new European system is based on cooperation between the national competent authorities of the member states and the EMEA. The EMEA acts as the focal point of the new system, coordinating the scientific resources made available by member state national authorities, including a network of some 2,200 European experts.

The EMEA is designed to coordinate the existing scientific resources of the member states, acting as an interface between the national competent authorities rather than as a highly centralized organization. The partnership between the EMEA, national authorities and the European Union institutions is central to the successful functioning of the European authorization procedure.

The European procedures

The new European system offers two routes for authorization of medical products:

Centralized procedure: Applications are made directly to the EMEA, leading to the granting of a European marketing authorization. Use of this procedure is compulsory for products derived from biotechnology, and optional for other innovative medicinal products.

Decentralized procedure: Applicable to the majority of conventional medicinal products. Applications are made to the member states selected by the applicant and the procedure operates by mutual recognition of national marketing authorizations. Where this is not possible, the EMEA is called on to arbitrate.

Opinions adopted by the EMEA scientific committees in either the centralized procedure or following arbitrations lead to binding decisions adopted by the European Commission.

Purely national authorizations remain available for medicinal products to be marketed in one member state.

Source: EMEA Status Report, 1999.

Exhibit 14.2 European Agency for the Evaluation of Medicinal Products (EMEA) mission statement

To contribute to the protection and promotion of human and animal health by:

■ Mobilizing scientific resources from throughout the European Union to provide high quality evaluation of medicinal products, to advise on research and development programmes and to provide useful and clear information to users and health professionals;

■ Developing efficient and transparent procedures to allow timely access by users to innovative medicines through a single European marketing authorization;

■ Controlling the safety of medicines for humans and animals, in particular through a pharmacovigilance network and the establishment of safe limits for residues in food-producing animals.

Source: EMEA, *About us*, at **www.eudra.org/aboutus.htm.**

Medicine Committee) is composed of two members nominated by each member state for a three-year renewable term. These members in fact represent the national regulatory authorities. Although Commission representatives are entitled to attend the meetings of the Committee, the Commission is no longer represented, no doubt to emphasize the independence of the CPMP.

In fact, the Committee has become more important, as well as more independent, since the establishment of the EMEA. In the new situation, the Committee members have greater incentives to establish EMEA's and their own international reputation, in competition with such bodies as the US Food and Drug Administration, than to defend national positions.

This change in the incentive structure of regulators operating in a transnational agency such as the EMEA corresponds to the distinction between 'cosmopolitans' and 'locals', introduced by Alvin Gouldner (1957–8) in his work on the sociology of the professions. Cosmopolitans are likely to adopt an international reference-group orientation, while locals tend to have a national or sub-national (for instance, organizational) orientation. Hence 'local' experts tend to be more submissive to the institutional hierarchical structures in which they operate than do 'cosmopolitan' experts, who can appeal to the standards and criteria of an international body of scientific peers.

Using Gouldner's terminology we may say that the EMEA creates a favourable environment for the transformation of national regulators from locals to cosmopolitans. It does this by providing a stable institutional focus at the European level, a forum where different risk philosophies are compared and mutually adjusted, and by establishing strong links to national and to extra-European regulatory bodies.

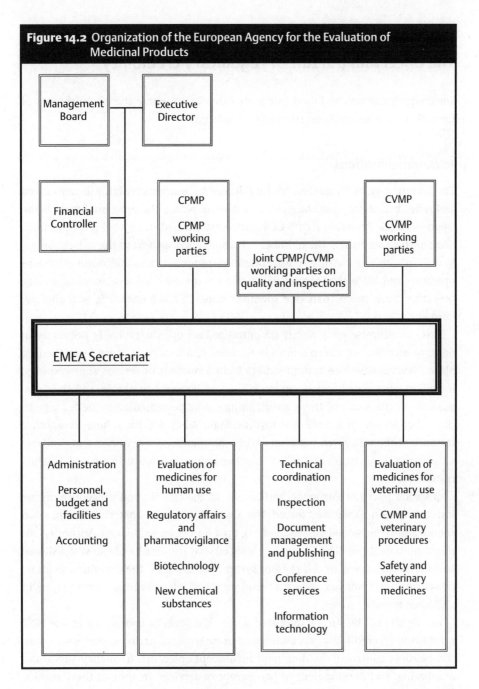

Figure 14.2 Organization of the European Agency for the Evaluation of Medicinal Products

The uncertain pursuit of regulatory credibility

Telecommunications and food safety are other areas where the establishment of European agencies has been seriously considered.

Telecommunications

The present regulatory framework for telecommunications is highly decentralized and relies heavily on comitology committees, of which the most important is the Open Network Provision (ONP) Committee established in 1990. One of the functions of this committee, the members of which are drawn from the national regulatory authorities (NRAs), is to arbitrate in disputes between telecommunications operators and NRAs that cannot be resolved at the national level, or that involve operators from more than one member state. The arbitration is not binding, however.

This compromise on a highly decentralized set-up was probably necessary in order to establish an internal market for telecommunications services in the first place. Nevertheless, the system suffers from a number of serious shortcomings, including poor coordination among NRAs and between the NRAs and the Commission. While some of these shortcomings may be remedied by better legislation, the deeper problems are institutional. What we have here is another instance of the mismatch between highly complex regulatory tasks and available administrative instruments, which has become a distinctive feature of EC-style regulation.

In spring 1997 the European Parliament, in the conciliation procedure on the Interconnection Directive, forced the Council to agree that the Commission should study the 'added value of setting up a European Regulatory Authority' for telecommunications. The EP further insisted that the results of the study should be used in the review of the present system. In response, the Commission asked two consulting firms to conduct a broad survey of telecommunications players in all fifteen member states.

The results of the survey indicated a very low level of confidence in the ONP committee. Its credibility was questioned in such crucial areas as interconnection, competition, control of the dominant incumbent operators, frequency allocation, numbering, and development of pan-European services. In spite of these results, the member states and the Commission decided to maintain the current system, albeit with a somewhat strengthened ONP Committee.

Food safety

The food sector is an area where EC regulation dates back to the earliest days of the Community. Policy on food safety is developed by the Commission, which is assisted by a large number of comitology and expert committees. This system of rule-making has proved to be inadequate. The BSE (mad cow disease) crisis exposed serious shortcomings in the overall coordination of European policies on agriculture, the internal market, and human health. The division of scientific tasks between committees of experts dealing with individual issues of animal and human health has been identified—among others by the EP—as contributing to the dangerous confusion between the pursuit of market or agricultural policy aims and the protection of human health (Everson and Majone 1999).

In the past the Commission had seriously considered the creation of a European Food Agency, but a political decision was taken towards the end of 1990 that the agency model would not be appropriate for the foodstuffs sector. Regardless, the idea of a European agency for food safety was resurrected in the wake of the BSE and other food scares. It received the endorsement of Commission President Prodi in speeches to the European Parliament in July 1999, and again in October 1999.

The idea is strongly supported also by the food industry. For example, Anthony Burgman, the co-chairman of the Anglo-Dutch multinational Unilever, has advocated a powerful and independent European Food Safety Agency, on the model of the US Food and Drug Administration. A strong European agency would streamline the testing and introduction of new food products which are now left to the member states, and help restore consumers' confidence after such episodes as the dioxin food scare in Belgium and the BSE crisis in the UK. Burgman warns that the absence of a powerful EU-wide regulatory body could leave European customers at the mercy of US food producers.[7]

The proposal for an independent European Food Authority advanced by the White Paper on food safety (Commission 2000)—and accepted by the member states at the Nice Summit of December 2000—falls far short of what Anthony Burgman and probably also President Prodi would have liked. The Authority is supposed to monitor developments touching upon food safety issues, provide scientific advice, collect and analyse information, and communicate its findings to all interested parties. Thus it is responsible for risk analysis and risk communication but has no regulatory powers. The possibility of future extensions of the Authority's competences is not excluded, but this concession is too reminiscent of the promises made to the EEA more than ten years ago, and still unfulfilled, to be credible.

Another good occasion to make clear institutional choices and credible long-term commitments has been missed. This is particularly unfortunate because of the serious credibility crisis in which Community regulation finds itself at present (Majone 2000). Any attempt to resolve this crisis must start from a clear understanding of the nature of the credibility problem.

Delegation and credibility

As was mentioned in an earlier section, an important reason for delegating powers to politically independent agencies is to enhance the credibility of a government's long-term policy commitments. The present section examines delegation as a strategy of regulatory commitment, and then applies the conclusions of this analysis to the current political situation in the EU. We start by examining how the commitment problem arises.

Political uncertainty and time inconsistency

Political uncertainty is the natural consequence of the democratic process. One of the defining characteristics of democracy is that it is a form of government *pro tempore* (Linz 1998). The time limit inherent in the requirement of elections at regular intervals implies that the policies of the current majority can be subverted, legitimately and without compensation, by a new majority with different and perhaps opposing interests. Because a legislature cannot bind a future legislature and a majority coalition cannot bind another, public policies are always vulnerable to reneging. This is a source of political uncertainty.

Time inconsistency is another serious threat to policy credibility. Time inconsistency occurs when a government's optimal long-run policy differs from its preferred short-run policy, so that the government in the short run has an incentive to renege on its long-term commitments. In the absence of a legally binding commitment, the government will use its discretion to pursue what appears now to be a better policy. However, if private actors anticipate such a policy change they will behave in ways which prevent policy-makers from achieving their original objective (Kydland and Prescott 1977).

For example, a policy of low inflation may be optimal over the long run, but at any time there can be short-run political gains from surprise inflation. If the policy-makers have the possibility of revising the original policy to achieve such short-term gains, private actors will recognize this and change their behaviour in such a way that the outcome is worse than if the original policy had always been adhered to. Of course, the phenomenon of time inconsistency is not unique to macroeconomic policy-making, but appears in any areas of discretionary policy-making where long-run and short-run objectives are not aligned.

In an increasingly interdependent world, credibility has become a crucially important aspect of public policy. Politicians have discovered that the best way to enhance the credibility of their long-term objectives is to delegate the implementation of those objectives to institutions operating at arm's length from government, such as independent central banks and regulatory agencies. An independent central banker is not accountable to the voters or to their elected representatives. Hence, he or she has no incentive to pursue time-inconsistent policies for short-run political gains. For instance, the Maastricht Treaty gives to the European Central Bank a very high level of political independence, which should guarantee the Bank's ability to pursue credibly the objective of price stability in the Union.

Similarly, the point of insulating regulators from the political process is to increase the credibility of a government's regulatory commitments. The delegation of regulatory powers to some agency distinct from the government itself is best understood as a means whereby governments can commit themselves to regulatory strategies that would not be credible in the absence of such delegation (Gatsios and Seabright 1989). In the same way, the commitment of the member states to the process of European integration would lack credibility without the delegation of significant regulatory powers to the European Commission and the Court of Justice. However, the progressive politicization of the Commission raises again the issue of credibility, this time at the European level.

The politicization of the Commission

The idea of reducing the democratic deficit of the EC policy-making process by assigning a larger role to the European Parliament, and in particular by involving the EP in the appointment of the Commission, is not new. However, the procedure introduced by Article 214 TEC contains a number of radical changes not only with respect to previous practices, but also with respect to the Maastricht Treaty. If under the latter Treaty the national governments could nominate a new Commission President only after consulting the EP, now their nomination must be approved by Parliament. Moreover, the President and other members of the Commission are subject to a vote of approval by the EP, as in classical parliamentary systems.

The link between the EP's term of office and that of the Commission is another institutional innovation. Since a newly elected Parliament takes part in nominating the Commission, any significant changes in the EP's composition can be reflected at the Commission level. Not surprisingly, influential European parliamentarians openly advocate a 'Parliamentary Commission', in which the composition and programme of the European executive would reflect the will of the current parliamentary majority. What appears to be certain is that in the future it will be virtually impossible for an individual Commissioner to remain in office against the wish of the majority in the EP.

An increasing level of politicization of EC policy-making becomes unavoidable as more and more tasks involving the use of political discretion are shifted to the European level. These new competences not only increase the administrative workload of the Commission, but also emphasize the Commission's political responsibilities. In this context, the demand for a greater role of the European Parliament becomes understandable. At the same time, one should not be blind to the risks which politicization entails for the credibility of EC regulatory policies.

A less technocratic, more politically accountable Commission may enjoy greater democratic legitimacy, but eventually it will have to face the same credibility problem of all democratic governments. The argument sketched in the preceding pages suggests that the delegation of powers to regulatory bodies distinct from the Commission itself, and enjoying significant decisional autonomy with respect to the Commission as well as the national governments, may provide a feasible solution to the credibility problem under the new political conditions prevailing in the Union. However, solving the credibility problem at European level requires some innovations in institutional design.

The network model

In spite of the preferences of some business leaders, public interest groups, and European parliamentarians for a centralized solution of the credibility problem, it is clearly impossible to transpose to the EU the American model of federal agencies operating independently from the regulatory authorities of the states. Regardless of what one thinks of the alleged legal obstacles to the adoption of such a model, it is certain that the member states would reject it. Their attitude could be different, however, towards a system where the national regulators are the components of an EU-wide network, coordinated by a European body independent from the Commission.

The relevant model is provided by the European System of Central Banks (ESCB), which is composed of the European Central Bank and of the national banks of the member states. According to the Maastricht Treaty, the ECB is completely independent from the other European institutions as well as from the member states, while the national banks must be independent from their respective governments as a condition of membership in the monetary union. Although, presumably, regulators would not be as independent as central bankers, the broad relevance of the ESCB model is increasingly recognized. Thus, two well-known financial experts, Jacques de Larosière and Daniel Lebègue, have suggested that the growing integration of markets 'could lead to the creation of a European system of national regulation in the same vein as the European Central Bank, with decisions taken centrally but applied nationally'.[8]

In fact, the new European agencies have not been designed to operate in isolation, or to replace national regulators. Rather, they are expected to become the central nodes of networks including national agencies as well as international organizations. To qualify as fully fledged regulatory networks, however, the European agencies and their national counterparts still need autonomous decision-maker powers, and a firmer legal basis of their independence.

For a transnational regulatory network to function properly, several conditions have to be satisfied: independence; a high level of professionalization of the regulators; a widely shared regulatory philosophy; a good deal of mutual trust. It is likely that these conditions will not be satisfied from the beginning. However, the very existence of the network provides an environment favourable to the development of the requisite properties. A national agency that sees itself as a member of a group of institutions pursuing similar objectives and facing analogous problems, rather than as a part of a large central bureaucracy pursuing a variety of objectives, is more motivated to defend its professional standards and policy commitments against external influences, and to cooperate with the other members of the network. This is because the agency executives have an incentive to maintain their reputation in the eyes of their international colleagues. Unprofessional, self-seeking, or politically motivated behaviour would compromise their international reputation and make cooperation more difficult to achieve in the future.

Thus, the function of a network is not only to permit an efficient division of labour and exchange of information. It is also to facilitate the development of behavioural standards and working practices that create shared expectations and enhance the effectiveness of the social mechanisms of reputational enforcement.

The issue of accountability

From a normative point of view it may be argued that the greater policy credibility made possible by delegating powers to independent agencies is not sufficient to compensate the consequent loss of democratic accountability. The delegation of regulatory powers to a transnational network is likely to raise even stronger doubts.

Even the present agencies are in many ways beyond the scope of public scrutiny, without any generalized administrative rules or standards laid down which they must observe, and the process by which they reach their conclusions are not subject to any external monitoring or review (De Búrca 1999: 77). This lack of clear mechanisms of accountability is highly problematic within a political entity whose legitimacy is often contested. It is perhaps an indication of a new awareness of the seriousness of this problem that the regulation,[9] which establishes the European Monitoring Centre on Racism and Xenophobia, confers jurisdiction on the ECJ to review acts of the Centre.

Accountability, or the lack thereof, has been a recurrent theme in the development of the regulatory state everywhere. The 'non-delegation doctrine' developed by the US Supreme Court in the early days of federal regulation was rather similar, in inspiration and practical consequences, to the Meroni doctrine formulated by the ECJ in the 1950s. The basic problem is always how 'to control and validate the exercise of essentially legislative powers by administrative agencies that do not enjoy the formal legitimacy of one-person, one-vote election' (Stewart 1975: 1688).

The century-old experience of the American regulatory state shows that the problem is not insoluble. The independence of American regulators has always been constrained and controlled in a variety of ways. To begin with, all agencies are created by congressionally enacted statutes and regulators are appointed by elected officials. The programmes they operate are defined and limited by the enabling laws. Furthermore, regulatory discretion is constrained by procedural requirements that have become increasingly stringent over time.

In sum, although the American agencies are not directly accountable to the people through the electoral and political processes, they are hardly free from procedural and substantive constraints imposing a form of accountability. Public accountability is provided by the requirements that the agencies promulgate rules to guide their discretion and give reasons for their decisions, by the extensive regime of legislative supervision and executive influence, by the opportunities for public participation that agency hearings afford, and by the pervasive discipline of judicial review. Thus, independence from direct political control does not mean independence from public accountability (Freedman 1978).

To a large extent, the strict procedural requirements which constrain the discretion of American agencies have been derived from the reason-giving requirement of the US Administrative Procedure Act. The framers of the European treaties were well aware of the importance of this requirement for institutions lacking direct democratic legitimation. Both the Treaty of Paris, establishing the European Coal and Steel Community, and the Treaty of Rome require European institutions to state the reasons on which their regulations, decisions, or directives are based. At the time these treaties were enacted there was no general requirement to give reasons in the law of the member states, so that these provisions were in advance of national laws. However, the European Court of Justice has shown itself to be quite prepared to impose the reason-giving requirement upon the national authorities in order that individuals are able to defend their rights under EC law. Hence the enactment of an EU Administrative Procedure Act—regulating agency decision-making and extending judicial review to all European agencies—would go a long way towards making independence and accountability mutually supporting, rather than mutually exclusive, values at national as well as European level.

Conclusions

One of the major institutional problems facing the EU today is that the structure of the Commission has remained essentially unchanged for more than forty years, and is proving increasingly inadequate to manage the growing complexity of Community regulation. The establishment of the new European agencies in the 1990s is a clear indication of functional needs, and interests, that are not satisfied or sufficiently integrated by the existing organizational arrangements. What has been achieved so far, however, is more in the nature of stop-gap measures, when not an exercise in symbolic politics, than credible long-term solutions. As the case of the Environment Agency reveals so clearly, political compromise has produced institutional designs characterized by ambiguous responsibilities, uncertain competences, and failure to tackle the enforcement problem.

However, the issue of independent and credible European agencies is still very much alive, as shown by the importance attached to it by the Commission White Paper on Governance, published in the summer of 2001. The vigorous internal debate stimulated by the preparation of this document has revealed that a growing number of Commission officials have abandoned the traditional non-delegation doctrine, and openly endorse the creation of strong regulatory agencies at European level. Such sentiments are widespread in the departments responsible for policy areas—such as transport, energy, telecommunications, financial services, and food safety—where the shortcomings of the traditional approach are most obvious.

Ironically, the growing popularity of the agency model is due not only to these shortcomings, but also to the progressive loss of prestige and influence by the Commission—a loss of status symbolized by the resignation of President Santer and the entire college of Commissioners, and confirmed by the unfavourable outcomes of most European summits after the late 1990s. To ambitious technocrats, with a long professional career still in front of them, an independent European agency promises a safe haven where they can apply their expertise without sacrificing their privileges as international functionaries. Hence industry, which generally favours greater harmonization of rule-making and enforcement, if necessary through the establishment of European regulatory agencies, now finds more receptive ears in some of the Commission's departments.

As we saw in the case of the environmental agency, the European Parliament also supports European agencies 'with teeth', as long as they do not undermine the EP's position in the legislative process. Now, the Parliament's role is potentially strengthened by the new tendency—visible in the new food safety agency and the proposed agencies for air and maritime safety—to create agencies no longer on the basis of the general Article 308 TEC, but of the specific treaty articles dealing with the policy area in which the agency would be operating. The reason this tendency is more favourable to the EP is that the more specific legal basis usually entails the application of the co-decision procedure, thus preserving EP's role as a co-legislator. By contrast, Article 308, which is a broad grant of additional powers to the Community, where these are thought to be necessary to attain one of the objectives of the Community, only requires that the Parliament be consulted.

Thus the strongest resistance to the establishment of European regulatory networks comes from the national governments and parts of the Commission—especially its Legal Service which sees itself as the guardian of the balance of power among Community institutions. However, a series of food scares and other regulatory debacles have so compromised the credibility of the traditional approach, both at national and European level, that it seems likely that even the last defenders of the status quo will eventually accept the necessity of radical institutional reforms.

Notes

1 Council Regulation No. 1210/90 of 7 May 1990.

2 Council Regulation No. 2309/93 of 22 July 1993.

3 Stated in case 9/56, *Meroni* v *High Authority* [1957–8] ECR 133.

4 Article 20 of Council Regulation 1210/90.

5 The new, simplified procedure was mandated by Directive 83/570.

6 See Regulation 2309/93

7 See *Financial Times*, 7 Sept. 1999, p. 2.

8 See *Financial Times*, 14 Sept. 2000, p. 17.

9 See particularly Article 15 of Regulation 1035/97.

Further reading

More detailed treatment of regulatory policies and institutions in the EU and in several member states may be found in Majone (1996). The credibility problem is analysed in Majone (2000) and, from the economist's perspective, in Gatsios and Seabright (1989). The volume edited by Craig and De Búrca (1999) is an excellent collection of essays by distinguished legal scholars on the evolution of EU law, including regulatory law, since the 1960s. Freedman (1978) still provides the most extensive discussion of the legitimacy of regulatory agencies. Although Freedman considers only US institutions, many of his arguments are general enough to be applicable to the European context.

Craig, P., and De Búrca, G. (1999) (eds.), *The Evolution of European Law* (Oxford: Oxford University Press).

Freedman, O. (1978), *Crisis and Legitimacy* (Cambridge: Cambridge University Press).

Gatsios, K. and Seabright, P. (1989), 'Regulation in the European Community', *Oxford Review of Economic Policy*, 5:37–60.

Majone, G. (1996), *Regulating Europe* (London: Routledge).

—— (2000), 'The Credibility Crisis of Community Regulation', *Journal of Common Market Studies*, 38/2: 273–302.

Web links

The web site **www.europa.eu.int** is the place to start any search for basic information on the institutions and bodies of the EU. For the different European agencies, offices, foundations, and centres, see specifically **www.europa.eu.int/ agencies/carte1_en.htm**.

Chapter 15

Social and Regional Interests: ESC and Committee of the Regions

Charlie Jeffery

Contents

Summary

The Committee of the Regions (CoR) was established over thirty years later than the Economic and Social Committee (sometimes called 'Ecosoc' or the ESC). Yet the two bodies have much in common. Both were established to bring in new expertise to European decision-making and given similar sets of consultative powers. Neither, though, has made an enduring impact. The ESC was rapidly marked down as an ineffectual body with weak powers and an unwieldy, disparate membership. The CoR has followed a similar trajectory and has at best yet to prove itself. One outcome has been the growing tendency of social and regional interests to pursue their concerns through other, more effective channels of access to European decision-making.

Introduction

The Economic and Social Committee (sometimes referred to as Ecosoc, here the ESC) is one of the founding institutions of the EU. It was created in the Treaty of Rome and launched in 1958 as a consultative body designed to bring in the advice of social and economic interests—above all business and labour—to European-level decision-making. The Committee of the Regions, a product of the Maastricht Treaty, had its inaugural meeting thirty-six years later in 1994. It too has an advisory role in EU decision-making and is comprised of representatives of local and regional authorities from all the member states.

For two institutions launched in such different eras the ESC and the CoR have a remarkable amount in common. The ESC was in most respects used as an institutional template for the CoR. The internal structures of the two bodies are similar, as are their advisory powers. For a short period in the mid-1990s they even shared a common administrative infrastructure. More fundamentally they had similar founding rationales: to mobilize additional input felt, at the time, to be valuable for the European decision-making process. In neither case, though, have observers been convinced that this rationale of added value has been delivered, not least because it has never been clear what *kind* of added value they should try to deliver. Are they primarily panels of experts there to help make better decisions? Or are they bodies that are genuinely representative of important interests in society, which would otherwise be neglected, in the routine course of interaction between member state governments and the 'core' EU institutions? If the latter, are they equipped to perform the classic role of democratic interest representation, that of building an interface between the political decision-making process and the citizens of the EU?

This 'role conflict' of technocratic expertise versus democratic representation forms a backdrop to this chapter. The chapter begins with an account of the factors that led to the ESC and CoR being set up. Though each is clearly a creature of a particular historical context—the post-war era of corporatist interventionism for the ESC, the more fluid dynamics of early 1990s 'multi-level governance' for the CoR—both were subject to competing technocratic and representative claims. Both were also set up in ways that limited the prospect of any *influential* role being developed. These limitations become evident in the chapter's discussion of the structure and composition of the ESC and CoR and the formal powers accorded to them by treaty. A look at the (changing) ways in which the two institutions have practised these powers over time then reveals the patterns of interaction they have had with the other key European institutions—Council, Commission, and Parliament.

A final section broadens the perspective. The ESC and CoR are not the only routes available for social and regional interests to bring their concerns to bear 'in Europe'. Both interest groups and regional and local authorities routinely use alternative routes to access EU decision-making. These alternative routes offer, for some at least, greater returns than working through the ESC or CoR and are logically given preference. To the extent that this happens, the credibility of the ESC and CoR just as logically suffers, creating a vicious circle. The ESC has, for most observers, never escaped this vicious circle. Whether the CoR can escape it still remains unclear.

The origins of ESC and CoR

The ESC and CoR were each fashioned in treaty negotiations held at critical stages in the European integration process. The Treaty of Rome, which established the ESC, built out radically from the narrow foundations of the European Coal and Steel Community (ECSC) to inaugurate a much wider project of economic integration. The Maastricht Treaty of 1992 was an ambitious response to market deepening, new global economic pressures, and, above all, the collapse of the iron curtain. At such critical moments as these, negotiating agendas are fluid and windows of opportunity for new and often unanticipated initiatives can emerge. The ESC and the CoR both fall into this category.

The idea of establishing an ESC as part of the new European Economic Community emerged only in September 1956 and was finally agreed just two months before the Treaty of Rome was concluded in March 1957 (Smismans 2000: 4). It was brought onto the agenda by two of the smaller players in the negotiations, Belgium and the Netherlands. Their aim was to reproduce the corporatist models provided by their domestic Social-Economic Councils—forums for consulting business and trade unions in economic policy-making—in the new EEC framework. The proposals fell on fertile ground, with all the other founding six except West Germany having similar domestic institutions (Lodge and Herman 1980: 267).

Two other factors argued for the ESC and led to its adoption against West German opposition. First, the idea of bringing in the expertise of the 'social partners' of business and labour to economic decision-making was consistent with both the predominantly economic logic of the early stages of the integration process and the prevailing climate of corporatist interest intermediation. 'Europe' could even lend its own example in the form of the Consultative Committee comprised of representatives of employers and workers (and also of traders and consumers), which had been established to support the work of the ECSC. Early Monnet-method strategies of 'spill-over' may also have played a supplementary role in garnering support for establishing the ESC: interest groups encouraged to 'learn' integration in one field of activity might be expected to develop an openness to further integrative steps elsewhere (Smismans 2000: 3; Lodge and Herman 1980: 265–6).

Second, the proposed EEC Assembly, the forerunner of the European Parliament, was to be indirectly elected, at least initially, and limited to a consultative role. As such it did not provide 'normal' parliamentary channels for bringing interest group influence to bear on European decision-making. In this sense some felt the ESC was needed as a supplementary *representative* body for the new Community, perhaps even 'as an incipient parliamentary-legislative assembly—the third organ in a tricameral legislature alongside the Council of Ministers and a European Parliament linked with the Commission' (Lodge and Herman 1980: 267).

A similar *mélange* of factors—with equivalent implications for establishing a clear sense of institutional purpose—lay behind the establishment of the CoR. The first was a change in the broad political context, heralded by the Single European Act of 1986 and sustained by the activist Commission presidency of Jacques Delors. The implication of deepening integration for regional and local governments was a much greater impact of European legislation in their fields of competence. In particular, regional and local governments across the Union were responsible for the on-the-ground implementation of many European policies. As the scope of these policies grew, regional and local governments were inevitably drawn in as desirable partners in policy-making. In certain fields, in particular structural policy after the reforms of 1988, this role became increasingly formalized, leading influential commentators to coin the term 'multi-level governance' (see Marks 1993).

If regional and local governments were increasingly drawn in 'from above' into this multi-levelled European decision-making process, there were at the same time new trends that operated 'from the bottom up' (Jeffery 2000: 8). Patterns of governance within the member states were being recalibrated in ways that upgraded the significance of sub-national governments. Globalization processes were felt to make redundant traditional forms of economic policy intervention by central governments and to require more differentiated economic strategies tailored to local and regional strengths. In parallel, the neo-liberal vogue in the 1980s for 'rolling back' the (central) state often did little more than shift the responsibility for state action to lower levels of government. And in some member states movements for regional autonomy (re)emerged to prominence. In each case the result was a growing capacity among regional and local governments to engage in policy-making processes, both at the domestic and the European levels. The new multi-level governance emerged, in other words, from the convergence of new trends of sub-national political mobilization launched from both 'above' and 'below'.

The institutional actors which supported the establishment of a Committee of the Regions at Maastricht can be distinguished by these 'top-down' and 'bottom-up' perspectives on the role of regional and local government. One key actor was the Commission. Its logic was impeccably 'top-down'. As the body responsible for the implementation of European legislation, but lacking its own implementation authorities on the ground, it needed partners for the implementation process. Sub-national governments fitted the bill, and as they became more heavily involved in European policy implementation there followed calls to regularize their input. The initial outcome was the creation by the Commission of its own Consultative Council of Regional and Local Authorities in 1988. The rationale behind the Consultative Council—'to improve the poor implementation of regional policy by member states by involving other stakeholders in its design and execution' (Warleigh 1999: 10)—was essentially the same technocratic impulse which had earlier argued for the inclusion of the economic expertise of interest groups, via the ESC, into economic integration policy.

In October 1990 the Commission went further and proposed that a body modelled on the Consultative Council be formalized in the treaty under negotiation in the pre-Maastricht Intergovernmental Conference (IGC) on Political Union. Just two months earlier the German Länder had tabled a parallel proposal for a 'Regional Council'. This was not intended by the Länder (just) as a fount of expertise for the Commission to draw on but rather, quite explicitly, as a *representative* body which would 'ensure that representatives of all Europe's regions can bring in specific regional interests to the legislative process at the European level' (Kilpert and Lhotta 1996: 224). In some of the more ambitious versions, the Regional Council was even envisaged—*pace* early views of the ESC's role—as a prototype for a 'third chamber' which would come to take a place in the European legislative process alongside Council and Parliament (Hoppe and Schulz 1992).

The idea of the Regional Council was one of the responses the Länder had developed to meet the challenges of the accelerated European integration process. They were concerned that post-SEA integration was cutting increasingly deeply into the policy fields for which they were responsible under domestic law, but without giving them compensatory rights of involvement in European decision-making. Faced with this loss of power, they were naturally keen to 'strike back' (Jeffery 1996a). The Regional Council was a key element of their thinking. The IGC on Political Union provided an opportunity to realize these aims. Unlike the parallel IGC on economic and monetary union (EMU), the IGC on Political Union did not have a clear and settled agenda. It emerged as a kind of add-on to existing, relatively advanced debates about EMU, effectively as a quid pro quo for German agreement to the French-led EMU agenda. With many issues as a result left open until the very last stages of the negotiations at Maastricht, there was considerable scope for agenda-setting. The Länder took this opportunity with gusto.

They did this in part through a series of domestic policy papers designed to bind the German central government to their view in the IGC negotiations. Having established a few years previously—in the ratification debates on the SEA—that they had a right of veto over the ratification of new European treaties, they had the wherewithal to make their views count. Judicious wielding of the possibility of veto helped ensure most Länder aims were adopted in the formal German position for the IGC.

The Länder also mobilized on a wider front. Their platform for the IGC resonated strongly with the aims of regional and (to a lesser extent) local governments elsewhere in the EU, which had also been affected by growing European incursions into their fields of responsibility. Working closely with other 'strong' regions in Belgium and Spain in particular, the Länder ensured that a range of other organizations including the Assembly of the European Regions, a Strasbourg-based lobby, and the European Parliament reiterated their demands in and around the IGC. These multiple pressures (Jeffery 1996a: 256–7) generated by the Länder coalesced with the Commission's proposals to force the Regional Council formally onto the IGC agenda in December 1990 and led, ultimately, to its adoption in the form of the Committee of the Regions in the European Summit at Maastricht one year later. What, of course, this odd alliance of 'top-down' *and* 'bottom-up', technocratic *and* representative agendas could not ensure was a clear sense of what the CoR was really for. Like the ESC it was launched into ambiguity.

The waters were muddied further by the structure and powers of the two bodies. In most respects the structure and powers of the CoR as decided at Maastricht were directly modelled on its elder sibling. This was no doubt in part a sheer administrative convenience adopted as a way of dealing quickly with one of the less important items on a crowded and poorly managed IGC agenda. It was also a clear political decision on the part of those outside the group of CoR advocates who did not wish to see the CoR, or the sub-national level more broadly, develop into genuinely influential policy actors. This, of course, was an implicit sideswipe at the ESC, which had been plugging along for over thirty years without wielding much influence on the course of European integration. The next two sections offer insights into why the ESC had failed to wield more influence, and, by implication, why the CoR was hampered from the outset.

The structure of ESC and CoR

Membership

The ESC has what can at best be called a diffuse membership. The vision of the Belgian and Dutch proponents of the ESC—a coherent forum of the 'social partners' of business and labour—was diluted at West German insistence. The result was a more broadly based body representing 'the various categories of economic and social activity, in particular, representatives of producers, farmers, carriers, workers, dealers, craftsmen, professional occupations, consumers and the general interest' (TEC Article 257).[1] These 'various categories' are combined in the ESC in three groups: I—Employers; II—Workers; and III—'Various Interests', a residual category which mops up the rest of the interest groups spectrum.

The number of members has grown from an initial 102 as a result of periodic enlargements, and currently stands—like the CoR membership—at 222, with each member state sending a delegation whose size is loosely linked with population size. This figure is due to rise to 344 in both ESC and CoR as the current group of applicant states joins the EU in the coming years.

ESC members are proposed by the member state governments and are appointed by the Council of Ministers (after the Treaty of Nice by qualified major-ity vote, beforehand unanimously) to serve four-year terms. Importantly, they are not mandated: in other words they are not expected directly to represent the interests of the interest group they belong to 'at home' (though, of course, many do see this as their role). However—not least because member states have differ-ent ways of selecting their ESC members—some members do not hold office in, or

Table 15.1 National delegations to ESC and CoR

Current members		Future members	
Country	No. of members	Country	No. of members
Germany	24		
United Kingdom	24		
France	24		
Italy	24		
Spain	21	Poland	21
		Romania	15
Netherlands	12		
Greece	12		
Belgium	12		
Portugal	12	Czech Republic	12
Sweden	12	Hungary	12
Austria	12	Bulgaria	12
Denmark	9		
Finland	9	Slovakia	9
Ireland	9	Lithuania	9
		Latvia	7
		Slovenia	7
		Estonia	7
Luxembourg	6	Cyprus	6
		Malta	5
Sub-total	222	Sub-total	122
Grand total after enlargement			**344**

even belong to, interest groups (Smismans 2000: 8). The membership of the Committee therefore provides only a patchy coverage of the possible spectrum of 'economic and social activity' across the EU. It also looks, at the start of the twenty-first century, a little anachronistic. Its categories of membership are those of the 1950s and have not been able to keep pace well either with changes in economic structure across the Union or with a picture of interest group politics which has been radically changed by new kinds of organization and activity, for example in the field of environmental protection or equal opportunities. The notion of the ESC as a *representative* body is therefore difficult to sustain.

The situation in the CoR is similar. For the regional lobby and the German Länder in particular its membership was also 'diluted'. The Länder vision had been for a body restricted to regional governments (notwithstanding the fact that this would have left a number of member states, including pre-devolution UK, unrepresented). With its interest in improving policy implementation, the Commission was by contrast interested in drawing the wider palette of sub-national government, both regional and local. The Commission view won out. The result has been a very diverse body bringing together representatives of sub-national governments in full-fledged federal states (from Germany, Belgium, and Austria), through to English district councillors and pretty much everything in between (Schöbel 1995: 30).

CoR members are unmandated, and appointed by the Council (also, post-Nice, by QMV) to four-year terms on the basis of proposals by member state governments. The latter choose their CoR delegations in as many different ways as there are member states. Until the Treaty of Nice, CoR members did not have to be electorally accountable. Unlike the ESC an equal number of 'Alternate Members' is appointed who can deputize when full members are unavailable.

Organization

The ESC and CoR have much the same form of internal organization. Presidents are elected for two-year periods along with Vice-Presidents (two in the case of the ESC, sixteen (!) for the CoR, including a 'chief' Vice-President who is in effect the designate for the next presidency). Supported by other officers, the President and Vice-Presidents form a Presidium (ESC) or Bureau (CoR) which organizes the Committee's business. This is carried out at two levels: in committee and in Plenary. The ESC currently has six standing committees, or sections plus a special temporary subsection on External Relations focused on EU enlargement. The CoR calls its committees Commissions, and currently has seven policy-focused Commissions, plus others focused on relations with other EU institutions and administrative questions. Standing committee membership is structured to reflect the wider composition of the ESC/CoR, balanced across the three Groups in the case of the ESC and across national delegations in the CoR. Both ESC and CoR members

Table 15.2 Standing Committees of the ESC and CoR

ESC Sections	Areas covered	CoR Commissions	Other areas covered
Section NAT	Agriculture, rural development, and the environment	Commission 1	Regional policy, Structural funds, economic and social cohesion, cross-border and inter-regional cooperation
Section ECO	Economic and Monetary Union and economic and social cohesion	Commission 2	Agriculture, rural development, fisheries
Section SOC	Employment, social affairs, and citizenship	Commission 3	Trans-European Networks, transport, information society
Section INT	The Single Market, production, and consumption	Commission 4	Spatial planning, urban issues, energy, the environment
Section TEN	Transport, energy, infrastructure, and the information society	Commission 5	Social policy, public health, consumer protection, research, tourism
Section REX	External relations	Commission 6	Employment, economic policy, Single Market, industry, small and medium-sized enterprises
ELA	Enlargement	Commission 7	Education, vocational training, culture, youth, sport, citizens' rights
		Commission on Institutional Affairs	Institutional affairs
		Committee for Administrative and Financial Affairs	Administrative and Financial Affairs

belong to at least one but (with minor exceptions) no more than two standing committees.

Whenever ESC or CoR have the task of drawing up an opinion, the Presidium/ Bureau assigns the task to the most appropriate standing committee. The latter in turn appoints a *rapporteur* to draft the opinion, who may be supported by a sub-committee or draw on the advice of an external study group. The ensuing draft is discussed and amended in the standing committee, then referred to the Presidium/Bureau for presentation to the Plenary. The ESC Plenary meets around ten times per year, that of the CoR around six times. The main business is to discuss and—if there is a majority—adopt opinions, though more general debates on other important issues within the Committees' remits are also held.

A 'civil service' headed by a Secretary-General supports the work of committees, Plenary and Presidium/Bureau in ESC/CoR. For the period between the CoR's foundation and the Treaty of Amsterdam of 1997, ESC and CoR shared common support services, such as translation, printing, and so on. Since 1997 these services have been formally separated (though most are still, in fact, shared). The ESC has over 500 administrative personnel, the CoR a little less than half that amount, and the budget for running both bodies is around €100 million. By comparison—and a clear indicator of relative importance—the European Parliament has some 4,000 officials and a budget of just over €1 billion.

Coalition-building

Both ESC and CoR have a diffuse and disparate membership. Some consideration is therefore needed of how different views are concerted in the process of drafting and issuing opinions. Both bodies, in fact, have a highly consensual style, issuing most of their opinions unanimously or at least with large majorities. Achieving consensus requires mechanisms or, more informally, coalition-building processes which coordinate and trade off the different interests and positions held by members. Consensus-building in the ESC is perhaps the more straightforward process (Nugent 1994: 237). It revolves around the three Groups: Employers, Workers, and Various Interests. These are organized in the ESC as quasi-political parties. As noted above, Section membership always reflects the balance between the three Groups, and they have their own secretariats. They meet collectively on a regular basis to discuss their views on ESC business, including voting intentions on opinions as they are being drafted in the Sections and before they are presented to the Plenary. Groups I and II are, predictably, more cohesive and therefore more capable of generating a clear view.

This Group-based concertation of opinion limits the number of competing voices in the Committee and makes it easier to achieve impressively high levels of consensus. Van der Voort (1997: 212 in Smismans 2000: 7) calculated that between 1978 and 1990 no less than 72.6 per cent of opinions were issued unanimously, and a further 18.2 per cent with overwhelming majorities. Cases where no agreement can be found between Groups, and the ESC is unable to issue an opinion are rare.[2]

The situation in the CoR is rather more complex. The basic units for concerting opinion at the launch of the CoR were the national delegations which, like the ESC Groups, are resourced by the CoR to meet regularly to discuss the Committee's work programme (Schwaiger 1997: 13). An alternative forum for concerting opinion has since emerged in the form of political parties. Four party groupings equivalent to (some of) those in the European Parliament began to meet consistently before plenary sessions during 1998: the Party of European Socialists (PSE), the European People's Party (EPP), the European Liberal Democrat and Reformist Party and the European Alliance. Revised rules of procedure adopted by the CoR in 1999 formalized this development by giving the party groups status and resources equivalent to national delegations (Switalska 1999: 93–5).

There are not just national and party-political cleavage structures in the CoR though. A number of loose regional groupings exist providing for cross-national exchange of views in the Mediterranean, the Nordic, and Alpine regions (Schwaiger 1997: 15). These periodically appear more generally as a 'north–south' divide focused on issues of structural funding and cohesion policy and on one memorable occasion over additives in wine (Farrows and McCarthy 1997: 29–30). A more enduring cleavage is that which exists between the different kinds of sub-national entity represented on the Committee; that is regional versus local or, perhaps more precisely 'strong' regions with legislative powers versus the rest (see Christiansen 1997). There is something of a debate about how important this cleavage is, with some arguing that there is 'no clear-cut division along these lines' (Schwaiger 1997: 15), others the opposite (Reilly 1997: 148–9).

A more general conclusion to draw is that the CoR is a body with a very fluid internal structure in which coalition-building is a complex, multi-dimensional enterprise. As it is also an enterprise that has adopted the same kind of consensual spirit as the ESC, decisions often need to be pitched at the lowest common denominator of cross-Committee acceptability (Farrows and McCarthy 1997: 31). Inherent in this is the danger of producing such anodyne opinions that the CoR's influence is minimal.

The powers of ESC and CoR

This section first sets out the formal powers given to ESC and CoR by Treaty, before turning to an account of how those powers 'play' in practice in interaction with the other main EU institutions.

Formal powers

The ESC was not generously endowed at the outset. The Treaty of Rome provided for mandatory consultation of the ESC by Council and Commission in certain specified fields and optional consultation in others. The Treaty of Amsterdam also opened up the possibility for ESC to be consulted by the European Parliament.[3] The list of areas where consultation is mandatory has expanded over time, in particular since the SEA. By 1997 the list included agriculture, the free movement of labour, internal market issues, economic and social cohesion, social policy, regional policy, the environment, research and technological development, employment policy, equal opportunities, and public health policy. Optional consultation where Council or Commission (and now Parliament too) 'consider it appropriate' can cover any other aspect of the Treaties. Initial aims on the part of the Dutch sponsors of the ESC to give the Committee a right of initiative, that is, the right to give opinions on issues not specified by Treaty or selected by Council or Commission, were not fulfilled until 1974 (and not confirmed by Treaty until Maastricht). In recent years around 150 opinions have been issued annually with 30–40 per cent of them arising from optional referrals, the same again from mandatory referrals, and the remainder from own initiative.

The right to give opinions does not extend to a right to have those opinions heard. Neither Commission nor Council (nor Parliament) are obliged to give feedback on ESC opinions, let alone take them into account. This rather limited conception of 'consultation' is further evidenced by the fact that the ESC does not have the right to draw up and amend its own internal rules of procedure, but has to have them approved by Council.

The CoR was given more or less the same set of powers, focused initially on the Council and Commission. Mandatory referrals naturally covered a rather different group of fields, reflecting the CoR's regional/local remit while the possibility of optional referral and of own initiative were the same as for the post-Maastricht ESC. Though the long-term pattern of opinions issued is not yet clear, the CoR is certainly presenting fewer opinions than ESC—around seventy per year—with a rather larger proportion (around 50 per cent) arising from its own initiative. The initial fields for mandatory referral comprised education, training and youth, economic and social cohesion, the Structural Funds, trans-European networks, public health, and culture. These were extended in the Treaty of Amsterdam to cover also aspects of employment policy, social policy, the environment and vocational training. Amsterdam also allowed Parliament to consult the CoR and gave the CoR the right—distinguishing it from the ESC—to adopt rules of procedure under its own authority. This in itself suggests the CoR has quickly established a qualitatively higher status than the ESC.

The ESC in practice

Despite the limited powers it had been given, there were confident expectations in the ESC both that 'its accumulated expertise would be valued and exploited by the EC's institutions' and that it would be able to develop a representative role as a 'mediator on behalf of national economic and social interests *vis-à-vis* the Commission and the Council of Ministers' (Lodge and Herman 1980: 269). Neither expectation was fulfilled.

The impact of the 'accumulated expertise' of the ESC was limited in the early years of the EEC in part by the nature of the early integration process, in part by the nature of its powers. Early EEC integration was typically a matter of detailed regulation of a gradual economic harmonization process in fairly narrow policy sectors. Though ESC input here might well have been valuable, it tended to be more or less invisible—not least because Commission and Council were not obliged to give any evaluation of what they thought of ESC opinions. The ESC also suffered from the tight timetable—sometimes as tight as ten days—between referral of an issue and the due date of an opinion. The Council in particular gave little scope for the ESC to undertake detailed consideration of issues. A more general problem was the point in the legislative process at which the ESC was consulted—generally at a relatively late stage when the main policy choices and directions were already well established and any debate was at the level of detail only.

In these circumstances the ESC was naturally keen to establish its own right of initiative. This would allow the Committee itself to set the timetable for deliberation and approach issues as they emerged onto the agenda rather than after their key points had already been set out. A first attempt to establish a right of initiative to draw up opinions on any matter of European competence at any time failed in the mid-1960s. A second was accepted by the member states in 1972 and incorporated into the ESC rules of procedure in 1974. The right of own initiative has typically been used to widen the focus of ESC deliberations away from matters of technical detail and towards more general agenda-setting. It has not, though, done much to change the wider pattern of the ESC's interactions with the other European institutions. To put it bluntly, there is little evidence to suggest that Council has ever taken the slightest notice of the ESC's opinion. At times it has been overtly hostile, most notably when a UK-led initiative in 1982 demanded a full-scale review of a body held to produce opinions too late, to express them too generally, and to be given too many optional referrals (Brüske 1983: 91). One reason for the Council's scepticism was no doubt because the ESC has generally tended to support the supranational agenda of the Commission and has therefore been prone to run up against the buffers of member state intergovernmentalism. The fact that ESC members carry no formal mandate—and therefore no guarantee of 'delivering' the interest group they hail from—may also play a role.

The ESC's support for a supranational agenda does not mean, though, that the

Commission has been much more open to ESC opinions. For Lodge and Herman (1980: 276–7) the Commission viewed the ESC as 'an unimportant and at times an irritating source of work because papers must be routed to it and because it is another body whose voice insists on it being heard'. There is little evidence that the Commission has become any less weary of the ESC since, no matter how much the ESC's own reports trumpet how great an impact it has had. As Dinan wrote more recently (2000: 153), though the ESC's 'output is a valuable and generally underused source of EU policy analysis', 'Council and Commission rarely heed its advice'. Former Commissioner Bruce Millan (1997: 9) echoed this evaluation (in a speech warning the CoR not to fall into the same trap):

The Economic and Social Committee . . . produces a lot of admirable reports, but again most of my fellow Commissioners, as far as I could see, paid no attention to what the Economic and Social Committee said. They did not consider it to be of any importance, and it would be a complete disaster if that were also to happen to the Committee of the Regions.

There are of course periodic exceptions to this rule of ESC non-influence. The most important example concerns what became the Social Charter adopted by all except the UK at Maastricht and later fully incorporated in the Treaty of Amsterdam. An ESC report on a 'Community Charter of Basic Social Rights' formed the basis of the Commission proposals on the Social Charter that were accepted at the Strasbourg European Summit in 1989. 'In this case the ESC set the agenda decisively, before the usual decision-making process began, for the first time in its history' (Brüske 1994: 345)—although what ultimately emerged as the Social Charter bore only a limited resemblance to what the ESC had first suggested!

The fields covered by the Social Charter—including pay, working conditions, freedom of association, health and safety at work, and workplace co-determination—might well be considered the 'natural' terrain of a body which had emerged as a European-level equivalent of national councils of business and labour organizations. Strikingly, though, the ESC itself has not been used as the forum for organizing 'Euro-corporatist' initiatives. A number of Tripartite Conferences were held during the 1970s which brought together European and national-level representatives of business and labour together with national and European officials to discuss matters of macroeconomic and social policy. The ESC had no role then, or in similar, shorter-lived discussions in the mid-1980s. Schmitter and Streeck (1994: 177) put this down to the composition of the ESC which, diluted by the amorphous 'Group III—Various Interests', was simply 'too cumbersome and insufficiently *paritaire* to bear the burden of leading the Community into the brave new world of social partnership'.

The fact that 'Euro-corporatism' effectively ignored Europe's corporatist institution is instructive and points to a wider reason for the ESC's marginal influence: interest groups had and have other channels at their disposal for influencing EU decision-making. Much more attention and resources are devoted by most interest groups—business, labour, and beyond—to influencing the positions their national governments take to the Council of Ministers, to lobbying the Commission and Parliament directly, or to working through the European-level peak organizations which also have direct routes into Commission and Parliament. Equally if Commission or Parliament want to mobilize technical expertise or policy implementation capacity, direct links to national or European peak organizations can provide them quickly and efficiently. If both interest groups and the key European institutions have these routes at its disposal, the potential added value of the ESC as a channel for influence is put clearly into perspective.

This question mark over the ESC's value raises questions not just about the institution as a forum for bringing specialist expertise to the EU, but about the notion of the ESC as a representative body. The absence of mandate and the patchy membership of the ESC always undermined its claims to 'supply' representativeness. Nor is there any clear 'demand' for a representative body among the interest group community and the other European institutions. Put simply, the idea of corporatist interest representation—despite the tripartite experiments of the 1970s and 1980s—was never one universally accepted across the EU and is now deeply anachronistic. It is all the more surprising, therefore, that the ESC has in recent years sought to relaunch itself with a (reformulated) representative rationale.

This reformulated rationale focuses on the concept of 'civil society' and is hung on the hook of the 'democratic deficit', and the need to close it. In the words of the ESC (2000: 2), the aim is 'to promote a greater commitment/contribution from civil society to the European venture, and to build and strengthen a Europe that is close to its public'. To this end the ESC has made greater use of open 'hearings intended to deepen contacts between the public and EU institutions' in developing its opinions. It has also developed a more explicit self-image as 'the representative of civil society organizations' which was reflected most ambitiously in a 'Convention' of 300 national, European, and international social organizations held in 1999 (Smismans 2000: 6, 14). However, it is not clear that many outside the limited circle of ESC addressees have taken much notice of these new initiatives.[4] It is hard to escape the conclusion that the new civil society emphasis is just another throw of the dice by an organization still searching for a role over forty years on from its launch.

The CoR in practice

This image of the ESC searching in vain for a significant role is one that has dogged the CoR through its short life. The parallels in structure, function, and powers it shared with the ESC meant that CoR's initial priority in developing its work was to demonstrate that it would not become an ESC mark two. Repeated warnings from friends of the CoR in the Commission—such as Bruce Millan (below)—who had helped bring the CoR into being in the first place, urged that the CoR needed quickly to develop a clear sense of purpose and a reputation for producing focused and useful opinions:

You should spend your time coming together, uniting your views . . . rather than squabbling among yourselves. It would give great pleasure to member states that are not enthusiastic about the Committee, and to the Council and even to the Parliament to some extent, if you spent time quarrelling among yourselves rather than putting forward views which you expect to be taken seriously by the Council and the Commission . . . The real danger for the Committee is that if it does not do its work well, it will not be taken seriously.[5]

In some respects the starting position for the CoR was a favourable one. Unlike the ESC it did not have to fight for years to be able to set its own priorities through the right of own initiative. It also had a broad and vocal coalition of early backers, including senior Commissioners but also the most powerful regional governments in the EU, the German Länder. The Länder had styled themselves as the architects of a new 'third', regional level in EU decision-making and envisaged the CoR as the key route in making this third level count (Jeffery 1996a).

These favourable conditions allowed the CoR to hit the ground running. Despite the difficulties of sharing administrative resources with the ESC it soon established a functioning organizational structure. As a result, its members were able quickly to swing into action, issuing over seventy opinions (including twenty-nine on CoR own initiative) in the first ten plenary sessions from March 1994 to January 1996. The main policy areas covered were regional policy, social policy, health, and education, with the CoR responding within the consultative timetable to referrals from Council and Commission (typically involving detailed policy questions), and using own initiative as a mechanism to set more general priorities for action (Farrows and McCarthy 1997: 32–6).

Impact is difficult to measure. It was significant, though, that the then Commissioner for Regional Policy, Monika Wulf-Mathies, committed the Commission in 1995—just eleven months after the CoR's launch—to extending the range of referrals beyond the mandatory areas required by Treaty. She also unveiled a code of conduct for Commission/CoR relations modelled on that between Commission and Parliament, which lifted the relationship with the CoR to a level above that enjoyed by the ESC. A succession of appearances at CoR meetings by a series of Commissioners also indicated that a positive relationship with the Commission was emerging (Jeffery 1995: 249). The most comprehensive academic analysis of the CoR's impact on the Commission by Switalska (1999: 53–61) confirms this picture: the Commission takes the CoR seriously, generally gives feedback on CoR opinions, and frequently takes CoR views on board.

A similar picture does not apply to the Council of Ministers, which has treated the CoR with 'benign indifference' (Warleigh 1999: 28), in particular refusing to give feedback on CoR opinions. The relationship with the European Parliament is a little more nuanced. Though there is frequent cooperation between CoR *rapporteurs* and their counterparts in EP Committees dealing with the same issues, there has been an underlying rivalry. This rivalry can be traced at one level to a policy turf battle, with the EP's Regional Affairs Committee covering much the same ground as the CoR. There is a deeper dimension, though, which can be traced back to some of the visions surrounding the creation of the CoR. In particular, the German Länder notion of a 'third level' had an implicit representative claim, which was confirmed in the CoR's discussions on the 1996–7 IGC, commenced soon after its launch. The Länder, with some support from Spanish and Belgian regions, revived the idea of the CoR as a potential 'third chamber' in the EU legislative process and called in the early IGC debates for the CoR to be given an explicit legislative role. They also proposed that the CoR itself be divided into two 'chambers', one for regional and one for local representatives, with the implication that the 'regional chamber' might take on that legislative role alongside Parliament and Council (Jeffery 1995: 254). Unsurprisingly such proposals soured relations with the EP, which was not keen on the idea of a competing legislative organ undermining its hard-won authority (Millan 1997: 10). Significantly, the EP had not by the end of 2000 made use of its power, established at Amsterdam, to refer matters to the CoR.

The debates in the CoR on the 1996–7 IGC are also instructive in a different sense. With the debate on the IGC starting so soon after the CoR's launch, the CoR was 'born into its own reform' and forced to confront the 'role-conflict' its original sponsors had thrust upon it: was it to be a representative body as the German Länder had hoped, or was it to be an expert body to be consulted wherever its expertise counted and could improve EU policy, as the Commission had envisaged (see Christiansen 1997: 51, 61–3)? It was on this issue of role that clear differences between the local and regional 'wings' of the CoR emerged in the IGC debates, with the former keen to propose to the IGC limited and incremental adjustments to the CoR's consultative powers, and the latter initially pressing for a fuller legislative-representative role. These differences were ultimately papered over in what the coordinator of a CoR Special Commission on the IGC called a 'compromise without consensus' (Kalbfleisch-Kottsieper 1995: 13). The outcome was a set of proposals for the IGC that for the most part was relatively anodyne (and easily accepted at Amsterdam). Where the proposals did move into more ambitious territory—for example on subsidiarity or on CoR access to the European Court of Justice—they had little chance of success precisely because it was clear that the CoR itself could hardly put together a united front in pursuing them (Reilly 1997).

The notion of 'compromise without consensus' points to a paradox inherent in the CoR's creation. On the one hand, its establishment was a triumph for the third level. On the other, its subsequent operation has provided a platform not just for those, like the German Länder, which were keen for better third-level representation, but also for the full, highly differentiated range of units of sub-national government across the EU. The CoR's contributions to the debates in the run-up to the Nice IGC in 2000 suggest a belated acceptance of the reality of this sub-national differentiation. The Committee, with a new leadership outside the 'founder generation' set out in a more modest tone more modest proposals designed to refine its place in the decision-making apparatus of the EU alongside the Commission, Council, and Parliament rather than to seek any broader recalibration of the Union in line with earlier three-level visions.

At the same time, the new CoR President, Jos Chabert, inaugurated a new debate about the CoR's rationale. Chabert (2000: 2–3) sought to change the CoR's image as 'a purely technical body', instead presenting it 'as a key component in the EU's quest for legitimacy'. This quest is, apparently, based on the notion that 'democratically elected local and regional representatives' such as those in the CoR can 'make the European institutions aware of the real, daily concerns of the people they represent' and that 'our citizens must be able to identify with their representatives as they do so'. Such a notion of legitimation through identification with popular representatives doing good works and, as a result, helping to bind the EU to its citizens is nice in theory. It accords well with the growing party-political logic that has begun to pervade the CoR's work in recent years. It rather runs into the sand in practice, though, in that very few European citizens have much grasp of the role their elected, sub-national actors play at the EU level. In this sense the CoR's 'citizens' agenda' echoes that of the ESC on civil society: a throw of the dice by a body trying to find itself a plausible purpose to which all of its disparate members might subscribe.

The ESC and CoR in context

It is clear enough from the discussion above that the ESC has never found itself a lasting niche in European decision-making, and that the CoR is having trouble establishing one. The combination of weak, consultative powers, unclear roles, and highly diverse memberships establishes an unenviable set of barriers which have to be hurdled if the ESC's interest groups or the CoR's authorities are to be able to exert any genuine collective influence—whether generated through technical expertise or a plausible claim to representativeness. The higher barriers to influence are, the more likely it is that social and regional interests will choose to use any alternative channels of influence open to them. The European decision-making process is both highly sectorized and multi-levelled. As a result, there are many different access points available for particular interests to press and realize their concerns.

The attractiveness of alternative access points has long been noted in the case of the interest groups gathered in the ESC (see Feld 1966; Mazey and Richardson 1989; Platzer 1999). Many interest groups—or even individual members of those groups—are well placed to exert influence over national government and, indirectly, the Council of Ministers. And, as the scope of EU policies has grown, a vast range of transnational Eurogroups and Brussels-based Euro-lobbyists has emerged, which seek to exert direct influence over Commission, Parliament, and Council (usually via its working groups). For most groups the choice between undiluted and direct access to some of the key nodes of the EU decision-making process and the consensual working style and (at best) diffuse impact of the ESC is fairly clear-cut. And, of course, the more that interest groups favour alternative routes, the harder it is for the ESC to establish itself as a plausible channel for influence.

This is not a new conclusion. It has been standard fare in assessments of the ESC for decades (see Brüske 1982: 107–8; 1994: 345; Wallace and Wallace 2000: 25). What is striking, though, is how much the same situation is beginning to emerge regarding the pursuit of regional interests in EU decision-making. Put starkly, the CoR has become a low priority for some regional interests because there are better ways of getting things done. A number of EU member states now have domestic policy formulation processes for EU matters that formally include sub-national governments in determining the member state position. These include Belgium, Germany, Austria, the UK (for Scotland, Northern Ireland, and Wales), and, to lesser extents, Italy and France. In the first four of these cases, regional governments have the right in some fields of policy to speak for the national delegation in the Council of Ministers. These national channels offer, needless to say, rather fuller opportunities for influencing EU decision-making than those of the CoR.

A case in point is that of the German Länder, joint progenitors of the CoR and erstwhile third-level visionaries. Since the CoR discussions on the 1996–7 IGC the Länder have in large part turned their backs on the CoR, bidding a 'farewell to the third level' (Jeffery 1996b) and helping shape EU decision-making primarily through domestic channels. The Länder priority, at the last two IGCs, has been maximizing the opportunities and returns from these domestic rights of input into EU decision-making, up to and including Council representation. This has shifted their focus away from general regional aims to specifically national ones (see Engel 1998: 178).

Alongside this kind of 'national' route into European policy, there are also channels of sub-national influence that act directly on 'Brussels'. Well over one hundred sub-national authorities maintain representative offices in Brussels designed to garner intelligence from, and communicate ideas to, Commission and Parliament. A vast range of transnational organizations bring together regions with shared sectoral or territorial interests to exert collective influence on the Commission in particular (Schmitt-Egner 2000). These transnational alliances are organized in part around the cleavage structures also evident in the CoR—but of course can present their shared concerns more directly, without having to negotiate a common denominator with other sets of regional interests as is the case in the CoR.

Conclusion

The CoR is, at best, one of a large number of channels open for regional interests to make a mark on Europe. It stands as institutional testimony to a high-water mark of common sub-national purpose achieved in the run-up to Maastricht. That common purpose has since evaporated—not least because it became evident how difficult it was to maintain common purpose in a Committee with such a disparate membership and such modest powers. Instead a much more complex pattern of multi-level governance has emerged in which sub-national governments pursue in a range of arenas—national, transnational, Brussels-focused, sometimes the CoR where it is expedient—highly individualized agendas designed to realize a set of specific territorial interests in EU policy-making. A similar situation applies for interest groups. They too have multiple channels of access and devise particular strategies to achieve their specific interests. These strategies may be directed at national governments or at the main European-level institutions, although the ESC will typically not figure very high on the Euro-institution list. In this sense the ESC is a frozen legacy of a constellation of factors that, in an earlier era of corporatist interest intermediation, seemed an appropriate way forward. Rapidly, however, it became anachronistic and is now more or less irrelevant. A decade or so on from its conception at Maastricht, it is difficult to see the CoR failing to follow the same path to anachronism and irrelevance.

Notes

1   Prior to the Treaty of Nice, the phrase 'representatives of the general public' was used instead of 'consumers and the general interest'. Otherwise, the constituencies of the ESC have remained unchanged since 1958.

2   A recent exception to the rule was an irresolvable difference of opinion between agricultural and consumer representatives on support levels for tobacco farming in 1999. See Commission 2000*b*, para. 1052.

3   This had happened only once by the end of 2000—cf. Commission 2000*b*, para. 1165.

4 Though the Commission did present an opinion to a 'convention of civil society' hosted by the ESC in Brussels in October 1999 (Commission 2000*b*, para. 1054).

5 Address at Queen's University Belfast, Nov. 1995

Further reading

Little has been published on the ESC. The best paper on the foundation and initial development of the ESC is Lodge and Hermann (1980). Smismans (2000) provides a solid update on more recent developments. Much more attention has been given to the CoR. Warleigh (1999) provides a solid overview, although an earlier special issue of *Regional and Federal Studies* (1997) is more incisive. A good wider analysis of EU interest group politics is Greenwood, Grote, and Ronit (1992); for a wider discussion of multi-level governance see the special issue of *Regional and Federal Studies* (1996).

Greenwood, J., Grote, J., and Ronit, K. (1992), *Organized Interests and the European Community* (London: Sage).

Lodge, J., and Hermann, V. (1980), 'The Economic and Social Committee in EEC Decision-Making', *International Organization*, 43/2: 265–84.

Regional and Federal Studies (1996), special issue on 'The Regional Dimension of the European Union', 6/2, summer.

Regional and Federal Studies (1997), special issue on 'The Committee of the Regions', 7/1, spring.

Smismans, S. (2000), 'The European Economic and Social Committee: Towards Deliberative Democracy via a Functional Assembly', *European Integration Online Papers*, 4/12 at **www.eiop.or.at/eiop/texte/2000-012a.htm**.

Warleigh, A.(1999), *The Committee of the Regions: Institutionalising Multi-Level Governance* (London: Kogan Page).

Web links

The ESC's web site at **www.europa.esc.eu.int** is well organized with a reasonable archive of ESC papers and publications. The CoR equivalent at **www.europa.cor.eu.int** has a less comprehensive archive but contains useful general information. Useful facts and figures on the work of the two bodies can be found in the Commission's annual General Report at **www.europa.eu.int/abc/doc/off/rg/en/2000** (and /1999, /1998 etc.).

Chapter 16
Conclusion

John Peterson and Michael Shackleton

Contents

Summary

Four basic themes emerge from close analysis of the EU's institutions. First, they are irrevocably interdependent: however much they compete, they are doomed to succeed or fail together. Second, their capacity to fulfil the core functions of the Union—providing leadership, managing policies, and integrating interests—is subject to new doubts, particularly in the context of imminent and radical enlargement. Third, EU member governments have recently developed a range of new institutional options for embedding the national into the European level of decision-making. Fourth, understanding collective governance in Europe requires close examination of how the EU's institutions operate and interact, with the new institutionalist literature offering valuable guides to such an analytical task. We conclude by raising the central question of whether the EU institutional structure can be made sufficiently accountable to European citizens for it to be seen as a legitimate purveyor of collective governance.

Introduction[1]

We began this analysis of the EU's institutions (see Chapter 1) by examining how the most fundamental, overriding goal of the Union—managing the enormous interdependence which links European states—created a demand for what William Wallace (2000) has called 'collective governance'. Collective governance logically requires institutions that work *collectively* to offer leadership, manage diverse tasks, and integrate interests in the pursuit of common goals. The EU's institutional system often seems to lack the capacity to foster truly collective action in the pursuit of shared goals, and moreover appears enormously complex, arcane, and far more convoluted than its counterparts at the national level. Yet, it is worth remembering that Europe remains an enormously diverse part of the world, featuring a varied range of densely populated states, whose histories are closely intertwined but marked above all by conflict (much of it bloody). Collectively governing Europe is not a simple business. The history of Europe is one of periods of cooperation interspersed (consistently) with its subsequent breakdown into conflict.

The historical focus of nearly all of this volume's contributions reminds us that European integration as a project began with strikingly narrow and overwhelmingly economic objectives: first, to manage jointly the production of coal and steel, and then, to develop a common market and free trade in other goods. Yet, the earliest moves to institutionalize European cooperation were never seen as final. They represented something new and unspecified, but definitely went beyond the intergovernmental cooperation of (say) the Council of Europe, with its limited agenda and resources and non-binding decision-making. From the beginning, EU institution-building had the decidedly political purpose of making European states ever more mutually dependent on one another.

In the half-century that it has existed, the EU has expanded to take on an enormous number of new tasks. It also has expanded its membership to become a far more diverse collection of states. No one could have imagined it ever forming such a broad political 'community' or 'union' at the beginning. Now, the EU is committed to admit far more and far more disparate new members than its institutional system was ever intended to accommodate. Logically, institutionalizing collective governance has become a steadily more politicized process, and one that dominates the calculations of European governments and increasingly touches the lives of European citizens, including many very far away from Brussels.

Recent moves to extend the EU's remit to matters of monetary, foreign, defence, and internal-security policies (amongst others) have led to more diverse institutional choices. Rather than simply framing the question as a straight up or down, black or white one—'do we want to *Communitarize* this policy sector or not?'—member governments have created a wider set of options for themselves. Deciding to make policy in the EU context is only a first step which leads to a set of further choices: 'do we Communitarize, *or* do we organize new cooperation using one of the many existing alternative institutional mechanisms *or* do we create an entirely new institutional solution?'

The stakes surrounding such choices are much higher now than they were in the 1950s. There are more players—more governments and affected interests, plus the EU's increasingly assertive institutions themselves—making compromises more difficult to strike. Moreover, the 'permissive consensus' that allowed bold steps forward in European integration without much public protest or even attention during most of the history of the EU is now gone. Citizens' sense of loyalty to the EU institutions is generally weak even if there is a somewhat stronger attachment to 'Europe' as a focus for collective action. Weak loyalties cannot be separated from increased institutional complexity. Most average citizens cannot help but be befuddled by the arcane language that has characterized the treaty changes of the last decade. It might be comforting to pro-Europeans, but almost certainly mistaken to think that the response of Irish voters to the Treaty of Nice in the June 2001 referendum, where a majority rejected the Treaty and a still larger number did not bother to turn out,[2] was an aberration. Much needs to be done before EU citizens truly identify with the institutions of the Union as 'their own'.

This volume has tried to cut through the complexity by encouraging acknowledged experts on each institution to approach it in a roughly similar way. The analyses have highlighted four basic themes. First, the EU's institutions are intensely and irrevocably interdependent. Regardless of how much they compete for power and influence amongst themselves, and how divided they are about where the EU is going, they are doomed to succeed or fail together. Second, the capacity of the institutions to continue to govern Europe collectively is being increasingly called into question, even in an EU of only fifteen member states. The prospect of further enlargement raises doubts about the ability of the system to generate policies that both work and are seen to work. Third, the process of embedding what is 'national' into what is 'European' has become a far more complicated process than it was when, say, the decision was taken in the 1960s to create a common agricultural policy to replace national agricultural policies. One result is that member governments have experimented with new forms of decision-making and even new kinds of *acquis*, such as the 'Schengen *acquis*' and the 'CFSP *acquis*,' to achieve collective governance. In doing so, they have compounded the EU's dizzying complexity. Fourth, without discounting the insights that alternative theoretical models bring to the study of the EU, this volume has shown that institutionalist theory has a lot to tell us about the EU. In particular, it reveals that an essential first step to understanding the politics of European integration is to understand the EU's inimitable and often mystifying institutions.

We develop each of these themes below, and conclude by grappling with perhaps the most urgent question facing students of the EU's institutional system: can it become a more accepted, respected pivot of political life in Europe? Or must it inevitably become a target of the same populist doubts, pressures, and protests to which other international organizations have become subject? We have no easy answers to these difficult questions. However, we can offer the essential argument that the EU's institutions are in the vanguard of efforts to legitimize international bodies that have become increasingly powerful regulators of economic and political life.

Institutional interdependence

A constant theme of this book has been that none of the institutions of the European Union is independent and free to act autonomously. All are interlinked and interdependent, especially with each other but also with national institutions in the member states. Every contribution to this volume has focused on the relationship between the institution(s) in question and its counterparts elsewhere in the EU system. The effect has been to highlight the *collective* responsibility that the Union's institutions and member states assume for EU policies. It is not only the members of the Commission's college (see Chapter 4) who must formally and publicly support all decisions of the Commission. More generally, if often informally, all components in the EU's institutional system—revealed as cogs in a *system*, or network of mutually reliant actors (see Keohane and Hoffmann 1991: 13–15)—are faced with a political obligation to justify publicly what the EU does and how it does it.

The character of this institutional interdependence has been shown in a variety of ways. First, as Kathleen McNamara points out in Chapter 8, even bodies that appear to be independent—and are assured a very large measure of independence in their statutes, such as the European Central Bank (ECB)—need links with the rest of the EU institutional system, and moreover the outside world, to prosper. To deny this need is to invite the opprobrium of other institutional actors and popular disillusion with what the EU does more generally. Witness the damaging (not least to the value of the euro) statement of the ECB President, Wim Duisenberg, to pleas for lower interest rates to spur economic growth in 2001: 'I hear but I do not listen.' It met with the ire of (particularly) the EP as well as many others beyond Brussels.

In fact, the design of the EU's institutional system virtually *demands* that actors within each of its individual institutions not only hear but also listen to their counterparts in the other institutions. Even the European Court (ECJ), whose deliberations remain shrouded in secrecy and which fosters an image of distant independence, ultimately depends on the good-will of the member states and their courts to implement its judgments. Whatever talk there may be of the decline, permanent or not, of the Commission, it is hard to see how the Council could prosper without a Commission strong enough to make suggestions, broker deals, and sometimes accept criticism for the results. In particular, the need for collective governance to maintain the Union's economic clout internationally is sometimes so clear that EU member governments are essentially obligated to defend the institutional system they have created, warts and all, when its basic authority is questioned. A good example was when all EU member governments publicly supported the Commission (or at least did not condemn it) after its highly controversial decision in 2001 to block the merger of two giant American firms—General Electric and Honeywell—in the face of the Bush administration's complaints that the EU was meddling 'outside their jurisdiction'.[3]

Of course, the reality of collective responsibility does not mean that turf-battling is not a primary feature of the EU's institutional system and one of its most harmful pathologies. At times, the EU's institutions can seem more concerned with expanding their own remits than with ensuring that the EU turns out effective policies. Yet, as much as they compete for turf, the Union's institutions also compete for credit for policies (such as the single market) that *do* prove to be effective. They also indulge in creative acts of 'blame displacement', denying their own responsibility for acts of fraud or set-backs such as the 2001 Irish referendum. Both kinds of behaviour simply reinforce how intertwined the fortunes of the EU's institutions—and, by extension, its member governments—have become over time.

Moreover, despite the blurring of lines of accountability in the EU (see our concluding section below), the institutions have become *collectively* accountable—probably increasingly so—for the work of the Union, and that at virtually every level. Within Council working groups, as Fiona Hayes-Renshaw points out (Chapter 3), as well as in Coreper—as shown by Jeffrey Lewis (Chapter 13)—national views are merged into an agreed position. Afterwards, national actors are staunchly reluctant to reveal to outsiders the range of views that preceded decision. The Council often collectively and stubbornly defends its common position in co-decision with the EP, even if it has been accepted with difficulty by some member states.[4] But after conciliation produces agreement, it becomes often very hard to separate out who was responsible for what. Michael Shackleton argues (Chapter 5) that co-decision has not only become something like the EU's template decision rule; it also has firmly established that most legislative decisions are made more or less collectively by the EU's three main legislative institutions—the Commission, Council, and Parliament. All are obliged to defend the outcome in the Court of Justice in the case of a legal challenge, thereby reinforcing the notion that Brussels as a whole produced the legislation. The more general point is that the future of the European project, to create a more prosperous and unified Europe, depends as never before on the ability of the EU's institutions to work together, as elements in a *system*, offering collective governance.

Capacity: decline or renewal?

A second underlying theme of the book has been the emergence of new questions about whether the EU's institutions are up to the jobs that they have been given. Even before the Union's membership expands radically to as many as twenty-five or thirty member states, it has become tempting to ask: has the EU's institutional system now worked about as effectively as it ever *could* or *will*? Even if it has fostered international cooperation of a kind unprecedented in modern history, with institutions designed to accommodate six member states and then adjusted to handle twelve to fifteen, must we now accept that it can never work as well with twenty-five or thirty? Are *immobilisme* and decline now inevitable? It is worth reviewing the arguments presented in this volume that give rise to such stark, even disturbing questions.

The leadership challenge

This book has highlighted the pluralistic, non-hierarchical character of the EU, and its lack of both government and opposition. No political party or coalition of parties can really claim to govern the Union. There is no cabinet, no true executive.[5] As de Schoutheete argues in Chapter 2, the European Council may seem to sit at the top of a pyramid structure, acting as a sort of Board of Directors for the EU. Proposals for renewing the Union's institutions during the 2000 IGC—from Fischer, Chirac, Blair, Lipponen, Amato, Herzog, etc., etc.—all urged that the capacity of European summits to impose their will on the rest of the EU's institutional system be strengthened. Yet, the single-mindedness of these proposals was more reflective of the EU's crisis of purpose than the ascendancy of the European Council, whose capacity to give strong political impulse to the Union's affairs is, in de Schoutheete's view, declining.

The EU sometimes seems woefully short on political leadership more generally. Leadership is a contested commodity in the EU, as we can see if we look at the various institutional candidates to provide it: the Commission, the Council presidency, the European Council, even (lately) the EP. Prodi's suggestion that the Commission was a proto-government met with howls of derision. The Council presidency can only act within a limited mandate and cannot go further than the other states will let it. The European Council meets only occasionally and for the equivalent of just over one working week per year. The EP continues to struggle to attract the loyalties of European citizens.

It might be argued that it is up to the EU's member governments, individually or in alliances with each other, to provide political direction to the European project. If we take this view, we inevitably end up asking whether past sources of leadership—such as the Franco-German alliance—can be resurrected. Two of the fundamental lessons of this volume help us to frame, if not answer, this question. First, we have seen that powers are now exercised more diffusely by the EU's institutions than ever before, making it more difficult for one member state or any group of them to give political impulses that resonate across the Union's institutional system. Second, it is clear that strong, decisive action at the EU level requires political agency from multiple sources—again, a strong Council requires a strong Commission—thus making principal-agent relationships ambiguous in the EU. In short, the evolution of the EU's institutional system casts new doubts on whether the EU of the future can rely on past sources of political leadership. And even if the Union has always relied on a sense of shared mission and purpose amongst its institutions for its success, it seems more reliant on collective institutional will now than ever before.

The management challenge[6]

The EU's lack of hierarchy has many pluses. It sustains participation by all parties because the policy agenda seems (in appearance, at least) remarkably open. No one wins all the time, and even losers in policy debates can become winners by shifting the agenda towards new policies that mitigate or cancel out past ones. Ultimately, collective governance is unsustainable in the absence of compromise: we can expect all to be willing to compromise today only if all can hope for better results, in view of their own interests, tomorrow.

Yet, the EU's lack of hierarchy creates problems of management as well as political drift. At earlier stages in its evolution, the EU's business might have been managed effectively by the Hallstein and Delors Commissions, or by its largest and most committed member governments (again, especially the French and German) when they held the Council presidency. Now, the reality is different. If it is accepted that optimal EU policy outcomes are possible only if objectives are clearly specified (because the EU must now do much more with only very limited capacities), then the Union's lack of any hierarchy of policy goals, as well as any body or institution able to impose one, are highly damaging. The Union has always operated a kind of consortium model of governance, in which much is left deliberately ambiguous to facilitate compromise. But there is usually a price to be paid in terms of efficient management—that is, setting priorities, following up past initiatives, ensuring effective implementation, and so on. The price often seems to rise inexorably as more voices must be accommodated at every turn, especially as the EU enlarges.

The EU's management problem has been scrutinized perceptively by Metcalfe (2000). Put simply, the EU's institutional system—whatever its virtues—is also a recipe for *undermanagement*. Regardless of how high and mighty the European Council looks to the untrained eye, much EU governance occurs in practice within horizontally structured and often highly autonomous policy networks which preside over individual policy sectors (see Peterson and Bomberg 1999: 21–8). The EU's main institutions are well represented in most of them (especially since co-decision has so substantially upgraded the EP's powers). Inter-institutional politics can be lively: agents representing the Commission, EP, and Council can be relied upon to defend their institutions' prerogatives and priorities staunchly.

Yet, responsibility is shared widely both for policy outputs and outcomes. As such, none of the EU's individual institutions has incentives to invest in the capacity of policy networks to manage the policy agenda. According to this view, the problems arising from the mismatch between the EU's aspirations and capabilities almost naturally become more severe over time since:

a combination of factors operating within the EU's institutional framework creates political incentives to take on more tasks while imposing constraints on the acquisition and development of capacities for managing them effectively. In the Council, political decision-makers too readily assume the existence of management capacities and governance structures to implement policies or dodge the difficult issues about who should provide them. The Commission has been more interested in staking out new territorial claims than insisting on the resources for discharging responsibilities effectively (Metcalfe 2000: 824).

Thus, the roots of the EU's management deficit are spread widely. One implication is that all of the Commission's recent efforts to make itself more organizationally efficient cannot, by themselves, produce more effective EU governance.

Weak management means poor coordination and a lack of clear priorities. Fiona Hayes-Renshaw's (Chapter 3) discussion of the General Affairs Council highlights its inability to set priorities and or coordinate across different EU policy sectors for EU policy-making. Perhaps some kind of permanent 'super-Council' of European Affairs Ministers could help close the management deficit. Yet, it remains difficult to foresee EU governments collectively biting the bullet and single-tasking senior, heavyweight cabinet ministers with the job of making the EU work better. To do so, they would have to defy the system of incentives that encourages all actors in EU decision-making to focus on winning today's policy argument, as opposed to ensuring that the policy agenda does not become too crowded or that yesterday's decisions are implemented properly.

The challenge of integrating interests

Until the 1980s, the task of integrating interests seemed a relatively simple one of integrating the *national* interests of its member states in narrowly circumscribed areas of policy marked out for collective governance, such as the CAP and external trade. Policy-making was an élite-driven exercise, more or less monopolized by national executives working with the Commission. The EP was an assembly of seconded national parliamentarians for whom 'Europe' was often a second-order priority. The Economic and Social Committee (ESC) was a pseudo-corporatist talking shop. Both the EP and the ESC were easily ignorable by the Council. The Commission was always less ignorable, and took pains to ingratiate itself with broad social and political interests while trying to integrate them into Europe-wide associations. But not until the Delors era did the Commission ever success-fully integrate transnational interests into its work to the point where it was able to 'use' them to challenge the Council or encourage member governments to accept its own policy agenda.

Now, of course, the challenge of integrating interests is far more acute. The EU's policy agenda has expanded enormously, and continues to do so. More societal interests both have a stake in EU policy-making and demand a voice in the process. One of us noted in the 1990s that the EU had (at the time) only recently been transformed from 'a system concerned with the *administration of things* to one con-cerned with the *governance of people*' (Shackleton 1997: 70; emphasis in original). That now seems like a very long time ago, especially given the EU's new role in providing public goods—such as money, defence, and policing—that only nation states provided back then. Yet, the Union has made far fewer and shorter strides towards integrating societal interests compared to the steps it has taken to subject new policies to collective governance.

Two caveats must be made here. One is that, as we have seen, the EU system does a remarkably proficient job of integrating the *institutional* interests of its main institutional players (which themselves could be viewed as effectively integrating *national* interests, narrowly defined). No important EU policy can be agreed—outside very few sectors such as competition or agriculture—without a very large measure of consensus spanning the Council, the Commission, and EP. Even the EU's newest institutions such as the CFSP planning unit, which privilege national interests and are overwhelmingly staffed by national officials, provide the Com-mission and EP with channels for input. Collective institutional responsibility for EU policy, which must be a central goal of any effective system of collective governance, is something the EU does rather well.

Second, the EU's institutional system has, over time, become increasingly innovative in the task of integrating different *sectoral* interests. One of the central features of the shift to so-called 'post-modern' political structures in response to globalization is the 'sectoral unbundling of territoriality in various functional regimes' (Ruggie 1998: 27). One outcome is the emergence of new policy-specialized, transgovernmental networks, populated by actors who have more in common with each other than with officials who specialize in *other* policy areas in their own nation states. The implication for the EU is that it now must integrate a far wider diversity of 'national interests' than was the case for most of its history.

On this test, again the EU scores quite well. Lewis (Chapter 13) portrays Coreper as a remarkably effective integrator of the interests of increasingly more divided and less single-minded national civil services, as well as an effective broker of 'political' and 'technical' interests. Majone (Chapter 14) is convincing in arguing that strong, independent agencies offer a potential mechanism for integrating functional interests in an era of 'sectoral unbundling'.

At the same time, Part III of this volume contains plenty of evidence to suggest that the European Union does not integrate many wider societal interests very effectively. Raunio (Chapter 12) starkly concludes that transnational party groups in the EP are very far from commanding the loyalty and support of European citizens, who generally do not understand the influence that pan-European party groups can have on EU policies. Jeffery (Chapter 15) strains to conclude that the ESC is even worth having, and views the Committee of the Regions as, at best, only one of a number of channels open for regional interests to make their mark.

The problem of the EU's limited capacity to integrate societal interests can easily be overstated. Those who view it as a major pathology of the Union sometimes neglect the essential distinction between *input* and *output legitimacy* (see Kathleen MacNamara's Chapter 8 on the ECB). Input legitimacy comes from ensuring that a large number of voices are heard in the policy process. Output legitimacy, more simply, comes from ensuring that policies work in the sense of bringing the greatest good to the greatest number of citizens. If the EU manages to produce policies that work, then it may not matter that much *how* they are made (see Scharpf 1999). Advocates of this view contend that however much the EU's policy remit has expanded, its competences remain tiny compared to those of its member states. What is less often stated, although implied by such arguments, is that integrating more interests into EU policy-making could well be counter-productive to output legitimacy, since the EU is already so fundamentally reliant on multi-tiered compromises within and across member states and its institutions.

The problem is that whatever comes out of the machine is inevitably going to be judged in part by how the system operates. In this sense, transparency has become especially important. Take, for example, the regulation on access to documents agreed during the Swedish Council presidency of 2001. The regulation, a breakthrough in key respects, was successfully agreed after negotiations between the Council and members of the European Parliament. However, ironically, many saw the regulation as the product of a backroom deal that was 'cut' in a way that showed utter disrespect for transparency as a value. After the Parliament approved a series of amendments to an original Commission proposal in November 2000, these amendments were simply set aside as the Council negotiated with a small coterie of MEPs into 2001. The result was a new version of the regulation, stripped of many of the changes originally voted through by EP, but presented as a *fait accompli* to the Parliament in April 2001, even though the co-decision procedure made it possible to continue the negotiations in conciliation. Whatever the merits of the regulation, or the advantages of finding agreement early in the procedure, there were considerable doubts as to whether the resulting legislative act relating to transparency[7] itself met the criterion of transparency. The legitimacy of the outcome was challenged on the basis of the nature of the process that led to it, as often happens in a system such as the EU, where a high premium is placed on consensus and compromise, and cutting deals that create no clear losers. Avoiding clear losers and integrating broad societal interests into EU decision-making are objectives that are, at best, in tension with one another and, at worst, fundamentally incompatible.

The prospects for renewal

Reform of the EU's institutional system to address problems of leadership, management, and representation remain firmly on the Union's agenda. Even if most member governments put a brave face on the new and dizzyingly complex institutional rules ushered in by the Treaty of Nice, most seemed chastened by the rejection of the Treaty by Irish voters in the 2001 referendum. Several (not least Tony Blair himself and the Belgian EU presidency of 2001) were willing to admit that the European Council could not carry on in the same way as before. The experience of successive IGCs, characterized by what Jeffery (Chapter 15) describes as 'crowded and poorly managed agendas', bolstered support for both agreement on some kind of EU 'constitution' as well as some kind of constitutional convention to negotiate one.

A fresh chance to realize such ambitions was created by the commitment, made at Nice, to convene another IGC in 2004. Yet, several member governments seemed exhausted by the experience of negotiating the Treaty of Nice, and averse to an incessant debate about institutional reform. The Prodi Commission did not seem capable of leading a debate on institutional renewal, particularly after Prodi committed yet another embarrassing gaffe by telling reporters on a visit to post-referendum Ireland that ratification of the Treaty of Nice was not necessary for enlargement to take place. The EP was less able to give a lead to the debate on institutional reform than it had been (remarkably) in the 1980s ahead of agreement on the Single European Act (see Corbett 1998).

Yet, there were good reasons to think that European integration was *not* stalled, the EU was *not* moribund, and its institutions were *not* doomed to atrophy. One was that the Union's policy agenda remained buoyant, if also marked by chronic underachievement. Another was the EU's proven capacity for improvisation (see

Peterson and Bomberg 1999: 58–9). Only when faced with a crisis, of the kind that was readily imaginable (institutionally) after the next enlargement, has the Union traditionally been able to innovate. Another good reason to think the prospects for institutional renewal were not so bleak was the 2004 IGC, which itself would more or less coincide with the next wave of enlargement.

A final reason was the wide variety of new methods for embedding the 'national in the European' that had been embraced, some quite successfully, in the late 1990s and after. Most eschewed the traditional Community method of decision-making, according to which the Commission (exclusively) proposes, the EP amends, and the Council disposes, much to the chagrin of admirers of the method. But they at least signalled that EU member governments remained willing to extend collective governance to the point of institutionalizing new policy co-operation, even if the new institutions were often strange and awkward creatures. The section that follows confronts these new, mostly 'open' methods of policy coordination and assesses their implications for the EU's institutional system.

Embedding the national in the European

One of the central themes of this book is how much more varied and complex the institutionalization of collective governance has become in Europe over time. The institutional diversity engendered by recent extensions of collective governance is striking. Take, for example, the arrangements for enforcing the Growth and Sta-bility Pact (Chapter 8), the 'dirty Communitarization' of justice and home affairs policy (Chapter 9), the 'Lisbon process' for the pursuit of economic reform (Chap-ter 4), or the mounting of a European security and defence policy (Chapter 10). Of course, we must be cautious not to lump together these and other non-traditional modes of collective governance, as significant differences exist between variants of the EU's policy process that have recently emerged (see H. Wallace 2000: 28). Yet, what most (if not all) have in common is that they preserve a role for indi-vidual member states which is stronger, more inscrutable, and less challengeable by the EU's common institutions than is the case under the Community method of decision-making.

In retrospect, we can see that the Community method, in its pure and unadulterated form, has been under threat since the early 1990s (see Devuyst 1999). Moreover, there is nothing new about the EU being used for narrow and ostensibly 'national' purposes 'to extend the policy resources available to the member states' (H. Wallace 2000: 28). But the increasingly frequent insti-tutionalization of collective governance in ways that explicitly preserve national prerogatives and priorities has been a spur to a burgeoning new literature on

'Europeanization' (see Börzel 1999; Bulmer and Burch 2000; Cowles *et al.* 2001; Radaelli 2000). Contributors to this literature have struggled to come up with a definition of Europeanization (much as institutionalists have strained to define 'institution'[8]) that is broad enough to convey the eclecticism of the process yet specific enough to be meaningful. Ladrech (1994: 69) does as good a job as any, defining Europeanization as a 'process reorienting the direction and shape of politics to the degree that E[U] political and economic dynamics become part of the organizational logic of national politics and policy-making'.

Even if Europeanization often seems a rather vague idea, it helps us come to grips with the relationship between the new, post-Maastricht politics of European integration and the recent institutionalization of new forms of policy cooperation. The preservation of national practices as national policy processes are Europeanized (and not Communitarized) could be viewed less as a *barrier* to the success of the European project than an essential *precondition* of its success. In an abstract sense (as well as, we suspect, an empirical one), it would be difficult to imagine cases in which any set of democratically elected governments would choose to transfer powers, in a way that at least appears straight and linear in eyes of many average citizens, from themselves to an international organization during a period when the secular trend is towards declining public support for the latter. Of course, the history of the EU is replete with evidence to suggest that the pooling and sharing of powers between states and the Union's common institutions has made the EU and its member states more powerful as a collective, in a way that defies any notion that power is a zero-sum commodity. Still, it is hardly surprising that we have not witnessed a straightforward Communitarization of policy areas, such as the CFSP, justice and home affairs, or employment policy, which have effectively been Europeanized instead. What is perhaps more surprising is that the trend towards *more* collective governance in Europe—albeit via methods that were unfamiliar until recently—has remained unbroken despite the disappearance of the 'permissive consensus'. Put simply, understanding why EU member governments have chosen to embed the national in the European in such a dizzyingly diverse number of ways starts with acknowledging that unless European governments can see their own practices and goals in some way reflected in Brussels policy-making, and can convince their citizens that this 'reflection' is genuine, they are unlikely to accept new shifts of competence to Brussels.

The general imperative to retain national levers of influence ('control' may be too strong a term) within the EU's institutions is abundant in this volume. Perhaps the prime illustration is the increasingly ubiquitous role of the European Council in the full range of what the EU does, even if de Schoutheete (Chapter 2) casts doubt as to how much it really controls (or even effectively monitors). Another is the debate about the role of national parliaments in EU decision-making, which (as Chapters 5 and 12 both make clear) is hardly a new one but which refuses to go away. The political need, acknowledged at Nice, for each member state to appoint one of their 'own' to the college of Commisioners is yet another example. Even the most ardent of federalists realize that sustaining the European project requires embedding the national in the European, because simply replacing the former with the latter simply does not happen any more (leaving aside rare, if important, exceptions, such as the replacement of national currencies by the euro).

Even where Europeanization has, over time, produced 'pure' and thorough-going Communitarization, levers for national influence have been retained and guarded very jealously. Monetary policy, as McNamara (Chapter 8) shows, is one such area: there is now a genuinely single currency, but the structures of the ESCB as well as the ECB itself reflect the imperative to preserve channels for national influence. Even the development of Community law reveals a similar pattern. It can be argued that the EU has achieved such strength as a legal system *only* because national courts are so intimately involved in interpreting and enforcing EU law, and because no democratic state can resist the injunctions of its own courts (see Weiler 1999).

It might be argued that there is not much that is really new about 'Europeaniza-tion'. EU member states—their governments, administrations, parliaments, and so on—have always been parts of the EU institutional system and not external to it. It is not difficult to find cases throughout the EU's history where member governments have taken cautious, tentative first steps towards policy cooperation before later deciding to fully Communitarize policy (environmental policy is a good example). None the less, some suggest that Europeanization has become an alternative to Communitarization as a response to pressures for collective govern-ance (see Laffan *et al.* 2000: 84–90). According to this view, European integration no longer has any teleology, or clear purpose or goal (if it ever had any at all). The EU is thus likely to become an increasingly more complex, differentiated, and polycentric institutional system over time.

Others portray Europeanization as a step on the path towards Communitariza-tion, as in the cases of JHA, environmental, and research policies. Advocates of this view argue that the emergence of new and different methods of embedding the national in the European does not imply that European integration has lost its purpose in institutional terms. They predict that 'the basic EU/EC set-up will remain and evolve as the major channel for dealing with an increasing number of public policies . . . .[because] no real alternative is available' (Wessels 2001: 215).

We lack the clairvoyance to predict with any certainty where the EU is headed in institutional terms. But it is clear that the EU has reached a crossroads in its institutional development, particularly with the prospect of a major enlargement in the near future. And we hope that this volume helps its readers to make up their own minds about whether Europeanization is something truly new that is replacing Communitarization, or merely signalling the inevitability of the latter over time.

EU institutions and the new institutionalism

If this book has grappled with one theoretical question above all others, it is: do institutions matter? In line with the teachings of the new institutionalist literature, we have seen that institutions—how they are constructed, how they work, and how they interact—are a powerful determinant of EU politics. A close reading of the contributions to this volume yields one heuristic point above all others: the process of collective governance in Europe cannot be understood without intimate knowledge of the EU's institutions, and how they work both individually and together as a system. The main themes that emerge from a careful scan across the full landscape of the EU's institutions are all, we would submit, central to the study of the EU more generally. They include:

■ the considerable scope for institutional *agency* in EU politics, which inevitably makes inter-institutional *competition* a primary feature of EU policy-making. We have seen that new mechanisms, such as trialogues and inter-institutional agreements, have had to be constructed to channel and control conflict between the EU's institutions over time. In one sense, fiercer inter-institutional competition is the product of the empowerment of the Commission and the EP after the 1980s (and the Court before and after that) to the point where the Council can agree relatively little of importance without their consent. As such, the main cleavages in EU policy debates are often as much inter-institutional as intergovernmental.

■ all actors in the EU's institutional system have *multiple identities*, which they must balance or at least reconcile in EU policy debates. Consider a few random, imagined examples. What motivates a centre-right (*Partido Popular*) minister from the Spanish Foreign Office who hails from the Basque country when the Council debates a move to centralize decision-making on the structural funds? What advice does an Irish *cabinet* official give to her Commissioner (for monetary policy) on a proposal to reprimand the Irish government for breaching the Growth and Stability Pact targets for budget deficit, and which incidentally sets a precedent for rapping future *coupables* on the knuckles? 'Actor-based' accounts of the EU policy process ascribe causal importance to questions of identity, particularly which of multiple identities ends up motivating the behaviour of individual actors (see works cited by Peterson and Bomberg 1999: 254). Regardless of how accurately (or not) such accounts portray EU policy-making, there is no doubt that the Union's institutions are a crucial, additional source of identity—along with nationality, party affiliation, and so on—for actors in EU policy-making. Its participants often go to considerable lengths to defend the prerogatives and dignity of 'their' institution in policy debates. One upshot is that the Council (in all of its forms) is a far from purely 'intergovernmental' institution. Another is that there exists plenty of scope for the defence of national interests within the Union's ostensibly 'supranational' institutions.

■ *path dependency*—the tendency for current policies and practices essentially to copy or resemble past ones—is powerful in the EU's institutional system. The centrality of path dependency to institutionalist theory makes the latter an impressive predictor of the extent to which the EU's institutions (and, equally if not more so, their *national* counterparts) often resemble generals meticulously prepared to fight the last war (see Peters 1999: 40). Witness the tendency of the Economic and Social Committee (see Chapter 15) to defend a corporatist model of state–society relations that was never accepted across Europe even in its heyday, or the resistance of national justice and home affairs ministries (see Chapter 9) to the obvious need to Europeanize cooperation in JHA policy. The persistence of the common agricultural policy (CAP) in a form that has not radically changed since the early 1960s cannot be explained without considering how each of the EU's institutions have developed dedicated organs—DG Agriculture, the Agriculture Council, the Special Committee on Agriculture, and so on—to defend it. Path dependency may be especially acute in a system that, after all, remains quite young, tends to be inward-looking, and relies heavily on past precedents—political and above all legal—to define the scope for future action. But the point is that the EU, along with national systems, often becomes trapped by previous decisions that it has made.

■ *principal-agent relationships* in the EU are often troubled and contested, with inevitable policy costs. Majone (Chapter 14) shows how member states have been unwilling to give new European agencies the degree of autonomy necessary to enable the system to be effective, not least because they remain stuck with outdated rules that limit the autonomy of European regulatory bodies from the Commission. In a lengthy list of policy areas—food safety, the CFSP, and financial control among them—half-hearted or disorderly delegation from member states to the EU's institutions (principals to agents) has produced confused or ineffective policy.

This survey of the EU's institutions, like the new institutionalist literature itself, might seem to paint a generally sombre, downbeat, pessimistic picture of modern political life. Prominent themes include inertia, pathology, inconsistency, turf battles, and so on. Yet, as is suggested by recent work that applies institutionalist theory to international organizations (see Keohane 1998; Peters 1999: 126–40), it is possible to view international institutions—including those of the European Union—as *the* leading purveyors of innovative solutions to the problems of modern governance. However much they are trapped by path dependency, the EU's institutions may have a better chance than European governments to develop, embrace, and promote long-term solutions to problems such as global warming, the ageing of the European workforce, fighting terrorism, or fostering democracy in the former Soviet Union. It is in the nature of politics that governments, whose calculations are always governed by four to five-year electoral cycles, have great difficulty in thinking beyond short-term time horizons and investing in policies which will only pay off long after the next election.

To illustrate the point, it is difficult to imagine that there would have been agreement at the Bonn climate change conference, which 'rescued' the Kyoto protocol in July 2001, if member states had not had EU institutions—the Commission and Council Presidency—to aggregate their national interests and push them to make politically difficult commitments to reduce emission levels. Even the EP seemed to have an impact on the Union's negotiating stance, and thus the conference's outcome, in Bonn. Appearing on the same platform with the Belgian energy minister (and President-in-office of the Council) and the Commissioner for environmental policy, the vice-chair of the Parliament's environment committee, Alexander de Roo, told a press conference in Bonn that the EU should take a hard line on tough issues such as nuclear energy. Asked by a journalist whether the three EU institutions spoke with one voice, the Belgian energy minister reportedly 'hesitated half a second and then simply said yes'.[9] In the end, a truly common European position at Bonn was essential in securing the agreement of states such as Japan and Canada that were reluctant to act without the United States.

In the case of global warming, as on other global issues, a crucial first step to achieving international policy agreement is to forge internal agreement within the EU. The institutional system of Union thus may be viewed as an essential and necessary (if by no means sufficient) element of collective governance at the global level. In this context, the new institutionalism trains us to think about how institutional traditions, such as those that have informed the creation and development of the EU's institutional system, reflect the values held most dear by societies. Despite its diversity, it could be argued that Europe shares a set of core values and thus an institutional tradition, in which 'the State is linked organically with society and society is significantly influenced by the nature of the State' (Peters 1999: 6). Whatever the inadequacies of the EU's institutions, which are often laid bare by the application of institutionalist theory, this basic principle offers at least a set of aspirations to guide institutional reform.

Conclusion: the accountability conundrum

If there is one single, burning question that arises from studying the EU's institutions, it may be the vexed accountability question: how can the Union's institutions become more accountable to European citizens and thus a more legitimate level of governance? It is hard to see how this conundrum can be solved with a dose of 'direct democracy', such as by directly electing the President of the Commission, empowering national parliaments in EU decision-making, or spending more to foster pan-European political parties. It might be rather easier to imagine the election of future European governments able and willing to do a better job of 'selling' the EU's institutions to average citizens. In time, the common line espoused by European leaders might be that the Commission, High Representative for the CFSP, the European agencies, and so on are necessary and public-spirited agents for governing Europe and defending its interests in an increasingly globalized world. So far, however, the post-Kohl and Mitterrand generation shows little inclination to take political risks to build or campaign for Europe, particularly when, as one senior EU official put it, the Commission often seems to be 'in a corner cowering and waiting for another Delors'.[10]

Arguably, the EU's accountability conundrum arises because member governments accept the need to pool sovereignty to achieve collective governance, but refuse to create straight, simple lines of accountability of the sort that allow citizens to throw out a government they themselves have democratically elected and substitute an opposition (see Peterson 1997). Going one step further, some might argue that the EU's institutional system is on the verge of breakdown, given the prospect of enlargement to include weak and poor states whose citizens are hungry for rapid economic development, combined with declining enthusiasm for the EU in Europe's more mature democracies. Generally, in the words of the Commission's (2001: 3) White Paper on 'European governance', 'people increasingly distrust institutions and politics or are simply not interested in them'. More particularly, citizens in Europe (and beyond) show signs of becoming ever more cynical about the ability of international organizations (IOs) to govern a globalized economy with equanimity and justice. The EU, according to this view, has become just another IO amongst others—such as the IMF, WTO, or G-8—that could not hold a major summit in the early twenty-first century without anti-globalist protests, thus symbolizing the widening gulf between governments and the governed.

Yet, the fact that the EU has become subject to the same kind of populist pressures which virtually all IOs face tells us something fundamental. It is that the problem of 'scaling up' democracy to suit a more interdependent and globalized world is by no means unique to Europe. Certainly, sovereign nation states have gone far further in Europe than those in any other region of the world to tie together their fates and opt for collective governance through common institutions. Still, the problem of subjecting governance at a level 'above' the nation state to democratic controls is one of the most vexing problems facing governments everywhere. Robert Dahl (1994), a shrewd student of democracy, has posed the problem as an essentially generic one. To simplify only slightly, the closer that governments work to the citizen, the more they must respond to the needs and preferences of average people. However, small-scale governments cannot hope to cope with problems such as global warming, the threat of terrorism, or humanitarian tragedies that are only solvable—if they are solvable at all—through the collective efforts of states working through international organizations. Above all, the problem of governing the global economy, in a political world where most governments believe in the virtues of open commerce, requires global rules and the adjudication of conflicting interests. In this context, the European Union may be seen as an essential, driving force behind the freeing of international trade, however much it frustrates its trading partners with its frequent back-sliding towards protectionism. At the same time, the EU remains a staunch defender of values that are easily trammelled by free trade, such as environmental protection or core labour standards. The European economy could be seen as a prototype for the global economy of the future, in which the main factors of production become basically borderless, but remain subject to effective (but light) regulation.

Taking the analogy further, the EU's institutions could be viewed as prototypes for global institutions that might one day govern something like a 'single', global market. It is easy to stretch this analogy too far, and to be seduced by the same naïve, Wilsonian vision of 'world government' that was widely embraced in the inter-war period, only to be exposed by realist IR theorists as intellectually bank-rupt in the 1950s. Yet, it was precisely then that the EU embarked on its extra-ordinary mission of institution-building in the pursuit of collective governance. One long-term effect, certainly foreseen by *none* of the EU's founding fathers, has been to mark out the EU's institutions as models suitable for emulation by other IOs that need to be made more accountable and legitimate in the eyes of average citizens.

In the view of Keohane (1998), the task of democratizing IOs is *not* much more challenging than was the task of creating and institutionalizing democracy at the domestic level during the passing of the era of the 'divine right of kings' in the seventeenth and eighteenth centuries. This view might be dismissed as overly naïve (and peculiarly American), but its existence shows us that there is much about the EU's institutional system that is admired (as well as much that is heartily disliked) internationally. It also reminds us that the Union's democratic conundrum reflects wider problems of democratizing global governance.

Moreover, compared to other IOs the EU appears to be a relatively 'democratic' and transparent one.[11] It over-represents its smaller member states in a way that, say, the United Nations or WTO never could. It does not discriminate against poorer states, as the IMF is frequently accused of doing. All of its constituent political units, at least for now, are entitled to representation in the college of Commissioners in a way that, say, the individual American states are not in the US cabinet. Maybe its most distinguishing feature is that it is subject to increasingly close and powerful scrutiny by the world's only democratically elected multinational parliament.

Moreover, it is worth recalling the view of the so-called 'new governance' school of policy analysts, for whom Majone (1996) is a primary spokesperson. According to this view, the EU's democratic deficit is easily overstated. The Union's competence is narrow and tiny compared to that of its member states. Many of the EU's core tasks of regulating economic activity are performed at the national level in many states by specialized agencies that are largely independent of political control. Some of the collective goods provided by the EU—free trade, fair competition, healthy food, a stable currency—cannot be provided without insulating policy-makers from short-term political pressures.

Even if we conclude that the new governance school is too complacent about the democratic deficit, there is reason to think that the problem of fragmented accountability alongside collective responsibility in the EU is beginning to be tackled by new and creative solutions. One is to subject all of the Union's institutions to standard sets of rules or procedures, or scrutiny by agents who are dedicated to a single task but responsible for applying it across the entire EU institutional system. A good example is the European Ombudsman, who has figured little in this book but has begun to appear as a quite important figure in forcing the institutions to march to the sound of a single drum on a range of issues of (mal)administration.[12] Or, as Laffan (Chapter 11) suggests, the empowerment of the Court of Auditors, and the creation of OLAF could be taken as evidence that, from a rather modest beginning, the EU has adopted a much tighter and uniform regime of financial control. Finally, we can see that Coreper now prepares ministerial deliberations, across what is finally beginning to resemble a truly 'single institutional framework', even in areas such as foreign policy and crisis management (see Chapter 10) which remain a long way from Communitarization.

We do not seek to deny that the EU's institutions suffer from severe problems, many of which could be considered 'pathologies', of the same kind that plague IOs generally. Especially given the EU's impending enlargement in the early twenty-first century, the Union's institutions often appear ill-suited to the modern tasks of European governance and more likely to stifle innovation than to encourage it. There is a clear need for analysts of the EU's institutions to embrace normative thinking about how the Union's institutional system could work better.

However, there is another side to the ledger. As we have seen, the EU's institutions—regardless of their problems, both collective and individual—often facilitate collective governance on divisive issues such as environmental protection, market liberalization, and the EU's relations with its near-abroad in a way that is often just short of miraculous. When the EU's institutions work well together, the Union's policy process takes on a sort of epileptic charm, much like good jazz music, blending European traditions, languages, experiences. It happens often enough, at least, to ensure that the European Union remains the champion of those who wish and hope for more and more effective collective governance internationally.

Notes

1 We are in considerable debt to Elizabeth Bomberg and Helen Wallace for their useful comments on earlier drafts of this chapter. Of course, we alone are responsible for any remaining errors or infelicities.

2 One of us, asked to state a view on the Treaty of Nice at a mid-town Dublin bar just before the Irish referendum, could only lamely state: 'I can't really justify the Treaty, but I can justify a "yes" vote for it.' The statement was greeted with howls of laughter. Turn-out for the Irish referendum was so low (about 30 per cent) that numerically more Irish citizens voted against the Treaty of Amsterdam in 1997 (in a referendum in which the Treaty was approved comfortably) than against Nice in 2001.

3 The US Treasury Secretary, Paul O'Neill, quoted in *Time*, 16 July 2001 (US edn.), p. 4.

4 The importance of this rule in the Council was underlined in the spring of 2001 when Germany withdrew its support from the common position that had been agreed unanimously one year earlier on the Takeovers Directive. This was the first time in the history of the EU that a member state had acted in this way and caused enormous consternation amongst other states, particularly when the European Parliament rejected the Directive in July 2001. Effectively, one member state had been able to overcome the opposition of the other fourteen.

5 As Weiler has argued tirelessly, the tiny share of EU policy which the Commission is responsible for implementing, and the almost as small percentage of the EU budget which it spends, means that it is far from being a true 'executive'. The Council has as much or more right to be termed the executive of the Union than does the Commission (Weiler 1999; see also Metcalfe 2000: 825).

6 We are particularly grateful to Helen Wallace for her perceptive comments on this section.

7 Official Journal L145 of 31 May 2001, pp. 43–8.

8 Note, for example, that almost every chapter in Peters's (1999) survey of different variants of institutionalism includes a section entitled 'what is an institution?', and manages to limit rational choice theorists alone to no less than four different, alternative definitions! (Peters 1999: 53).

9 Quoted in a letter to the editor by Alexander de Roo, MEP, printed in *European Voice*, 26 July–1 Aug. 2001.

10 Interview, Deputy Chef of *cabinet*, Brussels, 20 Mar. 2001.

11 For example, consider the contrast drawn by Emma Bonino, a former Commissioner, after violent protests at the 2001 G-8 Genoa Summit: 'The G-8 has no treaty and no transparency . . . Nobody knows what they stand for, which makes them quite different, from the institutional point of view, to the meetings of heads of state and government of the European Union' (quoted in *European Voice*, 26 July–1 Aug. 2001).

12 The Ombudsman has assumed extensive powers under Article 195 TEC to examine cases of maladministration, and more generally, has felt free to criticize the way in which the institutions operate. The institutions have in turn felt obliged to respond and to improve their working methods, such as recruitment procedures or their procedures for dealing with requests for information from the general public.

References

Abélès, M., Bellier, I., and McDonald, M. (1993), *Approche Anthropologique de la Commission Européenne*, unpublished report for the Commission.

Alabau I Oliveres, M. M., (1990), *Le Contrôle Externe Des Cours Des Comptes De L'Europe Communautaire*, Barcelona: University Institute for European Studies, Paper no. 1, Feb.

Alesina, A., and Summers, L. (1993), 'Central Bank Independence and Macroeconomic Performance: Some Comparative Evidence', *Journal of Money and Banking*, 25, May, 151–62.

Allen, D. (1998), 'Who Speaks for Europe?', in Peterson and Sjursen (1988).

—— (2000), *The Common Foreign and Security Policy of the European Union* (New York: Addison-Wesley).

Allison, G. T. (1971), *Essence of Decision: Explaining the Cuban Missile Crisis* (Boston: Little, Brown & Co.).

—— (1999), *Essence of Decision: Explaining the Cuban Missile Crisis*, 2nd edn. (London: Longman).

Anderson, J. (1997), 'Hard Interests, Soft Power, and Germany's Changing Role in Europe', in Katzenstein (1997: 80–107).

—— (1999), *German Unification and the Union of Europe: The Domestic Politics of Integration Policy* (Oxford: Oxford University Press).

Armstrong, K., and Bulmer, S. (1998), *The Governance of the Single European Market* (Manchester: Manchester University Press).

Arnull, A. (1999), *The European Union and its Court of Justice* (Oxford: Oxford University Press).

Attinà, F. (1990), 'The Voting Behaviour of the European Parliament Members and the Problem of the Europarties', *European Journal of Political Research*, 18/4: 557–79.

Ausschuss der Regionen (Committee of the Regions) (1997), 'Die Auswahl der AdR-Mitglieder: Verfahren in den Mitgliedstaaten', *AdR-Studien I—3.97, CdR 162/97 rev*.

Bainbridge, T. (1998), *The Penguin Companion to European Union*, 2nd edn. (Harmondsworth: Penguin).

Baldwin, R., and McCrudden, C. (1987), *Regulation and Public Law* (London: Weidenfeld & Nicolson).

Bardi, L. (1994), 'Transnational Party Federations, European Parliamentary Party Groups, and the Building of Europarties', in R. S. Katz and P. Mair (eds.), *How Parties Organize: Change and Adaptation in Western Democracies* (London: Sage), 357–72.

—— (1996), 'Transnational Trends in European Parties and the 1994 European Elections of the European Parliament', *Party Politics*, 2/1: 99–113.

Barnett, M. A., and Finnemore, M. (1999), 'The Politics, Power and Pathologies of International Organizations', *International Organization*, 53/4: 699–732.

Barrett, G. (1997) (ed.), *Justice Cooperation in the European Union* (Dublin: Institute of European Affairs).

Bay Brzinski, J. (1995), 'Political Group Cohesion in the European Parliament, 1989–1994', in C. Rhodes and S. Mazey (eds.), *The State of the European Union*, vol. iii: *Building a European Polity?* (Boulder, Colo.: Lynne Rienner), 135–58.

Begg, D. K., Giavazzi, F., and Wyplosz, C., (1997), 'Options for the Future Exchange Rate Policy of the EMU', *CEPR Occasional Paper*, No. 17.

Begg, D. K., De Grauwe, P., Giavazzi, F., Uhlig, H., and Wyplosz, C. (1998), 'The ECB: Safe at Any Speed', *Monitoring the European Central Bank*, 1 (London: Centre for Economic Policy Research).

Bell, D. S., and Lord, C. (1998) (eds.), *Transnational Parties in the European Union* (Aldershot: Ashgate).

Berman, S., and McNamara, K. R., (1999), 'Bank on Democracy: Why Central Banks Need Public Oversight', *Foreign Affairs*, 78, Mar./Apr., 2–8.

Bini-Smaghi, L. (1991), 'Exchange Rate Variability and Trade: Why is it so Difficult to Find Any Empirical Relationship?', *Applied Economics*, May, 927–36.

Blondel, J., Sinnott, R., and Svennson, P. (1998), *People and Parliament in the European Union: Participation, Democracy and Legitimacy* (Oxford: Clarendon Press).

Bloes, J. (1970), *Le Plan Fouchet et le problème de l'Europe politique* (Bruges: College of Europe).

Börzel, T. (1999), 'Institutional Adaptation to Europeanization in Germany and Spain', *Journal of Common Market Studies*, 37/4: 573–96.

Bowler, S., and Farrell, D. M. (1995), 'The Organizing of the European Parliament: Committees, Specialisation and Co-ordination', *British Journal of Political Science*, 25/2: 219–43.

—— —— and Katz, R. S. (1999a), 'Party Cohesion, Party Discipline, and Parliaments', in Bowler et al. (1999b: 3–22).

—— —— —— (1999b) (eds.), *Party Discipline and Parliamentary Government* (Columbus, Oh.: Ohio State University Press).

Bradley, K. (1988), 'The European Court and the Legal Basis of Community Legislation', *European Law Review*, 13: 379–402.

Brittan, L. (2000), *A Diet of Brussels: The Changing Face of Europe* (London: Little Brown & Co.).

Brown, L. (1995), 'Advocacy Coalitions and the Founding of the European Environmental Agency' (mimeo).

Brüske, E. (1982), 'Der Wirtschafts- und Sozialausschuss', in W. Weidenfeld and W. Wessels (eds.), *Jahrbuch der Europäischen Integration 1981* (Bonn: Europa Union Verlag), 107–19.

—— (1983), 'Der Wirtschafts- und Sozialausschuss', in W. Weidenfeld and W. Wessels (eds.), *Jahrbuch der Europäischen Integration 1982* (Bonn: Europa Union Verlag), 91–7.

—— (1994), 'Wirtschafts- und Sozialausschuss', in W. Weidenfeld and W. Wessels (eds.), *Europa von A-Z* (Bonn: Bundeszentrale für politische Bildung), 343–5.

Buitendijk, G. J., and Van Schendelen, M. P. C. M. (1995), 'Brussels Advisory Committees: A Channel for Influence?', *European Law Review*, 20/1: 37–56.

Buiter, W. (1999), 'Alice in Euroland', *Journal of Common Market Studies*, 322: 181–209.

Bulmer, S. (1994), 'The Governance of the European Union: A New Institutionalist Approach', *Journal of Public Policy*, 13/1: 351–80.

—— and Burch, M. (2000), 'The "Europeanization" of Central Government: The UK and Germany in Historical Institutionalist Perspective', in M. Aspinwall and G. Schneider (eds.), *The Rules of Integration* (Manchester: Manchester University Press).

—— and Wessels, W. (1987), *The European Council* (London: Macmillan).

Burghardt, G. (1994), 'The Potential and Limits of CFSP—Implementing Maastricht', *CFSP Forum*, No. 3.

Burley, A.-M., and Mattli, W. (1993), 'Europe Before the Court: A Political Theory of Legal Integration', *International Organization*, 47/1: 41–76.

Busch, P., and Puchala, D. (1976), 'Interests, Influence, and Integration: Political Structure in the European Communities', *Comparative Political Studies*, 9/3: 235–54.

Butler, M. (1986), *Europe: More Than a Continent* (London: William Heinemann).

Cameron, D. (1998), 'EMU after 1999: The Implications and Dilemmas of the Third Stage', *The Columbia Journal of International Law*, 4, Spring, 425–46.

Cameron, F. (1999), *Foreign and Security Policy of the European Union* (Sheffield: Sheffield Academic Press).

Campbell, J. (1983), *Roy Jenkins: A Biography* (London: Weidenfeld & Nicolson).

Carrington, P. (1988), *Reflect on Things Past* (Glasgow: Collins).

Chabert, J. (2000), 'Priorities for the 2000–2001 Period', at **www/cor.int.eu/speech/ speechchaberten.html**.

Checkel J. (1999), 'Social Construction and Integration', *Journal of European Public Policy*, 6/4: 545–60.

Chowdhury, A. R. (1993), 'Does Exchange Rate Volatility Depress Trade Flows? Evidence from Error-Correction Models', *Review of Economics and Statistics*, 75, 700–6

Christiansen, T. (1997), 'The Committee of the Regions at the 1996 IGC Conference: Institutional Reform', *Regional and Federal Studies*, 7/1: 50–69.

—— and Jørgensen , K. E. (1999), *The Amsterdam Process: A Structurationist Perspective on EU Treaty Reform*, mimeo, Aarhus: Department of Political Science.

—— and Kirchner, E. (2000) (eds.), *Committee Governance in the European Union* (Manchester: Manchester University Press).

—— Jørgensen, K. E., and Wiener, A. (1999) (eds.), *The Social Construction of Europe*, Special Issue, *Journal of European Public Policy*, 6/4.

—— —— —— (2001) (eds.), *The Social Construction of Europe* (London and Thousand Oaks, Calif.: Sage).

Chryssochoou, D. (2000), *Democracy in the European Union* (London and New York: I. B. Taurus).

Cini, M. (1996), *The European Commission: Leadership, Organisation and Culture in the EU Administration* (Manchester: Manchester University Press).

—— (2000), 'Administrative Culture in the European Commission: The Cases of Competition and Environment', in Nugent (2000: 73–90).

Claes, M., and De Witte, B. (1998), 'Report on the Netherlands', in Slaughter *et al.* (1998).

Cockfield, A. (1994), *The European Union: Creating the Single Market* (Chichester: Chancery Law Publishing).

Cohen, Benjamin J. (1998), *The Geography of Money* (Ithaca, NY: Cornell University Press).

Commission (1994), Press Release 39/94, 21 Nov.

—— (1995*a*), Schmidhuber Memo on Financial Management, Sec. 95.26.

—— (1995*b*), Report on the Operation of the Treaty on European Union, 10 May, Sec (95 final).

—— (1999*a*), 'Electronic Commerce in the Internal Market: A Proposal Presented by the Commission for a European Parliament and Council Directive on Certain Legal Aspects', available from **www.europa.eu.int/comm/dg15/comcom/newsletter/edition16-17/ page04-02_en.htm**.

—— (1999*b*), *The Formation of the New Commission: 2 Code of Conduct for Commissioners and Departments* (Brussels: European Commission).

—— (1999*c*), *Administrative Reform of the Commission: Statement of Purpose and Structure*, CG3 (1999) 1/4, 19 Oct.

—— (1999*d*), *Designing Tomorrow's Commission: A Review of the Commission's Organisation and Operation*, Brussels: European Commission, 7 July.

—— (2000*a*), *White Paper on Food Safety*, COM (1999) 719 final, Brussels, 12 Jan.

Commission (2000b), General Report 1999, at **www.europa.eu.int/abc/doc/off/rg/en/1999**.

—— (2000c), *Reforming the Commission: Consultative Document*, CG3 (2000) 1/17, 18 Jan.

—— (2000d), *Reforming the Commission: A White Paper*, Brussels: European Commission, 1 Mar.

—— (2000e), *Communication from the Commission: Matching the Commission's Activities With Its Human Resources: The Means to Match Our Objectives*, DOC/00/20.

—— (2000f), *Code of Good Administrative Behaviour for Staff of the European Commission in their Relations with the Public*, in *Official Journal*, 20 Oct., L267/64-6.

—— (2001), General Report 2000, at **www.europa.eu.int/abc/doc/off/rg/en/2000**.

Committee of Independent Experts (1999a), *First Report on Allegations Regarding Fraud, Mismanagement and Nepotism in the European Commission*, Brussels: European Parliament, 15 Mar.

—— (1999b), *Second Report on Reform of the Commission: Analysis of Current Practice and Proposals for Tackling Mismanagement, Irregularities and Fraud*, 2 vols., Brussels: European Parliament, 10 Sep.

Constantinesco, V. (1992), *Conseil Européen*, in Répertoire de Droit Communautaire (Paris: Dalloz).

Coombes, D. (1970), *Politics and Bureaucracy in the European Community: A Portrait of the Commission of the EEC* (London: George Allen & Unwin).

—— (1999), *Seven Theorems in Search of the European Parliament* (London: Federal Trust).

Corbett, R. (1993), *The Maastricht Treaty* (Harlow: Longman).

—— (1998), *The European Parliament's Role in Closer Integration* (Basingstoke: Macmillan).

—— Jacobs, F., and Shackleton, M. (2000), *The European Parliament*, 4th edn. (London: John Harper).

Coultrap, J. (1999), 'From Parliamentarism to Pluralism: Models of Democracy and the European Union's "Democratic Deficit" ', *Journal of Theoretical Politics*, 11/1: 107–35.

Council of the European Union (1996), *Council Guide*, vol. II: *Comments on the Council's Rules of Procedure*, Council Secretariat-General, DG F—Information Policy.

—— (2000), *Information Handbook of the Council of the European Union* (Luxembourg: Office for Official Publications of the European Communities).

Court of Auditors (1983), *Report in Response to the Conclusions of the European Council of 18 June 1983*, Official Journal C 287, 26, 24 Oct. 1983, 1–17.

—— (1995a), *Auditing the Finances of the European Union*, Luxembourg: Court of Auditors booklet.

—— (1995b), Report by the Court to the 'Reflection Group' on the Operation of the Treaty on European Union, Luxembourg: May 1995.

—— (1995c), Statement of Assurance Concerning the Activities Financed from the General Budget for the Financial Year 1994, Luxembourg, Nov. 1995.

—— (1996), Statement of Assurance Concerning the Activities Financed from the General Budget for the Financial Year 1995, 29 Nov. 1996.

—— (1997), Statement of Assurance Concerning the Financial Year 1996, *OJ* C 348, 18 Nov. 1997.

—— (1998a), Annual Report Concerning the Financial Year 1997, *OJ* C 349, 17 Nov. 1998.

—— (1998b), Special Report on UCLAF, *OJ* C 230, 22 July 1998.

—— (1999), Annual Report Concerning the Financial Year 1998, *OJ* C

—— (2000), Special Report of the EP's Political Groups, 2000/C/181/01.

Court of First Instance of the EC (2000a), Case T-17/00 R *Rothley and Others* v *Parliament*, ECR II-2085.

—— (2000b), Case T-178/98 *Fresh Marine* v *Commission*, ECR II-3331.

—— (2001), Case T-353/00 R *Le Pen* v *Parliament*, ECR II-125.

Cowles, M. G., Caporaso, J., and Risse, T. (2001) (eds.), *Transforming Europe: Europeanization and Domestic Change* (London and Ithaca, NY: Cornell University Press).

Cox, G., and McCubbins, M. (1993), *Legislative Leviathan: Party Government in the House* (Berkeley: University of California Press).

Craig, P., and De Búrca, G. (1999) (eds.), *The Evolution of European Law* (Oxford: Oxford University Press).

Cram, L. (1999), 'The Commission', in L. Cram *et al.* (1999: 44–61).

—— Dinan, D., and Nugent, N. (1999) (eds.), *Developments in the European Union* (London: Macmillan).

Cukierman, A. (1992), *Central Bank Strategy, Credibility and Independence: Theory and Evidence* (Cambridge, Mass.: MIT Press).

Curzon, V. (1974), *Essentials of Economic Integration: Lessons of the EFTA Experience* (London: Macmillan).

Dahl, R. A. (1994), 'A Democratic Dilemma: System Effectiveness versus Citizen Participation', *Political Science Quarterly*, 109/1: 23–34.

Damgaard, E. (1995), 'How Parties Control Committee Members', in H. Döring (ed.), *Parliaments and Majority Rule in Western Europe* (Frankfurt and New York: Campus and St Martin's Press), 308–25.

De Búrca, G. (1999), 'The Institutional Development of the EU: A Constitutional Analysis', in P. Craig, and G. De Búrca, (eds.), *The Evolution of European Law* (Oxford: Oxford University Press), 55–81.

De Clerq, W. (1990), *Europe Back to the Top* (Brussels: Roularta Books).

De Gaulle, C. (1970), *Discours et messages*, vol. IV: *Pour l'effort* (Paris: Plon).

Dehaene, J.-L., von Weizsäcker, R., and Simon, D. (1999), *The Institutional Implications of Enlargement: Report to the European Commission*, 18 Oct.

Deighton, A. (1997) (ed.), *Western European Union 1954–1997: Defence, Security, Integration* (Oxford: St Antony's College).

Delwitte, P., De Waele, J.-M., and Magnette, P. (1999), *A quoi sert le Parlement européen?* (Brussels: Editions Complexe).

den Boer, M., and Wallace, W. (2000), 'Justice and Home Affairs', in H. Wallace and W. Wallace (2000: 493–519).

De Ruyt, J. (1987), *L'Acte Unique Européen* (Brussels: Editions de l'Université Libre de Bruxelles).

Desmond, B. (1996), *Managing the Finances of the European Union: The Role of the European Court of Auditors* (Dublin: Institute of European Affairs).

Deutsch, K. W. *et al.* (1957), *Political Community and the North Atlantic Area: International Organisation in the Light of Historical Experience* (Princeton: Princeton University Press).

Devuyst, Y. (1999), 'The Community Method after Amsterdam', *Journal of Common Market Studies*, 37/1: 109–20.

de Zwaan, J. (1995), *The Permanent Representatives Committee: Its Role in European Union Decision-Making* (Amsterdam: Elsevier).

Dietz, T. (2000), 'Similar but Different? The European Greens Compared to Other Transnational Party Federations in Europe', *Party Politics*, 6/2: 199–210.

Dinan, D. (1999), *Ever Closer Union?: An Introduction to the European Community*, 2nd edn. (Boulder, Colo.: Lynne Rienner).

—— (2000) (ed.), *Encyclopaedia of the European Union* (London: Macmillan).

Dixit, A. (1989), 'Entry and Exit Decisions under Uncertainty', *Journal of Political Economy*, 97: 620–30.

Doutriaux, Y., and Lequesne, C. (2000), *Les Institutions de l'Union européenne*, 3rd edn. (Paris: Documentation Française, Collection Reflexe Europe).

Duchène, F. (1994), *Jean Monnet: The First Statesman of Interdependence* (London: Norton).

Duisenberg, W. (1998a), 'EMU: The Building of One Monetary System in the European Union', text of a speech delivered 16 Jan., Tokyo, Japan.

—— (1998b), 'The ECB: Independent, Transparent and Communicative', text of a speech delivered 16 Feb., Bankers Club Annual Banquet, London, England.

Dunleavy, P. (1991), *Democracy, Bureaucracy and Public Choice* (London and New York: Harvester Wheatsheaf).

Dyson, K., and Featherstone, K. (1999), *The Road to Maastricht* (Oxford: Oxford University Press).

Earnshaw, D., and Judge, D. (1997), 'The Life and Times of the European Union's Cooperation Procedure', *Journal of Common Market Studies*, 35/4: 543–64.

Easton, D. (1971), *The Political System: An Inquiry into the State of Political Science*, 2nd edn. (New York: Alfred A. Knopf).

The Economist (1998), 'Dominique Stauss-Kahn, Euro-Coach', 30 May, p. 54.

Edwards, G., and Spence, D. (1997a), 'The Commission in Perspective', in Edwards and Spence (1997b).

—— —— (1997b) (eds.), *The European Commission*, 2nd edn. (London: Cartermill).

—— and Wiessala, G. (1998–2001) (eds.), 'The European Union 1997, 1998, 1999, 2000' (Annual reviews of the *Journal of Common Market Studies*, chapters on justice and home affairs) (Oxford: Blackwell, 1998, 1999, 2000, and 2001).

Eichengreen, B. (1996), 'How to Avoid a Maastricht Catastrophe', *International Economy* (May/June): 16–20.

—— and Frieden (1995) (eds.), *Politics and Institutions in an Integrated Europe* (New York: Verlag Springer).

Eijffinger, S. C. W., and De Haan, J. (1996), 'The Political Economy of Central Bank Independence', *Special Papers in International Economics*, 19 (May) (Princeton: International Finance Section, Princeton University).

Emerson, M. *et al.* (1992), *One Market, One Money* (Oxford: Oxford University Press).

Engel, Christian (1998), 'Das "Europa der Regionen" seit Maastricht', in Franz H. U. Borkenhagen (ed.), *Europolitik der deutschen Länder. Bilanz und Perspektiven nach dem Gipfel von Amsterdam* (Opladen: Leske und Budrich).

ESC (2000), ESC Presentation Pamphlet' at **www.esc.eu.int/en/org/welcome.htm**.

European Court of Justice (1963), Case 26/62 *Van Gend en Loos*, ECR 1.

—— (1964), Case 6/64 *Costa* v *ENEL*, ECR 585.

—— (1973), Case 8/97 *Hauptzollamt Bremerhaven* v *Massey-Ferguson*, ECR 897.

—— (1977), Case 66/76 *CFDT* v *Council*, ECR 305.

—— (1979), Case 166/78 *Italy* v *Council*, ECR 2575.

—— (1980), Case 138/79 *Roquette Frères* v *Council*, ECR 3333.

—— (1985), Case 13/83 *Parliament* v *Council*, ECR 1513.

—— (1986a), Case 294/83 *Les Verts* v *Parliament*, ECR 1339.

—— (1986*b*), Case 34/86 *Council* v *Parliament*, ECR 2155.

—— (1987*a*) Case 45/86 ('GTP') *Commission* v *Council*, ECR 1493.

—— (1987*b*) Case 314/85 *Foto-Frost* v *Hauptzollamt Lübeck Ost*, ECR 4199.

—— (1988*a*) Case 68/86 ('hormones') *United Kingdom* v *Council*, ECR 855.

—— (1988*b*) Case 302/87 ('comitology') *Parliament* v *Council*, ECR 5615.

—— (1990*a*) Case C-70/88 ('Chernobyl') *Parliament* v *Council*, ECR I-2041.

—— (1990*b*) Case C-2/88 Imm. *Zwartveld and Others*, ECR I-3365.

—— (1990*c*) Joined Cases C-297/88 and C-197/89 *Dzodzi* v *Belgium*, ECR I-3763.

—— (1991) Joined Cases C-6 and 9/90 *Francovich and Bonafaci* v *Italy*, ECR I-5357.

—— (1992) Case C-295/90 *Parliament* v *Council*, ECR I-4193.

—— (1993*a*) Case C-41/92 *The Liberal Democrats* v *Parliament*, ECR I-3153.

—— (1993*b*) Joined Cases C-181 and 248/91 *Parliament* v *Council and Commission*, ECR I-3685.

—— (1994) Opinion 1/94 *Re the WTO Agreements*, ECR I-5267.

—— (1996*a*) Opinion 2/94 *Re Accession to the European Convention*, ECR I-1759.

—— (1996*b*) Case C-303/94 ('pesticides') *Parliament* v *Council*, ECR I-2943.

—— (1998) Case C-170/96 *Commission* v *Council*, ECR I-2763.

—— (2000*a*) Case C-387/97 *Commission* v *Greece*, ECR I-5047.

—— (2000*b*) Case C-376/98 *Germany* v *Parliament and Council*, ECR I-8419.

European Parliament (1997), Final Report and Recommendations, *Committee of Inquiry into the Community Transit System*, 19 Feb. 1997, A4-0053/97.

—— (1999), *Co-Governing after Maastricht: the European Parliament's Institutional Performance 1994–1999*, Directorate-General for Research, Political Series Working Paper 104, prepared by A. Maurer.

—— (2000), *Activity Report of the delegations to the Conciliation Committee for the period 1 May 1999 to 31 July 2000*, presented by Vice-Presidents Renzo Imbeni, James Provan, and Ingo Friedrich (to be found on Conciliation Committee section of EP web site).

Evans, P. (1993), 'Building an Integrative Approach to International and Domestic Politics: Reflections and Projections', in Evans *et al.* (1993: 397–430).

—— Jacobson, H., and Putnam, R. (1993) (eds.), *Double-Edged Diplomacy: International Bargaining and Domestic Politics* (Berkeley: University of California Press).

Everson, M., and Majone, G. (1999), 'The Role of Specialized Agencies in Decentralizing EU Governance: General Principles' (Florence: European University Institute), mimeo.

Farrows, M., and McCarthy, R. (1997), 'Opinion Formulation and Impact in the Committee of the Regions', *Regional and Federal Studies*, 7/1: 23–49.

Feld, W. (1966), 'National Economic Interest Groups and Policy Formulation in the EEC', *Political Science Quarterly*, 81/3: 392–411.

Fitzmaurice, J. (1975), *The Party Groups in the European Parliament* (Farnborough: Saxon House).

Fligstein, N. (1997), 'Social Skill and Institutional Theory', *American Behavioral Scientist*, 40/4: 397–405.

—— and Brantley, P. (1995), 'The 1992 Single Market Program and the Interests of Business', in Eichengreen and Frieden (1995).

—— and McNichol, J. (1998), 'The Institutional Terrain of the European Union', in Sandholtz and Stone Sweet (1998*b*).

Freedman, O. (1978) *Crisis and Legitimacy* (Cambridge: Cambridge University Press).

Frieden, J. (1991), 'Invested Interests: the Politics of National Economic Policies in a World of Global Finance', *International Organization*, 45, Autumn, 425–51.

Gagnon, J. E. (1993), 'Exchange Rate Variability and the Level of Trade', *Journal of International Economics*, 34, May, 269–87.

Galloway, D. (2001), *The Treaty of Nice and Beyond* (Sheffield: Sheffield Academic Press).

Garel-Jones, T. (1993), 'The UK Presidency: An Inside View', *Journal of Common Market Studies*, 31/2: 261–7.

Garrett, G. (1992), 'International Cooperation and Institutional Choice: The European Community's Internal Market', *International Organization*, 46/2: 533–60.

—— and Tsebelis, G. (2000), 'Legislative Politics in the European Union', *European Union Politics*, 1/1: 65–93.

Gatsios, K., and Seabright, P. (1989), 'Regulation in the European Community', *Oxford Review of Economic Policy*, 5: 37–60.

Ginsberg, R. H. (2001), *The European Union in International Politics: Baptism by Fire* (Oxford: Rowman & Littlefield).

Giscard d'Estaing, V. (1988), *Le Pouvoir et la Vie*, 2 vols. (Paris: Compagnie 12).

Gnesotto, N. (2000), *WEU Newsletter*, July (**www.weu.int/institute**).

Golub, J. (1999), 'In the Shadow of the Vote? Decision-Making in the European Community', *International Organization*, 53/4: 733–64.

Gomez, R. (1998), 'The EU's Mediterranean Policy: Common Foreign Policy by the Back Door?', in Peterson and Sjursen (1998).

—— and Peterson, J. (2001), 'The EU's Impossibly Busy Foreign Ministers: "No One is in Control" ', *European Foreign Affairs Review*, 6/1: 53–74.

Götz, H. H. (1998), 'The Crisis of 1965–66', in Loth *et al.* (1998: 151–62).

Gouldner, A. W. (1957–8), 'Cosmopolitans and Locals: Towards an Analysis of Latent Social Roles', I and II, *Administrative Science Quarterly*, 2: 281–306, and 444–80.

Grant, C. (2000), *EU 2010: An Optimistic Vision of the Future* (London: Centre for European Reform—CER).

Greenwood, J., Grote, J., and Ronit, K. (1992), *Organized Interests and the European Community* (London: Sage).

Grieco, J. M. (1995), 'The Maastricht Treaty, Economic and Monetary Union and the Neo-realist Research Programme', *Review of International Studies*, 21/1: 21–40.

Guéhenno, J.-M. (1992), 'Sicherheit und Verteidigung in Europa', *Dokumente*, 48/2: 121–7.

Guiraudon, V. (2000), 'European Integration and Migration Policy: Vertical Policy-Making as Venue Shopping', *Journal of Common Market Studies*, 38/2: 251–71.

Haas, E. B. (1958), *The Uniting of Europe: Political, Social, and Economic Forces, 1950–1957* (Stanford, Calif.: Stanford University Press).

—— (1960), *Consensus Formation in the Council of Europe* (Berkeley: University of California Press).

—— (1990), *When Knowledge is Power: Three Models of Change in International Organizations* (Berkeley: University of California Press).

Hall, P., and Franzese, R. (1998), 'Mixed Signals: Central Banks Independence, Coordinated Wage-Bargaining, and European Monetary Union', *International Organization*, 52, Summer, 505–35.

Hall, P. A., and Taylor, R. C. R. (1996), 'Political Science and the Three New Institutionalisms', *Political Studies*, 44/5: 936–57.

Halliday, F. (1983), *The Making of the Second Cold War* (London: Verso).

Hartley, T. (1999), *Constitutional Problems of the European Union* (Oxford: Hart Publishing).

Hay, R. (1989), *The European Commission and the Administration of the European Community*, Luxembourg: Office for Official Publications of the European Communities.

Hayes-Renshaw, F. (1999), 'The European Council and the Council of Ministers', in Cram *et al.* (1999: 23–43).

—— and Wallace, H. (1995), 'Executive Power in the European Union: The Functions and Limits of the Council of Ministers', *Journal of European Public Policy*, 2/4: 559–82.

—— —— (1997), *The Council of Ministers* (London and New York: Macmillan and St Martin's Press).

—— Lequesne, C., and Mayor Lopez, P. (1989), 'The Permanent Representations of the Member States to the European Communities', *Journal of Common Market Studies*, 28/2: 119–37

Heidar, K., and Koole, R. (2000a), 'Parliamentary Party Groups Compared', in Heidar and Koole (2000b: 248–70).

—— —— (2000b) (eds.), *Parliamentary Party Groups in European Democracies: Political Parties behind Closed Doors* (London: Routledge).

Helleiner, E. (1998), 'National Currencies and National Identities', *American Behavioral Scientist*, 41, August, 1409–36.

Henning, C. R. (1997), *Cooperating with Europe's Monetary Union* (Washington: Institute for International Economics).

Héritier, A. (1999), *Policy-Making and Diversity in Europe: Escape from Deadlock* (Cambridge: Cambridge University Press).

Hill, C. (1983), *National Foreign Policies and European Political Cooperation* (London: Allen & Unwin).

—— (1996) (ed.), *The Actors in Europe's Foreign Policy* (London and New York: Routledge).

Hill and Knowlton (2000), *The European Commission 2000-2005: One Year On* (Brusssels).

Hix, S. (1998), 'Elections, Parties and Institutional Design: A Comparative Perspective on European Union Democracy', *West European Politics*, 21/3: 19–52.

—— (1999a), 'Dimensions and Alignments in European Union Politics: Cognitive Constraints and Partisan Responses', *European Journal of Political Research*, 35/1: 69–106.

—— (1999b), *The Political System of the European Union* (Basingstoke and New York: Palgrave).

—— (2000) 'Parliamentary Oversight of Executive Power: What Role for the European Parliament in Comitology?', in Christiansen and Kirchner (2000: 62–78).

—— (2001), 'Legislative Behaviour and Party Competition in the EU: An Application of NOMINATE to the Post-1999 European Parliament', *Journal of Common Market Studies*, 39/4: 663–88.

—— and Lord, C. (1996), 'The Making of a President: The European Parliament and the Confirmation of Jacques Santer as President of the Commission', *Government and Opposition*, 31/1: 62–76.

—— —— (1997), *Political Parties in the European Union* (Basingstoke: Macmillan).

Hocking, B. (1999) (ed.), *Foreign Ministries: Change and Adaptation* (New York: St Martin's Press).

Hodson, D., and Maher, I. (2001), 'The Open Method as a New Mode of Governance', *Journal of Common Market Studies*, 39/4: 719–46.

Hoffmann, S. (1996), 'Obstinate or Obsolete: The Fate of the Nation-State in Europe', *Daedalus*, 95/3: 862–915.

Hoppe, U., and Schulz, G. (1992), 'Der Ausschuss der Regionen', in Franz U. Borkenhagen, Christian Bruns-Kloess, Gerhard Memminger, Otti Stein, *Die deutschen Länder in Europa* (Baden-Baden: Nomos).

Hoskyns, C., and Newman, M. (2000) (eds.), *Democratizing the European Union* (Manchester: Manchester University Press).

House of Lords, (1987), *Report on the Court of Auditors*, Select Committee on the European Communities, Session 1986/87, 6th report (HL 102).

—— (1989), *Fraud Against the Community*, Session 1988–89, (HL 27).

—— (1999), *Prosecuting Fraud on the Communities' Finances—The Corpus Juris*, 9th report, 18 May, **www.publications.pariamen98/99/Idselect/Ideucom/62/6202.htm**.

—— (2001), *The European Court of Auditors: The Case for Reform*, 12th Report, 3 Apr., **www.publications.pariamen98/99/Idselect/Ideucom/63/6302.htm**.

Howarth, J. (2001), 'European Defence and the Changing Politics of the European Union: Hanging Together or Hanging Separately?', *Journal of Common Market Studies*, 39/4: 765–89.

Huber, J., and Inglehart, R. (1995), 'Expert Interpretations of Party Space and Party Locations in 42 Societies', *Party Politics*, 1/1: 73–111.

Issing, O. (1999), 'The Eurosystem: Transparent and Accountable or Willem in Euroland' *Journal of Common Market Studies*, 37/3: 503–20.

Jackson, V., and Tushnet, M. (1999), *Comparative Constitutional Law* (New York: Foundation Press).

Jansen, T. (1998), *The European People's Party: Origins and Development* (Basingstoke: Macmillan).

Jeffery, C. (1995), 'Whither the Committee of the Regions?', *Regional and Federal Studies*, 5/2: 247–57.

—— (1996a), 'Towards a Third Level in Europe? The German Länder in the European Union', *Political Studies*, 44/2: 253–66.

—— (1996b), 'Farewell the Third Level? The German Länder and the European Policy Process', *Regional and Federal Studies*, 6/2: 56–75.

—— (2000), 'Sub-National Mobilization and European Integration: Does it Make any Difference?', *Journal of Common Market Studies*, 38/1: 1–23.

Jenkins, R. (1989), *European Diary: 1977–1981* (London: Collins).

—— (1991), *A Life at the Centre* (London: Collins).

Joerges, C., and Vos, E. (1999), *EU Committees: Social Regulation, Law and Politics* (Oxford: Hart Publishing).

Johansson, K. M. (1999), 'Tracing the Employment Title in the Amsterdam Treaty: Uncovering Transnational Coalitions', *Journal of European Public Policy*, 6/1: 85–101.

—— and Zervakis, P. (2001) (eds.), *European Political Parties between Cooperation and Integration* (Baden-Baden: Nomos).

Jørgensen, K. E. (1997a), 'PoCo: The Diplomatic Republic of Europe', in Jørgensen (1997b: 167–80).

—— (1997b) (ed.), *Reflective Approaches to European Governance* (Basingstoke: Macmillan).

—— (2000), 'Continental IR Theory: The Best Kept Secret', *European Journal of International Relations*, 6/1: 9–42.

Kalbfleisch-Kottsieper, U. (1995), 'Kompromiss ohne Konsens?' *EU-Magazin*, 6.

Kassim, H., Peters, G., and Wright, V. (2000), *The National Co-ordination of EU Policy: The Domestic Level* (Oxford: Oxford University Press).

Katzenstein, P. J. (1997) (ed.), *Tamed Power: Germany in Europe* (Ithaca, NY: Cornell University Press).

Keeling, D. (1998), 'In Praise of Judicial Activism. But What Does it Mean? And Has the European Court of Justice Ever Practised it?', in A. Roversi Monaco *et al.* (eds.), *Scritti in Onore di Giuseppe Federico Mancini* (Milan: Dott. A. Giuffrè).

Kenen, P. B. (1969), 'The Theory of Optimal Currency Areas: An Eclectic View', in R. A. Mundell and A. K. Swoboda (eds.), *Monetary Problems of the International Economy* (Chicago: University of Chicago Press).

Kennedy, T. (1998), *Learning European Law* (London, Sweet & Maxwell).

Keohane, R. O. (1998), 'International Institutions: Can Interdependence Work?', *Foreign Policy*, 110 (Spring): 82–96.

—— and Hoffmann, S. (1991) (eds.), *The New European Community: Decisionmaking and Institutional Change* (Boulder, Colo.: Westview Press).

Kilpert, H., and Lhotta, R. (1996), *Föderalismus in der Bundesrepublik Deutschland* (Opladen: Leske und Budrich).

Kinnock, N. (1999a), *Press Statement—29 September 1999*, Brussels: European Commission.

—— (1999b), *Some Strategic Reform Issues: Communication from Neil Kinnock to the Commission*, SEC (1999) 1917/2, 15 Nov., CG3 (1999) 7/6.

—— (1999c), *Commission Reform—Strategic Options Paper: Communication from Mr. Kinnock, in Agreement with Mrs. Schreyer and President Prodi, to the Commission*, 10 Dec., CG3 (1999) 10/6.

Kohler-Koch, B., and Eising, R. (1999) (eds.), *The Transformation of Government in the European Union* (London and New York: Routledge).

Kok C. (1989), 'The Court of Auditors of the European Communities: The Other European Court in Luxembourg', *Common Market Law Review*, 26: 345–67.

Kostakopolou, T. (2000), 'The "Protective Union": Change and Continuity in Migration Law and Policy in Post-Amsterdam Europe', *Journal of Common Market Studies*, 38/3: 497–518.

Kratochwil, F. (1993), 'Contract and Regimes: Do Issue Specificity and Variations of Formality Matter?', in V. Rittberger (ed.), *Regime Theory and International Relations* (Oxford: Clarendon Press).

—— and Mansfield, E. D. (1994), *International Organization* (New York: HarperCollins).

Kreppel, A. (1999), 'What Affects the European Parliament's Legislative Influence? An Analysis of the Success of EP Amendments', *Journal of Common Market Studies*, 37/3: 521–37.

—— (2000), 'Rules, Ideology and Coalition Formation in the European Parliament: Past, Present and Future', *European Union Politics*, 1/3: 340–62.

—— (2001), *The European Parliament and the Supranational Party System: A Study of Institutional Development* (Cambridge: Cambridge University Press).

Kydland, F. F., and Prescott, E. C. (1977), 'Rules Rather than Discretion: The Inconsistency of Optimal Plans', *Journal of Political Economy*, 85: 137–60.

Ladrech, R. (1994), 'Europeanization of Domestic Politics and Institutions: The Case of France', *Journal of Common Market Studies*, 32/1: 69–88.

—— (2000), *Social Democracy and the Challenge of European Union* (Boulder, Colo.: Lynne Rienner).

Laffan B. (1997a), *The Finances of the Union* (London: Macmillan).

—— (1997b), 'From Policy Entrepreneur to Policy Manager: The Challenge Facing the European Commission', *European Journal of Public Policy*, 4/3: 422–38.

—— (1999), 'Becoming a "Living Institution": The Evolution of the European Court of Auditors', *Journal of Common Market Studies*, 37/2: 251–68.

—— O'Donnell, R., and Smith, M. (2000), *Europe's Experimental Union: Rethinking Integration* (London and New York: Routledge).

Lanfranchi, P., and Lüthi, R. (1999), 'Cohesion of Party Groups and Interparty Conflict in the Swiss Parliament: Roll Call Voting in the National Council', in Bowler *et al.* (1999: 99–120).

Lavenex, S. (2001*a*), 'Migration and the EU's New Eastern Border: Between Realism and Liberalism', *Journal of European Public Policy*, 8/1: 24–42.

—— (2001*b*), 'The Europeanisation of Refugee Policy: Normative Challenges and Institutional Legacies', *Journal of Common Market Studies*, 39/5: forthcoming.

Lenaerts, K. (1992), 'Some Thoughts About the Interaction Between Judges and Politicians in the European Community', *Yearbook of European Law*, 12: 1–34.

—— (1993), 'Regulating the Regulatory Process: Delegation of Powers within the European Community', *European Law Review*, 18: 23–49.

Lequesne, C. (1993), *Paris–Bruxelles: Comment se fait la politique européenne de la France* (Paris: Presses Universitaires de la Fondation Nationale des Sciences Politiques).

—— (1996), 'La Commission Européenne entre autonomie et dépendance', *Revue Française de Science Politique*, 46/3: 389–408.

Levy R., (1990), 'That Obscure Object of Desire: Budgetary Control in the European Community', *Public Administration*, 68: 191–206.

—— (1996), 'Managing Value for Money Audit in the European Union: The Challenge of Diversity', *Journal of Common Market Studies*, 43/4: 509–29.

—— (2000), *Implementing European Union Public Policy* (Edward Elgar: Cheltenham).

Lewis, J. (1998*a*) 'Is the "Hard Bargaining" Image of the Council Misleading? The Committee of Permanent Representatives and the Local Elections Directive', *Journal of Common Market Studies*, 36/ 4: 479–504.

—— (1998*b*), *Constructing Interests: The Committee of Permanent Representatives and Decision-Making in the European Union*, University of Wisconsin at Madison, Ph.D. dissertation.

—— (2000), 'The Methods of Community in EU Decision-Making and Administrative Rivalry in the Council's Infrastructure', *Journal of European Public Policy*, 7/2: 261–89.

Lindberg, L. N. (1963), *The Political Dynamics of European Integration* (Stanford, Calif.: Stanford University Press).

—— and Scheingold, S. A. (1970), *Europe's Would-Be Polity: Patterns of Change in the European Community* (Englewood Cliffs, NJ: Prentice-Hall).

Linz, J. J. (1998), 'Democracy's Time Constraints', *International Political Science Review*, 19: 19–37.

Lipson, C. (1991), 'Why are some International Agreements Informal?', *International Organization*, 45/4: 495–538.

Lodge, J., and Herman, V. (1980), 'The Economic and Social Committee in EEC Decision-Making', *International Organization*, 34/2: 265–84.

Lohmann, S. (1999), 'The Dark Side of European Monetary Union', in E. Meade (ed.), *The European Central Bank: How Decentralized? How Accountable? Lessons from the Bundesbank and the Federal Reserve System* (Washington: American Institute for Contemporary German Studies).

Longley, L. D., and Davidson, R. H. (1998) (eds.), *The New Roles of Parliamentary Committees* (London: Frank Cass).

Lord, C. (1998*a*), 'Party Groups, EP Committees and Consensus Democracy', in D. S. Bell and C. Lord (eds.), *Transnational Parties in the European Union* (Aldershot: Ashgate): 204–17.

—— (1998*b*), *Democracy in the European Union* (Sheffield: Sheffield University Press).

Loth, W. (1998), 'Hallstein and De Gaulle: The Disastrous Confrontation' in Loth *et al.* (1998).

—— Wallace,W., and Wessels, W. (1998) (eds.), *Walter Hallstein: The Forgotten European?* (Basingstoke and New York: Macmillan and St Martin's Press).

Loughlin, M. (2000), *Sword and Scales* (Oxford: Hart Publishing).

Ludlow, P. (1992), 'Europe's Institutions: Europe's Politics', in G. F. Treverton (ed.), *The Shape of the New Europe* (New York: Council on Foreign Relations Press).

—— (2000), *A View from Brussels.* (No. 8) July 2000 (Brussels: CEPS).

—— (2001), *The European Council at Nice: Neither Triumph nor Disaster*, Background Paper, CEPS International Advisory Council, 1–2 Feb., Brussels.

Lynch, P. (1998), 'Co-operation between Regionalist Parties at the Level of the European Union: The European Free Alliance', in L. de Winter and H. Türsan (eds.), *Regionalist Parties in Western Europe* (London: Routledge), 190–203.

McCormick, J. (1999), *Understanding the European Union* (New York: St Martins Press).

McDonald, M. (2000), 'Identities in the European Commission', in Nugent (2000: 51–72).

McKinnon, R. I. (1963), 'Optimum Currency Areas', *American Economic Review*, 53: 717–25.

MacMullen, A. (2000), 'European Commissioners 1952–1999: National Routes to a European Elite', in Nugent (2000).

McNamara, K. R. (1998), *The Currency of Ideas: Monetary Politics in the European Union* (Ithaca, NY: Cornell University Press).

—— (2001), 'Where Do Rules Come From? The Creation of the European Central Bank', in A. Stone Sweet, N. Fligstein, and W. Sandholtz (eds.), *The Institutionalization of Europe* (Oxford: Oxford University Press).

—— (forthcoming 2002), 'Rational Fictions: Central Bank Independence and the Social Logic of Delegation', in a special issue on 'The Politics of Delegation', M. Thatcher and A. Stone Sweet (eds.), *West European Politics*, 25/1: forthcoming.

—— and Jones, E. (1996), 'The Clash of Institutions: Germany in European Monetary Affairs', *German Politics and Society*, 14/3: 5–31.

Mair, P. (1997), *Party System Change: Approaches and Interpretations* (Oxford: Oxford University Press).

Majone, G. (1996), *Regulating Europe* (London: Routledge).

—— (2000), 'The Credibility Crisis of Community Regulation', *Journal of Common Market Studies*, 38/2: 273–302.

Manners I. and Whitman, R. (eds.) (2001), *The Foreign Policy of the EU Member States* (Manchester: Manchester University Press).

March, J. G., and Olsen, J. P. (1989), *Rediscovering Institutions* (New York: Free Press).

—— —— (1995), *Democratic Governance* (New York: Free Press).

—— —— (1999), 'The Institutional Dynamics of International Political Orders', *International Organisation*, 52/4: 943–69.

March Hunnings, N. (1996), *The European Courts* (London, Cartermill).

Marks, G. (1993), 'Structural Policy and Multi-Level Governance in the EC', in A. Cafruny and G. Rosenthal, *The State of the European Community*, vol. ii.: *The Maastricht Debates and Beyond* (Boulder Colo.: Lynne Rienner).

—— (1996), 'An Actor-Centred Approach to Multilevel Governance', *Regional & Federal Studies*, 6/2: 21–36.

—— and Wilson, C. (2000), 'The Past in the Present: A Cleavage Theory of Party Response to European Integration', *British Journal of Political Science*, 30/3: 433–59.

—— Hooghe, L., and Blank, K. (1996), 'European Integration from the 1980s: State-Centric *v.* Multi-Level Governance', *Journal of Common Market Studies*, 34/3: 341–78.

Matthews, D. (1998), 'Pharmaceutical Regulation in the Single European Market', *Medicine and Law*, 17/2: 401–27.

Mattson, I., and Strøm, K. (1995), 'Parliamentary Committees', in H. Döring (ed.), *Parliaments and Majority Rule in Western Europe* (Frankfurt and New York: Campus and St Martin's Press).

Mayne, R. (1962), *The Community of Europe* (New York: W. W. Norton).

Mazey, S. and Richardson, J. (1989), 'Pressure Groups and Lobbying in the EC', in J. Lodge (ed.), *The European Community and the Challenge of the Future* (London: Pinter): 37–47.

Mendrinou, M. (1994), 'European Community Fraud and the Politics of Institutional Development', *European Journal of Political Research*, 26/1: 81–101.

Mentler, M. (1996), *Der Auschuss der Ständigen Vertreter bei den Europäischen Gemeinschaften* (Baden-Baden: Nomos).

Metcalfe, L. (2000), 'Reforming the Commission: Will Organisational Efficiency Produce Effective Governance?', *Journal of Common Market Studies*, 38/5: 817–41.

Millan, B. (1997), 'The Committee of the Regions: In at the Birth', *Regional and Federal Studies*, 7/1: 5–10.

Milward, A. (1992), *The European Rescue of the Nation-State* (London: Routledge).

Moe, T. M. (1990), 'Political Institutions: The Neglected Side of the Story', *Journal of Law, Economics and Organization*, 6/2: 213–53.

Monar, J. (2001), 'The Dynamics of Justice and Home Affairs: Laboratories, Driving Factors and Costs', *Journal of Common Market Studies*, 39/4: 747–64.

Monnet, J. (1976), *Mémoires* (Paris: Fayard).

—— (1978), *Memoirs* (New York and London: Doubleday and Collins).

Moravcsik, A. (1991), 'Negotiating the Single European Act: National Interests and Conventional Statecraft in the European Community', in R. Keohane and S. Hoffmann (eds.), *The New European Community: Decisionmaking and Institutional Change* (Boulder, Colo.: Westview Press), 41–84.

—— (1993), 'Preferences and Power in the European Community: A Liberal Intergovernmentalist Approach', *Journal of Common Market Studies*, 31/4: 473–524.

—— (1998a), *The Choice for Europe: Social Purpose and State Power from Messina to Maastricht* (London and Ithaca, NY: UCL Press and Cornell University Press).

—— (1998b), 'Europe's Integration at Century's End', in A. Moravcsik (ed.), *Centralization or Fragmentation? Europe Facing the Challenges of Deepening, Diversity, and Democracy* (New York: Council on Foreign Relations Press), 1–58.

—— and Nicolaïdis, K. (1998), 'Federal Ideals and Constitutional Realities in the Amsterdam Treaty', in G. Edwards and G. Wiesala (eds.), *The European Union 1997: Annual Review of Activities* (Oxford and Malden, Mass.: Blackwell for the *Journal of Common Market Studies*), 36: 13–38.

Morgenthau, H. J. (1948), *Politics Among Nations* (Chicago: Chicago University Press).

Mundell, R. A. (1961), 'The Theory of Optimum Currency Areas', *American Economic Review* 51: 509–17.

Narjes, K.-H. (1998), 'Walter Hallstein and the Early Phase of the EEC', in Loth *et al.* (1998).

Nelsen, B. F., and Stubb, A. (1998) (eds.), *European Union: Readings on the Theory and Practice of European Integration*, 2nd edn., (Basingstoke and Boulder, Colo.: Palgrave and Lynne Rienner).

Noël, E. (1966), 'The Permanent Representatives Committee', Lecture to the Institute of European Studies, Université Libre de Bruxelles on 19 and 21 April 1966, repr. in *A Tribute to Emile Noël: Secretary-General of the European Commission from 1958 to 1987* (Luxembourg: Office for Official Publications of the European Communities), 87–124.

—— (1967) 'The Committee of Permanent Representatives', *Journal of Common Market Studies*, 5/3: 219–51.

—— and Étienne, H. (1971), 'The Permanent Representatives Committee and the "Deepening" of the Communities', *Government and Opposition*, 6/4: 422–47.

North, D. R. (1990), *Institutions, Institutional Change and Economic Performance* (Cambridge: Cambridge University Press).

Norton, P. (1998) (ed.), *Parliaments and Governments in Western Europe* (London: Frank Cass).

Nugent, N. (1994), *The Government and Politics of the European Union*, 3rd edn. (Basingstoke and New York: Macmillan and St Martin's Press).

—— (1999), *The Government and Politics of the European Union*, 4th edn. (Basingstoke and New York: Palgrave).

—— (2000) (ed.), *At the Heart of the Union*, 2nd edn. (Basingstoke and New York: Palgrave).

—— (2001), *The European Commission* (Basingstoke and New York: Palgrave).

Nuttall, S. (1992), *European Political Cooperation* (Oxford: Clarendon Press).

—— (2000), *European Foreign Policy* (Oxford: Oxford University Press).

Oatley, T. (1997), *Monetary Politics: Exchange Rate Cooperation in the European Union* (Ann Arbor: University of Michigan Press).

Official Journal of the European Communities (issued most working days), Luxembourg: Office for Official Publications of the European Communities.

OLAF (2000), *First Report of the European Anti-Fraud Office (OLAF) on Operational Activities*, **www.europa.eu.int/commdgs/anti-fraud/index en.htm**.

Owen, D. (1996), *Balkan Odyssey* (London: Indigo).

Page, E. (1997), *People Who Run Europe* (Oxford: Clarendon Press).

Palmer, J. (2000), 'The European Union After Nice—One Step Forward, Two Steps Back?', *EPC Communications—Reports on Topical EU Issues*, 11 Dec. (available from **www.theepc.be**).

Patten, C. (2000), 'Towards a Common European Foreign Policy: How are We Doing?', Winston Churchill Memorial Lecture, Luxembourg, 10 Oct.

Paxton, J. (1984), *A Dictionary of the European Communities*, 2nd edn. (London: Macmillan).

Peers, S. (2000), *EU Justice and Home Affairs* (Harlow: Longman).

Perez Bustamante, R., and Palacio, A. (1998), *Los Consejos Europeos* (Madrid: Instituto Nacional de Administración Pública).

Persson, T., and Tabellini, G. (1994) (eds.), *Monetary and Fiscal Policy* (Cambridge, Mass.: MIT Press).

Peters, B. G. (1999), *Institutional Theory in Political Science* (London and New York: Continuum).

Peterson, J. (1995), 'Decision-Making in the European Union: Towards a Framework for Analysis', *Journal of European Public Policy*, 2/1: 69–93.

—— (1997), 'The European Union: Pooled Sovereignty, Divided Accountability', *Political Studies*, 45/3: 559–78.

—— (1999), 'The Santer Era: The European Commission in Normative, Historical and Theoretical Perspective', *Journal of European Public Policy*, 6/1: 46–65.

—— (2001), 'The Choice for EU Theorists: Establishing a Common Framework for Analysis', *European Journal of Political Research*, 39/2: 289–318.

—— and Bomberg, E. (1999), *Decision-Making in the European Union* (London and New York: Palgrave).

—— —— (2000), 'The European Union after the 1990s: Explaining Continuity and Change', in M. G. Cowles and M. Smith (eds.), *The State of the European Union*, vol. v: *Risks, Reform, Resistance and Revival* (Oxford and New York: Oxford University Press).

—— and Jones, E. (1999), 'Decision Making in an Enlarging European Union', in J. Sperling (ed.), *Two Tiers or Two Speeds? The European Security Order and the Enlargement of the European Union and Nato* (Manchester: Manchester University Press): 25–45.

—— and Sjursen, H. (1988) (eds.), *A Common Foreign Policy for Europe?* (London and New York: Routledge).

Piening, C. (1997), *Global Europe: The European Union in World Affairs* (Boulder, Colo.: Lynne Rienner).

Pierson, P. (1996), 'The Path to European Integration: A Historical Institutionalist Analysis', *Comparative Political Studies* 29/2: 123–63.

Platzer, H. (1999), 'Interessenverbände und europäischer Lobbyismus', in W. Weidenfeld (ed.), *Europa-Handbuch* (Gütersloh: Verlag Bertelsmann Stiftung), 410–23.

Pollack M. (1996),'The New Institutionalism and EC Governance: The Promise and Limits of Institutional Analysis', *Governance*, 9/4: 429–58.

—— (1997), 'Delegation, Agency and Agenda-Setting in the European Union', *International Organization*, 51/1: 99–134.

—— (1998), 'The Engines of Integration? Supranational Autonomy and Influence in the European Union', in W. Sandholtz and A. Stone Sweet (eds.), *European Integration and Supranational Governance* (Oxford and New York: Oxford University Press).

Posen, A. (1993), 'Why Central Bank Independence Does Not Cause Low Inflation: There is No Institutional Fix for Politics', in R. O'Brien (ed), *Finance and the International Economy*, 7 (Oxford: Oxford University Press).

Pridham, G., and Pridham, P. (1981), *Transnational Party Co-operation and European Integration: The Process Towards Direct Elections* (London: George Allen & Unwin).

Prodi, R. (1999a), *Speech to the European Parliament* (4 May), **www.europa.eu.int/comm/commissioners/prodi/speeches/040599_en.htm**.

—— (1999b), *Intervention of Mr. Prodi—Cologne European Council* (3 June), **www.europa.eu.int/comm/commissioners/prodi/speeches/030699_en.htm**.

—— (1999c), *Romano Prodi Announces Proposed New Team of European Commissioners*, Press Release, 9 July, **www.europa.eu.int/comm/newcomm/pr_en.htm**.

Puchala, D. (1972), 'Of Blind Men, Elephants and International Integration', *Journal of Common Market Studies*, 10/3: 267–84.

Putnam, R. (1988), 'Diplomacy and the Logic of Two-Level Games', *International Organization*, 42, Summer, 427–60.

Quermonne, J. L. (1999), *L'Union Européenne en quête d'Institutions Légitimes et Efficaces*, Report of a group from the Commissariat au Plan (Paris: Documentation française).

Quinlivan, A., and Schön, E. (2001), *Kinnock's Administrative Reforms: A Cultural Perspective*, Department of Government, University of Cork, Working Paper Series No. XIX.

Radaelli, C. (2000), 'Whither Europeanization? Concept Stretching and Substantive Change', Paper presented at the PSA, London: 10–13 Apr.

Raunio, T. (1997), *The European Perspective: Transnational Party Groups in the 1989–94 European Parliament* (Aldershot: Ashgate).

—— (1999), 'Always One Step Behind: National Legislatures and the European Union', *Government and Opposition*, 34/2: 179–202.

—— (2000a), 'Losing Independence or Finally Gaining Recognition? Contacts Between MEPs and National Parties', *Party Politics*, 6/2: 211–23.

—— (2000b), 'Second-Rate Parties: Towards a Better Understanding of European Parliament's Party Groups', in K. Heidar and R. Koole (eds.), *Parliamentary Party Groups in European Democracies: Political Parties behind Closed Doors* (London: Routledge): 231–47.

Ray, L. (1999), 'Measuring Party Orientation towards European Integration: Results from an Expert Survey', *European Journal of Political Research*, 36/2: 283–306.

Reilly, A. (1997), 'The Committee of the Regions, Sub-National Governments and the IGC', *Regional and Federal Studies*, 7/3: 134–64.

Rhodes, R. A. W. (1995), 'The Institutional Approach', in D. Marsh and G. Stoker (eds.), *Theory and Methods in Political Science* (Basingstoke and New York: Palgrave).

Rometsch, D., and Wessels, W. (1996) (eds.), *The European Union and Member States: Towards Institutional Fusion?* (Manchester and New York: Manchester University Press).

Rosamond, B. (2000), *Theories of Regional Integration* (Basingstoke and New York: Palgrave).

Ross, G. (1995), *Jacques Delors and European Integration* (New York and London: Polity Press).

Ruggie, J. G. (1993), 'Territoriality and Beyond: Problematizing Modernity in International Relations', *International Organization*, 47/1: 139–74.

—— (1998), *Constructing the World Polity: Essays on International Institutionalization* (London and New York: Routledge).

Salmon, J. (1971), 'Les Représentations et Missions Permanentes Auprès de la CEE et de l'EURATOM', in M. Virally *et al.* (eds.), *Les Missions Permanentes Auprès des Organisations Internationales*, vol. i (Brussels: Dotation Carnegie pour la Paix Internationale), 561–831.

Sanders, D. (1995), 'Behavioural Analysis', in D. Marsh and G. Stoker (eds.), *Theory and Methods in Political Science* (Basingstoke and New York: Palgrave).

Sandholtz, W. (1993), 'Choosing Union: Monetary Politics and Maastricht', *International Organization*, 46/1: 1–39.

—— and Stone Sweet, A. (1998*a*) (eds.), 'Integration, Supranational Governance, and the Institutionalization of the European Polity', in Sandholtz and Stone Sweet (1998*b*: 1–26).

—— (1998*b*) (eds.), *European Integration and Supranational Governance* (Oxford: Oxford University Press).

Santer, J. (1999), 'Thumbs Up to Reform', *Financial Times*, 26 Feb., p. 21.

Sbragia, A. (1991) (ed.), *Europolitics* (Washington: Brookings Institution).

Scharpf, F. (1999), *Governing in Europe: Effective and Democratic?* (Oxford and New York: Oxford University Press).

Schmitt-Egner, P. (2000), *Handbuch der Europäischen Regionalorganisationen* (Baden-Baden: Nomos).

Schmitter, P., and Streeck, W. (1994), 'Organized Interests and the Europe of 1992', in N. Ornstein and W. Streeck (eds.), *Political Power and Social Change* (Washington: AEI Press).

Schöbel, N. (1995), 'Der Ausschuss der Regionen—eine erste Bilanz', *Europäisches Zentrum für Föderalismus-Forschung Tübingen, Occasional Papers*, 4.

Schoutheete, P. de (1986), *La Coopération politique européenne* (Brussels: Labor).

—— (2000), *The Case for Europe: Unity, Diversity, and Democracy in the European Union* (Boulder, Colo., and London: Lynne Rienner).

Schwaiger, P. (1997), 'The European Union's Committee of the Regions: A Progress Report', *Regional and Federal Studies*, 7/1: 12–22.

Scully, R. M. (1997), 'Policy Influence and Participation in the European Parliament', *Legislative Studies Quarterly*, 22/2: 233–52.

Shackleton, M. (1997), 'The Internal Legitimacy Crisis of the European Union', in A. W. Cafruny and C. Lankowski (eds.), *Europe's Ambiguous Unity* (Boulder, Colo., and London: Lynne Rienner).

—— (1998), 'The European Parliament's New Committees of Inquiry: Tiger or Paper Tiger?', *Journal of Common Market Studies*, 36/ 1: 115–30.

Shackleton, M. (2000), 'The Politics of Codecision', *Journal of Common Market Studies*, 38/2: 325–42.

Shapiro, M. (1999), 'The European Court of Justice', in P. Craig and G. De Búrca (eds.), *The Evolution of EU Law* (Oxford: Oxford University Press).

Sherrington, P. (2000), *The Council of Ministers: Political Authority in the European Union* (London: Pinter).

Shonfield, A. (1973), *Europe: Journey to an Unknown Destination* (Harmondsworth: Penguin).

Shore, C. (2000), *Building Europe: The Cultural Politics of European Integration* (London: Routledge).

Siedentop, L. (2000), *Democracy in Europe* (Harmondsworth: Penguin).

Skocpol, T. (1985), 'Bringing the State Back In: Strategies of Analysis in Current Research', in P. B. Evans, D. Rieschemeyer, and T. Skocpol (eds.), *Bringing the State Back In* (Cambridge: Cambridge University Press).

Slaughter, A.-M., Stone Sweet, A., and Weiler, J. H. H. (1998) (eds.), *The European Courts and the National Courts* (Oxford: Hart Publishing).

Smismans, S. (2000), 'The European Economic and Social Committee: Towards Deliberative Democracy via a Functional Assembly', *European Integration Online Papers*, 4/12 at **www.eiop.or.at/eiop/texte/2000-012a.htm**.

Smith, H. (1995), *European Union Foreign Policy and Central America* (London: Macmillan).

Smith, J. (1999), *Europe's Elected Parliament* (Sheffield: Sheffield University Press).

Smith, K. E. (1999), *The Making of EU Foreign Policy: The Case of Eastern Europe* (Basingstoke: Macmillan).

Soetendorp, B., and Hanf, K. (1998), *Adapting to European Integration: Small States and the European Union* (London: Longman).

Solana, J. (2000a), 'The Development of a Common Foreign and Security Policy', speech at Diplomatia, Rome 26 June.

—— (2000b), 'Why Europe Needs the Military Option', *Financial Times*, 29 Sept., p. 21.

Soutou, G. H. (1992), 'Le Général de Gaulle et le Plan Rouchet', *De Gaulle et son siècle*, vol. V (Paris: La Documentation Française).

Spaak, P. H. (1969), *Combats Inachevés*, 2 vols. (Paris: Fayard).

Spence, D. (1991), 'Enlargement without Accession: The EC's Response to German Unification', *RIIA Discussion Paper*, 36 (London: Royal Institute of International Affairs).

—— (1995), 'The Co-ordination of European Policy by Member States', in Westlake (1995: 353–72.).

Stevens, A. with Stevens, H. (2001), *Brussels Bureaucrats? The Administration of the European Union* (Basingstoke and New York: Palgrave).

Stewart, R. (1975), 'The Reformation of American Administrative Law', *Harvard Law Review*, 88: 1667–813

Stone Sweet, A. (2000), *Governing with Judges* (Oxford: Oxford University Press)

—— and Caporaso, J. (1998), 'From Free Trade to Supranational Polity: The European Court and Integration', in Sandholtz and Stone Sweet (1998b).

Strasser D. (1992), *The Finances of Europe*, 7th edn. (Luxembourg: EC Official Publications).

Switalska, J. (1999), 'The Quest for Political Identity in the Committee of the Regions: Symbolism and Pragmatism', South Bank University, London, MA dissertation.

Taggart, P. (1998), 'A Touchstone of Dissent: Euroscepticism in Contemporary Western European Party Systems', *European Journal of Political Research*, 33/3: 363–88.

Taulègne, B. (1993), *Le Conseil Européen* (Paris: PUF).

Taylor, S. (2000), 'Prodi Commission fights back', *European Voice*, 12–18 Oct.: 8.

Teasdale, A. L. (1996), 'The Politics of Majority Voting in Europe', *Political Quarterly*, 67/2: 101–15.

Thelen, K., and Steinmo, S. (1992), *Structuring Politics : Historical Institutionalism in Comparative Analysis* (Cambridge: Cambridge University Press).

Thomassen, J., and Schmitt, H. (1999a), 'Issue Congruence', in H. Schmitt and J. Thomassen (eds.), *Political Representation and Legitimacy in the European Union* (Oxford: Oxford University Press), 186–208.

—— —— (1999b), 'Partisan Structures in the European Parliament', in R. S. Katz and B. Wessels (eds.), *The European Parliament, the National Parliaments, and European Integration* (Oxford: Oxford University Press), 129–48.

Thorn, G. (1984), *European Union or Decline: To Be or Not to Be* (Florence: European University Institute).

Tonra, B. (1997), 'The Impact of Political Cooperation', in K. E. Jørgensen (1997) (ed.), *Reflective Approaches to European Governance* (Basingstoke: Macmillan).

Torreblanca, J. (2000), *European Community and Eastern Europe, 1989–1993* (London: Ashgate).

Tsebelis, G. (1990), *Nested Games: Rational Choice in Comparative Politics* (Berkeley: University of California Press).

—— (1995), 'Conditional Agenda-Setting and Decision-Making inside the European Parliament', *Journal of Legislative Studies*, 1/1: 65–93.

Tugendhat, C. (1986), *Making Sense of Europe* (London: Viking).

Ungerer, W. (1993), 'Institutional Consequences of Broadening and Deepening the Community: The Consequences for the Decision-Making Process', *Common Market Law Review*, 30/1: 71–83.

United States Supreme Court (1803), *Marbury* v *Madison* 1 Cranch 137, 2d Lawyers' Ed. 60.

van Buitenan, P. (2000), *Blowing the Whistle: One Man's Fight Against Fraud in the European Commission* (London: Politico's Publishing).

van der Eijk, C., and Franklin, M. N. (1996) (eds.), *Choosing Europe? The European Electorate and National Politics in the Face of Union* (Ann Arbor: University of Michigan Press).

van der Voort, W. J. (1997), 'In Search of a Role: The Economic and Social Committee in European Decision-Making', University of Utrecht, Ph.D. thesis.

van Oudenhove, G. (1965), *The Political Parties in the European Parliament: The First Ten Years (September 1952–September 1962)* (Leyden: A. W. Sijthoff).

van Schendelen, M. P. C. M. (1996), 'The Council Decides: Does the Council Decide?', *Journal of Common Market Studies*, 34/4: 531–48.

Vedel, G. (1972), *Report of the Working Party Examining the Problem of the Enlargement of the Powers of the European Parliament ('Vedel Report')* (Brussels: Bulletin of the European Communities, Supplement 4/72).

Volcker, P. A. (1997), 'An American Perspective on EMU', in P. Masson, T. Krueger, and B. Turtelboom (eds.), *EMU and the International Monetary System* (Washington: IMF).

Wæver, O. (1995), 'Identity, Integration and Security: Solving the Sovereignty Puzzle in EU Studies', *Journal of International Affairs*, 48/2: 389–431.

Wallace H. (1980), *Budgetary Politics: The Finances of the European Union* (London: Allen & Unwin).

—— (2000), 'The Institutional Setting: Five Variations on a Theme', in H. Wallace and W. Wallace (2000: 3–38).

—— (forthcoming 2001), 'The Council: An Institutional Chameleon?', in *Governance*, 14: forthcoming.

Wallace, H. and Wallace, W. (1996) (eds.), *Policy Making in the European Union*, 3rd edn. (Oxford and New York: Oxford University Press).

—— —— (2000) (eds.), *Policy Making in the European Union*, 4th edn. (Oxford and New York: Oxford University Press).

—— —— and Webb, C. (1977) (eds.), *Policy-Making in the European Community* (Chichester: Wiley).

—— —— —— (1983) (eds.), *Policy-Making in the European Community*, 2nd edn. (Chichester and New York: Wiley).

Wallace, W. (1977), 'Political Cooperation: Procedure as Substitute for Policy', in H. Wallace *et al.* (1977).

—— (1983), 'Less than a Federation, More than a Regime: The Community as a Political System', in H. Wallace *et al.* (1983: 403–36).

—— (1996), 'Government without Statehood: The Unstable Equilibrium', in H. Wallace and W. Wallace (1996: 439–60).

—— (2000), 'Collective Governance', in H. Wallace and W. Wallace (2000: 523–42).

Waltz, K. (1979), *Theory of International Politics* (Reading, Mass.: Addison-Wesley).

Warleigh, A. (1999), *The Committee of the Regions: Institutionalising Multi-Level Governance* (London: Kogan Page).

—— (forthcoming) (ed.) *Understanding European Union Institutions* (London and New York: Routledge).

Watson, A. (1982), *Diplomacy: The Dialogue between States* (London: Methuen).

Webb, C. (1977), 'Introduction: Variations on a Theoretical Theme', in H. Wallace *et al.* (1977: 1–31).

Weigall, D., and Stirk, P. (1992) (eds.), *The Origins and Development of the European Community* (Leicester: Leicester University Press).

Weiler, J. H. H. (1981), 'The Community System: The Dual Character of Supranationalism'. *Yearbook of European Law*, 1: 268–306.

—— (1991), 'The Transformation of Europe', *Yale Law Journal*, 100: 2403–83.

—— (1998), 'Epilogue', in A.-M. Slaughter, A. Stone Sweet, and J. H. H. Weiler (eds.), *The European Courts and the National Courts* (Oxford: Hart Publishing).

—— (1999), *The Constitution of Europe* (Cambridge: Cambridge University Press).

—— (2000), 'IGC 2000: The Constitutional Agenda', in E. Best, M. Gray, and A. Stubb, *Rethinking the European Union* (Maastricht: EIPA).

—— (2001), 'Epilogue: The Judicial Après-Nice', in G. De Búrca and J. H. H. Weiler (eds.), *The European Court of Justice* (Oxford: Oxford University Press).

Werts, J. (1992), *The European Council* (The Hague: TMC Asser Institut).

Wessel, R. (1999), *The European Union's Foreign and Security Policy: A Legal-Institutional Perspective* (The Hague: Kluwer).

Wessels, W. (1997), 'An Ever Closer Fusion? A Dynamic Macropolitical View on Integration Processes', *Journal of Common Market Studies*, 35/2: 267–99.

—— (2001), 'The Millenium IGC in the EU's Evolution', *Journal of Common Market Studies*, 39/2: 197–209.

Westlake, M. (1991), 'The Community Express Service: The Rapid Passage of Emergency Legislation on German Unification', *Common Market Law Review*, 28: 599–614.

—— (1994), *Britain's Emerging Euro-Elite? The British in the Directly-Elected European Parliament, 1979–1992* (Aldershot: Dartmouth).

—— (1999), *The Council of the European Union*, rev. edn. (London: Cartermill).

White, B. (2001), *Understanding European Foreign Policy* (Basingstoke and New York: Palgrave).

Wiener, A., and Neunreither, K. (2000), 'Introduction: Amsterdam and Beyond', in K. Neunreither and A. Wiener (eds.), *European Integration After Amsterdam: Institutional Dynamics and Prospects for Democracy* (Oxford: Oxford University Press).

Williams, M. (1995), 'The European Parliament: Political Groups, Minority Rights and the "Rationalisation" of Parliamentary Organisation. A Research Note', in H. Döring (ed.), *Parliaments and Majority Rule in Western Europe* (Frankfurt and New York: Campus and St Martins Press): 391–404.

Willis, F. R. (1965), *France, Germany, and the New Europe, 1945–1963* (Stanford, Calif.: Stanford University Press).

Wilmott, P. (1984), 'The European Court of Auditors: The First Five Years', *Public Administration*, 62: 211–18.

Wurzel, R. (1999), 'The Role of the European Parliament: Interview with Ken Collins MEP', *The Journal of Legislative Studies*, 5/2: 1–23.

Index